W9-BRX-078

PREVENTING CATASTROPHE

PREVENTING CATASTROPHE

The Use and Misuse of Intelligence
in Efforts to Halt the Proliferation
of Weapons of Mass Destruction

THOMAS GRAHAM JR.
KEITH A. HANSEN

STANFORD SECURITY STUDIES
An Imprint of Stanford University Press
Stanford, California 2009

Stanford University Press
Stanford, California

Library of Congress Cataloging-in-Publication Data

Graham, Thomas
   Preventing catastrophe : the use and misuse of intelligence in efforts to halt the proliferation of weapons of mass destruction / Thomas Graham Jr., Keith A. Hansen.
      p. cm.
   Includes bibliographical references and index.
   ISBN 978-0-8047-6360-8 (cloth : alk. paper)
      1. Intelligence service—United States.   2. Weapons of mass destruction—Government policy—United States.   3. Nuclear nonproliferation—Government policy—United States.   I. Hansen, Keith A.   II. Title.
UB251.U6G73   2009
327.1'745—dc22   2008055817

Printed in the United States of America on acid-free, archival-quality paper.
Typeset at Stanford University Press in 10/14 Minion.

Special discounts for bulk quantities of Stanford Security Studies are available to corporations, professional associations, and other organizations. For details and discount information, contact the special sales department of Stanford University Press. Tel: (650) 736-1783, Fax: (650) 736-1784

*To the dedicated professionals in the
Central Intelligence Agency and in other
US intelligence agencies, along with their liaison
organizations abroad, who through
their remarkable work on nuclear, chemical,
and biological weapons proliferation
have made the world more transparent—
and thereby safer and more secure.
And to our grandchildren, who will benefit.*

Contents

Appendixes

Text Boxes

Preface and Acknowledgments

Each generation has its national security challenges. The invasion of Iraq in 2003 ostensibly over the issue of weapons of mass destruction (WMD) made clear that monitoring and limiting clandestine efforts to proliferate weapons of mass destruction are central to the national security of the United States in the twenty-first century. Endeavors to monitor and limit weapons of mass destruction programs in Iraq, Iran, and North Korea are representative of what policymakers will be facing in the future. However, dealing with the proliferation of nuclear, chemical, and biological weapons entails manifold challenges, from striving to understand the political/prestige and security motivations of countries for acquiring such weapons to monitoring the clandestine programs that are launched to provide such weapons. The stakes can be quite high in any attempts to limit or eliminate such programs, as we have witnessed in the case of Iraq.

As difficult as proliferation efforts by countries are to detect, understand, and stop, in almost all cases the scale of activities permits discovery and counteraction before programs, especially nuclear programs, are advanced enough to pose a real security threat to the United States. For example, the fact that India, Pakistan, Israel, and South Africa signaled from the outset that they were opposed to signing the Nuclear Non-Proliferation Treaty gave the international community fair warning that they had proliferation in mind. By contrast, the quest for WMD by terrorists compounds the urgency, and difficulties, of discovery because terrorists may make or obtain small quantities of nuclear, chemical, or biological weapon material from sources believed to be under control, such as in Russia, Pakistan, or North Korea. Moreover, the activities associated with small-scale clandestine efforts by non-state actors, such as terrorists, are even more difficult to detect and monitor than the proliferation efforts by nation-states. The consequences of missing such proliferation efforts, however, could be quite devastating: even if there is only a low probability that a nuclear weapon will be obtained and used by terrorists against US interests over the next ten years, it is not extreme to say that such an event would be a national catastrophe. Furthermore, the chance of a terrorist attack using chemical or biological weapons is more probable and more difficult to prevent than one involving nuclear weapons.

In our previous book, *Spy Satellites and Other Intelligence Technologies That Changed History*, we addressed the difficulties that US intelligence and policymakers faced during the Cold War in their efforts to monitor, understand, anticipate, and defend against the capabilities of Soviet strategic nuclear forces as well as Moscow's intentions with those weapons. We explained how the same intelligence capabilities that were developed to meet policy requirements regarding the Soviet strategic threat also provided the basis for negotiating and monitoring significant reductions in strategic arms, which greatly diffused the threat of nuclear war between the United States and the Soviet Union. Finally, we briefly addressed the post–Cold War challenge of adapting those intelligence capabilities to monitoring clandestine nucelar, chemical, and biological weapons proliferation in the twenty-first century.

The present book is our attempt to explain the challenges that US intelligence and policymakers now face in monitoring and limiting clandestine efforts by nation-states and non-state actors to acquire weapons of mass destruction. The United States has encountered difficulties in discovering which countries or non-state actors are attempting to acquire such weapons, and the problems of accurately characterizing those proliferation efforts are significant. The misunderstanding of Saddam's WMD programs in Iraq by the United States and the international community demonstrated the complexity of assessing the status of small, clandestine programs. As events have shown, not getting it right can have far-reaching domestic political and international repercussions, especially when policymakers have a strong bias for what they believe they must do.

Nuclear, chemical, and biological weapons that are commonly lumped together and referred to as weapons of mass destruction present different monitoring and policy challenges. While all such weapons programs represent serious threats, especially in the hands of terrorists, we will focus mainly on the proliferation of nuclear weapons, which pose the most destructive potential to world civilization.

Limiting clandestine WMD programs can be complicated by such factors as the complex intelligence-policymaker relationship, which is not always smooth and seamless, as the case of Iraq has underscored. We hope that the issues covered in this book will provide a better understanding of the challenges in discovering, limiting, and halting the proliferation of weapons of mass destruction.

Because national and international endeavors to confront proliferation activities are sensitive, particularly the use of intelligence capabilities, this presentation is necessarily general. The last thing we want to do is educate proliferators on how the United States and other countries go about uncovering and disrupting clandestine activities. We do believe, however, that enough may be said to eliminate some confusion from inaccurate public reporting on how the United States and other countries approach proliferation issues. Our goal in this book is to assist our country and the international community to meet this challenge and to avoid catastrophe.

We wish to express our gratitude to the following colleagues and experts, who took time to review and critique the manuscript, and in the process greatly improve it: Siegfried Hecker, now Codirector of CISAC at Stanford and former Director of Los Alamos National Laboratory; Sidney Drell, a prominent physicist and expert on technical nuclear issues, who has contributed much to US arms control and nonproliferation efforts; Hans Blix, former Swedish foreign minister, Director-General of the IAEA and director of UNMOVIC, the UN agency that carried out the inspections in Iraq immediately before the 2003 US invasion; Richard Kerr, former Deputy Director of Central Intelligence, who led the internal review of the Intelligence Community's analysis of Iraqi WMD programs; Robert Huffstutler, former Executive Director of CIA and career analyst of military affairs; James Goodby, former senior US arms control ambassador and also US representative in leading the effort to secure sites in Russia where nuclear weapons and fissile material were stored; Joseph Cirincione, prominent NGO leader for many years, currently president of the Ploughshares Foundation and one of the leading nongovernmental experts on WMD issues; David Koplow, professor of law at Georgetown University Law Center and prominent arms control expert; and Paul Pillar, currently a professor at Georgetown University and formerly the National Intelligence Officer for the Near East and South Asia. We also wish sincerely to thank Frances Eddy for her remarkable and indefatigable efforts in the development of the manuscript and its preparation for publication. Finally, we thank Geoffrey Burn, John Feneron and their associates at Stanford University Press as well as our editor, Jeffrey Wyneken, for their support during the publication process.

Foreword by Paul R. Pillar

Four and a half decades ago, President John F. Kennedy publicly mused about the possibility that fifteen to twenty-five countries would have nuclear weapons by the 1970s. This did not materialize, and it still has not. That such a worrisome scenario has not yet come to pass, however, provides no assurance that it will not still occur. The proliferation of nuclear or other unconventional weapons is a prime example of a security issue in which the seeds of threatening developments are always present, even though the circumstances that would cause some of those seeds to sprout are unpredictable.

Kennedy's comment should be remembered chiefly for underscoring three truths. First, proliferation of weapons capable of causing mass destruction has long been a matter of high concern and a priority of public policy. For the same reason, it is likely to continue to be a high-profile issue. Second, uncertainty in this subject abounds, and prediction is foolhardy. Kennedy wisely was not venturing a prediction but instead speaking about possibilities. And third, the future, predicted or not, can be shaped through policies, wise or not. The darker possibilities of unchecked nuclear proliferation did not materialize in the 1970s partly because of international efforts at arms control in the 1960s. These included a treaty to ban nuclear testing in the atmosphere, completed during Kennedy's presidency, and the Nuclear Non-Proliferation Treaty, which was signed later in the decade.

Public concern and policy deliberations will continue to be focused not only on weapons proliferation itself but also on efforts to reduce the inevitable uncertainty to a minimum and to form more accurate images of foreign programs to develop nuclear and other unconventional weapons. This inevitably will mean a focus on intelligence. Large—often unrealistically large—expectations get placed on intelligence to produce precise pictures of foreign programs. Such pictures are typically difficult to draw, partly because the programs are shrouded in assiduously maintained secrecy. The pictures become even more difficult to draw when intelligence is expected to project the future course of programs. In some cases this means anticipating decisions that foreign leaders have not yet taken, and which even the leaders themselves could not reliably predict. Whether the expectations are realistic or not, issues of intelligence are entwined with issues of proliferation. Much of the value of Thomas Graham and Keith Hansen's volume lies in providing a single integrated analysis of both.

The challenges posed to policy by the proliferation of nuclear and other unconventional weapons are multifaceted. The primary, but not sole, interest at stake is to reduce the chance of such weapons coming into the possession of those who would use them to do us harm. The traditional focus of concern has been states, especially "rogue" ones. Since the 1990s (when I was supervising analysis on terrorism within the US Intelligence Community), at least as much worry has been voiced about terrorist groups using unconventional weapons, to the point that it has become obligatory for political leaders to identify nuclear terrorism as the number one security threat to the nation. The policy challenges extend beyond keeping weapons out of hostile hands and to the larger consequences of any proliferation that does occur. These consequences include revisions to regional balances of power and the stimulation of still more proliferation on the part of regional rivals.

Difficult questions flow from these challenges, and Graham and Hansen explore several of them in depth. What are the motivations, for example, that attract regimes or terrorist groups to unconventional weapons? A full understanding of this subject is essential for crafting policies with a chance of retarding the spread of such weapons.

Regarding intelligence, a basic question is, how much more is it possible to know about foreign weapons programs, and how much are we unlikely ever to know, no matter how skillful and diligent are the intelligence efforts? An additional question, too often neglected, is how—and whether—intelligence is used in making policy. Too often intelligence on the topic of weapons proliferation (and on other topics) is assessed in isolation, with scorecards kept on how well or how poorly intelligence performs but with few stopping to ask how much difference this makes for the formulation and execution of nonproliferation policy—which is the only reason intelligence on the subject matters at all.

The unhappy experience of the George W. Bush administration's war against Iraq and how the issue of weapons of mass destruction played into the administration's campaign to win support for the war unfortunately has clouded these issues. As confirmed by my own experience in leading other work on Iraq by the Intelligence Community during this period, the ideal—and widely assumed—model of intelligence playing directly into the making of policy often diverges greatly from the reality. In the case of Iraq, weapons of mass destruction had much more to do with selling than with motivating the US decision to launch the war. Subsequent recriminations over the war have further obscured the issues and too often politicized the retrospective assessment of what intelligence did or did not do.

In other cases, policies genuinely concerned with nonproliferation are driven largely by factors other than intelligence. This is neither surprising nor inappropriate, particularly because nonproliferation sometimes conflicts with other foreign policy objectives—a conflict that became apparent in controversy over a US-Indian nuclear cooperation agreement that after much delay became ready for signature in 2008. The statesman must weigh all national interests at stake, and not act solely in response to what intelligence may say about a particular weapon program.

A virtue of Graham and Hansen's analysis is that it casts aside the political baggage and provides a clear exposition of how intelligence has addressed unconventional weapon programs in a variety of cases. Their book is neither an attack nor an apology but instead a careful examination of the possibilities and pitfalls of intelligence work on the topic. Most important, the authors do not offer just another scorecard drawn up in isolation but instead recognize that neither intelligence nor policy can be fully understood unless examined in conjunction with the other.

More broadly, this book is a lode of information for anyone seeking to learn more about proliferation of weapons of mass destruction and in particular nuclear weapons, and about what can be, and has been, done to check the spread of such weapons. Readers of this book will gain not only a wealth of information but also a sense of what ingredients are vital to an effective nonproliferation policy. And they will gain increased immunity to many of the misconceptions about the subject.

Paul R. Pillar
Georgetown University

PREVENTING CATASTROPHE

Introduction

The years since the US invasion of Iraq have witnessed a decline in public confidence in the US Intelligence Community's ability to understand and report on the proliferation of weapons of mass destruction (WMD) and in US policymakers' capacity to deal effectively with proliferation. Negative reactions to the US government's decision to use military force to remove the Saddam regime—which the administration stated was partly intended to eliminate Iraq's WMD programs—along with the lack of significant proof of the existence of such weapons, resulted in much acrimony and severe criticism of the Intelligence Community's ability to monitor accurately Saddam's clandestine efforts to produce or acquire nuclear, chemical, or biological weapons.

During this same period the Intelligence Community has been unable to judge definitively whether North Korea has an ongoing, clandestine uranium enrichment program, which could circumvent a shutdown of Pyongyang's plutonium weapon program. More recently, questions regarding Iran's efforts to develop nuclear weapons have been raised after the Intelligence Community, in a National Intelligence Estimate issued in late 2007, changed one of its Key Judgments on the status of Iran's nuclear weapon program. These episodes, especially Iraq (see Chapter 5), illustrate the confluence of intelligence and the world of politics in most foreign and national policies; furthermore, intelligence is often blamed for policy failures. Clearly, US intelligence on proliferation issues has sometimes been faulty, as in the case of Iraq's chemical and biological weapons programs in 2002. In the arena of nuclear weapon proliferation, however, the track record shows that intelligence has gotten it right more often than not, even to some degree in the case of Iraq (see Chapter 3).

Limiting the proliferation of nuclear weapons and other weapons of mass destruction and preventing their use is a top priority for the United States and the world community in the twenty-first century. With respect to nuclear weapons, this priority involves our national survival as surely as containing the Soviet nuclear threat did during the Cold War. The urgency is apparent in the amount of US and international effort in dealing with India, Pakistan, Libya, North Korea, Iraq, and Iran in the post–Cold War world.

However, the discussion of policy and intelligence interaction concerning WMD proliferation and of understanding the weapons themselves is often confusing and misleading. First, criticisms of the Intelligence Community often fail to take into account either the complex bureaucratic processes within the Intelligence Community that are designed to produce accurate and objective assessments or the interactions between the Intelligence Community and policymakers, who are responsible for formulating appropriate actions. The dynamics of these interactions are critical to successful policy-making, and the distinction between policy and intelligence must be understood (see Chapter 4). The best summary of how this bureaucratic process should work is contained in *Intelligence: From Secrets to Policy* by Mark Lowenthal. We add our perspective in the present book on how the intelligence-policymaker relationship generally unfolds to clarify the important distinctions between the roles and responsibilities of intelligence and policy. Using the Iraqi WMD episode as a case study (Chapter 5), we explain what can happen when the lines become blurred and the bureaucratic processes are corrupted.

Second, given the various types of weapons of mass destruction, important distinctions pertain to what is required for potential proliferators to develop, produce, acquire, and use them (for a discussion of the technical differences among WMD, see Appendix B). These distinctions complicate the challenges the United States and the international community face in monitoring and limiting proliferation. We hope to make clear the implications of these distinctions and describe the complexities in monitoring such weapons and limiting their proliferation, including within terrorist organizations. Suffice it to say here that it is the threat from nuclear weapons which rightly instills the greatest concern, as was evidenced in how US policymakers portrayed the potential threat of Iraqi WMD programs prior to March 2003 (see Chapter 5).

At least seven factors play into an analysis of clandestine efforts to obtain weapons of mass destruction, especially nuclear weapons. First, historical context is important for understanding the aspirations and motives of a country (or a terrorist group) seeking such weapons. Has a country been the user, or victim, of such weapons in the past, or is there a prevailing desire to achieve a particular status within a region or in the world community, which the pos-

What Are Weapons of Mass Destruction?

Insufficient care is generally taken to distinguish types of weapons. The term *weapons of mass destruction* is often misunderstood and used as a synonym for nuclear weapons. Almost always, however, *WMD* refers to nuclear, chemical, and biological weapons. It may also cover the means of delivery (missiles, aircraft, etc.). In the context of terrorism, of course, the means of delivery may be an individual person.

Nuclear bombs truly are weapons of mass destruction with their huge destructive power of blast, heat, and irradiation. Chemical weapons, however, are normally viewed by military planners as tactical or battlefield weapons. They can affect only a relatively small area although, like nuclear weapons, their effects are immediate. Biological weapons are unique in that they may have only a delayed impact, which allows the agents to be spread far.

Chemical and biological weapons are often referred to as the poor man's nuclear weapon because the infrastructure to produce them is cheaper and more easily obtained and concealed than that for nuclear weapons. Chemical and biological agents might more appropriately be called weapons of mass terror and casualties, rather than destruction. Chemical weapons have been used numerous times in tactical warfare and by terrorists, and US and Soviet militaries studied ways to militarize biological agents. In the hands of terrorists, of course, any of the three types of WMD, but especially nuclear weapons, would create panic and havoc.

Finally, weapons of mass destruction of any type not only require the critical ingredients (chemical agents, biological agents, or fissile nuclear material, which have to be stolen or produced), but they must also be weaponized (made to explode or be dispersed) and transported (perhaps by only a single human being, in the case of terrorists) to their intended targets. Thus, a whole system must be devised for such weapons to be useful.

session of the weapons will make possible? That India, Pakistan, Israel and, at least initially, South Africa refused to sign the Nuclear Non-Proliferation Treaty raised suspicions that each wanted to preserve the option to have nuclear weapons. All four eventually exercised that option. Second, what are the intentions of the leaders of such a country or a terrorist group? What do they hope to achieve through the acquisition of such weapons? Third, what actions of a country have raised suspicions? Has it been caught circumventing its obligations under an international treaty or convention that limits or bans the weapons? The difficulty of discerning between legal and illegal nuclear activities increases with the existence of civilian facilities, expertise, and enrichment or reprocessing capabilities, which can mask weapon program activities. Similarly, chemical and biological agents can be produced using legitimate civilian fertilizer or pharmaceutical laboratories. Even benign assistance in the field of nuclear technology for legitimate purposes, such as for research or power reactors, can lead to the clandestine use of nuclear expertise and material to develop weapons. Fourth, what industrial and resource base does a particular country have for the acquisition, production, and delivery of such weapons? Intentions may change from time to time within a country, but capabilities generally only improve. Fifth, what supply networks are available, whether they involve nation-states trying to sell expertise and technology or black-market efforts to peddle dangerous information, expertise, or materials to rogue states or terrorist organizations? Sixth, do relationships exist between certain countries and international terrorist organizations that might cause the countries to transfer weapons of mass destruction, or associated technologies, to such organizations? Finally, are certain countries particularly vulnerable to rogue operations or theft, which would put weapons of mass destruction or dangerous materials in the hands of terrorists? All of these factors, along with the capabilities of potential proliferators to deploy such weapons, must be examined by the Intelligence Community and communicated clearly to policymakers, who then gain an appreciation for the intentions, capabilities, and potential threat of any clandestine proliferation effort. (One of the more comprehensive reviews of international WMD proliferation efforts is *Deadly Arsenals: Nuclear, Biological, and Chemical Threats* by Joseph Cirincione.)

Before we can adequately explore the Intelligence Community's effort to understand and report on proliferation efforts, such as the amount of progress Saddam's regime had made in reconstituting its WMD programs prior to 2003, it will be important to explain in a bit of detail the dynamic relationship between intelligence and policymaking in the United States. Therefore, after a review of the significant differences among the various types of weapons of mass destruction and the reasons that countries and terrorist groups seek nuclear, chemical, or biological weapons capabilities (Chapter 1), a discussion of the challenges we face in detecting and monitoring clandestine WMD programs (Chapter 2), and an examination of the record of the US Intelligence Community in monitoring nuclear, biological, and chemical proliferation activities (Chapter 3), we explain the proper role of intelligence and how it supports and interfaces with policy efforts to thwart proliferation activities (Chapter 4). The discussion should provide readers with a better understanding of what, and how, US intelligence reported in the case of Iraq, as well as how its judgments were used (Chapter 5). Finally, this book describes the tools, both national and international, available to the United States in its efforts to limit and, if possible, reverse proliferation activities (Chapter 6). We hope this book will provide some lessons and a better appreciation for what will be involved in future efforts to monitor and inhibit the proliferation of clandestine WMD programs.

1   Motivations of Countries and Terrorists to Acquire WMD

Countries and terrorist groups seek weapons of mass destruction, especially nuclear weapons, for various reasons. According to Sidney Drell and James Goodby (*The Gravest Danger*), the cases of North Korea, Iran, and Iraq suggest that prestige and national security—through parity or regional dominance—has been the driver behind efforts to acquire nuclear weapon capabilities. To assert that a state is interested in nuclear weapons for security reasons usually means for strategic parity or deterrent purposes; for example, with Pakistan, to offset the superior forces of India, or with Israel, initially to nullify the numerical advantages of its Arab neighbors' conventional military forces. Some states believe that just by possessing nuclear weapons they will be perceived as the dominant state in their region. Iran is a case in point. The possession of nuclear weapons might enable Tehran to dominate at least its part of the Middle East. For purposes of *prestige*, nuclear weapons also have political value: a state in possession of nuclear weapons can be perceived as a great power. India is a case in point, while Japanese diplomats have complained that Japan is treated like a second-class nation in the international arena and is excluded from important diplomatic meetings because Japan does not have nuclear weapons.[1]

One can argue that it was Saddam's WMD effort that ultimately led to Iran's decision to pursue nuclear weapons, although we believe that Iran probably has had other motives, such as prestige under the Shah, hostility with Israel after the 1979 revolution, and possibly deterrence against US military action. The defense of national sovereignty is a powerful motivation, and both Iran and North Korea appear to have pursued nuclear weapons for that reason.[2]

While the term weapons of mass destruction normally includes chemical, biological, and nuclear weapons, the principal attention should be on nuclear weapons (see Appendix B). Chemical and biological weapons should more properly be considered weapons of mass casualties; they do not have the same destructive power as nuclear weapons. Chemical weapons affect only a limited area when employed, and military forces have defenses against them. Biological weapons are essentially terror weapons (even the party deploying the weapons has little control over them once their use is initiated because of the possibility that infected individuals would travel and spread the disease before knowing they themselves were infected), and in advanced countries public health services may be able to develop defenses against them. However, while a first attack with biological weapons in an advanced country likely could be contained, it nevertheless would draw vast quantities of antidotes to the area where the biological agent was used. A series of attacks could place a heavy toll on the responder community (or country) and cause widespread panic. Moreover, the broad extent of international travel could spread a disease to other countries. No other weapon has a comparable capacity to create catastrophe anonymously.[3] Even so, the use of nuclear weapons could be a potential "game changer": they are overwhelmingly destructive through blast and intense heat; they can change the relationship between states; they can be controlled by the deploying party; and there is little defense against them. Nuclear weapons are truly a thing apart, and terrorist groups, such as al-Qaeda, dream of obtaining such a weapon.

States are also motivated to acquire nuclear weapons for strategic deterrence. The security issues may be regional, such as with India and Pakistan, or more global, as with the United States, the Soviet Union, France, the United Kingdom, and China, especially during the Cold War. For other countries, such as Iran and North Korea, which deeply mistrust the West and fear that the United States will act impulsively and aggressively against their interests, their likely calculation is that nuclear weapons provide at least some deterrent value. After all, they saw how the United States and the Soviet Union used their nuclear arsenals to deter each other from initiating nuclear aggression during the Cold War. However, if unconstrained, the nuclear weapon programs of North Korea and Iran could lead to further nuclear proliferation within their respective regions and might actually decrease their security.

The Political Value of Nuclear Weapons. It became apparent early on that nuclear weapons, with their enormous destructive capacity and indiscriminate effects, could not be used as primary weapons of war; rather they were weapons of deterrence or of last resort. Nevertheless, nuclear weapons took on political value. The possession of nuclear weapons came to be seen as indicative of great-power status for a country, distinguishing it from states that did not

The Power of Nuclear Weapons

The atomic bomb used against Hiroshima at the end of World War II had an explosive power of 12.5 kilotons, the equivalent of 12,500 tons of TNT. Central Hiroshima was completely destroyed and over 200,000 people were either killed outright or died later from radioactive poisoning—out of a total urban population of approximately 330,000 people. Yet this device was soon dwarfed by later weapon developments.

In the mid-1950s, the United States and the Soviet Union were testing nuclear weapons in the megaton range, 1 megaton being the equivalent in explosive power of 1 million tons of TNT. For comparison, it perhaps could be said that 1 megaton is roughly equivalent to a TNT-loaded freight train that stretches from New York to Los Angeles. In the 1960s, the United States deployed missiles in underground silo launchers around the country, each with a 9-megaton warhead. Just one of these weapons, if detonated at the Washington Monument, had the capability to more or less destroy Washington, D.C., out to the Capital Beltway in every direction—a radius of approximately 15 miles. The United States routinely carried multiple bombs on its B-52 bombers, each with the explosive power of 25 megatons. One of these bombers thus carried more explosive power than was used by all sides in World War II. The Soviet Union deployed intercontinental missiles with nuclear warheads comparable to such bomber weapons. In 1961, breaking a three-year moratorium on nuclear testing, the Soviet Union tested a nuclear weapon with an explosive yield of more than 50 megatons, scaled down from 100 megatons because of concerns over possible effects.[4]

It became apparent that the potential destructive power of nuclear weapons is limitless. While more sophisticated nuclear weapons are possible only for a highly industrialized and advanced state, a crude weapon of the Hiroshima type—built on the simple gun design—is within reach of any nation that can acquire the appropriate nuclear material, in this case highly enriched uranium.

have such weapons. For example, the five permanent members of the United Nations Security Council are the five nuclear weapon states recognized by the Nuclear Non-Proliferation Treaty. The political value of nuclear weapons was graphically demonstrated by Britain and France many years ago. In February 1958 British Prime Minister Harold Macmillan, referring in a television interview to the British nuclear weapon program, said that "the independent contribution [of British nuclear weapons] . . . puts us where we ought to be, in the position of a great power."[5] In a speech in November 1961, French president

Charles de Gaulle asserted that "a great state" that does not have nuclear weapons when others do "does not command its own destiny."[6] Further, after the May 1998 Indian nuclear tests, Indian prime minister Vajpayee announced, "We have a big bomb now. India is a nuclear weapon state."[7] President Lula of Brazil declared during his first successful election campaign for president in 2002 that what Brazil needs is respect and in this world the only way a state gains respect is through economic, technological, and military strength, which includes the acquisition of nuclear weapons.[8] Such assertions, of course, are not lost on countries such as North Korea and Iran.

Major Nuclear Weapon states

The international community generally recognizes five nuclear weapon states (China, France, the Soviet Union/Russia, the United Kingdom, and the United States), which was codified in the drafting of the Nuclear Non-Proliferation Treaty in the late 1960s.

The *United States* acquired nuclear weapons at the end of World War II as a result of the Manhattan Project, which began in the early 1940s. The project had been established by President Roosevelt in response to urging by Albert Einstein and other scientists. Most of the scientists who advocated this course were émigrés from Nazi Europe; they greatly feared that, given the quality of German nuclear physics, Hitler would get the bomb first and use it to dominate the world. Eventually, this concern became the driving force in establishing the national nuclear weapons laboratory at Los Alamos, New Mexico. The United States and Britain did their best to frustrate possible German programs, bombing the heavy-water plant in Norway, conducting elaborate espionage efforts, and so on. The US program paused after the close of World War II but then resumed, responding to the beginning of the Cold War, and thereafter to the Soviet nuclear buildup.

The *Soviet Union* reacted to the United States in the 1940s with its own nuclear weapon program. It largely stole the technical capability from Los Alamos by means of its atomic spy ring and tested its first nuclear device in 1949, early in the Cold War. President Harry Truman had mentioned to Stalin at the Potsdam Summit, in 1945, that the United States possessed a new, highly destructive weapon. While Stalin appeared to show no interest in Truman's information, he understood; on his return to the Soviet Union, Stalin energized the Soviet program, which soon was led by Igor Kurchatov. Eventually the Soviets constructed an enormous nuclear infrastructure, which included a number of secret cities whose only function was to contribute to the Soviet nuclear weapon program.

After a time the US program, as well as the Soviet program, developed a momentum that seemed unstoppable, and a vast arms race between the United States and the Soviet Union came into being. The United States ultimately built more than seventy thousand nuclear weapons and at the peak had more than thirty thousand weapons deployed. The Soviet Union built some fifty-five thousand weapons and maintained forty-five thousand nuclear weapons in the field for a number of years.[9] As a result of the competition and large commitments, the United States and the Soviet Union became the world's nuclear superpowers, a status that held great political and military significance for half a century.

The nuclear weapon arms race and the associated threat of thermonuclear confrontation was created and sustained by mutual worst-case assumptions, which came to pose grave danger, not only to the two countries but to the world community. Even as early as the 1960s this danger was well understood: during the all-encompassing strategic arms race, both countries deployed land-based and submarine-based missiles that were maintained on hair-trigger alert and were capable of delivering nuclear weapons with pinpoint accuracy in thirty minutes or less. Once launched, these missiles were not recallable; many incidents over the years ran the risk of causing one or the other country to mistakenly launch its weapons. In the end, the arms race bankrupted the Soviet Union, and it cost the United States around five and a half trillion dollars. If any of the incidents had led to launches, even resulting from erroneous information, world civilization could have been destroyed. The risks associated with nuclear deterrence were total.

The *United Kingdom* was the partner of the United States in the Manhattan Project and thus privy to the secrets of the program. Britain decided to deploy nuclear weapons shortly after World War II and conducted its first test in 1952. In the wake of the dismantlement of its empire, and its high personnel and material costs in World War II, possessing nuclear weapons was Britain's key to maintaining its great-power status. Interestingly, Canada was also part of the Manhattan Project, but it did not feel the need to build nuclear weapons. Canada's security could rely on the country's relationship with the United States, and Canada did not have the political need to be perceived as a great power. Even so, for many years afterward, Canada was regarded as an advanced nuclear state and was included in important East-West meetings of the 1950s along with Britain and France. For example, Canada was included as a member of the Subcommittee of Five of the United Nations Disarmament Commission (the United States, the United Kingdom, France, the Soviet Union, and Canada), which was the first forum to address the discontinuance of nuclear weapon testing, in the 1950s.[10]

France was motivated by the same consideration as Britain's, although in France the issue of whether to become a nuclear weapon state was far more controversial. Several governments of the Fourth Republic after World War II were opposed to nuclear arms because they feared that if France developed nuclear weapons, Germany would as well. For many French leaders it was more important to deny nuclear weapons to Germany than it was to gain them, and great-power status, for France.[11] This concern lessened somewhat as West Germany undertook obligations never to acquire nuclear weapons. However, the French questioned the reliability of the US nuclear umbrella, worrying that the United States would not risk nuclear strikes on its own soil to defend France. Finally, in 1955, Premier Mendes-France decided to build the bomb;[12] the first test was conducted in the Sahara Desert in 1960, by which time the Fifth Republic, led by General de Gaulle, was in place. President de Gaulle made no secret of his view that possessing the "bomb" would ensure great-power status for France. So, while it could be said that the United States and the Soviet Union acquired nuclear weapons for their security, Britain and France acquired them for status as well as for security.

China began pursuing nuclear weapons in the 1950s, leading to its first test in 1964. In the early years of the program, China received substantial help from the Soviet Union as a "fraternal" Communist state. This changed abruptly during the last years of the 1960s, and the once fraternal relationship turned toward hostility, nearly leading to war. China pursued nuclear weapons largely for security reasons, namely, hostility toward the Soviet Union and fear of possible nuclear blackmail by the United States over Taiwan. Indeed, China had engaged in a serious military conflict with the United States during the Korean War. However, China has not shown much interest in great-power status based on the prestige of being a nuclear weapon state, and has thus far followed a policy of minimum nuclear deterrence.

Proliferate States

Beyond the five earliest nuclear weapon states, four other countries currently have nuclear weapons: India, Israel, North Korea, and Pakistan. As discussed in this section, a number of other countries have the potential to acquire nuclear weapons should they deem it necessary for national security (see Appendix C).

India was the first of these states to test a nuclear explosive device—a so-called peaceful nuclear explosion—in 1974. It is uncertain when the Indians actually weaponized their nuclear devices, but in 1998 they tested the "bomb" overtly to demonstrate that India had become a nuclear weapon state. India has always appeared more interested in the prestige factor of nuclear weapons. Although a security issue with China exists, for nearly twenty-five years India appeared content to possess nuclear weapon technology without building or testing weapons, despite being on the opposite side of the Himalayas from several hundred Chinese nuclear weapons. Since the Bharatiya Janata Party came to power and conducted nuclear tests, in 1998, India has emphasized that it is now a nuclear weapon state and therefore an important country.

Pakistan, in contrast, developed nuclear weapons for its security (against India), although its program antedated the first Indian test by several years. Prime Minister Zulfikar Ali Bhutto is reported to have said after the disastrous Pakistani defeat at the hands of India in 1971, which led to the dismemberment of Pakistan, that his country would build nuclear weapons even if the people had to "eat grass."[13] There was no obvious Indian nuclear weapon capability to offset at the time, but there was India's great conventional military superiority, which had been the cause of Pakistan's defeat. By 1998 the situation was different in that India had just conducted five nuclear weapon tests, indicating that it would weaponize and declare itself a nuclear weapon state. Pakistan responded with six test explosions and made the same declaration as to its status.

Israel's nuclear weapon program appears to have been driven entirely by security motivations, given its isolation in the Middle East. From the beginning of the Israeli program in the 1950s and for many years afterward—indeed many years after the initial nuclear weapon capability was attained in 1967—Israel's nuclear weapons have been an important part of its security, despite the risk that its nuclear capabilities would be emulated by others in the region. The Israeli program was conceived by Prime Minister Ben Gurion on the proposition that after the Holocaust Israel should never rely on anyone else for its security.

However, after four successful wars with its Arab neighbors, the possession of nuclear weapons no longer seemed necessary to ensure its survival.

As a result of its program, Israel refused to sign the Nuclear Non-Proliferation Treaty (NPT) and some friction with the United States resulted. During a 1969 visit of Prime Minister Golda Meir to Washington, she explained to President Richard Nixon why Israel had to have nuclear weapons and could not sign the NPT. She pledged not to test or to publicly acknowledge Israel's possession of such weapons. Nixon apparently accepted this explanation and the reality that a nuclear Israel was a fait accompli.[14]

Today Israel, with the help of the United States, enjoys vast superiority in conventional forces over any possible foe. Israel has never been interested in nuclear weapons for prestige; up to the present it still has not formally admitted that it possesses nuclear weapons but rather follows a policy of ambiguity—despite the fact that Israel is now considered to be an advanced nuclear weapon state, more like France than like India.

North Korea pursued nuclear weapons for mixed motives. On the one hand, it is a garrison state (somewhat like Israel), which since the collapse of the Soviet Union has appeared to be obsessed with its security, indeed its survival. And North Korea still faces formidable US military forces in the region. Its remaining supporter in the region, China, extended diplomatic recognition to South Korea, but the United States has not yet responded in kind to North Korea. On the other hand, North Korea has signaled for fifteen years that it would be willing to trade its nuclear weapon program for concessions from the United States: diplomatic recognition, removal of sanctions, a security guarantee, Western-supplied light-water nuclear reactors for energy, and money. It is unfortunate that the United States has taken so long to respond effectively; North Korea now may have built up to ten nuclear weapons, which likely will not be given up for a long time. In 2008, the United States and North Korea were finally moving in a direction that had a reasonable chance of eventually denuclearizing North Korea, although this process stalled in late 2008 (see Chapter 3).

Other Efforts to Acquire Nuclear Weapons. Several other countries sought, achieved, or are seeking nuclear weapon capabilities. Initially, *Iran* was threatened by Iraq's nuclear weapon program, but current Iranian leaders may well view nuclear weapons as insurance against an attack by the United States—an insurance Iraq did not have in 2003. But it is difficult to see a scenario in which Iran, which already has conventional superiority in the region, would use nuclear weapons against its neighbors. Some concern exists about the disparate nature of the Iranian state, where, for example, the Revolutionary Guards might not adhere to policy set by the senior leaders of government. Beyond this concern, some argue that a nuclear weapon capability would give Iran perceived dominance in the Middle East, which it appears to see as its destiny. Iran sees itself as the heir to the Persian Empire, a legitimate great power, and nuclear weapons are the *indicia* of great-power status, as Britain, France, and, to some extent, India have illustrated. For Iran, then, prestige is arguably a major motivator.

Both *Iraq* and *South Africa* had nuclear weapon programs, which were motivated primarily by security. Saddam Hussein thought he could dominate the Middle East and keep Iran in check. However, by about the mid-1990s, the Iraqi nuclear weapon program had been eliminated through inspections by the International Atomic Energy Agency working alongside the United Nations Special Committee in the wake of the 1991 Gulf War (see Chapter 5). The former white-minority South African government at one point possessed six nuclear bombs and apparently believed, misguidedly, that nuclear weapons would protect it against Soviet-inspired communist attack from its neighbors. South Africa gave up its weapons voluntarily so that it could reintegrate itself into the world community. It also seems clear that the outgoing government did not want to pass a nuclear arsenal on to the incoming black-majority government.

In the case of *Libya*, motivations seem harder to discern; perhaps Qadhafi was merely a maverick seeking prestige. *Brazil* once pursued nuclear weapons for prestige and may again one day. *Argentina* was similarly motivated but largely in response to Brazil. *Ukraine* briefly had nuclear weapon status and attempted to retain the strategic nuclear weapon systems left by the Soviets in its territory following the collapse of the Soviet Union. In Ukraine's view, it would naturally have emerged as the "France of the East." But Ukraine gave up this notion once it became convinced that it otherwise would never be accepted as part of the world community. It agreed to become a nonnuclear weapon state; however, it insisted on formal security guarantees from Russia, Britain, France, and the United States. Both *Belarus* and *Kazakhstan* had similarly "inherited" nuclear weapons when the Soviet Union collapsed, but Russia (with some help from the West, and with much less difficulty than with Ukraine) successfully persuaded both countries to return the weapons to Russia and, along with Ukraine, to join the international community as nonnuclear weapon states.

In the 1960s, it appeared as if nuclear weapons might spread all over the world. President John F. Kennedy expressed his belief that by "1970 . . . there

---

Nuclear Weapon Programs: Country by Country

Those That Have Nuclear Weapons:
 China, France, India, Israel*, North Korea**, Pakistan, Russia, United Kingdom, United States

Those Suspected of Having Nuclear Weapon Programs:
 Iran, Syria

Those That Had but Renounced Nuclear Weapon Programs:
 Argentina, Belarus, Brazil, Egypt, Iraq, Kazakhstan, Libya, Romania, South Africa***, South Korea, Spain, Sweden, Taiwan, Ukraine, Yugoslavia

Those Having the Potential to Develop Nuclear Weapons:
 Algeria, Argentina, Australia, Austria, Belgium, Brazil, Bulgaria, Canada, Chile, Egypt, Finland, Germany, Hungary, Indonesia, Italy, Japan, Mexico, Netherlands, Norway, Poland, Romania, Slovakia, South Africa, South Korea, Spain, Sweden, Switzerland, Taiwan, Turkey, Ukraine.[15]

 *Israel has never publicly acknowledged having nuclear weapons.
 **North Korea tested a nuclear weapon, but it is uncertain how many weapons it has.
 ***Under the white-minority regime, South Africa had six nuclear weapons in its arsenal, but Pretoria gave them up prior to handing power over to the black-majority government.

---

may be 10 nuclear powers instead of 4, and by 1975, 15 or 20," which he regarded "as the greatest possible danger and hazard."[16] Had such proliferation happened, there might have been more than *forty* nuclear weapon states today: over forty countries have nuclear reactors of some type, and many of these countries, if sufficiently motivated, could become nuclear-capable were they to gain expertise and the ability to enrich uranium to a weapons-grade level.[17] Such proliferation would have created a nightmarish world. Nuclear weapons would have been so widespread that it would be increasingly difficult to keep them out of the hands of terrorists, and every conflict would run the risk of "going nuclear." Truly, the survival of the international community would have been in the balance every day.

Countries Possessing Chemical and Biological Weapons

 During the twentieth century, the world witnessed the use of both chemical and biological weapons by several countries in warfare, particularly dur-

---

Biological or Chemical Weapon Programs: Country by Country

Those Suspected of Having Offensive Biological Weapon Programs:

Israel, North Korea, Russia (probably China, Egypt, Iran, Syria; possibly India, Pakistan)

Those That Renounced Offensive Biological Weapon Programs:

Canada, France, Germany, Japan, Russia, South Africa, United Kingdom, United States[18]

Those Suspected of Having Chemical Weapon Programs:

Egypt, Israel, North Korea, Syria (probably China, Iran; possibly Myanmar, Saudi Arabia, South Korea, Taiwan, Vietnam)

Those That Renounced Chemical Weapon Programs:

Albania, Belarus, Canada, France, Germany, India, Italy, Japan, Kazakhstan, Libya, Russia, South Africa, South Korea, Ukraine, United Kingdom, United States, Yugoslavia[19]

---

ing World Wars I and II. Today, despite conventions banning such weapons, clandestine chemical and biological weapons programs are believed to operate in a number of countries. Because these programs have a lower profile, it is more difficult to be sure which countries continue to possess one or the other. At last count, some nine countries are suspected of having biological weapon programs, and eleven are suspected of having chemical weapon programs.

Potential Terrorist Acquisition and Use of WMD

While it might be difficult for any terrorist organization to acquire and use a nuclear weapon, it cannot be ruled out; a radiological weapon is probably more feasible. The potential for terrorists possessing and using chemical or biological weapons is a realistic threat, which must be considered. Although terrorists have not used these weapons in any significant degree, except by terrorists in Japan in 1995 (as discussed in Chapter 3), both types of weapons appear to be well suited for covert use.

Chemical Agents. Chemical agents (poison gas) are proven weapons of war, but they are weapons against which well-trained and well-equipped troops can nevertheless fully protect themselves. Civilians will ordinarily not be protected; population centers are particularly vulnerable to chemical attacks by terrorists. According to one analysis, some seven hundred chemical plants operate nationwide in the United Sates. The biggest chemical threat may be the transit of the approximately one hundred thousand 90-ton tank cars containing toxic gases, such as chlorine or anhydrous ammonia, which are shipped each year across the United States. The release of these chemicals in an attack, depending on where it happens, could result in the death or serious injury of over one hundred thousand people.[20] In post-Saddam Iraq numerous attacks using chlorine gas have been used by sectarian terrorists. If the Aum Shinrikyo terrorists who attacked the Tokyo subway system in March 1995 had used a higher concentration of sarin gas than they did that morning (for example, a 70–80 percent pure mixture rather than the 30 percent pure mixture that was used), there could have been deaths and injuries in the tens of thousands instead of the actual twelve deaths and five thousand injuries (see Chapter 3).[21]

It is surprising that similar attacks by al-Qaeda or other groups have not been conducted around the world. One has to wonder why this is the case. The December 1984 accident (or sabotage) at the Union Carbide pesticide plant in India released a cloud of chlorine gas that killed at least five thousand people immediately and injured tens of thousands more. With memories of 9/11 fresh in mind, it is now conceivable how terrorists, through sabotage, could turn hazardous chemicals, which are located in most countries, into weapons of terror.[22] Perhaps the Aum Shinrikyo experience in Japan points to the relative difficulty of producing weaponized biological agents, but this group did succeed in deploying the chemical agent sarin (see Chapter 3).

Biological Agents. Unlike chemical weapons, which have been used in numerous military campaigns, biological weapons are not particularly useful as battlefield weapons. To spray an oncoming force with an agent that will make them sick several days later is unlikely to diminish the vigor of an attack. Yet, the strategic use of biological agents such as anthrax, botulinum toxin, or smallpox could be a threat to civilian populations. As we stated previously, the failure of the well-funded Aum Shinrikyo terrorist group to weaponize and deploy virulent strains of botulinum toxin and anthrax demonstrates significant technical hurdles with biological weapon development.[23]

The first successful terrorist incident involving biological agents in the United States occurred in The Dalles, Oregon, in 1984. The religious cult Rajneesh, to discourage and retaliate against community opposition to its development plans, disseminated salmonella bacteria in the salad bars of ten restaurants. They infected about 750 people, but none died. A second bioterrorist

Anthrax Attack in the United States

According to the FBI, just weeks after the September 11, 2001, terrorist attacks by al-Qaeda, army bacteriologist Dr. Bruce E. Ivins, working at Fort Detrick, Maryland, anonymously sent anthrax-tainted letters to several lawmakers on Capitol Hill and to members of the media in New York and Florida. Besides paralyzing part of the US postal system and forcing the temporary closure of several congressional offices, the attack killed five people and another seventeen were sickened from exposure to anthrax spores. The victims included postal workers and others who came into contact with the letters.

This attack appeared to have been motivated by revenge for program cutbacks and was also the product of an unstable personality. The FBI began investigating the incident and early on identified the US Army Medical Research Institute of Infectious Diseases, the US government's biodefense laboratory at Fort Detrick, Maryland, as the likely source of the anthrax used. The bureau reportedly scrutinized twenty to thirty scientists who might have had the knowledge and opportunity to send the anthrax letters. Ultimately, the bureau closed in on Ivins, a scientist who had worked at Fort Detrick for eighteen years and who had coauthored numerous anthrax studies. Ivins committed suicide in late July 2008 before the FBI could bring formal charges against him and obtain an explanation for the attack.[24]

attack in the United States occurred in the fall of 2001 when, allegedly, an army research biologist stationed at Fort Detrick, Maryland, mailed a small number of anthrax-tainted letters, causing widespread evacuation of government offices and crippling part of the US postal system for months. Five people died, and seventeen others were infected and sickened. The attacks exhibited one of the wide range of covert delivery options available to bioterrorists; raised questions about source and the ease of acquiring biological agents; and exposed the widespread vulnerability of population centers to such weapons.

As noted above, casualties from the use of biological weapons against civilian populations by states or by terrorist groups might be contained in first-world countries with modern public health systems, resulting in significant, but not overwhelming damage. However, multiple attacks, coming one after another, could strain systems to their cracking point and sow devastating panic. Moreover, the resulting diseases could be spread unknowingly around the globe, given the anonymous nature of the agents and the ubiquity of international travel. Many biological agents are available, such as Marburg, plague, Ebola, botulism, anthrax, and synthetic viruses.[25] In third-world countries with limited public health capability the effects likely would be devastating. The anthrax attack in the United States in 2001 demonstrated how easily someone on the inside of a biodefense laboratory could on his or her own (or by supplying a terrorist organization) cause panic and death among the civilian population.

Nuclear Weapons. Returning to the issue of nuclear weapons, the question of terrorists' motivations in acquiring such weapons is different from that of states. Terrorists' motivations to acquire actual nuclear weapons, radiological dispersal devices, chemical weapons, or biological weapons are more or less an attempt to advance whatever political agenda an organization may have by sowing terror with the most horrific weapons that can be obtained. While all types of weapons of mass destruction may be sought by one or more terrorist organizations, nuclear weapons, again, are in a special category. Osama Bin Laden has said that the acquisition of nuclear weapons by al-Qaeda is a "religious duty."

This being the case, one must ask why terrorists, particularly al-Qaeda, have not detonated some kind of nuclear device. Various kinds of terrorist attacks continue to be orchestrated around the world by al-Qaeda and other organizations. Indeed, in July 2005, terrorists conducted the worst attack on London since the Nazi raids during World War II; fifty-two commuters on three subway lines and one bus were killed.

Some argue that terrorist organizations, including al-Qaeda, are tactically conservative and risk-averse from an operational standpoint. While they do not hesitate to risk their lives, they avoid futile operations, especially ones that use an actual intact nuclear device such as a bomb or missile warhead. Crude nuclear devices, such as a gun-type device like the weapon used against Hiroshima, could probably be fabricated by an organization such as al-Qaeda, but terrorists still need to get their hands on nuclear fissile material. State-owned and controlled stockpiles of fissile material remain the most likely gateways to nuclear terrorism. However, unless a nation-state gives fissile material to a group, security may be too great to steal it, and the price may be too high. Thus, al-Qaeda may have decided that the bar is too high for such an operation, unless something unforeseen makes obtaining the required material, and a nuclear attack, more feasible. (For a discussion of the challenges terrorists face in producing nuclear or radiological weapons, see Appendix C.)

We cannot be sure, but we can hope that US and international efforts to monitor and limit proliferation have been at least partly responsible for the absence of nuclear material thus far in terrorist attacks. The good news is that a complicated chain of events must take place for a terrorist organization to obtain nuclear material, fabricate even a crude device, and deploy it success-fully. To carry out a nuclear attack, the terrorist organization must successfully complete each step in the process. For a country to defend against an attack, it need disrupt only one step of the process. With nuclear attacks, then, the odds may work against terrorists and for the defenders.[26]

Should al-Qaeda or any of its associated organizations nevertheless acquire weapons of mass destruction, especially nuclear weapons, these organizations have made it clear that they will use them. Their motives have nothing to do with security or prestige but rather with a political agenda.

2   Detecting and Monitoring Clandestine WMD Programs

The strategic challenge and threat posed by the Soviet Union during the Cold War spurred US intelligence to develop capabilities to monitor and analyze large and technically sophisticated strategic nuclear forces, as well as conventional forces, which include chemical and biological weapons systems. In addition, the growth in the number of nuclear weapon states in the 1950s and 1960s (United Kingdom, France, and China), the "peaceful" Indian nuclear test in 1974, the efforts by other countries to develop a nuclear deterrent against hostile neighbors, and the actual use of chemical weapons during the Iran-Iraq war in the 1980s required the Intelligence Community to look well beyond the Soviet Union vis-à-vis the proliferation of nuclear weapons and other weapons of mass destruction.

Intelligence Support to Policymakers

Before describing how the Intelligence Community tackles the proliferation problem, we must briefly explain the steps normally required to produce intelligence that is useful to policymakers. Understanding this process is critical to an appreciation of how the IC strives to meet the challenges the United States faces around the world. Except for the issue of warning, in which the Intelligence Community must take the initiative to collect and analyze data so that policymakers can avoid surprises, the normal intelligence cycle begins with the needs of policymakers (see Appendix E). Intelligence is a service activity; it responds to the information needs of policymakers, but it neither recommends nor promotes policy options. Thus, it is the responsibility of policy officials to identify their requirements, and the responsibility of intelligence officials to respond to those requirements. If the Intelligence Community does not have sufficient information, then it must initiate collection efforts to obtain it.

Once the information is in hand (at least as much as is obtainable), it is processed, because raw intelligence data, whether imagery, signals or communications, or in some cases human source reporting, are usually not in a form that is directly useful to policymakers. Then the information is analyzed and merged with all sources of information, whether openly available or obtained through intelligence channels. The analysts' job is to critique the available information and the reliability of its sources, discern credibility and plausibility, reach judgments based on all available information, and then organize the information and judgments so that they respond to policymaker needs and can be easily digested by policy consumers. Finally, the information is passed to

---

US Intelligence Community

The US Intelligence Community (IC) comprises the executive-branch agencies and organizations that conduct a variety of intelligence activities to satisfy the requirements of the policy community. Many of these organizations were instrumental in developing—along with the help of US industry—and utilizing the necessary intelligence capabilities for understanding Soviet military forces during the Cold War, and they remain critical in monitoring the military capabilities of a number of countries under international arms control and nonproliferation agreements, as well as the activities of international terrorist groups.

The IC is currently composed of sixteen organizations. Those that focus, at least in part, on military, nonproliferation, and strategic nuclear issues include the Central Intelligence Agency; the National Security Agency; the Defense Intelligence Agency; the Bureau of Intelligence and Research of the Department of State; army, navy, marines, and air force intelligence services; the National Geospatial-Intelligence Agency; the National Reconnaissance Office; and the Department of Energy. The others include the Federal Bureau of Investigation (for domestic counterintelligence and counterterrorism activities); the Department of Homeland Security; the Coast Guard; the Department of the Treasury; and the Drug Enforcement Administration.[1]

Members of the Intelligence Community advise the director of national intelligence (DNI) through their representation in a number of specialized bodies. These include the National Counterterrorism Center and the National Intelligence Council. The Intelligence Reform Act of 2004 created the DNI position to provide better coordination and communication among the components of the community to meet the intelligence challenges of the twenty-first century (see Appendix D).

What Is Intelligence?

In the context of US national security, *intelligence* can be defined as information or insights provided to policymakers in support of their deliberations on and implementation of foreign and security policies. Such information is often unique and unavailable to policymakers from any other source. At times, intelligence combines what is publicly available or what is learned through diplomatic channels with clandestinely acquired information to confirm, clarify, or perhaps contradict what otherwise might be taken as an accurate understanding of a given situation.

To produce relevant and timely intelligence the Intelligence Community normally conducts collection, processing, analysis, production, and dissemination activities—all in response to the requirements of policymakers in the executive and legislative branches of government. Much of the intelligence produced is classified because of the sensitive sources and unique methods used to clandestinely collect and analyze information. Open-source information (newspapers, public broadcasts, and speeches) also makes a major contribution to intelligence judgments. Most of the sixteen members of the US Intelligence Community collect or analyze only foreign intelligence; the FBI and the Department of Homeland Security alone are chartered to conduct intelligence activities within the United States and against US citizens. All intelligence activities are regulated by US laws and monitored by oversight bodies within both the executive and the legislative branches.

Intelligence is provided to policymakers in various forms: as current reporting, in-depth analysis, warning of potential threats, or as estimates or forecasts of how international events may unfold. Intelligence can cover political, economic, military, social, humanitarian, environmental, or other issues of importance to US foreign and security policy. Disseminating intelligence is normally done through written or oral presentations, depending on the recipient as well as the urgency of the issue.

Covert Action. Despite misleading media portrayals and public perceptions, covert actions (political, economic, or paramilitary efforts to influence the affairs of foreign nations) normally occupy only a small share of the IC's resources and efforts. Covert action is not truly intelligence but rather policy implementation. When neither diplomacy nor the use of military force is deemed an appropriate or effective tool to achieve US national security objectives, policymakers may resort to covert action. From its creation in 1947, the Central Intelligence Agency has been responsible for planning and executing covert actions using clandestine means that hide US involvement. Such actions must be ordered and authorized by the president.

the requesting policy official (most likely along with many others) in a timely manner. As we will explain in Chapter 5, this system of providing objective intelligence is not perfect; it can suffer from weak sources, insufficient analytic rigor, and mistakes in judgment on the part of the Intelligence Community, and it can be perverted by the heavy hand of policy consumers. If the response is less than complete or satisfactory, then the process begins again until the Intelligence Community has exhausted its resources or until the information would no longer be useful (see Chapter 4).

Early during the Cold War, US policymakers realized that the lack of good intelligence on Soviet military capabilities and intentions made planning difficult and would possibly waste resources in reacting to phantom threats. Further, the potential danger of conflict through miscalculation was increased by assuming worst-case scenarios in situations where there was inadequate understanding of Soviet motives and intentions. Thus, policymakers in the executive branch and members of Congress insisted on receiving better intelligence information and analyses to avoid miscalculation and overreaction. As a result, they pushed for enhancements to the Intelligence Community's collection and analytic capabilities in partnership with US industry.

Monitoring the Soviet Threat

As one of the initial steps to create the US Intelligence Community under President Truman, the Central Intelligence Agency (CIA) was established in 1947 to coordinate and centralize analysis of all-source intelligence. The CIA was directed also to conduct clandestine human source collection efforts (espionage) to infiltrate and report on the activities, capabilities, and intentions of the USSR, its satellite partners, and the international communist movement.

The CIA soon found the task of recruiting Soviet and other communist agents with appropriate access to be difficult, given police state control and effective intelligence services under communist rule. As a result, the Eisenhower administration initiated the development of remote technical collection systems to monitor Soviet activities and at least reduce the uncertainty regarding Soviet military capabilities and intentions, which plagued US military planning and procurement decisions. Almost every administration that followed provided the resources to enhance intelligence collection and analytic capabilities against the perceived Soviet threat.

The US Intelligence Community was thus eventually able to establish a relatively accurate baseline understanding of Soviet military force capabilities. It is important to say "relatively" because the intelligence record during the Cold War was certainly not perfect. At times the Intelligence Community either over-estimated or underestimated the capabilities (the number of weapons or their technical qualities, such as ranges, accuracies, or lethality) of Soviet weapon systems, especially those of strategic bombers and intercontinental-range bal-listic missiles. These episodes often resulted in, or fed, ongoing debates within the policy community or led to strife between parts of the policy community and the Intelligence Community. It was, of course, just as important to un-derstand Moscow's strategic intentions, and the difficulty of doing this often led to interagency battles among intelligence analysts and among policymakers regarding how to interpret Soviet behavior, statements, and at times their ac-tual military capabilities. There were no crystal balls and, without good human source information, Soviet intentions could only be inferred.

The resulting ambiguities and uncertainties, along with Soviet efforts to de-ceive and hide their intentions, actions, and capabilities, made accurate judg-ments a real challenge. The limitations of intelligence support to policymakers continue to the present. It should not be a surprise then to anyone when the Intelligence Community's analyses and judgments do not always prove to be unanimous or accurate.

Monitoring WMD Proliferation

Even as the Intelligence Community was developing sophisticated and com-prehensive capabilities to monitor increasingly capable Soviet military forces, some resources were also focused on proliferation issues. Proliferation, it turns out, posed a challenge of a different kind, for the clandestine nuclear weapon programs of smaller countries lacked the large infrastructure and signatures as-sociated with the Soviet (and to some extent the Chinese) industrial enterprises and military forces. Thus, some of the capabilities developed to monitor Soviet forces were less capable of monitoring small, clandestine nuclear weapon pro-grams as well as other WMD programs. The fundamental difference was due to the factors described in Chapter 1: small, clandestine programs, especially those involving chemical or biological agents, are often hidden in dual-purpose facilities using dual-purpose equipment, and nuclear weapon programs can be masked by legitimate civilian nuclear programs and facilities. Further, prolifer-ating countries generally do not deploy large WMD stockpiles requiring large infrastructures, which reduces the tip-offs of suspicious activity that technical collection systems, particularly imagery satellites, can normally provide. This challenge is compounded by the international sale and transfer of knowledge, technology, and equipment, much of which is legitimate but which can be re-channeled into clandestine activities (see Appendix F). Moreover, monitoring the technical and financial activities of some relatively developed countries, such as China, as well as countries such as North Korea, is no small task. And when clandestine transfers and activities involve non-state actors, such as the A. Q. Khan black-market nuclear proliferation network or international ter-rorists, the small signature and diffuse nature of the transactions increase the complexity of the monitoring task (for details on the A. Q. Khan network, see Chapter 3).

The United States and other like-minded countries have had to devise unique methods of collecting intelligence against would-be proliferators. One means that has become increasingly available is commercial satellite imagery, such as from Google Earth. The US National Geospatial-Intelligence Agency (NGA), which is charged with analyzing imagery on behalf of the entire Intel-ligence Community, is using commercially available, high-definition satellite photos to supplement what can be collected by the more capable US govern-ment reconnaissance satellites. One report in 2008 indicated that NGA was helping to fund an advanced commercial satellite being launched by GeoEye. However, there is a downside to this new tool: countries have stepped up efforts to conceal sensitive facilities, and terrorists also can make good use of such imagery. For example, in August 2006, the Islamic Army in Iraq reportedly cir-culated an instructional video on how to aim rockets at US military sites using Google Earth. And images from Google Earth and other commercial sources have been found in safe houses used by al-Qaeda and other terrorist groups.[2]

Unfortunately, every disclosure, whether official or unofficial, of US moni-toring capabilities gives proliferators new advantages in their efforts to deny information on their clandestine activities. This appears to have been the case with India's nuclear test preparations in 1998 (see Chapter 3), and it certainly muddied the waters as intelligence organizations in the United States and other countries tried to sort out the status of Saddam Hussein's WMD programs af-ter 1998, when UN inspectors were denied further access (see Chapter 5). The Iraqis under the Saddam regime became experts in concealing their clandestine activities from both inspectors and remote technical collection systems.

Clandestine Human Sources. Because of the intrinsic limits on traditional

Concealment of Clandestine WMD Programs

Efforts to hide clandestine military programs are part of the "cat and mouse" game that countries play to gain advantage over their adversaries or to avoid international condemnation. State and non-state actors undertake measures to deceive those who would collect against their covert activities or discover the location of covert facilities. During the Cold War the Soviet Union and the United States took steps to mask sensitive military capabilities, and a number of other countries have done the same with their clandestine efforts to develop weapons of mass destruction.

As commercial satellite imagery and rapid communications have become available and have joined ever more sophisticated technical collection capabilities, those who wish to hide their clandestine programs and facilities have become more adept at doing so. Saddam Hussein used sophisticated concealment and denial measures to hide his nuclear, biological, and chemical weapons programs from the United States and international inspectors. Other proliferators, such as North Korea, Iran, and Syria, have done the same.

Following the exposure of Iran's undeclared nuclear activities by an opposition group, Tehran has undertaken extensive efforts to provide false cover stories and to conceal, bury deeply underground, and sanitize its nuclear infrastructure against snooping satellites and forensic environmental sampling by IAEA inspectors. Along similar lines, Syria tried to conceal its nuclear reactor at Al-Kibar with a false façade (hiding the reactor inside an ordinary-looking building with no external cables or other indicators of ongoing nuclear activity, such as a telltale cooling tower) both before Israeli aircraft destroyed the facility and then afterward by removing indicators of the reactor before IAEA inspectors could arrive.

technical collection systems, the focus in targeting and collecting against small, clandestine programs often comes back to human sources. In many proliferation situations, there are no external observables; only human sources can gain access to people or facilities. Thus, an emphasis on clandestine human collection has reemerged against countries—and their suppliers—seeking nuclear weapons or other WMD capabilities.

As always with this type of intelligence collection, finding human sources with relevant access and vetting their motivations and information is a significant challenge. Most people are not inclined to spy against their own countries, unless they are suffering a severe setback or disappointment in their lives, want revenge against their government for some grievance or, as at times during the Cold War, are driven by ideology to cooperate with the intelligence services of other countries. Thus, potential agents must be carefully scrutinized to ascertain their access to valuable information as well as their reliability and suitability. When the goal is to infiltrate terrorist cells, where killing (especially American citizens) is a badge of honor, the challenge becomes even greater and more dangerous.[3]

Sophisticated technical and human collection operations always face counterintelligence efforts by the intelligence and security services of the target countries. It turns out that many of the most effective, and therefore damaging, agents working against both sides during the Cold War were volunteers, who did not need the foreign intelligence service to convince them to spy. For example, the Soviets had sympathetic US spies (e.g. the Rosenbergs) in the Manhattan Project in World War II and sympathetic British spies (e.g. Messrs. Philby, Burgess, and Maclean) in the early days of the Cold War. On the other side, officers on the Soviet General Staff voluntarily provided critical military information to the United States and United Kingdom during the Cold War. At the end of the Cold War and into the post–Cold War era, Aldrich Ames, a career CIA officer, and Robert Hanssen, a career FBI officer, volunteered to provide the Soviet Union, and later Russia, with an invaluable one-two punch in access to US domestic and foreign intelligence. The damage to US national security, the Intelligence Community, and its foreign agents was staggering. Sensitive national security secrets, and human lives, were lost.[4]

While terrorist organizations do not typically have the resources to spy on the United States in the same way, sleeper cells certainly use their access to scout out potential weaknesses and targets for future attacks. And countries such as North Korea and Iran, which desire to develop weapons of mass destruction, have at least some capacity to recruit agents to steal technical or other secrets. It has become well known that China has made numerous attempts to steal technical, particularly nuclear, secrets to advance its nuclear arsenal.

Even in the post–Cold War era, then, the United States must be diligent in protecting its national security secrets and conscientious in protecting its facilities and population centers from terrorist plotting and potential attacks. It must also continue to use its sophisticated remote technical collection systems, to the extent possible, to monitor proliferation activities. It follows that the United States must safeguard the technical and operational details of its collection systems, along with its human agents.

International Inspections. When the United States does not have a physical

Impact of Foreign Spying on US Intelligence Capabilities

Foreign efforts to collect US national security information during the Cold War were extensive, and many of these clandestine efforts continue to the present day. The Soviet Union and its Eastern European allies were particularly aggressive. Foreign intelligence services also tried to neutralize US efforts to collect information on their activities, particularly those dealing with military forces and programs for weapons of mass destruction.

Soviet efforts to collect information on US-recruited spies, reconnaissance satellites, and other classified collection systems as well as efforts to conceal their own activities from detection were aided, unfortunately, by US nationals who gave away key information. In the arena of imagery, William Kampiles, a young, immature CIA officer, gave the Soviets in 1978 the operating manual for the new KH-11 reconnaissance satellite system, which allowed the Soviets (and possibly other countries with which the Soviets shared their intelligence) to strengthen their countermeasures.[5] Countries that are intent on clandestinely developing weapons of mass destruction typically attempt to conduct their activities in a manner that makes it difficult for remote technical monitoring systems, particularly satellites, to be effective. (For a discussion of the challenges posed in the past by the clandestine proliferation efforts of India, Iran, Iraq, Israel, North Korea, and South Africa, see Chapter 3.)

Satellite imagery is not the only technical means of collection that espionage and countermeasures can affect. In the 1980s it was discovered that the Walker spy ring had compromised US Navy communication codes, thereby compromising signals intelligence (SIGINT) capabilities as well as naval operations.[6] Moreover, a government contract employee, Christopher John Boyce, compromised a SIGINT satellite system seemingly out of spite against the CIA in the 1980s.[7] All of these espionage cases were gifts to the Soviet Union and, at least in part, to other countries striving to hide their activities from the United States and the international community.

The damage to US intelligence collection and operations by foreign espionage activities has continued well into the new century. Some of the most damaging foreign spying against the United States has taken place after the Cold War, by Russia, China, and other countries. As mentioned above, two US intelligence officials, Aldrich Ames of the CIA and Robert Hanssen of the FBI, betrayed the United States by volunteering their services to the Soviet Union during the Cold War. Their betrayal continued into the post–Cold War era; they each provided sensitive intelligence information for over a decade. Ames was caught in the mid-1990s, and Hanssen only in 2002. Both were counterintelligence experts, which meant that they were able to divulge the names of agents working for US intelligence and to thwart US efforts to catch foreign, especially Russian, spies. Significant damage resulted to US human collection efforts during and after the Cold War, and a number of those working clandestinely for the United States lost their lives.[8] Moreover, Ames had access to a variety of other intelligence information within the CIA, including published national intelligence estimates, some of which addressed proliferation issues. This compromised how and what US intelligence understood about some proliferation activities. Sergei Tretyakov, who served as the deputy head of the Russian mission to the United Nations in New York until his defection in 2000, claims that Russian intelligence operations against the United States are just as active now as during the Soviet period.[9]

In addition to Russia, a report prepared for Congress in 2002 listed China, France, India, Israel, Japan, and Taiwan as among the most active collectors against the United States. Further, in 2001, an analyst working for the Defense Intelligence Agency was arrested for having spied for Cuba for seventeen years. US officials had to assume that any intelligence she passed to the Cubans was likely shared with other countries. The revelation of such significant foreign spying activities following the Cold War made the US Intelligence Community revise personnel and security procedures, among other measures.

Israel. In April 2008, the FBI somewhat belatedly arrested Ben-ami Kadish, a US Army mechanical engineer, on charges of having spied for Israel from 1979 through 1985. Kadish was suspected of having reported to the same Israeli handler as had Jonathan Jay Pollard, a US civilian working for the navy, who pleaded guilty in 1986 of spying for Israel. Apparently because of his belief that the United States was not sharing enough intelligence with Israel, Pollard volunteered to provide intelligence reports, imagery, and information about weapon systems (presumably of Soviet origin).[10]

China. As part of a government-wide response to revelations about Chinese spying in 1999, particularly against US nuclear facilities, the FBI created an intelligence directorate to strengthen its counterintelligence efforts against both foreign spies and terrorists.[11] In 2008, the FBI arrested two Chinese intelligence agents— one who passed secrets on every planned US military sale to Taiwan for the next five years, and the other who passed defense industrial secrets on the space shuttle and on other military and civilian aircraft programs over an eighteen-year span. For example, Chi Mak, who was sentenced in early April 2008, acknowledged that he had been placed in the United States more than twenty years earlier in order to burrow into the defense-industrial establishment to steal secrets. According to a *Washington Post* account, US intelligence and Justice Department officials claim the Mak case represents only a small facet of an intelligence-gathering operation that has long been in place and is growing in size and sophistication. The Chinese government has deployed a diverse network of professional spies, students, scientists, and others to systematically collect US know-how.[12] And according to Assistant Attorney General Kenneth Wainstein, such arrests marked only the latest Chinese attempts to gain top-secret information about US military systems and sales. He described China as "particularly adept, and particularly determined and methodical in their espionage efforts."[13]

presence in a particular country, such as in Iraq prior to 2003, it must rely more than normally on intelligence provided by other countries or information provided by the international community, such as through international inspections. For example, following the 1991 Gulf War, the United States gained many of its insights into Iraq's WMD programs from international inspections conducted by the United Nations (UN) and International Atomic Energy Agency (IAEA). The United Nations Special Commission (UNSCOM) was created in 1991 and was made responsible to the Security Council directly, not to the UN Secretary-General. It was given predominance over the IAEA also, which created unnecessary conflict; however, this was gradually overcome by the professionalism of the two staffs.[14] The IAEA completely dismantled the Iraqi nuclear weapon infrastructure, and the special commission eliminated most of the Iraqi chemical and biological weapons programs. However, once Saddam refused to continue inspections in 1998—after the inspectors were temporarily withdrawn to permit a bombing campaign against Iraq by the United States and the United Kingdom—the United States had to rely more heavily on remote technical collection, defectors, and the liaison intelligence services of those friendly countries still represented in Iraq. The nature of clandestine WMD programs, as described in Chapter 1, limits the utility of overhead imagery. Depending on

---

Liaison Intelligence Relationships

An issue that has risen to the fore is the reliance the United States had to place on liaison intelligence information to understand the truth about Saddam's WMD programs. Although the US relationship with British and German intelligence services was highlighted, the fact that US intelligence has such relationships is not news. Indeed, these relationships, especially with Britain, have existed since the advent of the US Intelligence Community in the late 1940s. They even preceded and were in part responsible for the establishment of the post–World War II peacetime intelligence effort by the United States.

Britain's intelligence station, located in New York City, was instrumental in bringing the United States into World War I and in sharing intelligence information with the United States on Germany. Sir William Wiseman was the head of the station and in some ways became more influential with President Woodrow Wilson than was the British ambassador in Washington. Weisman was considered to be the most influential "agent of influence" the British ever had.[15] Similarly, during the run-up to World War II, a British intelligence officer, Sir William Stephenson, played an influential role in persuading President Franklin D. Roosevelt to come to the aid of Britain against Hitler's Germany.[16] As is appropriate for a true secret agent, some of Stephenson's published biographical information has been challenged. In 1976 a Canadian author, William Stevenson, who is not a relation, published a biography of Stephenson entitled *A Man Called Intrepid;* however, some statements in the book have been questioned.

During World War II, one of the most robust areas of cooperation was in signals intelligence; the British had broken the German Enigma code, and the United States eventually broke the Japanese diplomatic and naval codes. During the fighting in Europe, the United States and Britain continued to share intelligence as they joined forces to defeat Hitler, and British intelligence helped teach US intelligence how to function, particularly in clandestine operations and covert actions, in support of the French resistance. As a result of Stephenson's initiatives and the intelligence cooperation during the war, a special, close Anglo-American intelligence relationship developed, which continues today.[17]

Since World War II, US intelligence liaison relationships have expanded well beyond the British to countries such as Australia, Canada, Germany, France, Israel, and others. Most intelligence services have liaison relationships to increase their capabilities, especially in areas where they may not have unilateral access.[18] Each service has its own strengths and weaknesses, dependent largely on the priorities of its government and national security requirements. Therefore, individual intelligence services must decide, depending on the issue in question, whether another intelligence service can contribute unique information for its own policymakers.

Using liaison intelligence information for policy decisions can be, of course, a two-edged sword. While the information may be unique, the receiving service is normally one step removed from the source and at times does not have direct access to that source, depending on the closeness of the liaison relationship. Thus, as we said previously, the recipient service's ability to determine the credibility of the information and reliability of the source is reduced. Furthermore, the recipient country always runs the risk of being the target of disinformation—either by the source or by the liaison service providing the information. A senior US official is quoted as having said, "There is no such thing as friendly intelligence agencies. There are only the intelligence agencies of friendly powers."[19] Thus, intelligence services and policymakers must be cognizant that an ulterior motive may lie behind the liaison information; the receiving service must do all it can to corroborate the information it receives.

the stage of development, some activities related to nuclear weapon programs are identifiable, but earlier stages of research and development can be hidden within structures as can the production of chemical and biological precursors and agents. And the intercept of critical conversations among individuals is always fortuitous.

The 1998 Iraq case was instructive, however, in highlighting the challenges encountered in managing long-term inspection surveillance of a major proliferator. The bombing campaign known as Operation Desert Fox, carried out in 1998 by the US and UK air forces, destroyed the consensus in the Security Council over how to proceed in Iraq. The bombing was carried out as punishment for Iraqi noncooperation with the special commission, about which the chairman of UNSCOM had complained in a letter to the Security Council. France, Russia, and China then wanted the disarmament phase of Iraq terminated and the sanctions eased. To them, the special commission seemed increasingly a UK-US operation.[20] As a result, it was easier for Saddam to refuse re-admittance to the inspectors. Political coalitions among nations are always fragile, and care must be taken to preserve them.

Liaison Information. At times, because of the nature of hostile regimes involved in proliferation efforts, such as Saddam's Iraq, North Korea, and Iran, the United States does not have a physical presence in the country and therefore is severely limited in its ability to recruit local agents who have access to information of interest to US policymakers. As mentioned earlier, in addition to any information the United States can collect unilaterally, it is often necessary to rely heavily on the information provided by the intelligence services of friendly countries that do have a presence and at least some access, including through their own recruited agents. However, the use of liaison information puts the United States one step removed from vetting the credibility and trustworthiness of the sources. "Curve Ball," a German-run agent, is a case in point (see Chapter 5).[21] Also, the Intelligence Community must determine the motivations of the liaison service in sharing this information to rule out an attempt to feed false information to the United States.

Technical Collection. As mentioned earlier, technical collection systems are sophisticated but can be limited in their ability to collect against clandestine activities, which often are conducted inside small, nondescript, or dual-purpose structures. Thus, the Intelligence Community has made a concerted effort to adapt its imagery (IMINT) and signals intelligence (SIGINT) capabilities to new tasks. Overhead imagery, principally from reconnaissance satellites, can provide information on activities on the ground or at sea that increase suspicions regarding illicit activities. The growing availability of commercial satellite imagery has dramatically increased the amount of photographic coverage of areas of interest to the international community. However, images capture only activity at the moment; following a pattern of activity may be required before the alarm bells go off. In intercepting signals, such as phone conversations, the information gained may be specific and helpful; however, the intercept of conversations tends to be fortuitous, especially as individuals of interest become more sophisticated, as in changing cell phones periodically to prevent being tracked.

In the technical arena the Intelligence Community must not only stay on top of modern technology but analysts must be ever more imaginative in devising ways to look at information and make sense of the tidbits that are collected. The US government must encourage creativity and provide resources to the Intelligence Community to keep up with developments and hopefully stay ahead of them.

Tracking and understanding the flow of dual-use information and technology has already been mentioned. This requires cooperation among intelligence agencies and the clever combination of human and technical intelligence collection capabilities to build synergies that can track and make sense of what proliferators are up to. It is easy to see how human source, imagery, and signals intelligence could work together to piece together a puzzle, at least in principle. However, this requires not only experts on individual countries who understand what they may be striving to achieve but also analysts who understand international bank transfers and money flows, as well as technical experts who understand which technologies are of interest and which countries have them. Not unlike the Cold War challenge of understanding Soviet strategic nuclear forces and Moscow's intentions, today's challenge of monitoring clandestine programs requires a sophisticated and well-managed effort by diverse experts and collection disciplines to follow and make sense of the complex web of activities that go into any proliferation effort. A key challenge in the post–Cold War era is the significant expansion in the number and diversity of foreign players.

Open-source Information. A problem that gets too little attention is the collection and analysis of the enormous flow of open-source information. At times, such as in the case of North Korea, more information comes from open sources than from clandestine intelligence sources. The revolution in open-source information, due to technical advances in communications such as Google Earth, in-country blogs, and the extensive use of cell phones, is overwhelming to any collection and analytic effort. Even though the US Intelligence Community has for decades collected and analyzed foreign broadcast activities, sifting the wheat from the chaff is increasingly difficult, as is sorting through what information is true versus what is intended to mislead. As during the Cold War, a certain psychological warfare is conducted by rogue states as well as terrorist groups, especially al-Qaeda, to influence world opinion and undermine international nonproliferation efforts through misinformation and deception.

Analysis. Rarely is newly collected information passed directly to policymakers in its raw form. It must be processed so that analysts can review and consider its relevance and validity in the context of all other information available to the Intelligence Community. Thus, the process of responding to policymakers' needs for information requires careful analysis and presentation. This means that the Intelligence Community must maintain close relationships with policymakers in order to respond to their needs appropriately and, if possible, anticipate what will challenge them in the future. Policymakers are generally well-informed and capable individuals and would not ask the Intelligence Community for assistance if they already knew the answers to the questions they ask. The fact is that they can never have expertise on all of the issues they are required to work on. So the job of responding to policymakers' needs is inherently difficult, and generally responses cannot be made with absolute confidence because of the unknowns and complexities of the issues. (A thorough discussion of the challenge of producing helpful analysis for policymakers may be found in chapter 6 of *Intelligence: From Secrets to Policy,* by Mark M. Lowenthal.)

Intelligence analysts typically are experts in their areas of responsibility and provide information from all sources relevant to the issues they cover. Analytic expertise ranges from political, economic, military, and technical to anthropological, ecological, environmental, medical, and psychological. Analyzing sophisticated military forces and proliferation efforts requires good technical expertise to understand the activities of concern. The potential consequences of incorrectly assessing a state or non-state's technical capabilities and activities are substantial. Moreover, recognition of the indirect ways that funds can be transferred internationally in support of clandestine proliferation or terrorist activities calls for analytic expertise in the banking and commercial arenas. Finally, the advent of terrorist and proliferation activities centered in the Middle

East and South Asia makes having skill in the languages of those regions a clear requirement. Unfortunately, as in the early days of the Cold War, it takes time to recruit and train analysts in the required skills.

In addition to having expertise, the primary responsibility of analysts is to know what has been reported in the past and how additional reporting will help policymakers have a more complete and accurate understanding of the country or issue on which they are working. Thus, Intelligence Community managers not only are required to manage collection efforts, but they must also guide, review, and critique the work of their analysts so that individual agencies, or the Intelligence Community as a whole in the case of interagency analyses, can ensure that the community is providing the most comprehensive and thoughtful intelligence on a given subject. Collegial review and coordination among analysts is essential to be sure that all relevant information and views are presented. As explained in Chapter 4, the packaging of analysis in a form and length that will be most effective in communicating with policymakers is also critical.

Coordination. The coordination of views and interpretations, both within the Intelligence Community and with outside experts, is a fundamental part of the analytic process. It ensures that relevant information is brought to the table; it also helps to work through possibly contradictory pieces of information or analyses, and it exposes individual or institutional biases that may exist. The value of coordination was evident in the divergent views expressed in the NIE produced on Iraq's WMD programs in the fall of 2002 (see Chapter 5).

However, a significant reality in the intelligence business is that not all information should be seen by everyone. The compartmentalization of information from especially sensitive sources must be protected and access limited. Indeed, prior to the adjustments in the organization of the Intelligence Community and information sharing among agencies, which followed the terrorist attacks of 2001, a strict legal wall separated foreign and domestic intelligence. The fear had been that privacy and civil liberties would be threatened by any intelligence agency that had both domestic and foreign intelligence responsibilities. This wall resulted in insufficient sharing of intelligence between the FBI, which is responsible for the collection of domestic intelligence, and the rest of the Intelligence Community, which is responsible for foreign intelligence. Establishing the Department of Homeland Security's Intelligence Division, among other measures, has significantly improved the integration of local, domestic, and foreign intelligence.

At some point in the process of formulating judgments, senior managers and analysts must have a full deck of cards to ensure that the most informed judgments are made and passed on to policymakers. Moreover, sharing sensitive information within the Intelligence Community as well as with policymakers must be done with the assurance that sensitive sources and methods will be protected—and not exposed to justify a particular policy or win a policy battle. Sharing such information with the public requires even more discernment. This is where unauthorized leaks and press reports of intelligence information can be so damaging.

Because all intelligence analysis is intended to be relevant, timely, and objective, neutralizing bias and preventing the politicization of analyses are essential. If policymakers suspect that intelligence analysis is slanted to promote a particular policy outcome, the analysis surely will be discounted or dismissed by at least some policymakers, and the intelligence officers involved in producing the analysis will be suspect. Unfortunately, the discounting of analysis can occur no matter how hard the Intelligence Community tries to avoid bias. Likewise, policymakers at times hype intelligence provided by stretching the judgments to help sell their policies (see Chapter 5). The Intelligence Community puts great effort then into ensuring, as far as possible, that its analysis is free of personal, institutional, and political bias, and that it is not policy-prescriptive. Along with this task is the onus of presenting to policymakers information or judgments when they are in conflict with policy preferences and will not be well received. It is the job of the Intelligence Community to "tell it like it is," as far as that is understood, and not to soft-peddle or spin its analysis to please the preferences of policymakers.

This does not mean that intelligence analysts are forced to agree on everything so as to present only single judgments or judgments that represent the lowest common denominator of agreement. To the contrary, when uncertainties (usually due to incomplete information) lead to differing interpretations, then the substantive differences and the reasons for them must be explained. Policymakers normally develop policies that in themselves contain less than one hundred percent certainty of success, so they need to understand where significant gaps of intelligence information lie as well as differences of analytic judgment and the level of confidence analysts have in their judgments. Intelligence analysts therefore must report what they do not know, as well as what they know and believe to be true. Even if actionable intelligence is not available, the Intelligence Community must provide what it knows as clearly as possible so that policymakers can determine how much weight to give the resulting intelligence judgments.

Since collected intelligence is rarely complete and void of ambiguity, analysts normally work with information gaps and corresponding uncertainties. Thus, they must be taught to think "outside the box" to avoid falling into the trap of "group think," which is fostered by uncritical mind-sets. Moreover, they must make informed judgments based on incomplete data. Sorting through available information and clearly explaining one's assumptions are important but can be difficult, as will be discussed in the case of the Intelligence Community's effort to understand Saddam's WMD programs (see Chapter 5). In that example, history, past practices, and intentions together created a context for interpreting ambiguous and incomplete information in a particular way. Policymakers, who are generally absorbed by intense efforts to solve problems, often appreciate a fresh look at the data the Intelligence Community can provide so that they can consider new ways to approach difficult situations. (At times, however, their patience for "fresh looks" is limited.)

Dissemination. Finally, the timeliness and form of intelligence reporting are important. Intelligence analysis, no matter how good, misses an opportunity to inform policymakers if it is not presented when needed and in a form that is easily absorbed. This means that the Intelligence Community does not have the option to decline responding because of lack of data. This was somewhat the case in 2002 when the Intelligence Community produced an estimate of Iraq's WMD capabilities despite the lack of new intelligence (see Chapter 5). Intelligence must report what it knows, however limited, and apply informed analytic judgments to bridge the gaps in information and then present the results in time to help policy deliberations. Even a limited response can give policymakers a fuller understanding of the situation they are facing, but it can also provide a false understanding of the situation. So that busy policymakers can easily grasp the message and underlying substance, there are multiple formats for written analyses as well as videos and oral briefings. The appropriate level of detail depends on the intended audience: the president normally receives relatively short and concise analyses, while support staffers who are experts in the various fields want and receive much more detail. How the Intelligence Community communicates sometimes can be as important as what it communicates.

In the US Intelligence Community, the CIA, the Defense Intelligence Agency (DIA), and the Bureau of Intelligence and Research (INR) perform all-source analysis; the CIA generally has the largest number of analysts working on a subject matter, save military analysis, which is the primary purview of DIA. This means that these organizations receive information from all collection disciplines and try to make sense of the whole array of data. Therefore, the sharing of information, except for that of the highest sensitivity, is a normal practice, and the all-source analysts frequently interact with the primary national collection agencies—the National Security Agency (for signals intelligence) and the National Geospatial-Intelligence Agency (for imagery intelligence). Analysts are also supported by the intelligence components of the four military services as well as by experts within other departments, such as the Departments of Energy and Treasury (for more on the Intelligence Community, see Appendix D).

Assessing Motives, Intentions, and Capabilities. To discern whether a country or a terrorist organization is pursuing or has a clandestine WMD program, analysts must address different aspects of the problem, including the following: (1) what might be motivating a country or group to seek nuclear weapons or other WMD capabilities? (2) what are the intentions of that country or group in doing so? and (3) what, if any, capabilities is that country or group trying to obtain, or what does it already have? Depending on the question asked, the Intelligence Community tries to obtain information using the most appropriate collection discipline. Regarding intentions, human sources typically will have the best chance of success, assuming access is possible. If agent access is not possible, then perhaps communication intercepts, if available, will work. For capabilities that include physical signatures, such as buildings or equipment, imagery collection is probably the best source because activities can be observed over time.

For example, in some cases the first indication of a clandestine nuclear weapon program can come from a chance spotting of items or activities that are normally associated with such programs. In other cases, intelligence might be obtained regarding the desires of a country or group to have such weapons, but no signs of an actual program have yet been detected. In either case, analysts are looking for the other pieces of the puzzle to corroborate any information in hand in an effort to make sense of the whole and to postulate what might be transpiring. In addition, understanding the context of the detected activities (past efforts or actions, as well as clear attempts at concealment, denial, or deception) may allow analysts to infer that a clandestine effort is underway. All of these factors must be included in the management of collection and analytic efforts in order to compensate for areas of uncertainty and to bridge gaps where the information is spotty or even contradictory.

As explained in Chapter 5, intelligence analysts were swayed heavily in their judgments by the Saddam regime's past practices and motivations, even when there was little new evidence of WMD activity in Iraq. Saddam was clearly using concealment, denial, and deception practices to thwart access and understanding by inspectors as well as collection efforts by remote sensors. Despite the fact that the inspections that resumed in late 2002 and early 2003 had failed to turn up any evidence, even at suspected locations, and that unaccounted items may have been the result of poor accounting on the part of the Iraqis, it was difficult to accept the lack of concrete, current evidence as proof that such programs and materials did not exist. Some inspectors suspected concealment of prohibited items. In retrospect, it is unfortunate that alternative explanations for Iraqi behavior were not considered more thoroughly.

Understanding Cultural and Historical Context. Along with the factors just described, good intelligence analysis must be rooted also in a realistic understanding of a country's cultural and historical traditions. Nothing can replace the insights that are gained by knowing the language and having studied, worked, or traveled in a country or region. Understanding how the citizens of a country think about life, how they relate to one another, and how they relate to the outside world are all clues to what might be motivating their leadership. That is one reason why open-source information often plays a significant role in intelligence analysis. What leaders say, what their papers print, and what their radio and television programs broadcast are all clues as to how a people are perceiving and reacting to the outside world. Moreover, in a culture where lying and deception may be normal, one must factor that reality into the analysis. When members of the Intelligence Community feel particularly weak in these areas, they are wise to seek out the assistance of members of the academic or business community who have relevant experience in specific countries. No avenue of potential insight and understanding should be ignored.

It should be clear that good understanding of clandestine proliferation activities goes beyond the detection of actual weapons themselves. While unambiguous detection is the ideal, in most cases the information obtained about clandestine programs is more indirect, and it can come from either the supply or demand side—hopefully from both. As mentioned earlier, the effort to understand ambiguous and spotty information particularly with regard to dual-use facilities and materials is often compounded by efforts to deny such information. Effective collection and good analysis require appropriate expertise, sophistication, care, and persistence. Nevertheless, the risk is high that intelligence understanding will be incomplete, that policy needs will not be fully satisfied, and that intelligence assessments will contain some errors. But as discussed in Chapter 3, the overall track record in monitoring nuclear proliferation activities thus far (despite the setback in Iraq) has been relatively good.

3   The Track Record
Against Clandestine Proliferation

Over the past six years, the public has been bombarded with articles about the failure of the US Intelligence Community, particularly the Central Intelligence Agency, to assess accurately the status of Saddam Hussein's nuclear, chemical, and biological weapon programs. Some of this criticism is justified. (For an explanation of how this failure in Iraq came about, see Chapter 5.) Overall, however, the performance of the US Intelligence Community over the decades has been on target more often than not in assessing the status of clandestine nuclear weapon programs in individual countries. The effort against nuclear proliferation has always had the highest priority, although special attention has been paid to some countries' efforts to develop clandestine chemical or biological weapons programs. One perennial problem has been the priority given to the use of scarce intelligence collection and analytical assets—which often are diverted to monitor crises—to understand the activities, intentions, and capabilities of a diverse collection of nations, most of which are not open to rigorous monitoring (see Appendix G). With non-state actors, the track record in monitoring clandestine proliferation efforts is less clear; little is known publicly about the success the United States has had against efforts by terrorist organizations to obtain nuclear, chemical, or biological weapons. It is prudent, therefore, that we discuss separately the track record in monitoring the clandestine efforts of nation-states from the record with non-state actors. However, the two did come together in the case of the A. Q. Khan black market nuclear proliferation network, which we discuss at the end of this chapter.

Monitoring Proliferation by Nation-States

The experience of the US Intelligence Community in South Asia is mixed. It seems that US scientists and intelligence knew almost as much about the nuclear program in Pakistan as did Pakistani scientists.[1] This is in contrast with significant surprises from India in 1974 and 1998 (though there were successes in 1981 and 1995). The United States apparently has tended to examine India less critically than more-threatening countries because it is a parliamentary democracy. Pakistan, however, would always be scrutinized more closely because it has been ruled often by a military dictatorship and because of its proximity to more unstable and dangerous areas to the north.

India. The possibility of a nuclear explosive test by India had been widely discussed for years within the US government prior to the 1974 Indian test.[2] Several intelligence assessments in the latter part of the 1960s and early 1970s concluded that India could rather easily move from a peaceful nuclear program to a military one; and if it decided to do so, it could conduct a nuclear test within a short time. For example, in 1972 an assessment concluded that over the next several years the chances that India would conduct a test were about even; and that while India could conduct a test on short notice, no firm intelligence existed that it had decided to do so.[3] The drilling in the spring of 1974 at Pokhran, the designated test site, was thought to be related to a search for water or perhaps oil. Thus, the Indian nuclear test on May 18, 1974, was a surprise.[4] Although US intelligence understood the details of India's program well, the bottom line was that US intelligence did not expect a test in 1974. Since US policymakers were not warned in advance, the option of using diplomatic means to prevent the test was unavailable. The primary reasons for the inability to predict the actual test was the low allocation of collection assets for the task along with the paucity of inside information.[5]

A different and more favorable outcome occurred some years later. In 1981, Indira Gandhi returned to office as prime minister. In May 1982, in response to a proposal from Indian nuclear scientists, she authorized two nuclear tests. However, she called them off within hours. Shortly before, India's foreign secretary, Maharaja Krishna Rasgotra, had been in Washington and learned that the United States had information on preparations for the two planned tests at Pokhran. When Rasgotra met with US Undersecretary of State Lawrence Eagleburger, Eagleburger asked him about the test preparations and wanted to know what was going on in Pokhran. When Rasgotra returned to India, he briefed Prime Minister Gandhi on this meeting and told her that there would be trouble if India conducted a nuclear test. Gandhi, who had earlier that day authorized the two tests, abruptly cancelled them.[6] US intelligence had placed collection against India higher on the priority list than in the past.

In 1992, then Director of Central Intelligence Robert Gates told a congressional committee that while there was no evidence that India had weaponized and assembled nuclear weapons, "such weapons could be assembled quickly." In the spring of 1995, in response to military scientists who wanted to conduct a nuclear test, Indian Prime Minister Rao authorized the preparation of test shafts at the Pokhran nuclear test site. During the months that followed, US intelligence closely followed these preparations. By November, scientific and technical activity appeared to increase. On December 15, 1995, the US ambassador, Frank Wisner, called on the private secretary of Prime Minister Rao and indicated that a test by India could bring sanctions from the United States. President William Clinton telephoned the prime minister soon after. The Indian foreign minister publicly denied that India was planning a test. Thus, for the second time, timely intelligence had prevented an Indian nuclear test.[7]

In 1998, however, the outcome was different. In March, the Bharatiya Janata Party (BJP) for the first time had sufficient success in parliamentary elections to form a government. During the electoral campaign, the BJP had made it clear that if they were successful and formed a government, they would test nuclear weapons and build a nuclear weapon arsenal. On May 11, India carried out three tests at Pokhran, according to an announcement by Prime Minister Vajpayee later that day, and conducted two more tests on May 13. While the actual number and yields of the nuclear tests carried out by India would remain the subject of controversy for years (the readings of monitoring devices in the West showed fewer tests with lower yields than claimed by the Indian government), India no doubt had carried out nuclear tests, and US intelligence had not given policymakers advance warning. Even though it is doubtful that with advance warning from the Intelligence Community a US demarche would have dissuaded the Indians from testing, Senator Richard Shelby, chairman of the Senate Select Committee on Intelligence, described this disconnect as "a colossal failure."[8] Given that the new Indian government had indicated its intent to test, however, it seems unreasonable to lay all of the blame for preventing the tests on the Intelligence Community's failure to provide tactical warning of the time and place.

But why had this failure happened? The Indian government in the previous months had engaged in an effective campaign of disinformation, and there was a tendency to believe that the BJP's statements were only campaign rhetoric. In late March 1998, senior foreign policy advisor N. N. Jha had reassured officials at the American embassy that over the next three to six months his government would be reviewing Indian national security policy and had no plans for weapon tests. The US ambassador to the United Nations, Bill Richardson, was similarly reassured by Prime Minister Vajpayee in April, in New Delhi.[9]

Indian concealment activities at the test site included burying cables, placing camouflage netting over the test area, and conducting as many operations as possible at night or when reconnaissance satellites were not overhead. On the night of May 5, army personnel laid the cables at the various shafts and then covered their tracks, replacing vegetation and trying to make the area appear undisturbed. The Indians also took advantage of the May sandstorms that occur in the area to hide from US satellites. They monitored the winds carefully to be sure that any artificially created mounds created by bulldozers were aligned with the wind to make the mounds appear to be naturally created. Vehicles used for activities at night were always back in the same assigned places by day so as not to disclose increased vehicle movement. Information on the impending tests was known only to a few officials and those actually working on the project. The Indian Intelligence Bureau ran a vigorous counterintelligence program, so that the CIA was unable to recruit a single person who knew anything about the tests. And NSA also could come up with nothing, because India's nuclear weapon establishment communicated through encrypted digital messages relayed via small dishes through satellites.[10]

Director of Central Intelligence George Tenet promptly appointed a review panel headed by former vice chairman of the Joint Chiefs of Staff Admiral David Jeremiah to investigate the Intelligence Community's failure to detect Indian test preparations. The panel presented a report in June making a number of recommendations. A key recommendation was to reorder intelligence collection priorities so that important issues such as nuclear weapon programs in India and Pakistan would be treated with the same urgency as monitoring so-called rogue states, such as Iran and North Korea. Since the 1998 tests, the US Intelligence Community has carefully monitored India and Pakistan as the countries have proceeded to weaponize, so that the nuclear programs and capabilities of the nuclear arsenals in India and Pakistan are well understood.[11] Experts estimate that by 2005 India may have produced between 334 and 504 kilograms of weapons-grade plutonium, enough to produce between 75 and 110 nuclear weapons (based on 4–5 kilograms of plutonium per weapon).[12]

Pakistan. After the Indian tests of May 1998, US intelligence analysts believed that Pakistan would without doubt soon respond in kind. On May 14, Director Tenet informed the House and Senate intelligence committees that preparations for an underground test by Pakistan in the Chagai Hills region had been detected by US intelligence. In the coming weeks the United States, through diplomatic means, including telephone calls from President Clinton to Pakistani prime minister Sharif, tried hard to dissuade Pakistan from carrying out nuclear tests. But the tests—six in all—did take place on May 28 and May 30. Pakistan's tests came as no surprise to US intelligence, not only because the Indian tests made the Pakistani tests almost inevitable but also because of very effective monitoring of the nuclear program in Pakistan for many years.[13]

In 1987, Abdul Qadeer Khan, director of the Kahuta uranium enrichment facility who is sometimes referred to as the father of the Islamic bomb (and who later would be caught running a black market nuclear proliferation network—see later in this chapter), declared that Pakistan already possessed a nuclear weapon capability. He said in a press interview that "what the CIA had been saying about our possessing the bomb is correct."[14] The United States had blocked Pakistan's purchase of a reprocessing plant from France in the 1970s, but in 1975 Dr. Khan essentially stole centrifuge enrichment technology from a subcontractor of URENCO in the Netherlands, where he had worked for several years, brought it to Pakistan, and with government backing, built a uranium enrichment facility at Kahuta near Islamabad.[15] By the 1980s, the US government was aware of all of this. US intelligence also learned that, beginning in 1987, Pakistan began constructing nuclear weapon cores.[16] Thus, by 1987 the US government knew that Pakistan either possessed a nuclear explosive device or all the components to make one. The United States was also aware that China had passed to Pakistan a design for a 20-kiloton nuclear weapon, which had been tested at the Chinese test site, and that Pakistan was manufacturing triggering devices very similar to Chinese devices by the mid-1980s.[17] By May 1990, the US government had concluded that Pakistan possessed one or more nuclear weapons; by 1994, the government believed that Pakistan possessed enough nuclear material for six to eight nuclear weapons and could probably make one or two more weapons a year.[18] Over time, the US Intelligence Community had gained a good understanding of the Pakistani program due to an effective combination of overhead reconnaissance and the successful recruitment of spies with access to the Pakistani program. Thus, there have been no real surprises from Pakistan with respect to its program, either in 1998 or at any other time. One possibly disturbing note: some believe that on September 11, 2001, the United States may have known the location of Pakistani nuclear weapons but General Musharraf had these locations changed a few days later.

Israel. Israel made its decision to acquire nuclear weapons only a few years after the founding of the state. The first prime minister, David Ben-Gurion, believed that after the Holocaust, Israel could rely only on its own strength and nothing else to ensure survival. To him this meant, among other things, nuclear weapons, and to this end he established the Israeli Atomic Energy Commission in 1952.[19] In 1956 Israel decided as a first step to acquire a small research reactor from the United States. However, soon a better opportunity came its way: in July 1956 President Gamal Abdel Nasser of Egypt announced the nationalization of the Suez Canal. Britain and France decided on a military response, and France inquired whether Israel would be willing to join. Israel decided to join in the operation at least partly in the hope of getting a better deal on a nuclear reactor from France than from the United States.

Before the commencement of the operation against Egypt, France agreed to sell a research reactor to Israel. After the collapse of the Suez expedition, Israel asked France for an upgraded sale, in particular a reactor similar to the 40-megawatt reactor at Marcoule, France, which would produce a significant amount of plutonium every year. France agreed to supply a plutonium-producing reactor to be built at Dimona, which became the center of Israel's nuclear weapon program. Israel also requested that Saint Gobain Nucleaire build an underground plant attached to the reactor, which would include a reprocessing facility to extract plutonium from the Dimona reactor's spent fuel. France agreed to do this, and an agreement for the sale was signed a year later, in mid-1957. The reactor was to be used for "peaceful purposes." The sale agreement made no reference to the reprocessing plant; this was covered by a separate contract. Not long after, France provided Israel important information on the design and manufacture of nuclear weapons.[20] The heavy water required for the reactor was purchased in early 1959 in a third deal, this time with Norway, and Israel again promised to use the material for peaceful purposes only.[21]

By the time of the heavy-water purchase from Norway, construction of the nuclear facility was underway; later in 1959, excavation work for the reprocessing plant had begun. The nuclear reactor at Dimona was completed in the early 1960s and the reprocessing plant, by 1965. The first plutonium from the reactor was separated in 1965; by the time of the 1967 Six-Day War, Israel had two or three nuclear devices in its possession.[22]

The US Intelligence Community became interested in the Israeli program early on and by the late 1950s was convinced that Israel was engaged in a secret nuclear weapon program. The CIA learned of Norway's heavy-water sale to Israel, and there were reports that Israeli observers were present at France's first nuclear weapon tests. Through surveillance by U-2 aircraft, imagery of the construction project became available in 1958. By 1960, the US government considered Dimona to be a "probable" nuclear weapon development site. In late 1960, Secretary of State Christian A. Herter of the outgoing Eisenhower administration presented to the Israeli ambassador the US Intelligence Community's consensus that Israel was building a facility at Dimona that could not be intended solely for peaceful purposes and that could be interpreted to be for weapons production. The ambassador pleaded ignorance and said he would seek instructions.[23]

On December 20, the ambassador replied to Herter that what was being built at Dimona was a small research reactor, which would be used solely for peaceful purposes. The US government was not convinced. President-elect Kennedy asked Herter which nations he thought would be most likely to join the nuclear club in the near future. Herter replied, "India and Israel."[24] President Kennedy became convinced of a very real risk that nuclear weapons would sweep all over the world, and that Israel presented the greatest short-term danger in this regard. In the end, if the United States could not effectively say no to its ally Israel, how could it say no to Germany? And if Germany ever should acquire nuclear weapons, the Soviet Union quite likely would convert the Cold War into a "hot" war. Accordingly, during his time as president, Kennedy put considerable pressure on Israel not to build nuclear weapons.

After taking office in January 1961, Kennedy pressed for inspections, and within a few months Israel allowed an inspection of Dimona, with occasional inspections continuing to 1969. During these inspections the Israelis successfully pulled the wool over the eyes of US inspectors and concealed the true purpose of Dimona: all US inspections concluded that Israel was engaged only in peaceful nuclear research. The US inspectors were led to believe that the reactor at Dimona was a small research reactor rather than the large plutonium producer it actually was; the reprocessing plant was never found. Officials at the CIA and the State Department remained skeptical, however. After all, Israel continued to refuse to sign the Nuclear Non-Proliferation Treaty! While all US government agencies believed that Israel had the capability to build a nuclear weapon quickly if it so chose, there were differences of view as to whether it had actually done so. This was the situation in 1969 when inspections ended.

By 1974, however, views had changed, and a national intelligence estimate of that year concluded that Israel had already produced nuclear weapons. On March 11, 1976, the CIA deputy director for science and technology, Carl Duckett, participated in an off-the-record briefing for members of the American Institute of Aeronautics and Astronautics. He was asked about Israel's nuclear capability and responded that the CIA's estimate was that Israel possessed between ten and twenty nuclear weapons.[25] By the 1980s, the estimate had increased to twenty to thirty nuclear weapons.[26]

All of this was subsequently knocked into a cocked hat, however, as a result of the disclosures (an interview accompanied by photographs) by Mordechai Vanunu, a former employee at Dimona. The intelligence he provided, which was published by the *London Times* on October 5, 1986, revealed that the nuclear weapon program in Israel was much larger than US intelligence had realized. It was consistent with an arsenal of one hundred to two hundred nuclear weapons and disclosed an Israeli capability to build thermonuclear weapons. Thus, although the US Intelligence Community provided policymakers early warning of an Israeli nuclear weapon program in the late 1950s, the size of the program ultimately was vastly underestimated.[27]

South Africa. South Africa's white-minority government first began mining uranium in 1944, and it substantially increased production in the 1950s. In 1965, construction began on the Safari-1, a 20-megawatt research reactor acquired from the United States under the Atoms for Peace program; it became operational in 1967. In 1965, some South African politicians, most notably Prime Minister Hendrik Verwoerd at the inauguration ceremony for Safari, implied that South Africa should have nuclear weapons. A small uranium enrichment program had begun a few years earlier, and in the mid-1960s it was moved to Pelindaba, the site of Safari, to permit more sophisticated experiments. In 1970, construction began on a pilot enrichment plant, called the Y plant, at Valindaba, near Pelindaba, which became operational in 1974. That same year, Prime Minister John Vorster authorized the construction of the first nuclear device—a gun type device. (The unsophisticated Hiroshima gun design requires that a small quantity of highly enriched uranium be simply propelled up the barrel of a cannon-like device to collide with a second piece of HEU at the cannon's muzzle, forming a super-critical assembly and starting an explosive nuclear chain reaction.) A test site was located in the Kalahari Desert.

In the 1970s, South Africa, one of the world's major uranium producers, became of increased interest to US intelligence. Focus was on the Safari reactor and new means of uranium enrichment, which had been announced by the South African government. The Safari research reactor was under IAEA safeguards, which, of course, the unacknowledged Israeli reactor at Dimona never was. In 1974, in a special US intelligence estimate covering Israel, Taiwan, and South Africa, South Africa was judged unlikely to develop a weapon program in the 1970s, even though it possessed enrichment technology that would permit such a decision. The estimate judged further that a weapon program would be pursued only if a serious threat from one of South Africa's neighbors was perceived.[28]

In 1977, South Africa was preparing to conduct a nuclear weapon test at its Kalahari test site and began to drill boreholes and lay cables to carry out this objective. To act as a cover, a test of a new conventional rocket launcher was also scheduled nearby. However, the cover was destined to fail, as a Soviet reconnaissance satellite passed over the test site in early July. After the photographs were analyzed in Moscow, a second satellite was deployed over the site on July 20 for a closer look. When these photographs had been analyzed, the Soviet government sent a personal message from General Secretary Leonid Brezhnev to President Jimmy Carter that South Africa was planning a nuclear test in the Kalahari Desert, and it asked for the US government's help in stopping the test. US intelligence apparently had not independently detected the test preparations, and the US government went into crisis mode, secretly flying a small plane over the site. According to a report in the *Washington Post*, officials were "90 percent certain" that the Soviet analysis was correct.[29]

An interagency study was also commissioned, which concluded that South Africa might well back down from a test, as it had no overriding reason to test at that time, but the South African government would be unlikely to give up its efforts to acquire nuclear weapons. The Soviet government was informed that the US government agreed with its assessment on August 14. The British, French, and West German governments were also asked to help in the diplomatic offensive. South African denials continued for a while, but by August 21 the South African government agreed to give the assurance demanded by the United States. At a press conference on August 23, President Carter announced that "South Africa has informed us that they do not have and do not intend to develop nuclear explosive devices for any purpose, either peaceful or as a weapon" and "the Kalahari test site which has been in question is not designed for the test of nuclear explosives, and that no nuclear explosive test will be taken in South Africa, now or in the future."[30]

South Africa did not carry out a nuclear weapon test at the Kalahari site, although a mysterious double flash of light emanating from the South Atlantic was detected by a US VELA satellite in 1979. The double flash of light is a normal signature of a nuclear explosion. For years there was disagreement within the US government as to whether this event had been a nuclear weapon test. If it had been a test, was it Israeli, South African, or a joint test?[31] It is generally accepted that the event could not have been a South African test, as South Africa did not possess a nuclear device that would have been appropriate for such a test—judged to be between 3 and 5 kilotons—in 1979. However, in 1997 after the change in South African governments, a South African official stated that the 1979 incident had been a joint South African–Israeli test. The credibility of the official's statement, which has never been acknowledged by Israel, is bolstered by reports of Israeli–South African cooperation on nuclear issues and by the fact that the previous white-minority South African government had continued to build nuclear weapons through the 1980s, until President F. W. de Klerk stopped the program in 1989 and ordered the existing weapons destroyed. The South African government invited IAEA observers to witness the weapons' destruction prior to turning power over to the black-majority government in the early 1990s.[32]

In all, South Africa built six nuclear weapons (a seventh device was under construction) with a yield of 20 kilotons each, using the gun design with highly enriched uranium. The gun design is sufficiently uncomplicated that testing is not required to be confident that the device will detonate near the expected yield. This program was kept entirely secret from US intelligence and other intelligence services. However, an internal CIA report did state that while no direct evidence of a South African nuclear weapon program was available, it was the judgment of the analysts that South Africa either possessed nuclear weapons or could construct them quickly. The CIA also knew that South African scientists expected a yield of 20 kilotons should there be a test.[33] South Africa joined the Nuclear Non-Proliferation Treaty in 1991 after destroying its weapons pursuant to orders from President de Klerk, but only in 1993 did de Klerk publicly disclose the South African program in a speech to the Parliament. In summary, with respect to South Africa, US intelligence had strong suspicions of a program, but as noted, it was the Soviets who detected the test site preparations in 1977, and final confirmation of the program came from the South Africans. In 1979 US intelligence did detect what was later confirmed to be a test.

Libya. Between 1970 and 1990, Libya made numerous attempts to acquire a nuclear weapon capability. In 1970, Muammar Qadhafi sent a senior official to China to attempt to buy a nuclear weapon. He was politely rebuffed. For a time Libya tendered a standing offer of one million dollars in gold to anyone who would deliver an atomic bomb. In 1973, Libya reached a secret agreement with Prime Minister Ali Bhutto to finance the Pakistani nuclear weapon program in exchange for full access to the technology. Pakistan took the money for some years but never delivered a nuclear weapon capability to Libya. Libya also attempted to buy a research reactor from the United States, but after this acquisition was blocked, it did buy one from the Soviet Union in 1975—under Nuclear Non-Proliferation Treaty safeguards. This reactor became operational in 1981. Libya continued to press India and Pakistan for help in acquiring nuclear weapons to no avail.[34]

Over the years, US intelligence followed Libya's efforts to develop a nuclear weapon both internally and by purchase. Several Intelligence Community studies regarded the Libyan domestic program as rudimentary, plagued with poor leadership, and unlikely to produce a nuclear weapon in the foreseeable future. However, it was judged in the mid-1980s that it was important to pay attention to Libya, because Qadhafi again might try to buy a nuclear weapon capability.[35]

Libya continued in a desultory fashion to try to develop or acquire a nuclear weapon, but after many years, Qadhafi had nothing to show for his efforts. In 1995, he decided to try again. The Libyans approached A. Q. Khan and offered to buy from him the complete capability to develop and construct nuclear weapons. The Khan network reached agreement with Libya and made initial deliveries in 1997—twenty centrifuges and parts for more—which would permit Libya to begin research. The Khan network was expanded to carry out the Libyan deal with final agreement reached in 2000.[36] Establishing facilities in Malaysia and elsewhere, the network went into production itself to manufacture the equipment requested by Libya. Khan sent enrichment equipment and actual nuclear material to Libya. By 2002 Libya had assembled a few centrifuge machines and had been supplied with a design for an atomic bomb. By 2003, all was beginning to come together.

Meanwhile, the Central Intelligence Agency had been working closely with Britain's MI6 in the Libyan case. By 2003, penetration of the Khan network was leading to growing concerns about what Libya, among other countries, was receiving. Something needed to be done; how to roll up the Khan network and stop the transfers was the subject of debate in London and Washington. Sources had to be protected, and it was necessary to be sure of getting the whole network. (A fuller discussion of the activities of the A. Q. Khan network and international efforts to thwart its transfers can be found later in this chapter.)

For years Qadhafi had been eager to move out of the international isolation he found himself in—for economic and political reasons—and he had initiated contact with the United States as early as 1999. In March 2003, Qadhafi secretly approached the British government with a proposal that he was prepared to negotiate on Libya's weapons of mass destruction, not just its nuclear program but its chemical and biological weapons programs as well. Libya had long possessed a worrisome chemical weapon capability. Months of difficult negotiations followed, involving the CIA, MI6, and key figures in the Libyan government. The March 2003 invasion of Iraq may have been the tipping point, as Qadhafi might have thought he would be next, but it is more likely that he had already concluded that he needed to change his relationship with the international community. The negotiations dragged on until September, and then the tip-off came that a ship named the *BBC China* was headed for Libya from the Khan network with key technology for the Libyan nuclear weapon program. The German-owned ship was stopped and searched in Italy before it arrived in Libya. Crates containing equipment—centrifuge components—were opened and their contents confirmed. It was clear to the Libyans that British and American intelligence knew exactly what they were doing. The game was up, and within two weeks Libya admitted the first Western inspectors to visit the key WMD sites.[37]

Iraq. It was Saddam Hussein himself who was the driving force behind Iraq's efforts to seek weapons of mass destruction, especially nuclear weapons. The Iraqi Atomic Energy Commission had been established in 1959, and the Nuclear Research Center at Tuwaitha, near Baghdad, began operating a very small research reactor acquired from the Soviet Union in the late 1960s. In 1974, French Prime Minister Jacques Chirac visited Iraq, and this led to the signing of an agreement two years later between Iraq and the French nuclear industry. Pursuant to this contract, Iraq was to receive, among other things, a 70-megawatt research reactor similar to the Osiris reactor at the French nuclear research center at Saclay. Accordingly, the French called it the Osiraq reactor (from *Osiris Iraq*), although Saddam Hussein renamed it the Tammuz [July] I, commemorating the revolution that had brought the Baath Party to power in Iraq in July 1968.

The reactor was subsequently modified to be a 40-megawatt light-water nuclear materials testing reactor (MTR). Despite Iraqi claims that the plant was for peaceful use, it was an unusual choice: the MTR design is useful for doing analytic tests with established reactor programs, but not particularly useful to countries that have no established reactor program—unless they are interested in producing plutonium to make a bomb.[38] The reactor was to be operational by late 1981. The Iraqis insisted on highly enriched uranium fuel (the standard fuel for an MTR), although the French at the private urging of the Israelis had offered them low enriched fuel. Highly enriched uranium of course could be made into nuclear weapons.[39] And the spent fuel from this large research reactor could be reprocessed for plutonium for weapons—just as at Dimona in Israel.

Over the years Israel became increasingly worried about Osiraq. Saddam himself proclaimed that Iraq's pursuit of a nuclear reactor was part of "the first Arab attempt at nuclear arming." Iran attacked and damaged the site with two F-4 phantoms on September 30, 1980, shortly after the outbreak of the Iran-Iraq War.[40] Then on June 7, 1981, shortly before Osiraq was to become operational, Israel launched an air attack, utilizing six F-14s and six F-15s, and destroyed it.[41]

The Israeli opposition criticized the attack on Osiraq, but the government judged it important to carry out a strike before the reactor was "live" to avoid radiation fallout.[42] Then–opposition leader Shimon Peres is critical of the strike to this day, claiming that it drove Iraq to enhance and hide its nuclear weapon program. Indeed, in the aftermath of the Osiraq raid, Baghdad continued its pursuit of nuclear weapons but by a different, clandestine route. This time it was to be by means of uranium enrichment. In the next few years, at least six secret nuclear weapon laboratories were established at Tuwaitha, and by 1988 Iraq was prepared for a major expansion of its nuclear weapon program.

In 1990 came the invasion of Kuwait by Iraq, followed in early 1991 by the expulsion of Iraqi forces from Kuwait and the defeat of its forces by the United Nations coalition led by the United States. In this 1991 ("First") Gulf War the central objective of the United States, along with most members of the international community, was to keep the Iraqis from further advances toward the Saudi Arabian oil fields while driving them out of Kuwait. But a secondary objective also made this war possible: to eliminate Iraq's nuclear weapon program. The US Intelligence Community had believed this program existed, in spite of the failure of the IAEA to find anything significant during NPT safeguards inspections over the years. It is fair to note that neither the United States nor the IAEA (and presumably Israel) had successfully detected the extent of the program until UN inspections began after the 1991 Gulf War.[43]

On March 2, 1991, the UN Security Council passed the first of ten postwar resolutions dictating to Iraq what it was to do following the defeat of its army. The Security Council decided to make a clean sweep of Iraq's weapons of mass destruction programs. It mandated the IAEA to eliminate any Iraqi nuclear program infrastructure, and it established a new special commission (UNSCOM) to destroy the large stocks of chemical and smaller stocks of biological weapons possessed by Iraq.

The IAEA rather quickly discovered, despite Iraq's noncooperation, that the nuclear facility at Tuwaitha was far larger and more extensive than had been imagined and that Iraq could likely have constructed a nuclear weapon in two or three more years. After a huge effort, the IAEA believed by 1996 that it had entirely destroyed this nuclear infrastructure, in spite of the obstacles placed in its path from time to time by the Iraqi government. However, given that Iraq retained capable nuclear scientists and knowledge that could not be destroyed, subsequent reconstitution could not be ruled out. Likewise, the special commission was of the view that much progress had been made in eliminating the stocks of chemical and biological weapons by the mid-1990s; but since chemical and biological weapons can be produced in facilities that have normal commercial uses, it was not possible to ensure against future clandestine production.

In 1998, Saddam Hussein refused to continue the inspections by both the IAEA and the special commission after UNSCOM director Richard Butler had ordered UN inspectors out of Iraq in preparation for extensive US-UK aerial bombings. As a result, during the next four years international concern grew that Iraq might attempt to reconstitute its nuclear program and resume production of chemical and biological weapons. However, imports into Iraq remained under very tight control; Iraq was under constant remote technical intelligence surveillance; and it was subjected to periodic aerial bombardments by the United States and United Kingdom under UN auspices.

There never was a high probability of Iraq significantly reconstituting its nuclear weapon program; this would have required large, recognizable facilities. Further clandestine production of chemical and biological weapons, however, was possible. Yet Iraq had no means of delivering such weapons: its missile capability was minimal; Iran had essentially stolen its air force after the 1991 Gulf War (when Saddam had dispatched his planes there to avoid their destruction); and its military establishment remained in tatters. Nevertheless, uncertainties regarding Saddam's WMD programs grew as time moved on without the aid of further inspections (see Chapter 5).

North Korea. The North Korean interest in acquiring nuclear weapons goes back many years. Agreements were signed on nuclear research in 1956 and 1959 with the Soviet Union and in 1959 with China. The North Korean dictator Kim Il Sung in 1964, after the first Chinese nuclear weapon test, sent a delegation to China seeking assistance in developing nuclear weapons. As with Libya's attempt a decade later, the effort was unsuccessful. Kim Il Sung tried again, unsuccessfully, to secure nuclear weapon technology from China in 1974 at a time when the Republic of Korea was exploring the nuclear weapon option. Finally, reportedly in the late 1970s, Kim gave the order to his government to build nuclear weapons on its own.[44]

The Soviet Union had sold a small, 2–4 megawatt research reactor to North Korea in the 1960s, which was sited near Yongbyon, and North Korean and Soviet scientists also established a nuclear research center there. In the early 1980s, North Korea began work on a significantly larger research reactor in the 20–30 megawatts-thermal range (providing about 5 megawatts-electric output). The Yongbyon reactor has been referred to both as a 25-megawatt (thermal) and a 5-megawatt (electric) reactor. The reactor was designed for dual purpose—producing heat and electricity as well as plutonium. In recent publications it has been most commonly described as a 5-megawatt (electric) reactor, and so it will be described in this book.[45] In 1986, the reactor began operating. By 1991, the nuclear program in North Korea had considerably expanded with uranium mining being conducted at two locations, nuclear research at several locations, the 5-megawatt research reactor in operation, and construction underway on a 50-megawatt (electric) reactor at Yongbyon as well as on a 200-megawatt (electric) reactor in Taechon.[46] These two reactors were designed to produce a significant amount of electricity along with substantial plutonium. Together, they could produce nearly 300 kilograms of weapons-grade plutonium per year.[47]

All of this, of course, was of considerable interest to US intelligence. In 1989, a CIA analysis concluded that North Korea was rapidly expanding its nuclear activities and that it might be willing to risk international opposition to gain (with the aid of nuclear weapons) a decided advantage over South Korea. In June 1989, the United States identified what appeared to be a reprocessing plant at Yongbyon. Secretary of State James Baker in a speech in San Francisco in October asserted that "nuclear proliferation, notably North Korea's reactor program, remains a danger." US intelligence was on top of this one. By 1991, intelligence in Washington estimated that North Korea was three to five years (perhaps a bit more) away from a weapon. Some of the facilities at Yongbyon appeared complete. Then, at the end of 1991, the two Koreas agreed on the denuclearization of the peninsula. This seemed to provide for a respite in tensions, but it lasted only a few months.[48]

In early 1992, North Korea finally signed its NPT Safeguards Agreement with the IAEA, having joined the treaty under Soviet pressure in 1986. A number of inspections followed, largely focused on the 5-megawatt reactor at Yongbyon and the 50-megawatt plant under construction. Also included was the 200-megawatt reactor under construction at Taechon, north of Pyongyang. Early in the inspections process, the IAEA found discrepancies in North Korea's safeguards declaration. IAEA inspectors discovered that what North Korea had declared to be a "radioisotope laboratory" was actually a reprocessing plant. North Korea had previously denied that it possessed a reprocessing facility; but on a visit in May, IAEA director-general Hans Blix was shown a partially completed structure called a radio-chemistry laboratory, which as he later said in a press conference in Beijing, when completed and in operation "would certainly in our terminology be called a reprocessing plant." North Korea admitted to having produced a small amount of plutonium from damaged fuel rods. However, the IAEA gathered samples of nuclear waste and on analysis concluded that more than the admitted 90 grams of plutonium had been reprocessed. Further, during their visit in late 1992, Director-General Blix and the IAEA inspectors became suspicious of two apparent nuclear waste storage areas at the Yongbyon facility and asked to inspect them. This request was denied.

In late February 1993, the IAEA board approved a strongly worded resolution requesting a "special inspection" of the two sites, which it believed (based on satellite imagery) would reveal evidence of undeclared plutonium production.[49] The Board in effect gave North Korea thirty days to comply with the resolution and permit the inspections. North Korea immediately rejected the inspections request, and on March 12, not long after this announcement, North Korea gave the required three-month notice of withdrawal from the NPT and halted further inspections by the IAEA. This of course did not end the matter. A few weeks later the IAEA board approved a resolution forwarding the North Korean case to the UN Security Council for consideration of sanctions.[50]

The intelligence, when combined with scientific analysis, caused the US Intelligence Community to take ever stronger views of the nuclear threat from North Korea. In February 1992, Director of Central Intelligence Gates told the House Foreign Affairs Committee in public session that North Korea could have a nuclear bomb in "a few months to as much as a couple of years." His successor, R. James Woolsey, Jr., said in November 1993 that US intelligence agencies had believed "for some time" that North Korea "would have enough nuclear material for a weapon and perhaps two."[51] Meanwhile, in the spring of 1993, the United States and North Korea agreed to negotiate; in June, on the last day of the NPT ninety-day withdrawal notice period, North Korea cancelled its withdrawal from the NPT. The negotiations concluded at the end of 1994, assisted by the intervention of former President Jimmy Carter with the North Korean dictator, Kim Il Sung, when both parties signed the Agreed Framework. This agreement took place even though the two parties had come close to war in the spring of that year over North Korea's decision to pull the fuel rods out of its 5-megawatt reactor without permitting IAEA inspection, raising the risk of the reprocessing of the fuel, which, it was believed, contained enough plutonium for up to five or six nuclear weapons. The United States had informed the North Koreans that if they began the reprocessing of the spent fuel, it would destroy the reprocessing plant with cruise missiles. The North Koreans replied that if the United States did that, they would turn Seoul into a "sea of fire." Under the Agreed Framework the fuel rods stayed in the spent fuel pond and the reactor ceased operations, all under the watchful eyes of IAEA inspectors.[52]

From the conclusion of the Agreed Framework in October 1994 until January 2003, the nuclear situation in North Korea remained largely static on the surface. The Clinton administration made an abortive attempt to settle all remaining nuclear issues in late 2000—the Agreed Framework was intended to accomplish this but did not, as the United States and its Western associates never fully implemented it. Early in the Bush administration, any further negotiation was rejected, and President Bush included North Korea as a member of the "Axis of Evil," along with Iraq and Iran, in his State of the Union speech in January 2002. The Intelligence Community consensus by 2001 was that North Korea had one or two nuclear weapons, as Deputy Director of Central Intelligence John McLaughlin stated in a speech in August.[53]

There were also concerns within the Intelligence Community as early as 1999 that North Korea was pursuing a covert uranium enrichment program in circumvention of the Agreed Framework. There was a widely shared view that while the Agreed Framework had frozen North Korea's existing nuclear weapon program, it had not prevented Pyongyang from retaining its supply of plutonium and possibly embarking on another route to acquire weapon-grade nuclear material. By 2001, there were strong suspicions that such a program existed. It was believed that the A. Q. Khan network and Pakistan had delivered the necessary assistance to North Korea.[54]

By the fall of 2002, the United States had what it believed was "irrefutable evidence," most likely from what it learned from penetration of the A. Q. Khan network smuggling ring, that North Korea possessed a covert program to produce nuclear weapons through uranium enrichment—contrary to the Agreed Framework.[55] At a meeting in Pyongyang on October 3, 2002, Assistant Secretary of State James A. Kelly presented to Vice Minister Kim Gye Gwan the US position that President Bush had been prepared to have serious discussions with the Democratic People's Republic of Korea (DPRK) about improving the US–North Korean relationship (after vetoing Secretary Colin Powell's proposal the year before to continue the negotiations pursued by President Clinton in 2000), but that this would no longer be possible because of the DPRK's uranium enrichment program. A repeat performance with the vice minister occurred the next morning followed by a meeting between the US delegation and the North Korean First Vice Minister Kang Sok Ju. He delivered a long monologue in which he asserted that contrary to Article 3 of the Agreed Framework, the United States, by declaring North Korea to be a member of the Axis of Evil; by announcing a policy of preemptive strike; and by including North Korea among the potential targets for a nuclear attack, was actively threatening North Korea with nuclear weapons. Thus, North Korea had to modernize its military as much as possible. He acknowledged that the United States had said that the DPRK had begun a uranium enrichment program for the production of nuclear weapons; he then said that the DPRK was prepared to develop and manufacture even more weapons and needed to get on an equal footing with the United States.

Even though Kang did not explicitly admit to an enrichment program, all members of the US delegation concluded from listening to his remarks that he had unquestionably if tacitly acknowledged a highly enriched uranium (HEU) weapon program. The United States accordingly decided to terminate heavy fuel-oil shipments to North Korea under the Agreed Framework and to persuade its allies, Japan and South Korea, in the Korean Peninsula Energy Development Organization to support this policy. The DPRK has subsequently and consistently denied having an HEU program.[56]

The October 2002 confirmation was the turning point in US relations with North Korea. At the beginning of the Clinton administration it had estimated that North Korea had enough plutonium to make perhaps one or two nuclear weapons. In 1993, the United States had been prepared to go to war to stop further reprocessing for plutonium, but the Clinton administration subsequently believed it had a process in place to deal with North Korea. But now, in 2002, the situation had become unconstrained. During the following several years, the Bush administration sat idly by, hoping for the ultimate collapse of the North Korean government, while the DPRK conducted two reprocessing efforts extracting enough plutonium for five to six additional nuclear weapons in 2003, and two more in 2005. This was added to the plutonium gained in 1989 from a three-month shutdown of the 5-megawatt reactor, likely enough for one to two nuclear weapons. The reactor made enough plutonium for approximately one nuclear weapon per year. Thus, the estimated total for North Korea increased to 8–10 nuclear weapons.[57]

As a result of the developments described above, in December 2002 North Korea expelled the IAEA inspectors, and in January 2003 it withdrew from the NPT and announced that it would reprocess the spent fuel rods in storage and restart the 5-megawatt reactor. North Korea then began making public statements about its nuclear weapon program, including the reprocessing of spent fuel rods from the Yongbyon reactor, apparently to influence certain private Americans in the hope that they would in turn influence the US government. This led to uncertainty regarding North Korea's activities and differences of interpretation in how much reprocessing had taken place.

By April 2004, US intelligence revised its estimate of the North Korean nuclear arsenal upward to eight nuclear weapons.[58] In the spring of 2005, there were concerns that a nuclear weapon test was being planned. Nothing came of this, however, and in September 2005, with the United States downplaying the HEU issue, North Korea agreed in principle to terminate its nuclear program as part of the negotiations in the ongoing Six-Party Talks, which had begun the year before among the United States, North Korea, China, Russia, South Korea, and Japan. Given the lack of progress in the talks, the United States returned to a harder line, and a long period of stalemate followed, leading up to North Korea conducting a nuclear weapon test on October 9, 2006. Intelligence estimates indicated that it was unsuccessful—an attempted 4-kiloton test resulting in probably less than a 1-kiloton explosion. A short time afterward, apparently after pressure from China assisted by effective diplomacy from US Ambassador Chris Hill, North Korea signed an agreement in early 2007 to close down its 5-megawatt reactor at Yongbyon and to begin negotiating the termination of its nuclear program. In July 2007, the reactor was closed down in the presence of IAEA inspectors.

The closure was a useful first step, but a long road to denuclearization still lay ahead. The North Koreans had undertaken in the agreement to provide an accounting of their nuclear program by the end of 2007, but by March 2008 they had failed to do so. Even as Pyongyang and Washington exchanged accusations about who was holding things up and not following through, optimism remained that eventual denuclearization was possible. Indeed, in July 2008, negotiators from the Six-Party Talks agreed on initial steps to verify North Korea's nuclear disarmament, which required the complete dismantling of the nuclear facility at Yongbyon, this being in exchange for deliveries of fuel oil and other economic aid.[59]

The press has reported some intelligence estimates judging that the North Korean arsenal has reached ten weapons. As noted earlier, North Korea extracted enough plutonium in 2003 to build five to six nuclear weapons and in

2005 enough for two more. These should be added to the one or two weapons that were suspected prior to the freeze established by the 1994 Agreed Framework.[60] Throughout this long effort US intelligence agencies have provided the government with as much information from the darkness of North Korea as possible to help policymakers understand what the North Koreans are saying publicly as they try to influence international opinion.

President George W. Bush came to office with a visceral negative reaction to the North Korean dictator Kim Jong Il (who had replaced his father, Kim Il Sung, when he died in the mid-1990s). In a press conference as late as five years into his presidency (April 28, 2005), President Bush seemed to go out of his way to attack Kim Jong Il. While he said nothing new, his attack had the effect of undermining his newly appointed negotiator, Ambassador Chris Hill, in the Six-Party Talks with North Korea. The president volunteered that "Kim Jong Il is a dangerous person. He's a man who starves his people. He's got huge concentration camps. And . . . there is concern about his capacity to deliver a nuclear weapon."[61]

After the long stalemate in the Six-Party Talks, North Korea's nuclear test in October 2006 demonstrated the DPRK's possession of plutonium and some level of expertise. This act appeared to be too much for China, which put pressure on North Korea to come to a settlement on its nuclear program. Under pressure, North Korea agreed to a set of obligations on nuclear disarmament in February 2007, one of which they carried out promptly: the disabling of the Yongbyon reactor so that it could make no more plutonium. This was a major step forward.

As 2007 proceeded, progress was made in disabling the reactor and understanding the size and scope of the DPRK program. There were now many US and other Western technical experts in the DPRK. North Korea agreed to make a comprehensive declaration of its nuclear weapon program by the end of 2007. In exchange Washington agreed to take North Korea off its list of state sponsors of terrorism, which would lift certain sanctions against the DPRK. The deadline was not met, but North Korea finally did make a declaration in June 2008. The declaration had considerable information on the plutonium program but nothing on the uranium enrichment program—and nothing on any DPRK role in building a research reactor in Syria capable of producing significant quantities of plutonium (the reactor was destroyed by Israeli warplanes in September 2007). The president gave notice of his intent to remove the DPRK from the terrorism list, but when at the end of the forty-five-day notice period North Korea had not yet agreed to a comprehensive verification arrangement to review the data in the declaration, the president let the notice period expire without taking any action. In early September 2008, Washington reiterated that it would not take the DPRK off the list until it agreed to verification arrangements. However, on September 8, after weeks of insisting that North Korea knew what it needed to do to be removed from the State Department's list of state sponsors of terrorism, US officials admitted that they had communicated this precondition only verbally.[62]

On September 3, the DPRK announced that it would restore and restart its plutonium-producing Yongbyon reactor. On September 4, 2008, North Korea began to move equipment, which appeared to indicate that it would try to restart the Yongbyon reactor and make more plutonium.[63] The Bush administration made an extensive written verification arrangement an important objective, insisting on full access to "any site, facility or location" deemed relevant to the DPRK nuclear program. David Albright, the US nuclear expert, said it amounted to a "verification wish list" and that Iraq had agreed to such a plan "only after it was bombed." North Korea after an initial rejection replied with a counter proposal in which it agreed to a number of US demands but objected to two key elements—visits to undeclared facilities and the taking of samples. So by mid-September the DPRK disarmament negotiations were at an impasse, inspectors were to be barred, and there were indications that within a week the DPRK would resume reprocessing for plutonium.[64]

However, the situation changed in early October. North Korea barred inspectors from the Yongbyon reactor and threatened to resume the production of plutonium. The US then decided that the DPRK had shown progress and announced that a verbal understanding had been reached on a verification arrangement which, according to the United States, included potential access to facilities not included in Pyongyang's declaration and permission for inspectors to take environmental samples from facilities to determine how much plutonium had been produced. No text of the claimed agreement was ever released.[65] On the strength of this President Bush ordered on October 11 the removal of the DPRK from the State Department state sponsors of terrorism list. Inspectors were readmitted, and it appeared that the disarmament discussions were back on track. However, on December 11, North Korea balked at agreeing to a written verification plan, possibly in a move to see how the newly elected Obama administration would approach the issue. Earlier on November 12 North Korea had refused to allow outside inspectors to take samples from its main nuclear complex at Yongbyon saying in a statement by the Foreign Ministry that it had never agreed to such sampling.[66] The December action effectively ended the disarmament process with North Korea for the Bush administration.

Iran. The nuclear program in Iran has a long history. The Shah was interested in developing a substantial nuclear power capability, which made the nuclear weapon option possible through the reprocessing of spent fuel (under the table). The Atomic Energy Organization of Iran was established in 1974, and in 1976 the Shah's government reached agreement with Siemens of Germany to build two reactors at Bushehr near the border with Iraq. After the Islamic Revolution, Ayatollah Khomeini opposed the pursuit of nuclear weapons, on religious grounds. Toward the end of the devastating 1980–88 Iran-Iraq War, however, he apparently changed his mind. Germany declined to return after the end of the war, and Iran invited Russia to rebuild the two reactors at Bushehr, which had been badly damaged during the war. This began a close Russian-Iranian commercial relationship in the nuclear arena, which has continued to the present and explains, at least in part, why Russia was initially reluctant to agree to UN Security Council sanctions on Iran. Meanwhile, already by the 1980s, A. Q. Khan had been in contact with the Iranian leadership.[67]

Despite constant pressure from the United States, Russia persevered with the project and announced its completion in 2004. Nevertheless, Russia delayed delivering fuel for the reactor complex and indicated that its reliable supply obviated the need for Iran to begin domestic production of fissile material.

The United States has been concerned about the Iranian nuclear program for many years and has tried numerable times, with limited success, to reduce Russia's involvement in it. In 1992, Director of Central Intelligence Gates testified to Congress that Iran was seeking nuclear weapons and might acquire them by the year 2000. Iran was attempting to purchase sensitive nuclear technology from Argentina and China; these sales were blocked by the United States as a result of diplomatic approaches to the two countries. As the years passed, increased intelligence on the Iranian nuclear sites was made available to the IAEA.[68]

During the 1990s, the Iranian program seemed to have slowed down somewhat. After inconclusive IAEA visits in 1991 and 1994, the Iranian case disappeared to some degree from the radar screen.[69] The United States continued its pressure on Russia and China not to sell nuclear technology to Iran asserting that Iran was seeking the capability to construct a nuclear weapon. The demands appeared to have some effect; by 1997 the Clinton administration claimed that Iran would not be in a position to build a nuclear weapon before 2005.[70] Until 2000, however, the US government was unaware of the expanding cooperation between Iran and the A. Q. Khan network. Tehran was acquiring centrifuges for uranium enrichment from Khan for its enrichment facilities at Natanz. And, of course, it was not reporting these acquisitions to the IAEA as required by its NPT Safeguards Agreement.

In 2002, the existence of the proposed heavy-water reactor at Arak, along with the enrichment facilities at Natanz, were revealed to the world by the National Council of Resistance of Iran, the political arm of People's Mujahedin, known as the MEK.[71] The MEK had been a terrorist organization operating in Iran for many years and was listed by the United States as such. The MEK was expelled in the 1980s to Iraq, where it became a wholly owned subsidiary of Saddam Hussein. Thus, the source was somewhat suspect, but the facts were real.

The Natanz facility, construction of which began in 2000, included a pilot enrichment plant, which could house some one thousand centrifuges, and a large underground facility eventually intended for perhaps fifty thousand centrifuges, where Iran could enrich on an industrial scale and ultimately produce enough highly enriched uranium for up to twenty to thirty nuclear weapons a year.[72] Also, Iran has been pursuing plans to construct a heavy-water 40-megawatt thermal reactor at Arak, not far from Natanz, which could produce plutonium sufficient for perhaps one or two nuclear weapons a year. The production of plutonium, however, would require a reprocessing facility, and none has yet been detected. However, many of Iran's facilities are under cover or underground and thus not easily detectable by satellite imagery.

Disclosure of the nuclear facilities led Iran to agree to IAEA inspections at Natanz and Arak and other places, which greatly improved US intelligence understanding of the program in Iran. Overhead collection was increased as well. But even with the on-site inspections and expanded surveillance, the United States did not learn much. The general assessment at that time was that Iran was five to ten years away from the capability to construct a nuclear weapon. By 2006, Iran had only a few more than 160 centrifuges operating. And even though, according to the Iranians, that number increased to 3,000 in 2007, the Iranian program appeared to be proceeding slowly.

With increased IAEA inspections and Iran's admission of violating its Safeguard Agreement (its nonreporting of the acquisition of enrichment technology), Iran also agreed to enter into negotiations with the European Union (EU), represented by Britain, France, and Germany. The EU sought Iran's agreement to suspend enrichment, which Iran was unwilling to do for more than a brief period. Iran has insisted that its program is peaceful, and it took a somewhat harder line in negotiations after the election of Mahmoud Ahmadinejad as president in 2005. Negotiations were very much on again, off again; over time the United States was able to influence the EU and forge a consensus among the Permanent Five members of the UN Security Council to pass resolutions sanctioning Iran—one in late 2006 and a second in the spring of 2007. A third was passed in early March 2008.

While Iran appears to make efforts to reach a settlement with the EU and the IAEA, it remains adamant that it will not suspend enrichment again. The United States seemingly has not been willing to offer Iran the same "carrots" (diplomatic relations and guarantees against attack) that it has offered North Korea. Washington may believe that such incentives would not work with the current Iranian leadership. Meanwhile, the domestic audience in Iran has become convinced that Iran's nuclear program is essential to Iran's development.[73] George Perkovich said, in 2005, "The nuclear issue in Iran, as in most countries, is an elite affair. . . . [They believe that] the nuclear issue is about modernity, prowess, national superiority, and anti-colonialism. . . . Most discussants in Iran argue that nuclear weapons would do Iran little good, but that Iran should acquire nuclear technology in order to modernize."[74] David Albright pointed out in 2006 that "it is vital to understand what Iran has accomplished, what it still has to learn, and when it will reach a point where a plan to pursue nuclear weapons covertly or openly could succeed more quickly than the international community could react. . . . Iran must foreswear any deployed enrichment capability and accept adequate inspections. Otherwise we risk a seismic shift in the balance of power in the region."[75]

Shift in US Intelligence Judgments on Iran's Nuclear weapon program. After monitoring Iran's nuclear activities and reporting for some years that Iran was pursuing a nuclear weapon program, the US Intelligence Community publicly issued in December 2007 an unclassified version of the Key Judgments from a new National Intelligence Estimate (NIE). The unclassified Key Judgments revised the community's earlier (2005) judgments on the status of Iran's nuclear weapon program. According to the new judgments, Iran had halted its weaponization efforts in 2003, although its efforts toward enrichment and delivery had continued apace (for the unclassified Key Judgments of the NIE see Appendix H). (*Note: The three key components of a nuclear weapon program are obtaining fissile material—highly enriched uranium or plutonium; manufacturing a nuclear device using such material; and the ability to deliver the device to a target, usually by aircraft or missile. The 2007 judgments claim that only one of the three steps—weaponization or manufacturing of a nuclear device—was halted in 2003.*) Some feared that the new NIE findings would undercut the Bush administration's ability to marshal international support against Iran's effort to enrich uranium. For several years, US and foreign intelligence, coupled with inspections and reports by the IAEA, had spurred efforts by US policymakers, several European Union countries, and the UN Security Council to bring pressure on Iran to halt its efforts to enrich uranium out of suspicions that it intended to build nuclear weapons. Contrary to fears raised by some after the release of the unclassified Key Judgments, additional sanctions were passed by the UN Security Council. Thus, the administration's efforts against Iran did not seem to suffer a setback due to the release of the NIE's findings. Iran had consistently resisted pressure, arguing that it was doing only what was permitted under the Nuclear Non-Proliferation Treaty and that it needed low-enriched uranium to fuel its nuclear power reactors.

The issuance of the unclassified judgments at the very time that the administration was urging additional pressure on Iran raised questions on whether the new intelligence judgments were the result of internal or external political pressure. On the one hand, some postulated that intelligence analysts were using the NIE's judgments to undermine the Bush administration's policy on Iran because of the NIE debacle on Iraqi WMD a few years earlier.[76] On the other hand, some surmised that the timing of the release reflected an effort by those in Congress who opposed the Bush administration's policy on Iran and who feared it might resort to the use of military force. They therefore asked for the declassification of the NIE's judgments to embarrass the administration. The facts as we understand them do not seem to corroborate either theory. No details regarding the basis of the new intelligence judgments have been made public other than the claim that Intelligence Community leaders decided it was time to reexamine the judgments from the 2005 NIE and report any newly available information.

The Principal Deputy Director of National Intelligence stated in a memorandum attached to the unclassified NIE on Iran that the decision to release conclusions from an NIE was based on weighing the importance of the information to public discussions about US national security against the necessity to protect classified information, especially the sources and methods used to collect intelligence. He claimed that the decision to release this particular version of Key Judgments on Iran was made when it was determined that doing so was in the interest of US national security. He explained that the Intelligence

Community is on record publicly with numerous statements based on the 2005 NIE, which judged that Iran was pursuing a nuclear weapon program, so it was important to release information on the changes in the IC judgments to ensure an accurate presentation. He concluded by confirming that the unclassified judgments are consistent with those in the classified document. However, almost nothing is said in the unclassified release about the sources of information that underlie the new judgments, which is consistent with his point about protecting sensitive sources and methods. The unclassified version does report that due to ambiguities there are differences of opinion within the Intelligence Community on the levels of confidence associated with the new judgments.

Having experienced the political consequences of pursuing a policy in late 2002 and early 2003 that later was found to be based, at least in part, on faulty intelligence regarding the status of Saddam Hussein's WMD programs, President Bush reportedly had begun questioning Intelligence Community judgments on Iran's nuclear weapon program after becoming uncomfortable with the limited intelligence. At the same time, some in Congress began asking for a new intelligence estimate to update the judgments made in 2005. The Intelligence Community reexamined its judgments, and the result was quite surprising: after an additional scrub of old and new data, the Intelligence Community reported that Iran had apparently shut down, or at least suspended, the weaponization part of its nuclear weapon program a few years earlier. The new judgments naturally posed a significant challenge to the Bush administration's policy on Iran, and White House officials seemed skeptical at first. President Bush is quoted as having said that "you want to make sure it's not disinformation."

The Intelligence Community reportedly set up a "red team" to determine whether the new information could be fake, but the IC concluded it was not. According to news reports, because of the political sensitivity of the findings, the Director of National Intelligence planned to keep the judgments classified, presumably to avoid dragging intelligence into another political debate over the administration's foreign policies. He apparently reversed his decision given the flurry of official discussions on the implications of the new judgments, which led to fears that the classified judgments would be leaked, leading to charges of an official cover-up.[77]

In an apparent effort to put the new NIE in context, the Scope Note issued along with the unclassified judgments states that the estimate assesses the status of Iran's nuclear program and the program's outlook over the next decade and focuses on the following questions: (1) what are Iran's intentions toward developing nuclear weapons? (2) what domestic factors affect Iran's decision making on whether to develop nuclear weapons? (3) what external factors affect Iran's decision making? (4) what is the range of potential Iranian actions with respect to the development of nuclear weapons and the decisive factors that would lead Iran to choose one course or another? and perhaps most importantly (5) what is Iran's current and projected capability to develop nuclear weapons, along with its key chokepoints and vulnerabilities? The Scope Note emphasized that this NIE does not assume that Iran intends to acquire nuclear weapons but rather assesses Iran's capability and intent (or lack thereof) to acquire nuclear weapons, taking into account Iran's dual-use uranium fuel cycle and nuclear activities that are at least partly civil in nature. Finally, the Scope Note states that the Intelligence Community examined information available as of October 31, 2007.[78]

As a sign that at least some lessons had been learned since publication of the October 2002 NIE on Iraq's WMD programs (see Chapter 5), the unclassified version of the NIE on Iran also provides readers an explanation of the estimative language used in the judgments and how the Intelligence Community describes its levels of confidence in the judgments that are made. This is clearly an effort to prevent a misreading of the new judgments. Some argue that lack of clarity and precision was a problem in the case of the Iraqi WMD estimate.

Setting aside for a moment the substantive judgments of the Iran NIE, we note that the unclassified version also included a statement that under the DNI the Intelligence Community has undertaken a number of steps to improve the NIE process. In addition to being more precise about the level of confidence surrounding the judgments reached, the IC has adopted new procedures to integrate formal reviews of source reporting and technical judgments (individual agencies are now required to submit formal assessments of the sources used in developing their judgments). This appears to be in reaction to some criticisms of the 2002 Iraq NIE (see Chapter 5 regarding the sourcing of judgments). While the unclassified version of the Iran NIE is largely devoid of source discussion, which is to be expected to protect sensitive sources and methods of collection and analysis, we understand that appropriate details were provided in the classified version given to US policymakers.

It is important to examine carefully how the 2007 judgments differ from those of 2005. The main Key Judgment made in the new NIE states, "We judge with *high confidence* that in fall 2003, Tehran halted its nuclear weapons program" (its nuclear weapon design and weaponization work and covert uranium conversion-related and uranium enrichment-related work). "We also assess with moderate-to-high confidence that Tehran at a minimum is keeping open the option to develop nuclear weapons." This is not a reversal of a previous position but rather a new position; the 2005 NIE did not take a position on this issue. Left unchanged were the judgments that uranium enrichment development continued and that as a result Iran would have enough fissile material to build a nuclear weapon in early-to-mid next decade. The key factor in a nuclear bomb program is the production of fissile material, not nuclear weapon design work. And once it has sufficient nuclear material, Iran most likely could resume its weaponization efforts rather quickly, if it has not done so already. The NIE goes on to state seven more Key Judgments regarding the status of Iran's technical capabilities and prospects for producing a nuclear weapon, if it decides to resume such an effort. In addition, the NIE contains a side-by-side comparison of how the new judgments compare to those made in May 2005 (see Appendix H).

IAEA Judgments on Iran's Nuclear Program. Even with the publication of the latest US intelligence judgments regarding Iran's nuclear weapon program, which appear to make Iran less threatening, the International Atomic Energy Agency (which has watchdog responsibilities for actions taken under the Nuclear Non-Proliferation Treaty, to which Iran is a party) continues to voice concern about Iran's nuclear activities. In a report by the IAEA's Director-General to the board of governors on August 30, 2007, the agency concluded as follows: (1) it has been able to verify the nondiversion of declared nuclear material in Iran; however, since early 2006 the agency has not received the type of information Iran had previously provided, and as a result the agency's knowledge about Iran's current nuclear program is diminishing; (2) contrary to decisions of the UN Security Council, Iran has not suspended its enrichment-related activities and has continued construction of facilities of concern; and, (3) Iran needs to build confidence in the peaceful nature of its nuclear program so that the agency can provide assurances not only regarding declared nuclear material but, equally importantly, regarding the absence of undeclared nuclear material and activities. The Director-General warned that without full implementation of an Additional Protocol designed to prevent a repeat of Iran's undeclared activities for nearly two decades, the agency cannot credibly assure the absence of undeclared nuclear material and activities in Iran. Finally, the Director-General urged Iran to implement all the confidence-building measures required by the UN Security Council.[79]

In February 2008, IAEA Director-General ElBaradei circulated a report updating developments in Iran since his 2007 report. In the new report he claimed that good progress had been made in clarifying outstanding issues with Iran's past nuclear activities with the exception of its alleged weaponization studies. He added that the IAEA must make sure that Iran's current activities are exclusively for peaceful purposes. To that end the IAEA has been asking Iran to conclude an Additional Protocol to ensure that there are no undeclared nuclear activities. The Director-General concluded that Iran's undeclared nuclear activities for over two decades has undercut international confidence about Iran's future intentions with its nuclear program.[80]

What should one make of these reports—the revised US intelligence judgments and the IAEA reports? With respect to substantive judgments reached, one should not gain great comfort in the Intelligence Community's assessment that Iran has stopped work on a portion of its nuclear weapon program. As former Assistant to the President for National Security Affairs and Secretary of State Henry Kissinger wrote in mid-December 2007, the concern about Iran's nuclear weapon program has three components: the production of fissile material, the development and production of bombs or warheads, and the development of missiles with increasing range to carry warheads. The new NIE seems to be reporting that Iran has suspended only the engineering (design, weaponization, and covert enrichment of uranium) aimed at the production of warheads. It is clear from the IAEA report mentioned earlier that doubts remain about the benign nature of Iran's uranium enrichment efforts.

In late 2008, the *New York Times* reported that Iran had produced 630 kilograms of low-enriched uranium—enough for one bomb if properly purified through additional enrichment.[81] Kissinger reminds his readers that it is the enrichment activity by centrifuges that has been the source of international debate and effort to halt Iran's nuclear weapon activities (as we observed earlier). Moreover, the NIE does not say how close Iran was to completing a bomb before it suspended that portion of its nuclear weapon program, and it expresses only "moderate confidence" that the suspension has not been lifted. Finally, Kissinger believes the release of this unclassified version of the Iran NIE undermines the Intelligence Community's avoidance of public advocacy and participation in a partisan debate.[82]

Kissinger's points are well taken; the international community should not derive much comfort in the revised NIE judgments that appear to reduce the potential nuclear threat from Iran. While Iran may have pulled back somewhat from its plans to become a nuclear weapon state, it has not in fact terminated its nuclear weapon program but only suspended some of the relevant work, perhaps just temporarily. Because the Intelligence Community was not clear or precise enough in stating its primary new judgment, the importance of the revision of 2005 NIE conclusions has been misconstrued and misrepresented by those who opposed the Bush administration's policy on Iran or who feared possible US military action against Iran. During February 2008 testimony, DNI Mike McConnell seemed to admit that the NIE was not written as clearly as it should have been. When testifying before the Senate Select Committee on Intelligence (SSCI), McConnell echoed Kissinger when he outlined three parts to an effective nuclear weapon capability: (1) production of fissile material; (2) effective means of delivery, such as ballistic missiles that can reach Africa and Europe; and (3) design and weaponization of the warhead. He confirmed that the recent NIE assessed that Iran halted only warhead design and weaponization, along with covert efforts to produce fissile material, in 2003. He emphasized that the Intelligence Community remained concerned about Iran as a nuclear weapon threat.[83]

The United Kingdom's Analysis of Iran's Nuclear Program. In early March 2008 the British government claimed that Iran could still be developing a nuclear weapon and called into question the US intelligence finding that work on a nuclear bomb had ceased in 2003. Apparently reflecting the results of an independent British analysis, an unidentified British diplomat said that "I haven't seen any intelligence that gives me even medium confidence that these programmes haven't resumed." He pointed to the evidence that had been presented to the IAEA in February; the UK's representative to the IAEA, speaking on behalf of Britain, Germany, and France, said that Iran's cooperation with the agency had been abysmal.[84] Iranian President Ahmadinejad dismissed such information as either fabricated or irrelevant and refused to enter any new talks with the European Union about Iran's nuclear program.[85]

Where Is Iran Headed? Iran continues to want to enrich uranium, which would give it an inherent ability to produce weapons-grade nuclear material. Indeed, on April 8, 2008, President Ahmadinejad announced that Iran had tested a new advanced centrifuge and had begun installing six thousand of them at its uranium enrichment plant in Natanz. The public display of this technological breakthrough is in clear defiance of US and UN demands that Iran stop enrichment efforts.[86] And as was evidenced by its public display of a space launch vehicle in early 2008, Iran is building longer-range missiles that could be used to deliver nuclear weapons. The debate over the 2007 NIE has focused on only part of the weapon issue: in two of its seven other judgments, the Intelligence Community concluded that "Iranian entities are continuing to develop a range of technical capabilities that could be applied to producing nuclear weapons" and "We assess with high confidence that Iran has the scientific, technical and industrial capacity eventually to produce nuclear weapons if it decides to do so." In his SSCI testimony, McConnell added that the Intelligence Community believes that the earliest possible date Iran technically could be capable of producing enough fissile material for a weapon is late 2009, although that is unlikely. The unclassified Key Judgments stated further, "We judge with moderate confidence Iran probably would be technically capable of producing enough highly-enriched uranium for a weapon sometime during the 2010–2015 time frame."

We note that in early 2009 the IAEA issued yet another report on the status of Iran's nuclear program in which it reported that its latest inspections had discovered that Iran had enriched more uranium (about one-third more) than it had reported showing that Iran had not suspended its enrichment activities despite UN demands. As a result, Iran now had amassed more than a ton which, if further purified, would be enough for one nuclear bomb.[87]

Was US Intelligence on Iran Politicized? It is comforting to see that the Intelligence Community, at least in the production of national estimates, is striving to be more precise in its judgments. As we discuss in Chapter 5, more rigor in vetting sources and clarity in stating judgments might have avoided some of the discord that resulted from the 2002 NIE on Iraq's WMD programs. However, partisan politics is always at play, and the Intelligence Community can never completely avoid being the "whipping boy" in a political debate or the "fall guy" for an ill-conceived or failed policy. Kissinger ends his article observing that the executive branch and Intelligence Community have gone through a rough period with accusations of politicization and policy biases, and he questions the wisdom of releasing these unclassified judgments. He believes that the recent unclassified Key Judgments only intensify the controversies and that policymakers and Congress should assume responsibility for their judgments without involving intelligence in their public justifications.

Finally, we view any accusation that "intelligence analysts" used the NIE to get back at the Bush administration shows ignorance of how NIE's are produced. As discussed in Chapter 4, analysts do not decide by themselves what judgments are reached and reported to policymakers. They offer their best informed judgments, but any individual or organization biases are largely neutralized through a review process in which senior IC managers determine that an NIE appropriately addresses the issue in question and provides objective judgments with appropriate explanations of the limit of consensus and confidence within the Intelligence Community.

Beyond the politics of Washington decision making, as we discuss in Chapter 4, the US Intelligence Community must continue to do all it can to monitor, correctly assess, and clearly report on suspected proliferation activities, while policymakers must use intelligence reporting responsibly and take into account other sources of information, such as IAEA inspections, when dealing with potential nuclear weapon proliferation activities. It is impractical to expect that intelligence will not be drawn into political or policy debates; the Intelligence Community must explain its judgments and, to the extent possible, the basis for those judgments. It must also strive to demonstrate that its analysis, judgments, and reporting have not been politicized by one side or the other.

Sudan. This failed state had served as the home of Osama bin Laden as well as the training ground for al-Qaeda before bin Laden moved his base of operations to Afghanistan in the 1990s. Following the terrorist bombings of two US embassies in neighboring Kenya and Tanzania on August 7, 1998, US intelligence had spotted what could have been a dual-use pharmaceutical plant in Khartoum producing chemical weapons for terrorist use. The Intelligence Community apparently had only limited information about the Shifa facility and made no judgment on whether it was producing precursors for chemical weapons. Nevertheless, President Clinton ordered missile strikes on August 20, 1998, against the plant and against a terrorist training base 100 miles south of Kabul, Afghanistan. The Sudanese government charged that US intelligence had been faulty—that the plant was strictly a source for human and veterinary medicines—and it proceeded to bring legal charges against the United States, calling on the UN Security Council to investigate the US claims.[88] President Clinton responded only that there was "compelling evidence that further attacks (beyond the two embassy bombings) were planned by a network of Islamist terrorists," and US officials declined to discuss the controversy publicly.[89]

Such incidents demonstrate the risks that actions based on limited intelligence can have in halting the proliferation of small, clandestine WMD programs. Because the intelligence leading to the strikes in Sudan was so sensitive that it could not be discussed publicly, the United States lost credibility regarding its actions.

Syria. In late 2007, Syria came on the public radar scope as another country possibly attempting to develop a nuclear weapon capability. On September 6, 2007, Israel—implementing a unilateral government decision (as it had in Iraq in 1981) to use military force to halt suspected nuclear proliferation—conducted an air raid on a facility named Al Kibar in northern Syria, 90 miles from the Iraqi border. Satellite imagery suggests it could have been a small nuclear reactor under construction and similar in design to the 5-megawatt, gas-cooled, graphite-moderated reactor at Yongbyon in North Korea, the reactor that has been of central concern in international efforts to denuclearize North Korea. The US Acting Deputy Assistant Secretary of State for nuclear nonproliferation told reporters on September 14 that there had been a number of Koreans at that location.[90]

If in fact a nuclear reactor had been secretly under construction, it would call into question Syria's commitments under the Nuclear Non-Proliferation Treaty and its Safeguards Agreement with the International Atomic Energy Agency. It would also call into question North Korea's pledge to halt any export of nuclear weapon technology and contravene that state's obligations under UN Security Council Resolution 1718 of October 14, 2006. Some have suspected Syria also of having received assistance from the A. Q. Khan nuclear proliferation network.[91]

Even though Syria has never been credited with having a nuclear weapon program, this is not the first time that one has been suspected. At one point during the George W. Bush administration, congressional testimony on this subject was cancelled when the Intelligence Community expressed concern that Undersecretary of State John Bolton was prepared to assert stronger claims about Syria's program than was warranted by the available intelligence.[92]

The Bush administration had reportedly been skeptical prior to the Israeli attack in September 2007 that the facility, which had been observed by reconnaissance satellites since 2001, was a nuclear reactor built with North Korea's assistance. However, in late April 2008, the CIA reportedly testified in closed session to Congress on what it believed to be the facts about the facility bombed by Israel. According to unconfirmed reports, the testimony asserted that the facility had a tall, boxy structure like those used to house gas-graphite reactors; a video secretly taken prior to the Israeli raid showed that the Syrian reactor's core design was the same as that of the North Korean reactor at Yongbyon. The video reportedly also showed North Koreans inside the unfinished reactor, which convinced the Israelis to destroy it, although it is not clear how the individuals were identified as North Korean.[93]

US intelligence officials were quoted as having high confidence that North Korea had aided Syria but only low confidence that the facility was meant for weapon development. In his first public comment on the facility, then CIA Director Michael Hayden stated that a plutonium reactor was within weeks or months of completion, that it was similar in size and technology to North Korea's Yongbyon reactor, and that it could produce enough nuclear material to fuel one or two weapons a year.[94] However, outside experts have claimed that the US disclosure did not amount to proof of an illicit nuclear weapon program because there is no sign of a reprocessing plant for converting spent fuel from the reactor into weapons-grade plutonium.[95]

The Intelligence Community admitted basing its low-confidence judgment regarding an association between the facility and weapon development on the lack of an identifiable plutonium reprocessing capability in the region of Al Kibar. Also absent was an identifiable means for Syria to manufacture the uranium fuel needed to operate the reactor. However, the Intelligence Community claimed that the absence of power lines and switching facilities needed for a facility to provide energy increased suspicion that the facility was not being built for peaceful purposes. Moreover, based on information it began to collect in 2001, the community could conclude that nuclear cooperation between North Korea and Syria had begun as early as 1997. The evidence included multiple visits to Syria by senior North Korean nuclear officials and a suspected cargo transfer from North Korea to the reactor site in 2006.[96]

While the United States and Israel concluded in 2007 that the Syrian facility was part of a clandestine nuclear weapon program, German and British news analysts postulated another possibility: the facility was part of a multinational nuclear weapon effort led by Iran, in which Syria and North Korea were collaborating. According to this hypothesis, Syria, with assistance from North Korea, would produce nuclear fuel and supply it to Iran.[97] Moreover, the reactor under construction in Syria with North Korean assistance was even more questionable than Iraq's Osiraq reactor destroyed by Israel in 1981. The Osiraq reactor had been openly purchased from France, declared and subject to IAEA monitoring. The Syrian reactor, by contrast, was being secretly built, deliberately concealed, and was undeclared. The physical characteristics were also different. The Osiraq reactor was appropriately sized and designed for nuclear research and with difficulty could have been used to produce plutonium without detection by IAEA inspectors. The Syrian reactor was modeled on a reactor specifically designed to produce plutonium for nuclear weapons.[98] However, the Director-General of the IAEA claimed in late 2008 that the traces of uranium found at the Al Kibar site did not provide conclusive evidence that there had been a reactor there.[99]

Whatever the truth turns out to be about the Syrian facility, it would be wise for the United States, Israel, and the IAEA to be alert to any effort by Syria, following Iraq's example after Israel's raid on its Osiraq facility, to move to an even more clandestine nuclear weapon program. Moreover, the three will need to work together more closely to ensure effective monitoring in Syria.

Soviet Union/Russia. The international community has typically given lower priority to monitoring clandestine chemical and biological weapons programs because they have been perceived as less of a threat to international peace than nuclear weapons. A number of countries have pursued such weapons mainly for potential battlefield use against neighboring or regional enemies. However, in addition to Libya and other countries, an incident involving the Soviet Union in the late 1970s attracted the attention of the United States and international community.

Because of their Cold War rivalry, the United States and the Soviet Union were concerned about each other's efforts to develop chemical and biological weapons. Each closely monitored the activities of the other, which was difficult because the development of agents could take place within otherwise legitimate chemical and pharmaceutical facilities. The principal concern was the possible use of such weapons in a conventional war in Europe between NATO and Warsaw Pact forces. There was also some apprehension that one or the other might figure out a way to deliver biological agents to international distances. Thus, the United States and the international community raised a red flag when suspicions arose in the late 1970s that the Soviets had an ongoing clandestine program for offensive biological weapons.

In 1979, five years after the Biological Weapons Convention (BWC) entered into force, the international community learned of a laboratory explosion in Sverdlovsk (now Ekaterinburg), which apparently had released deadly anthrax spores and caused a number of deaths. The United States learned of this incident essentially through intelligence means—the interviewing of defectors—and the information suggested that the Soviets were violating the BWC. The Soviet Union denied the claims, and it took the United States and international community until the early 1990s to induce the Russian Federation, which had inherited the program, to finally acknowledge what turned out to be a massive violation and to halt the program (see Chapter 6).

Monitoring Clandestine Proliferation by Non-State Actors

Efforts to detect, follow, and understand the proliferation activities of non-state actors, such as the A. Q. Khan black market nuclear proliferation network and international terrorist organizations, are even more challenging than those for individual nation-states described above. Non-state entities do not generally own territory or have facilities that can be monitored, at least by normal remote intelligence technical means. It takes the on-scene assistance of local police or others to detect and monitor any suspect activity. However, non-state actors often depend on the assistance of nation-states, or entities within those states, which means that the monitoring of suspect nation-states may lead to the detection of their support to terrorists.

In a fall 2008 speech, IAEA Director-General Mohamed ElBaradei stated that the number of reports of radioactive material stolen around the world during the previous year was disturbingly high. Although the total amount of material missing was not enough to build one nuclear device, ElBaradei said that the possibility of terrorists obtaining nuclear or other radioactive material remains a grave threat. Most of the concern centers on countries of the former Soviet Union.[100]

Thus far, little has been made public regarding efforts by the United States or other countries to follow and disrupt proliferation activities of international terrorists. We suspect that the successful detection of such activities is so sensitive that governments do not want to alert non-state actors to their tracking methods. From time to time, however, one reads about the arrest of individuals supposedly handling some type of nuclear, chemical, or biological item. The Aum Shinrikyo incident in Japan in the early 1990s and the anthrax attack in Washington, DC, in 2001, are examples. And quite a bit has now been written about the A. Q. Khan network. It is important to understand how intelligence and policy came to uncover that network's nuclear proliferation activities.

A. Q. Khan Network. Abdul Qadeer Khan was once described by CIA Director George Tenet as "at least as dangerous as Osama Bin Laden."[101] After completing his university studies in Pakistan, the young A. Q. Khan headed to Europe for a graduate education. He studied in West Berlin, the Netherlands, and Belgium, where he received his PhD in 1971. Shortly thereafter, he went to work for a subcontractor of URENCO in the Netherlands, where he had access to sensitive information relating to uranium enrichment and the nuclear fuel cycle. Traumatized by Pakistan's defeat in the 1971 war with India, he volunteered as, in essence, a spy in 1974. Khan secretly transferred centrifuge plans and other sensitive information to which he had access at URENCO to Pakistani agents; he returned to Pakistan in 1975. Toward the end of his stay in the Netherlands, Khan's activities were discovered by the Dutch security service.

The Dutch government was prepared to move against him; however, the CIA urged that this not happen so that they could learn more about his activities and associates. This was the first time that an opportunity to stop Khan was passed up. There were to be more such opportunities.

In less than a year Khan was able to establish the Engineering Research Laboratories (ERL) and begin playing a significant role in the Pakistani nuclear weapon program while reporting directly to Prime Minister Ali Bhutto, not to the Pakistan Atomic Energy Commission. Later that year, ERL established its secret plant at Kahuta, not far from Islamabad, Pakistan's capital, and Khan began helping Pakistan acquire nuclear weapons.[102]

In 1976 Khan embarked on a shopping spree to acquire nuclear weapon technology for Pakistan's program. A Pakistani colleague served as his purchasing agent in Europe. Equipment critical to Pakistan's program was often concealed in large shipments with no nuclear application, and customs passed on whole lots without proper inspection. But some items on the shopping list were unquestionably designed for a nuclear plant, such as a large and complicated system of pipes and vacuum valves to feed uranium hexafluoride gas into centrifuges. A Swiss company was prepared to sell this system to Khan after the Swiss government indicated that it would not require an export license. Several months later three Pakistani C-130 cargo planes arrived in Switzerland to transport this machinery to Pakistan. A German firm agreed to build a fluorine plant in Pakistan, an important step in the production of uranium hexafluoride. A Dutch firm sold to Khan 6,500 tubes manufactured of hardened steel for centrifuge rotors.[103] These purchases could be made easily as they were not on the so-called IAEA Zangger Committee list of items for which export licenses should be required. Complete centrifuge units were on the list, but individual components such as vacuum tubes were not.[104] Lastly, Khan called on the fraternity of European engineers, salesmen, and middlemen whom he had known during his URENCO days to come to Pakistan and train the "local boys" on the sophisticated machinery being assembled at Kahuta.[105]

Khan first appeared on the CIA's radar screen in Islamabad in early 1976. Near the end of 1977 there was information that construction had begun at Kahuta on a huge installation said to be for uranium enrichment.[106] By 1979, experts at the CIA realized that Khan had assembled everything he needed to construct his own centrifuge plant. ERL was renamed Khan Research Laboratories (KRL) in 1981, and so it has remained. Khan made a major contribution to Pakistan's development of nuclear weapons, leading to a nuclear weapon capability by the end of the 1980s. He became known by some as "the father of the Islamic bomb." US intelligence closely followed Khan's work, but what wasn't known for over a decade was that Khan had emerged, after the maturity of the program in Pakistan, as a worldwide middleman of nuclear proliferation.

In a historic decision in 1979, President Carter accepted National Security Advisor Brzezinski's argument that the importance of defeating the Soviets in Afghanistan outweighed the objective of stopping Pakistan's nuclear program. In January 1980 Carter proposed in his State of the Union address that existing sanctions against Pakistan should be eased off and the focus of attention be on preserving its territorial integrity. Four years previously, as recounted earlier, the CIA had decided to let Khan escape Dutch arrest so that it could keep track of the Pakistani nuclear program. Now Carter and Brzezinski were giving Pakistan carte blanche to pursue nuclear weapons in exchange for help against the Soviets in Afghanistan. This decision caused long-term damage to American nonproliferation policy, as did Ronald Reagan's statement during the 1980 election campaign that the Pakistani nuclear weapon program was none of our business.[107]

By 1982, the US State Department had concluded that Pakistan was intent on acquiring nuclear weapons; Kahuta was too large for research and development. A 1983 intelligence report confirmed that Pakistan was on course to develop a nuclear weapon. The CIA and the State Department delivered the truth about Pakistan to President Reagan and his advisors, but they chose to ignore it in favor of working with Pakistan to defeat the Soviets in Afghanistan.[108]

By the late 1980s, Khan had less need for his outside suppliers, but his outside suppliers still needed business. This led to Khan's sales outside of Pakistan. Since the Pakistani program was converting to more-modern P-2 centrifuges, Khan had a large stockpile of older P-1 machines to sell. The Khan ring began to attempt sales to Iran, Iraq, North Korea, and Libya.

Khan made an unsolicited offer to sell Iran uranium enrichment technology, which came to fruition in the mid-1990s. In the early 1990s he supervised the transfer of uranium enrichment technology to North Korea by Pakistan in exchange for designs and parts of North Korea's Nodong missile, which became known as the Gauri in Pakistan.[109] What's more, in the late 1990s, the Khan network made an agreement with Libya to transfer a complete package of material and equipment, along with a design of a weapon, which would lead Libya to a nuclear weapon capability.[110]

Initially, close attention was not paid to Khan as a potential proliferator beyond Pakistan. US intelligence only began to learn of possible transfers to North

Korea in the late 1990s. Khan's transfers to Iran came to light after the 2002 revelation of the existence of the Natanz and Arak facilities. But through various means Washington was beginning to catch on to Khan. The first test of the Gauri missile revealed the likelihood of Pakistani–North Korean cooperation. Khan's travels in Africa apparently in search of uranium also raised suspicions. In the late 1990s, information on the developing relationship with Libya began to emerge as US intelligence obtained a good idea of how the Khan network operated. However, the initial thinking was that the network existed to serve Pakistan only. Knowledge about transactions on behalf of other countries came only later.

Although the Reagan administration had looked the other way politically as Pakistan was developing its nuclear weapon program and focused instead on the Soviet-Afghan war, it nevertheless closely followed the program. In the 1980s, the CIA and British Intelligence learned that Khan had obtained a design for a Chinese nuclear weapon tested in 1966 (which he many years later supplied to the Libyans and probably the Iranians). The CIA's penetration of the Pakistani program was so complete that as early as 1984 the agency could show a scale model of the Pakistani bomb to the country's foreign minister. And by 1989, a CIA official could say that "the President of the United States knew more about Pakistan's nuclear program than the prime minister of Pakistan."[111] However, the CIA and the US government didn't fully understand that Khan was using his program to support other countries, most importantly Iran, North Korea, and Libya. In addition, in October 1990, Khan sent an emissary to Baghdad to offer a package of nuclear weapon technology. The Iraqis were interested, but no action was taken, and the 1991 Gulf War took place a few months later.

In the late 1990s, the Libyan project caused Khan to buy more nuclear-related technology in Europe and elsewhere. When reports first came in, it was assumed that Khan was buying for Pakistan's program. A far greater concern was intelligence that Khan was increasing his cooperation with North Korea to include enrichment technology. The CIA suspected Khan in 1993–94 of setting up a barter with North Korea to trade longer-range missile plans in exchange for uranium enrichment technology. Khan was determined to acquire a nuclear weapon delivery vehicle that could cover all of India. The CIA was aware of a number of trips by Khan to North Korea and also of many Pakistani transport aircraft traveling there. However, while the CIA had detected Khan's work with North Korea, it was not as fortunate with Khan's cooperation with another troublesome regime—Iran.[112]

In early 2000, the CIA was able to recruit one of the key figures in Khan's illegal supply ring. By the spring of 2000, the CIA had obtained proof that two of the most dangerous regimes in the world—the militant clerics in Iran and the international terrorist sponsor in Libya—were pursuing nuclear weapons with Khan's assistance. This, coupled with what was already known about Khan and North Korea, made Khan's threat to the United States and the world undeniable.[113]

Still the US government did not move against Khan and his network. The CIA, the State Department, and officials at the White House argued that more could be learned by delaying action. And in the subsequent year, even more was learned, particularly about the burgeoning deal with Libya. In the Libyan arrangement, as indicated earlier, Khan had agreed to transfer virtually an entire nuclear weapon program: centrifuges, bomb design, and fabrication facilities. Because of the size of the Libyan contract, it became necessary to build dedicated construction facilities in Malaysia. The new Bush administration did not press President Musharraf of Pakistan to act; the CIA and the administration were following the same passive response as before, namely, watch and wait.[114]

However, in the fall of 2000 President Musharraf initiated his own investigation and decided the time had come to stop "this dirty business," as one of his advisors put it. On March 10, 2001, Khan's career in Pakistan's nuclear industry came to an end; he was retired from Kahuta, and he was appointed to a job without responsibilities as the special advisor to the president on strategic affairs.[115]

This did not stop Khan, however; he simply relied more on his network. The development of a complete nuclear weapon program for Libya continued at his facility in Malaysia, as did the frequent trips to North Korea to assist with the uranium enrichment program there. The CIA and British intelligence, having so deeply penetrated the network, were fully aware of all of this. When, in August 2002 at a National Press Club briefing in Washington, the National Council of Resistance of Iran blew the cover on the Iranian program, Khan immediately realized that he was in serious trouble, as IAEA investigations could reveal that he had provided the prototypes and blueprints for Iran's program, which now was running largely on its own.

As mentioned earlier, for some years Libya's Qadhafi had recognized his need to change his ways and move out of international isolation, but it wasn't until 2003 that Qadhafi was prepared to deal. Negotiations began in the spring but bogged down until the fall, when interception of the ship *BBC China* carrying thousands of components for centrifuges from Malaysia to Libya made it possible to confront the Libyans with evidence; Qadhafi then agreed to negotiate an end to Libya's WMD programs.

Legal and Political Tensions in Monitoring A. Q. Khan's Network

During the summer of 2008, details of the US effort to monitor and defeat the A. Q. Khan proliferation network's attempts to supply nuclear designs and equipment to Libya and Iran came to public light. The effort appears to have been an intelligence success, but it also demonstrates how intelligence efforts to discover and monitor clandestine proliferation activities can lead to international political and legal complications.

According to a *New York Times* article, in 2000 the CIA recruited three Swiss businessmen to track and undermine Khan's activities. Friedrich Tinner and his two sons had a long-standing commercial relationship with Khan going back to the 1970s. Supplying precision manufacturing gear, they had the technical expertise to aid Khan's development of centrifuges, to produce fuel for Pakistan's nuclear weapon program and for secret shipment to Libya and Iran.

Despite their sophistication, remote technical sensing devices, such as imagery satellites, can be fooled by deceptive measures; but a well-placed mole inside a clandestine network can help get to the truth. This was the value the Tinners reportedly provided to the United States. Gary Samore, who at the time headed the National Security Council's nonproliferation office, stated that the CIA relationship with the Tinners was significant because it confirmed US suspicions based on other information, particularly about Iran's nuclear efforts. In addition, the posting by Khan of Urs Tinner (one of the sons and the one originally approached by the CIA) in Dubai (Khan's principal transshipping point) led to information enabling the seizure of centrifuge parts bound for Libya, and CIA was able to secretly cripple other mechanical and electrical gear shipped to recipient states (such as Iran) on behalf of Khan to slow down the progress of the clandestine nuclear weapon programs in such countries.

After Khan's confession that his clients included not only Libya but also Iran and North Korea, it became clear that his network of clients was considerable. But the sabotage carried out by the CIA had been effective. When inspectors from the International Atomic Energy Agency (IAEA) traveled to Iran and Libya, they discovered vacuum pumps that had been cleverly damaged so that they would not work. A power supply shipped to Iran was also found to be defective.

The Tinners were eventually arrested for exporting illegal equipment. In the investigation, the Swiss along with other European authorities uncovered the Tinners' intelligence association with Washington. The legal case against the Tinners immediately raised tensions between efforts to prosecute and efforts to protect sensitive sources. Swiss authorities sought information from Washington, but the

(continued on page 84)

(continued from page 83)

State Department apparently wanted the Tinner files destroyed to stem further nuclear proliferation, and according to the *New York Times*, the CIA wanted to protect its sensitive sources (the Tinners) and methods. One former US official is to have said that "if a key source is prosecuted, what message does that send when you try to recruit other informants?"

In August 2007, the Swiss government cancelled its criminal case against the Tinners and destroyed the Tinners' electronic files and holdings. The father, Friedrich Tinner, was released from jail in 2006, son Urs (the key CIA contact) in December 2008, and his brother Marco in January 2009.[116] The justification given was to ensure that the information did not reach the hands of a terrorist organization or rogue state. The move led to a political and legal uproar on the part of some Swiss and European officials, who claimed that the justification was unwarranted because the files could have been preserved and protected. The *New York Times* article did not mention the role of Swiss intelligence, which undoubtedly is as concerned about nuclear proliferation as the CIA and may also have argued against the retention of the Tinner files and against the Tinners' prosecution. Neither do we know what the IAEA's position or preferences were in this matter. According to the *Times* account, the CIA has declined to comment on the Tinner case, but a CIA spokesman called the disruption of the Khan network a genuine intelligence success.[117]

This episode demonstrates the difficulties of collecting intelligence against clandestine proliferation operations and protecting the information obtained. While the documents might have been helpful to Swiss prosecutors and to the IAEA and others who wanted to know more about the extent of Khan's activities, undoubtedly the files were thoroughly examined by experts before they were destroyed. In the Tinner case, there appears to have been a policy judgment that protecting future intelligence collection efforts was of higher priority than prosecuting criminals.

Once Qadhafi decided to come in from the cold, the United States had the opportunity to break the Khan network and put an end to his career. CIA Director George Tenet confronted President Musharraf with US intelligence in New York in September 2003. Tenet insisted that Musharraf close down the Khan operation by arresting Khan. Seizure of the *BBC China*, forced Musharraf to act. Khan publicly confessed, but Musharraf pardoned him and placed him under long-term house arrest. Many of Khan's associates were arrested and jailed at least for a time. The credit for ending this threat goes to the US and British intelligence services. But the enormity of the Libyan program and the potential for actually building a bomb was a dramatic demonstration of the dangers of permitting Khan to operate all those years, even while being watched by the CIA.[118]

Because the A. Q. Khan network was international, involving several countries suspected of wanting nuclear weapon programs, various concerned countries had to work together to monitor and analyze the extent of the nuclear proliferation activities being carried out. Cooperation was required to piece together the intelligence and to develop policy efforts that would be successful in stopping further proliferation. Even then, significant proliferation had taken place before the network was properly understood or before measures were taken to halt its activities.

Aum Shinrikyo Sect. Although Osama bin Laden has claimed it his religious duty to obtain weapons of mass destruction, especially nuclear weapons, the best example we have of a terrorist organization's efforts to develop and deploy biological and chemical weapons is the case of the Aum Shinrikyo terrorist sect in Japan in the early to mid-1990s.

Terrorist Attack Using Chemical Agents

During the morning rush hour on March 20, 1995, passengers on Tokyo's subway system began reporting strange smells in subway stations and on subway cars. Soon passengers began collapsing on subway station platforms, sick and dying. Fire department emergency assistance teams raced to the scene, and before it was over, eleven people had died and more than five thousand had been injured. Several subway stations and several subway lines seem to have been affected. It was not long before this incident was identified as a poison gas attack, and by 11 A.M. the chemical agent was identified as the nerve gas sarin. Ultimately, the Japanese terrorist sect Aum Shinrikyo was found to be the perpetrator of the attack and was brought to justice.

A nerve agent attacks the human central nervous system, leading quickly to vomiting, convulsions, and death. It has only one function—to kill people. Sarin gas is odorless and colorless in its pure liquid state, but it will kill the average human being in less than fifteen minutes if even a tiny drop penetrates the pores of the skin. In the currency of chemical weapons, sarin is old technology. There are more than a hundred ways to make sarin, chemists say, and its formula is accessible in university libraries and on the Internet.

In the late 1980s and 1990s, a fanatical religious sect, Aum Shinrikyo, came into being and grew powerful in Japan at the local level. It was led by a self-styled guru named Shoko Asahara, who became obsessed with the approach of Armageddon—doomsday—as he saw it. When Armageddon failed to happen as expected, Aum Shinrikyo decided to make it happen. Members of the sect went shopping in Russia for weapons of mass destruction to bring about the end of the world. The idea was that Asahara would be installed as "holy emperor" after the destruction of the Japanese state.

The Aum Shinrikyo cult had made repeated attempts to produce and weaponize lethal biological agents (botulinum toxin and anthrax) for use against Japanese civilians. The sect bought land in Australia as a possible test range and sought technology in the United States. However, the cult's extensive efforts to develop biological weapons failed, so they resorted to developing chemical agents for their attacks.

The sect looked in Russia for chemical weapon formulas and the expertise to make biological weapons, as well as nuclear weapon technology. It was able to acquire the formulas for the chemical nerve agents sarin and VX. Aum Shinrikyo established a factory near Mount Fuji, where quantities of sarin as well as some VX were produced.

In June 1994, the sect decided to do a field trial in the Japanese mountain town of Matsumoto. A small team went to this town near evening on June 27. They had with them a quantity of newly produced sarin of a rather pure quality. The plan was to release the gas from a spray tank, which in fact was done. However, the members of the terror team were nervous about handling sarin in such a pure state, and they also failed to make allowance for the wind. The attack degenerated into confusion, and the attackers fled. Nevertheless, seven residents of nearby buildings died and nearly sixty were hospitalized.

All of this took place without any of the world's intelligence services being aware of what was unfolding; the Japanese police had no good sense of what was happening in their own backyard. As a registered "religious" organization, Aum Shinrikyo enjoyed substantial autonomy under Japanese law.

Thus the stage was set for the attack on March 20, 1995. The plan was to release sarin gas on five subway cars on three lines, all of which fed into the downtown Tokyo station of Kasumigaseki. Sect members carried bags of the gas onto the cars, hidden under newspapers, and placed them on the floor under their seats. They then punctured the bags with the tip of their umbrellas and jumped off the train. Fortunately, because of the difficulties encountered by the team in Matsumoto, the sarin used in this hoped-for doomsday attack was considerably watered down, only about 30 percent pure, and much less potent than the gas used during the release in Matsumoto. Once again, the attack was carried out somewhat clumsily, and not all the bags were punctured.

As a result, the terrorists did not achieve their objective of killing thousands and paralyzing the government, thereby hastening the advent of doomsday. However, as D. W. Brackett states in his book *Holy Terror*, "Although more than five thousand were injured, the death rate—eleven people—was surprisingly low for a nerve-gas attack. That was due in large part to the relative weakness of the sarin—estimated by chemists to have been only thirty percent pure—and the crude method used to disperse it. Had the gas been stronger—say, seventy or eighty percent pure—and its method of dispersal more effective, the death and injury toll could easily have soared into the tens of thousands." Even so, the resulting deaths and injuries demonstrated a grim truth: even when poorly produced and disseminated, chemical weapons can be devastatingly effective.[119]

The Aum Shinrikyo terrorists did not achieve their goals, and the Japanese police rapidly obtained evidence that enabled them to destroy the cult. However, the attack did demonstrate two things: fanatical religious cults can be perpetrators of extreme violence, and weapons of mass destruction can be obtained and effectively used by terrorists. The two attacks brought to the fore the ease with which terrorists can obtain at least some chemical weapons and use them against unsuspecting populations.[120] This case also demonstrates that developing biological agents is somewhat more difficult even for a well-funded group.

Perhaps equally important, the incident shows how small, clandestine efforts to develop and deploy chemical and biological agents can take place under the radar of normal police and intelligence monitoring activities. Cooperation between local police forces and national intelligence organizations is required to detect and monitor the relevant activities of such groups. It appears that no one pieced together the efforts of this sect to secure expertise and agents in Russia or access to land in Australia. To be sure, the targets of the attack were Japanese, not nationals in other countries, as with al-Qaeda, but there was an international aspect to the sect's activities. What is surprising is that more attacks along these lines by other terrorist groups, especially al-Qaeda, have not occurred. Granted, reports have circulated of chlorine gas being dispersed in sectarian violence in Iraq, but up to the present there have been no reports of a group such as al-Qaeda supporting or launching a significant attack using chemical or biological agents.

4   Intelligence Community–Policymaker Relations: Playing as a Team?

Good national security policy depends on good intelligence in support of policy deliberations and implementation. But it also requires policymakers who know how to use intelligence properly without misusing or compromising it. When the intelligence-policymaker relationship works well, the chances of having good policy decisions are greatly increased. When that relationship is less than optimum, which can happen for a variety of reasons, policy is likely to suffer. (Mark Lowenthal's *Intelligence: From Secrets to Policy* provides a concise discussion of this important relationship; see chapter 9 therein.)

Unfortunately, the role that intelligence should play and the contribution that it can make to national security policy are not well understood by the general public (and at times even by some policymakers). Given Hollywood's portrayals of intelligence activities and frequent press coverage of "intelligence failures," confusion and misinformation abound on the nature of intelligence and its legitimate role in supporting policymakers. Even the distinction between intelligence and policy is generally not understood. The extent to which the intelligence-policymaker relationship is misunderstood or otherwise perverted can affect popular perceptions of US intelligence capabilities, and it can affect the success of US policy, including efforts to limit the proliferation of weapons of mass destruction.

The US National Security Community

The US national security apparatus consists of three major players: policymakers (executive branch), the Intelligence Community, and Congress. Defining and promoting US national security policy is the prerogative of the president and his National Security Council (NSC). Although Congress pays close attention and frequently questions administration officials, it is the role of the president and his national security advisors to devise policies that ensure the national security of the United States. The policy community considers options and makes policy; the Intelligence Community (IC) provides intelligence to support the policy-making process; and Congress oversees and critiques the entire process. Policymakers often consult with members of Congress during this process, and the Intelligence Community provides substantive support to Congress in parallel with its support to policymakers in the executive branch.

Policy Community. In making national security policy, the president is supported by the NSC, which is comprised of the heads of the key policy departments and agencies, principally State, Defense, Energy, Treasury, Homeland Security, and Justice. The Director of National Intelligence (formerly the Director of Central Intelligence) and the Chairman of the Joint Chiefs of Staff are advisors to the NSC. The president and council are supported by a staff of professional experts, many of whom are on loan from the various national security departments and agencies. They serve under the direction of the president's national security advisor. It is the task of this staff, with support from the various departments and agencies, to solicit intelligence and to prepare policy options for members of the council to consider in advising the president on the best course of action for the issue of the moment.

Intelligence Community. The US Intelligence Community came into existence with the National Security Act of 1947, which established the NSC, the position of Director of Central Intelligence (DCI), and the Central Intelligence Agency (CIA). Since then, successive administrations have expanded and modified the Intelligence Community's structure to meet evolving policy requirements. Most recently, the Intelligence Reform Act of 2004 put the Intelligence Community under the Director of National Intelligence (DNI), which replaced the DCI position. The DNI has responsibility for coordinating the work of sixteen different agencies and serving as the president's senior intelligence advisor. The DNI's staff is responsible for ensuring that priorities are set, pulling together and coordinating intelligence from all agencies, and ensuring that sufficient information sharing is taking place among the key players. All IC entities except the CIA belong to policy departments and are therefore referred to as departmental intelligence components. Their primary support is to their home agency and department head, but they also have a corporate responsibility to support each other with relevant information. Some have unique collection capabilities, such as for signals intelligence (National Security Agency, or NSA), imagery intelligence (National Geospatial-Intelligence Agency, or NGA), and human source intelligence (National Clandestine Service/CIA), which means that they have a corporate role to play as well. A majority of the IC entities come under the Department of Defense because of the need to support military operations in the field. Only the CIA is totally independent of any policy agency; it was created in 1947 to provide coordinated, all-source information to the president and members of the NSC (see Appendix D).

Congress. In addition to their control of the government's budget, congressional committees continually oversee and critique the programs and activities of the policy and intelligence communities. The committees are focused on foreign policy, defense policy and procurement, government operations, and intelligence. Only since the mid-1970s have there been standing committees in both houses devoted to the oversight of the Intelligence Community (see Appendix I). And in the succeeding decades, members of Congress have become avid consumers of intelligence as well as overseers of its budgets and programs.[1]

The Intelligence-Policymaker Relationship

The intelligence function is to provide timely, relevant, and objective information to those responsible for developing and executing US national security policy (see Chapter 2). Intelligence is not policy! By its very nature, intelligence exists to support policymakers, not to recommend, advocate, or make policy. It is a fact that policymakers can formulate policy without the assistance of intelligence; sometimes they choose to ignore the intelligence they receive. In contrast, intelligence has no reason to exist apart from supporting the policymaking process. In the most fundamental sense, intelligence is a service activity that responds to the information needs of policymakers. Both the policy and intelligence communities are integral players in the US national security arena, and they both interact with Congress on these issues.

Competing for Policymaker Focus. Often the pace of events and difference in personalities affect how the intelligence-policymaker relationship unfolds. The relationship is not automatically successful, and it takes effort on both sides to make it work.

Most policymakers want and value the support they receive from the Intelligence Community (IC) and try to forge a positive working relationship with one or more components of the IC. Policymakers also seek information from other sources to support their initiatives. Generally speaking, policymakers have extensive experience and contacts, but they cannot be experts on all issues on which they must work; thus, they tend to listen and give credence to those they know and trust. Therefore, intelligence officials must work hard to earn the confidence of new policymakers, who come into office with changes in administrations and perhaps with little or no experience in Washington, especially in working with sensitive intelligence. Building confidence is normally accomplished by establishing personal rapport with policy officials and by providing information and analysis that is relevant, timely, and objective. It generally falls to intelligence officials to take the first steps to explain what the IC can and cannot provide as well as to offer assistance.

Differing Cultures. Policymakers and intelligence officials work within distinct cultures. It is not a matter of one being the "bad guy" and the other, the "good guy"; both need to perform their functions and cooperate to achieve the common good for the nation's security. In our experience, such cooperation is more often the case than not. Generally speaking, policymakers are action oriented and are under pressure to promote successful policies. They are often at odds with one another given their different departmental affiliations and perspectives on how to achieve the articulated goals of the president. As such, they are almost always looking for information that supports their policy preferences and contributes to their success. It is fair to say that policymakers typically seek information from multiple sources when they are trying to understand a situation and devise an appropriate policy. Once they settle on a policy, they naturally look for information that will support that policy. If they are less than objective and lack professional integrity, they will dismiss good intelligence that does not help them sell their policy to Congress, to allies, or even to the American public.

In contrast, intelligence officers are trained to provide the best intelligence available whether or not it enhances the prospects for a policy to succeed. As much as humanly possible, intelligence officers must overcome their own biases (they all, of course, have private views on policy issues) by providing objective, apolitical analyses. The Intelligence Community strives to neutralize personal or institutional biases in intelligence judgments and reporting through conscientious management and the reporting of alternative views. And intelligence officers must be willing to deliver the "bad news" to policymakers when they know their analyses and judgments will not be happily received.

Policymakers tend to be optimists as they strive to achieve their policy ends, while intelligence officers are often more cautious and skeptical because of their effort to analyze all facets of a situation and to look for pitfalls. This cultural difference often results in policymakers questioning the veracity of the IC's analysis, although that can be an appropriate response. Policymakers have the right and responsibility to pose hard questions regarding the intelligence they receive. However, when policymakers undercut the credibility of judgments or analysts because the information does not support their bias or policy preference, the situation can become seriously dysfunctional.

New policymakers, especially if they have no experience working with intelligence, can have unrealistic expectations of the IC. Such expectations range from the Hollywood fantasy that intelligence officers know everything and can do anything to an extreme skepticism that the IC knows anything useful. If a policymaker arrives on the scene with strong political biases or even animosity toward the Intelligence Community, perhaps as a result of past negative experience, then intelligence officials can have difficulty establishing an ideal working relationship. In a worst-case scenario, a few policymakers will not ask for intelligence or will ignore the intelligence they receive, choosing to believe their own trusted sources of insight. We will see in Chapter 5 the impact this approach had on some in the Bush administration prior to the commitment of US forces in Iraq in 2003.

Because of this "new policymaker" phenomenon, intelligence officials must do what they can to educate policymakers and manage their expectations to avoid disappointment or disillusionment. Intelligence officers have an imperative to be transparent and explicit in sharing with policymakers what they know and what they do not know. Explaining important gaps in intelligence information is critical to policymakers in their policy deliberations. Equally important is the need for the intelligence to expose alternative views that may exist within the IC on the issues analyzed. More often than not, gaps and uncertainties accompany any finished intelligence provided to policymakers. When they exist, there is the possibility of credible alternative interpretations of what the information means and how the future may unfold. The IC must make informed judgments, but it also must make clear alternative explanations or future outcomes when they exist. Finally, the IC must allow policymakers the opportunity to challenge information and judgments in order to understand how confident the IC is in what it is saying. At times, from their interactions with foreign officials, policymakers will be aware of tidbits that have not been given to intelligence analysts. A good policy-intelligence dialogue will get all relevant information and views on a situation out on the table for a comprehensive review.

Policymakers sometimes have offered their perspectives on this important and delicate relationship with intelligence. Many value close, professional relationships with intelligence officers and the opportunity to view information on an issue from a different perspective. For example, former ambassador Robert Blackwill, who served on the NSC staff as the Warsaw Pact and the Soviet Union were collapsing, commented that his relationship with CIA's analysts on Eastern Europe was critical to his understanding and promoting US interests during this turbulent period. By establishing a close working relationship with intelligence, he was able to request and receive analyses and information that were tailored to his needs rather than sift through larger reports for the few nuggets that mattered to him. He added that he valued the CIA's analysis in particular because CIA analysts were not otherwise working for one of the policy agencies engaged in interagency policy battles.[2]

Reporting Intelligence Findings to Policymakers

The final stage of the intelligence cycle is providing finished intelligence (analyzed data and judgments) in a way that meets the needs of policymakers. Intelligence in its raw state, such as images of objects of interest or intercepts of conversations of important foreign nationals, is at times passed without being incorporated into a finished piece of analysis if the data is clear enough and meets an urgent need. However, even then the intelligence requires some expert explanation to ensure that the recipient understands the context and what is being indicated by the picture or intercept.

Providing information and responses that are relevant to the questions asked, timely enough to be helpful, and seen as objective (void of individual, institutional, or policy biases) is the goal of the Intelligence Community. This intelligence mantra—relevant, timely, and objective information—requires some explanation. First, most policymakers in the national security arena (especially in times of crises, which are frequent) are working with tight deadlines and under stress. Thus, they look for information that can help them when they need it. Good analysis, therefore, is that which focuses on the issue of the moment and which arrives in time to inform policy deliberations and decisions. The good news is that the Intelligence Community gears itself to respond to tight deadlines, knowing that information provided after a decision has been made is not helpful nor generally appreciated. With regard to objectivity, the term itself can be subjective. What is objective in one person's view can be seen as biased in another's. Even though the Intelligence Community strives to prevent politicization (that is, outside policy preferences influencing its judgments) and to neutralize personal and institutional biases, no intelligence product is ever viewed by policymakers as totally pure. The Intelligence Community must take every precaution to avoid prescribing policy or introducing ideological biases in its judgments, and must understand that consumers of intelligence are always reading information through their own biased lenses. Policymakers generally assume that intelligence officers are as politicized as they are.

Beyond these considerations, how the intelligence is provided can influence greatly how well policymakers receive it. Thus, the Intelligence Community puts considerable energy into finding out how individual policymakers prefer to receive their intelligence. To borrow terminology from the private sector, the Intelligence Community studies and devises ways to "market its products to its consumers." However, most of this effort focuses on learning how individual policymakers consume information (reading, oral briefing, watching a video). Some consumers are avid readers while others prefer to have someone talk them through the analysis to be able to ask questions in real time. The Intelligence Community ensures that all its customers are able to ask follow-on questions. More often than not, the response to one question leads to another question, so that the interaction between intelligence and policy is dynamic and continuous.

How information is written and communicated can be as critical to effectively informing policymakers as the substance it contains. Considerable effort is thus put on producing concise and easily readable text so that busy readers can quickly grasp the essence of the analysis and judgments. The President's Daily Brief (PDB), which has undergone various redesigns and reformats in response to the preferences of successive presidents, is the most obvious specially tailored product. The PDB was established in the early 1960s to permit the busiest of all US policymakers, the president, to read unique intelligence in a manner and quantity that he could readily consume, and to have "one-stop shopping." All presidents since John F. Kennedy have been provided this tailored daily intelligence product. Because policymakers at different levels require varying degrees of detail, products such as National Intelligence Estimates (NIEs) often contain tailor-made summaries, which are appropriate for the different levels of readership.

Single-Agency Reports. Some analyses (commonly referred to as single-agency analyses) are produced by individual intelligence agencies and components, while others, such as NIEs, are written as interagency (Intelligence Community) products. Single-agency products are written especially for the policymakers within specific departments, such as the secretaries of State and Defense (or their subordinates), and respond to their specific requirements. These products may also contain specialized intelligence, such as signals intelligence (SIGINT) collected and analyzed by the National Security Agency or imagery intelligence (IMINT) collected and analyzed by the National Geospatial-Intelligence Agency. And each of the military service intelligence organizations necessarily gathers intelligence to support its service's unique military activities and operations at the tactical level. In contrast, the CIA was created to be independent of any policy agency so as to serve the whole national security community, particularly the White House, and to gather and analyze information from all sources in as unbiased a manner as possible.

Whether single-agency or interagency products, all analyses are coordinated to some degree and reviewed before being disseminated. Within individual agencies, analysts with related expertise are called on to provide peer reviews so that obvious omissions of evidence or perspectives may be corrected. Each level of management necessarily reviews the substance of the analysis to ensure quality control and ascertain that all relevant experts have been involved and that the analysis is being presented in the most effective manner. In the end, the intelligence presented almost always represents a corporate effort, not the judgments of an individual analyst.

Interagency Reports. Intelligence Community products, such as NIEs, require even more extensive coordination and review than single-agency reports because their findings represent those of the entire Intelligence Community. In addition to being reviewed within the individual agencies, as with single-agency products, interagency products must be reviewed at the corporate community level. Depending on the import of the analysis, the Director of National Intelligence and the heads of all principal agencies may meet as the National Intelligence Board to discuss and pass on the final product. Because the chances are good that there will be differences of analytic judgment on one or more aspects of an issue, interagency products must clearly note where the substantive differences are and why they exist. Such differences represent alternative interpretations and normally reflect gaps and uncertainties in the available information. Informed judgments regarding these uncertainties may differ, but it is incumbent on senior IC managers to ensure that the differences are not a reflection of bias but rather represent plausible alternative interpretations of the evidence in hand. Most importantly, it is the duty of the IC's leadership to ensure that all products are relevant (responsive to needs), timely (disseminated in time to inform the decision-making process), and objective (free of internal or externally imposed biases).[3]

A National Intelligence Estimate is an attempt to discern reality; it is not a learned essay on an academic subject. Thus, it must contain informed judgments made in assessing and analyzing facts derived from intelligence collection. The so-called facts are often the subject of disagreement as to whether and to what extent they are credible. Assessments of particular facts must be qualified to reflect differing assessments of raw collected intelligence. In effect, then, an NIE must often say, "It is our assessment that such and such is the case and our judgment that this factual situation, if correctly analyzed, can mean such and such." But when agreement on judgments cannot be reached, one or more components of the Intelligence Community will insert an alternative view on the information or the judgments reached by the majority of IC components.

Of overriding importance in any interagency product is that the Intelligence Community gets the facts and its judgments as right as possible. Many NIEs form a significant part of the background knowledge of the policy community. As such, some may have a large impact on the policy process, although only a very few have a profound effect. In speaking "truth to power," then, the story told in a particular NIE must be as careful, thorough, clear, and accurate as possible. But having said this, again one must keep in mind the purpose of an NIE. It is not an academic exercise designed to address a subject with many caveats and allowing for many eventualities, as in the manner of British weather reports; it is a document addressing a specific subject in order to inform policymakers, give them a better understanding of the issue and factors involved, and bound the limits of plausible explanations or future outcomes, so as to provide the basis for the best policy decision possible.

Even though the facts of a subject may be far from clear and their explanation uncertain, the Intelligence Community should draft NIEs that are clear and comprehensive and that set forth a coherent story based on the best judgments that can be made. There can be caveats, but IC analysts and managers should not be afraid of being wrong in making their best judgment. The language used to convey information and judgments should be precise, the sources identified to the degree they can be, and the characterization of facts and implications expressly made. Only then can policymakers be well informed and more likely able to make sound policy decisions.

Combating Politicization

One frequently hears accusations that intelligence has been politicized—that under pressure it has spun its judgments to accommodate policy preferences and pressure. The Intelligence Community continually debates how closely intelligence officers should work with their policy counterparts to provide good support yet avoid the politicization of intelligence. Former DCI Richard Helms called attention to this concern in the context of providing Intelligence Community support in the late 1960s and early 1970s to the launching, negotiating, and monitoring of nuclear arms control agreements.[4]

From the beginning of the CIA's creation by the National Security Act of 1947, a "red line" was established to prevent intelligence officers from recommending policy and to prevent policymakers from influencing intelligence judgments to suit their policy needs. At a roundtable held at Georgetown University in late 2003, former intelligence officers and policy officials discussed this issue. They concluded that during the Cold War the boundary was usually observed, because the Intelligence Community had a near monopoly on sensitive information about the Soviet Union and was able to offer its findings and judgments to policymakers, who then decided how to deal with the issues at hand. However, in the post–Cold War world, policy support requirements have increasingly blurred the purity of that separation, at least at the tactical level. Both in increased support to military operations in places like Kuwait, Iraq, and Afghanistan as well as in the war against terror, intelligence officers have found themselves increasingly "embedded" with policymakers to provide the intelligence required in fast-moving situations. During the roundtable, a former policymaker noted that the old divide between policy and intelligence is blurred if not gone, due in part to technology that now allows raw intelligence to be provided to policy consumers at the tactical level (as to military soldiers in the field). Policy officials armed with raw reporting no longer hesitate to shape intelligence.[5]

However, at the national level (mainly in Washington, DC), the traditional lines of demarcation are generally followed. Intelligence officers continue to be taught to observe the red line to avoid losing credibility. Once an intelligence officer has stepped over the policy line, he or she will no longer be seen as objective and therefore trustworthy, at least by some policymakers. Of course, that intelligence may be viewed as more trustworthy if it supports the policymaker's position. Over the past sixty years most directors of central intelligence have

National Intelligence Estimates

Within the Office of the Director of National Intelligence (ODNI) is the National Intelligence Council (NIC), which is a collection of senior intelligence analysts known as National Intelligence Officers (NIOs) and their staffs, who are responsible for key areas of substantive focus. The NIOs lead the Intelligence Community's production of interagency analyses and estimates on their areas of expertise and responsibility. For example, the NIO for strategic forces and nuclear proliferation took the lead on the 2002 National Intelligence Estimate (NIE) on the status of Iraq's WMD programs (see Chapter 5), with support from the NIO for the Near East and South Asia.[6] A similar group of senior analysts most likely directed production of the NIE on Iran's nuclear weapon program, the Key Judgments of which were issued in an unclassified form in December 2007 (see Chapter 3).

One of the tasks of NIOs is to know their policy customers and determine when an interagency effort, such as the production of an NIE, is appropriate and potentially useful. Of course, policymakers (or members of Congress) may request an NIE at any time. Once a product is determined to be needed, the responsible NIO produces a "draft terms of reference" outlining the thrust of the NIE and invites all agencies to send representatives to an interagency meeting. At that meeting the NIO determines who in the IC has the requisite expertise to prepare the draft document and sets the schedule for the review, coordination, and production process, which includes the substantive content, format and presentation that will meet the needs of policymakers (for more detail on the NIE process, see Appendix J).

After receiving and reviewing the incoming draft to ensure its completeness and responsiveness to the policy question, the NIO circulates it to agency representatives and calls for their coordinating review. Depending on the length and complexity of the draft and substantive differences over judgments, the coordination process can take hours, days, or weeks. The NIO's responsibility is to ensure that the NIE presents all substantive facts, represents and explains any differences of view, and clearly notes gaps and uncertainties in the information and judgments. In addition, most forward-looking NIEs discuss alternative future scenarios. Because no one knows what the future will bring, NIEs should attempt to bound the future with reasonable alternatives so that policymakers can focus their attention on the most likely range of outcomes.

Next, the NIO makes sure that the NIE is well organized and optimally presented. This usually means that after a transmittal letter from the DNI, the reader will find Presidential Bullets (one page of tightly condensed judgments that may also appear in the President's Daily Brief), Key Judgments, which bring forth the most important findings and conclusions of IC analysts, and then the Main Text, which includes all the detailed substance and arguments that support the Key Judgments. This structure allows the various levels of policy readers to go into as much depth as they choose. Normally, senior policymakers will read the Key Judgments and perhaps selected portions of the Main Text, while lower-level policy experts will read the detailed analysis along with any backup material provided.

Once the draft is fully coordinated by the intelligence analysts, the NIO asks for a meeting of the National Intelligence Board, which is chaired by the DNI and includes the heads of all agencies, to determine collectively whether the NIE is ready to be given to policymakers. This is not a rubber-stamp exercise but rather an opportunity for agency experts and senior IC managers to have one last shot at ensuring that the analysis is complete and responsive. If it is deemed so, then the NIE is formally published and distributed to the appropriate policymakers under the signature of the DNI, which shows that it is a community product.[7] If not, NIEs can be remanded back to the NIO and participating agencies to correct the deficiencies noted. Once an NIE is cleared for publication and release by the DNI, the judgments are briefed to the president and senior policymakers. The NIOs and others make certain that copies are delivered to policy and congressional customers who have a legitimate need to know. At times, delivery will be in person to guarantee that the recipient fully understands the substance and nuances of the judgments as well as the confidence with which the Intelligence Community has made them.

In a preface to the unclassified summary of the NIE on Iran's nuclear weapon program issued in December 2007, the Office of the Director of National Intelligence included an explanation of the nature of NIEs and the process that produces them. The ODNI explained that since the Intelligence Reform Act of 2004, the DNI and Intelligence Community have undertaken a number of steps to improve the NIE process. These include the following: (1) new procedures to integrate formal reviews of source reporting and technical judgments; specifically, the directors of the National Clandestine Service (CIA), NSA, NGA, and DIA and the Assistant Secretary/INR are now required to submit formal assessments that highlight the strengths, weaknesses, and overall credibility of their sources used in developing the critical judgments of the NIE; and (2) more-rigorous standards in explaining what intelligence judgments mean, along with the confidence levels associated with judgments, to clarify the reasons for any differences in judgments within the Intelligence Community and to display those differences in the Key Judgments section of the NIE.[8]

In our experience NIEs are normally produced in a moderate number—perhaps two per month on average—because of their complexity and importance; this rate is much less frequent than for the daily current intelligence publications. Exactly when NIEs are produced depends of course on policy needs for a consolidated and authoritative Intelligence Community assessment on a given subject. The public dissemination of either declassified Key Judgments or an unclassified version of Key Judgments from a particular NIE is quite infrequent. The public release of Key Judgments from the NIEs on the Iraqi WMD and Iranian nuclear weapon program during the past several years has probably made releases seem more frequent than they really are. It should be noted that the more detailed Main Texts of those NIEs, which contain the specifics about sensitive sources and the detailed analysis supporting the judgments, have not been (and are normally not) released for obvious reasons.

played it straight, but some have discovered this pitfall. During the Johnson administration DCI John McCone found himself in a tough situation when CIA analyses called into question the success of the administration's policy in Vietnam and pit the CIA against both the Department of Defense and the White House. He ultimately fell into disfavor and resigned as DCI when his offer of advice on the Vietnam war ran against the president's preferred policy.[9] During the Nixon administration Richard Helms found himself being squeezed by the Pentagon, which sought to hype the threat posed by Soviet strategic nuclear forces to support US military programs.[10] To the dismay of the Intelligence Community, both McCone and Helms gave in to the pressure and agreed to tone down IC judgments to be less contrary to administration policy (see Appendix K for details).

Some have argued that giving William Casey a cabinet position in the Reagan administration in addition to his role as intelligence advisor to the president and National Security Council compromised his DCI position. And DCI Robert Gates, who had a close association with the strongly anti-Soviet Casey during the 1980s, was dragged through a tough confirmation process by the Senate in 1991 under accusations that he had compromised himself and intelligence analysis with an anti-Soviet bias and by hyping the Soviet threat. In contrast, his successor as DCI, James Woolsey, was so distant from policy and from President Clinton that he finally resigned, in part because of his lack of access.[11] Most recently, some believe that George Tenet became too close to President George W. Bush, which led to his being less objective, cautious, and willing to provide unwelcome analyses than he should have been when reporting the IC's levels of certainty on the reliability of information about the existence of weapons of mass destruction in Iraq (see Chapter 5).[12]

The Vietnam controversy during the Johnson presidency, followed by the controversy regarding Soviet strategic capabilities and objectives during the Nixon administration, is now joined by the Iraqi WMD controversy during the George W. Bush administration as clear examples of the occupational hazards that US intelligence officers often face. The judgments they deliver do not necessarily enjoy careful, rational study but may be misused or disappear into a highly political, sometimes chaotic, process when other forces and sources of information carry the day in the making of policy.

Politicization of intelligence analysis is not just a problem of policymaker pressure; biases can crop up from within the Intelligence Community itself. Everyone has biases, but professional intelligence officers are trained to sublimate their personal biases in executing their duty to supply objective intelligence. In addition, good management practices and the process of coordinating intelligence analysis are used to neutralize individual biases. Unfortunately, biases can also become institutionalized. The various components of the Intelligence Community, especially those serving departmental masters, must continually fight against institutional bias that supports their department's policy position. Once again, the production of interagency analysis, such as National Intelligence Estimates, is one way the IC attempts to identify and eliminate such biases from its analyses. In a speech to the CIA after becoming the Director of Central Intelligence and having weathered the aforementioned bruising confirmation process, Robert Gates warned against politicization, especially from within. He defined politicization as "deliberately distorting analysis or judgments to favor a preferred line of thinking irrespective of evidence." He explained that politicization can result from products being forced to conform to policymakers' views, management pressure to drive a certain line of analysis or substantive viewpoint, changes made in tone or emphasis to favor a certain outcome, or limits on the expression of alternative views. He called for good management practices and discipline from intelligence analysts and managers to protect judgments from being swayed by internal or external pressure and biases.[13, 14]

Policymaker Disregard for or Misuse of Intelligence. Policymakers may tend to disregard, misuse, or mischaracterize the intelligence they receive, when they are so committed to a course of action that they refuse to listen to contrary information. No intelligence officer likes to bring bad news to policy consumers, particularly those with whom he or she has been closely working, but intelligence officers are obliged to report what they believe to be the truth about a situation whether it supports or detracts from the policy preference.

Some less than honest policymakers will do all they can to undermine the credibility of unwished-for intelligence, including the integrity and objectivity of the intelligence officer presenting the analysis. Other policymakers will put their own spin on the intelligence to win support for their policy preference. This can often lead to confusion, especially when the debate goes public while the actual intelligence reported to policymakers must remain out of the public domain. Still other policymakers will disclose, and even compromise, the intelligence they have received to bolster their case in public. Intelligence is misused at times by both policymakers within the administration and by members of Congress. In Chapter 5 we examine how some policymakers spun the intelligence on aspects of Iraq's WMD programs to bolster their case for the urgency of removing Saddam Hussein by military force.

One of the most disappointing events is when policymakers choose to disregard or ignore intelligence information or judgments that do not fit the way they want the world to be. For example, the Intelligence Community produced an estimate in 1991 forecasting the breakup of Yugoslavia; this was at a time when policymakers were consumed with the breakup of the Warsaw Pact, the imminent collapse of the Soviet Union, and Iraq's military occupation of Kuwait. Even though the IC's forecast was accurate, it did not match what policymakers wanted to see transpire. They chose to largely ignore the IC's warning and pursued in vain their efforts to keep the Yugoslav factions together. One can argue that the NIE should have explored the possibility of different outcomes, however unlikely the IC might have judged them to be. In any case, this episode demonstrates that even when intelligence gets it right, successful policy decisions do not necessarily follow.

Domestic Politics, A Necessary but Troublesome Reality. We live in a democracy; thus, all important subjects, regardless of their sensitivity, become part of the political process. In the post–Cold War era this is more true than ever before: intelligence issues often become front-page news and end up as part of the political debate. From time to time Key Judgments from NIEs become political issues. Examples abound: intelligence judgments since the early 1990s as to the number of nuclear weapons that North Korea may or may not have produced have been very much part of the political debate; and the intelligence judgments from 2005 and 2007 on Iran's efforts to develop a nuclear weapon have been an important part of the subsequent domestic political debate over what policy to pursue with Iran.

Many officials in political positions within the government have adopted the "New York Times rule": Never put anything in writing, no matter how highly classified the document, that you wouldn't want to see on the front page of the *New York Times*. While it is important that the drafters of NIEs be frank, judgments from NIEs inevitably risk being leaked to the press for political reasons. This can happen within the executive branch, usually at the political level in the White House or the Department of Defense, or it may come from congressional committees. Protecting sensitive intelligence is of utmost importance; unfortunately, our democratic society must cope with a permanent risk that highly classified information which can affect the outcome of policy debates or which is important to understanding specific political issues will, sooner or later, become public knowledge. With Iraq and Iran we have seen NIEs released and their judgments used as ammunition by both those who support and those who oppose a given policy.

And, of course, some claim that intelligence information should be open to public debate. The American people, they argue, pay for intelligence through their tax dollars, so the Intelligence Community cannot be beyond the political process. As a result of this and other factors, many intelligence activities become exposed and polarized. Here also there are many examples. In the five or so years before the election of President Reagan, intelligence reports analyzing the military strength of the Soviet Union were distinctly less alarmist than those that followed in the early 1980s. The change was sufficiently marked that it could not have been the result of new information; the emphasis was different. In large measure the change grew out of the charges made by conservatives in the mid-1970s that the Intelligence Community had consistently underestimated both the intentions and capabilities of the Soviet Union.[15] If sound policy is to be pursued within the public earshot, nonpolitical intelligence reporting is essential, and sensitive intelligence sources and methods must be protected. (An excellent book for understanding "threat inflation" during the Cold War is *The Arsenals of Folly* by Richard Rhodes, published in 2007.)

Complications from Congressional Oversight. The intelligence budget is large, more than $40 billion a year. The House Permanent Select Committee on Intelligence (HPSCI) and the Senate Select Committee on Intelligence (SSCI) are the authorizing committees for this budget, and they also exercise substantive oversight on intelligence programs and activities (see Appendix I). For example, they review collection programs and analysis techniques, and they propose laws that govern certain activities, such as electronic surveillance, that might involve US citizens. These committees established review procedures through the federal courts under the Foreign Intelligence Surveillance Act (FISA) of 1978 to govern the legality and permissibility of intelligence wiretaps.[16] The Director of Central Intelligence (now the Director of National Intelligence), along with the directors of various other intelligence agencies such as the National Security Agency, must brief these two committees regularly on the issues of the day. Briefings are important because these committees oversee the proper functioning of the Intelligence Community on behalf of the American people. What's more, convincing briefings are necessary by the Director of National Intelligence or the Director of the CIA, for example, if they hope to do well in the budget process. The legislative branch, moreover, must be well informed if it is to make sound decisions in approving program and budget requests. Unfortunately, when senior intelligence officers have failed to develop good relationships with the leadership of the House or Senate intelligence committees, the results have been much to the detriment of their agencies and the US government as a whole.

One of the more recent important demonstrations of the oversight function was the investigation by the Senate Select Committee on the use of intelligence in Iraq before the war. This report criticized the Intelligence Community for its failure to give an accurate account of the status of Iraq's WMD programs. Unfortunately, the report turned out to be a highly partisan product. Senator Pat Roberts, the Republican who was chairing the committee at the time the report was released, promised a second report on the role of the White House in influencing and using intelligence on Iraq, but he did not pursue a second report. Subsequently, under the new Democratic chairman of the committee, Senator John Rockefeller, the SSCI issued a report on the Intelligence Community's warnings, in January 2003, on the consequences of the removal of Saddam Hussein.[17] And only in 2007, under Senator Rockefeller, did the SSCI release its report on how senior government officials used the intelligence provided on Iraq's WMD programs.[18]

The Challenge Posed by Leaks. As stated earlier, a well-known phenomenon of Washington politics is the leaking of classified information, whether sensitive intelligence or policy deliberations, to influence policy debates or public opinion. Such leaks, which are almost always intentional, come from the executive branch as well as from Congress. To the extent that they compromise sensitive intelligence sources and methods they, at a minimum, make the job of providing objective intelligence analysis difficult. At the extreme, they can lead to the loss (or even death) of important human sources or the loss of capabilities of expensive and sophisticated technical collection systems. Leaks can undermine efforts to monitor and limit the proliferation of nuclear weapons and other weapons of mass destruction. Unfortunately, very few leakers are ever caught and prosecuted, given that the risks to national security from legal proceedings can be as great as the damage from the leaks themselves. And leaks can complicate the Intelligence Community's working relationships with both the Congress and executive branch agencies, including the White House, particularly if either branch is attempting to use leaked intelligence to undermine or embarrass the other.[19]

Policymaker Misuse of Intelligence on Iraq. Policymakers are always looking for information to support their policies. In the case of Iraq, which we discuss in detail in Chapter 5, the problem was the administration's desire to use intelligence to manipulate the public and gain support for a predetermined policy. For various reasons the Bush administration was determined from its earliest days to invade Iraq and overthrow Saddam Hussein. As Paul O'Neill, the former Treasury secretary recounts in his memoir told to reporter Ron Suskind in *The Price of Loyalty*, at the second National Security Council meeting of the administration, in 2001, Defense Secretary Donald Rumsfeld asserted that removing Saddam Hussein would "demonstrate what this country is all about." Iraq could be changed into a new country, and that would solve everything. The president, according to O'Neill, responded, "Fine. Go find me a way to do this."[20] Thus, the selective use of intelligence, expanded, distorted, and hyped, was used as a device to mold public opinion. As Deputy Defense Secretary Paul Wolfowitz said, "Weapons of Mass Destruction was the one issue we could all agree upon."[21]

As we discuss in Chapter 5, the Intelligence Community did make some mistakes in its analysis and reporting on the situation in Iraq, particularly with regard to the existence of chemical and biological weapons stockpiles, the aluminum tubes issue, and not coming out stronger against the Niger contract for yellow cake. However, the mistakes were at least in part attributable to the superheated atmosphere created by the White House, and there was consistent subtle pressure on the IC to tell the White House what it wanted to hear. (Policymakers often only ask the question to which they want answers.) Vice President Cheney made many trips to the CIA apparently in an effort to help the agency reach the outcome he wanted—intelligence judgments that would support the Bush administration's decision to use military force to remove Saddam. Beyond the consequences of policymakers misusing intelligence, however, the real lesson from Iraq is that in the absence of strong, accurate intelligence, the likelihood of major policy mistakes increases dramatically.

Intelligence is rarely perfect, and over the years some intelligence judgments have been overstated and others understated. Such errors can affect public opinion and reduce confidence in the capabilities, if not the integrity, of the Intelligence Community. For example, the "bomber gap" and "missile gap" in the late 1950s, both of which proved to be nonexistent, affected public attitudes as well as congressional views toward the Soviet Union. Today, the public's opinion of the US Intelligence Community has been molded in part by criticisms of intelligence reporting on the nuclear ambitions of Iraq, Iran, and North Korea.

5   Intelligence on Iraqi WMD
Programs and Policy Reactions

The road leading up to the US decision to use military force against Saddam Hussein in March 2003 was complex and multifaceted. Intelligence had only limited influence on that decision. To understand what transpired, particularly the role that intelligence played, we must break the episode into discrete parts: first, the US Intelligence Community's beliefs about the facts on the ground in Iraq, particularly on the status of Saddam's clandestine WMD programs; second, policymakers' preferences and how they chose to receive and use the intelligence information given to them; and third, the international community's beliefs, including what UN and IAEA inspectors had uncovered, or not uncovered, and their conclusions about Iraq's WMD programs. Finally, one must treat nuclear, chemical, and biological weapons individually, even while public discourse often confuses them. As we stated in the Introduction, important distinctions among these weapons must be kept in mind when reviewing the Iraqi or, indeed, any other case.

Efforts to Monitor Saddam's WMD Programs

As mentioned briefly in Chapter 3, the Intelligence Community had been following Saddam's efforts to acquire WMD capabilities for two decades. But its effort to achieve an accurate understanding of the status of Iraq's WMD programs in late 2002 was hindered by a variety of factors. Everyone knew that Saddam had previously used chemical weapons against Iran and on his own Kurdish population; his regime had a long history of using concealment and deception to spoof national and international efforts to monitor his clandestine programs; contrary to UN Security Council resolutions, he refused to resume inspections by international experts in 1998 following the temporary withdrawal of inspectors for a planned US-UK bombing campaign; and his regime failed to account for the WMD material and agents that had previously been in his inventory. Although unaccounted items did not prove that weapon stockpiles still existed, they nevertheless did cast doubt on the reliability of the regime's statements and reporting. Moreover, the United States lacked any physical presence in Iraq following the 1991 Gulf War, which severely limited the Intelligence Community's ability to recruit and run human agents inside the country.

Thus, the United States was forced to rely heavily on information from émigrés, defectors, and liaison intelligence services. Many of the Iraqi émigrés and defectors provided incomplete or biased information, in some cases to persuade the United States to take steps they hoped would bolster their futures. Although at least a few US intelligence officers participated in the UN Special Commission (UNSCOM) inspection teams prior to 1998, we found no evidence that any participated directly in the United Nations Monitoring, Verification and Inspection Commission (UNMOVIC) teams in early 2003. The latter teams, however, were guided at least in part by information from US intelligence (and presumably from intelligence from other countries), but the UN teams failed to turn up concrete evidence of reconstituted WMD programs.[1] It is unclear how much credence US policymakers gave to the inconclusive reports of UN inspectors. What seems clear is that by then, policy decisions on Iraq had been made.

It is no secret that no love was lost between Saddam and the United States after he was forced to retreat from Kuwait in 1991. The United States, and presumably other like-minded countries, tried all means possible, save military force prior to 2003, to remove Saddam from power. Presidents George H.W. Bush, William Clinton, and George W. Bush all authorized covert actions to depose Saddam; none of them succeeded. Meanwhile, Saddam clearly tried every means, including bribing UN officials, to keep funds flowing into his coffers in part with the hope of eventually reconstituting his WMD programs.[2] In addition, concealment, denial, and deception practices were an integral part of the Iraqi regime's modus operandi; they affected all facets of life, influenced the regime's relationships with the outside world, and negatively impacted the work of inspectors and US efforts to monitor remotely efforts to reconstitute Saddam's WMD programs. One author prophetically concluded in 1998 that "Saddam's continuing challenges to the U.N. inspection regime, kept alive the possibility of eventual U.S. military action that might lead to his removal."[3] When military action was finally launched in March 2003, most US and inter-

The Iraqi WMD Episode: A Snapshot

The Intelligence Community's efforts to understand and accurately report on the status of Saddam's WMD programs and how that information affected policymakers prior to the introduction of US military forces in 2003 provide an important case study of the intelligence process and its support of the policy community.

The 1991 Gulf War Legacy. Everyone knew that at one time, at least, Saddam's Iraq had possessed chemical weapons: during the 1980s he had used them against Iranian forces and his own Kurdish population. And it was not a mystery that Saddam was pursuing a nuclear weapon capability—witness the 1981 Israeli air strike against his nuclear research reactor at Osiraq discussed in Chapter 3. This facility was large enough to produce significant quantities of plutonium, and Israel apparently concluded that acquiring plutonium was Saddam's goal. However, after the Israeli attack, Iraq began to create the capability to produce weapon-grade uranium, rather than plutonium, as the means for gaining nuclear weapons. Saddam increased his nuclear weapon workforce from five hundred to seven thousand over the next five years.[4] Nevertheless, the international community and the United States were surprised at how much progress Iraq had made when UN and IAEA inspectors were able to examine its nuclear weapon program following the 1991 Gulf War. As a consequence of those inspections, an effort was made to dismantle the nuclear weapon facilities, along with the chemical and biological weapons programs. By 1998, IAEA reports to the UN Security Council still raised questions about Saddam's nuclear weapon program, but they found no inconsistency with Iraq's declarations. However, Saddam never provided a complete accounting for his WMD-associated material, especially in the chemical and biological weapons arena.

The Situation Before 2003. Following the temporary withdrawal of inspectors in 1998 due to planned US and British airstrikes, Saddam barred further inspections. The international community was thus denied considerable ground truth on Saddam's efforts to reconstitute his WMD programs. Everyone believed that his intentions were to do so. The international community subsequently learned that he had skimmed off sizable funds from the Oil for Food Programme, circumventing sanctions to help finance the reconstitution of Iraq's WMD capabilities. However, it is unclear how much of these funds he used to reconstitute the WMD programs—some believe very little. Meanwhile, the United States and other countries were trying to track his progress through indirect human sources (defectors, émigrés, and liaison reporting), whose reliability and whose accuracy in reporting could not be fully determined. Saddam's regime had demonstrated its sophistication in concealing its activities from inspectors; moreover, the rampant practice of concealment and deception in Iraq made it extremely difficult to know who was telling the truth or who actually knew the truth about Iraq's reconstitution efforts. And because most of the nuclear, chemical, and biological work took place in laboratories, US remote technical monitoring capabilities were generally unhelpful in monitoring Saddam's progress. Even so, no one was inclined to doubt reports of his attempts to move ahead, especially on chemical and biological weapons programs. Unfortunately, the United States subsequently learned that some of the information, particularly from liaison sources and defectors, was misleading or just plain wrong. As we explain later, it is regrettable that US intelligence did not do a more thorough job of investigating and reporting on the credibility of some of the sources. The UN inspections that resumed in early 2003 threw further doubt on these sources and their reports.

Intelligence Judgments. Based on the history of the Saddam regime, his efforts to deceive, his incomplete accounting, and his intentions, intelligence analysts reached what most people at the time believed was the reasonable judgment that he was in fact attempting to reconstitute his WMD programs. In late 2002, the uncertainty was regarding how much progress he had made. No one believed he had yet obtained or was close to producing nuclear weapons, and the IAEA reported that it had found no evidence of a reconstituted nuclear weapon program. But all believed that Saddam probably had chemical and biological warfare agents waiting to be used. However, prior to the introduction of military forces in early 2003, UN inspectors were becoming dubious even about that. In a March 2004 interview, former United Nations Monitoring, Verification and Inspection Commission (UNMOVIC) director Hans Blix stated that by "January 2003, we had performed quite a lot of inspections to sites which were given by intelligence and they had not shown any weapons of mass destruction, so we began to be doubtful."[5] There is no public evidence that with this new information in mind the US Intelligence Community reexamined its October 2002 judgments about the status of Saddam's WMD programs. Even now, years after the beginning of US military operations, which provided new opportunities to investigate, no significant evidence for such weapons has been uncovered. It appears that the IC considerably overestimated the regime's progress in reconstituting its WMD programs.

Policy Use of Intelligence. Two of the justifications for the use of US military force to remove Saddam were his possession of WMD capabilities and the threat that he might support terrorist use of such capabilities. Although the IC found

(continued on page 110)

(continued from page 109)

no convincing evidence for the actual development of nuclear weapons or of a connection between Saddam's regime and international terrorists, some US policymakers tended to hype these two threats far beyond what the intelligence would support. Subsequently, it became clear that some policymakers had chosen to ignore the IC's analysis in favor of other sources that provided better support for their policy preferences. Despite the fact that the IC judged there was no imminent nuclear threat (as opposed to Saddam's chemical and biological weapon stockpiles), such a threat was what some policymakers pointed to. In response to the failure subsequently to find evidence for a threat from reconstituted nuclear, chemical, or biological weapon programs, policymakers have tended to blame the IC for bad analysis when in fact the policymakers knew what they wanted to do and were looking for support from various sources to bolster their case.

Implications. The studies and reports conducted on the Intelligence Community's performance have focused on three issues: (1) inadequate, misleading, and bad human source information; (2) analysis that was based largely on assumptions and old information with insufficient vetting of new information, along with a rigid mind-set; and (3) insufficient critical review and management of the analytical process that led to the judgments in the 2002 NIE. These reports have presented no evidence of direct politicization of the intelligence judgments by policymakers, yet the IC's judgments certainly were exploited, and sometimes simply ignored. Notwithstanding, there appears to have been an unfortunate reluctance by the IC to offer alternative explanations or scenarios to expose the uncertainties it faced.

It is incumbent on the Intelligence Community to learn from this episode to avoid making similar mistakes in the future. The IC owes its best effort to policymakers and to the nation. With regard to the selective use of intelligence by policymakers, the Iraqi episode is not unique. Good intelligence-policymaker relationships are critical for good policy, but there will always be some policymakers who will use only the information that supports their policy preference and ignore that which does not. The Intelligence Community must maintain its integrity by being objective, bold, and professional in reporting what policymakers need to know—even when they do not want to hear it.

national experts expected some evidence of Saddam's WMD programs to soon be uncovered. As is now well known, no chemical or biological stockpiles were found.

Nuclear Weapons. As we mentioned in Chapter 3, US and international concerns that Saddam was attempting to develop a nuclear weapon capability go back a couple of decades and were not something new in 2002. Indeed, in 1991 following Desert Storm and the resumption of IAEA inspections and the initiation of UN inspections, it was discovered that Iraq had progressed more in its nuclear weapon program than had been believed. This discovery sent shock waves throughout the nonproliferation community and led to the institution of more-stringent safeguards and inspection guidelines between the IAEA and its member states (see Chapter 6). It also caused the US Intelligence Community to reexamine its approach to understanding how clandestine nuclear programs can be developed. The subsequent discovery of the extent of the A. Q. Khan nuclear proliferation network has had a similar effect.

Despite the fact that Iraq had ratified the Nuclear Non-Proliferation Treaty in 1969, under which it pledged to place all of its nuclear materials and facilities under IAEA safeguards, the international community learned that Saddam had pursued a covert, multibillion-dollar nuclear weapon program. As mentioned earlier, Iraq apparently had first tried the plutonium route, but after the Israeli bombing of the Osiraq research reactor in 1981, it switched to a uranium enrichment program. This program relied heavily on foreign contractors who were willing to circumvent export controls and sell design information on early Western-type calutrons. By 1991, Iraqi experts had also secretly separated small amounts of plutonium at the IAEA-safeguarded facility at Tuwaitha.

Although prior to the US military intervention in 2003 the threat from Iraq's nuclear weapon program received the most play from policymakers and some others, it seemed clear by the time Saddam barred inspectors from returning in 1998 that the International Atomic Energy Agency's dismantlement, monitoring, and verification efforts, along with the damage from Operation Desert Storm, had entirely eliminated Saddam's nuclear weapon program.[6] However, without ongoing inspections, which the United Nations and United States were unable to implement, there was some concern by 2002 about how much Saddam had progressed in reconstituting his overall WMD program. The Iraq Survey Group's final report in 2004 stated: "Saddam wanted to end sanctions while preserving the capability to reconstitute his weapons of mass destruc-

UN Inspections of Iraq

Through Resolution 687 of April 3, 1991, the UN Security Council established the terms and conditions for a formal cease-fire between Iraq and the coalition of Member States cooperating with Kuwait. Section C of this resolution dealt with the elimination, under international supervision, of Iraq's weapons of mass destruction and ballistic missiles with a range greater than 150 kilometers, together with related items and production facilities. It also called for measures to ensure that the acquisition and production of prohibited items were not resumed. The UN Special Commission (UNSCOM) was set up to implement the nonnuclear provisions of the resolution and to assist the International Atomic Energy Agency (IAEA) in the nuclear area. The special commission was headed by Ambassador Rolf Ekeus, a highly capable senior Swedish diplomat; one of his principal assistants was Robert Gallucci, who later became US Assistant Secretary of State and negotiator of the Framework Agreement with North Korea. The IAEA at the time was headed by Dr. Hans Blix, who later, in 2002 and 2003, would serve as the director of the United Nations Monitoring, Verification and Inspection Commission (UNMOVIC). One of his principal assistants was David Kay, an effective US inspector and later the first leader of the Iraq Survey Group.

The UN Special Commission's main purpose was to monitor and verify Iraq's compliance with its unconditional obligation not to use, retain, possess, develop, construct, or otherwise acquire any weapons or related items prohibited under section C of Resolution 687. Under its Resolution 715 of October 11, 1991, the Security Council mandated the special commission to implement the plan for ongoing monitoring and verification of peaceful chemical and biological activities along with limited ballistic missile development. The council also requested the commission to assist and cooperate with the IAEA in implementing the plan for ongoing monitoring and verification in the nuclear field.

Iraq was obliged to provide, on a regular basis, full, complete, correct, and timely information on activities, sites, facilities, material, or other items, both military and civilian, that might be used for purposes prohibited under Security Council resolutions. UNSCOM and the IAEA had the right to carry out inspections, at any time and without hindrance, of any site, facility, activity, material, or other items in Iraq. They could conduct inspections unannounced or at short notice and inspect on the ground or by aerial surveillance any number of declared or designated sites or facilities.

Iraq initially failed to state its recognition of, or to act upon, its obligations. Only in June 1992 did Iraq give UNSCOM initial declarations concerning non-nuclear activities that needed to be monitored. And only in late 1993 was the commission able to establish the monitoring activities to be carried out from its Baghdad Monitoring and Verification Centre. This arrangement lasted until 1998, when as stated earlier Saddam refused to allow inspections to resume after the temporary withdrawal of the inspectors due to the forthcoming US-UK bombing campaign against Iraq.

After this halt in inspections and in response to increased concerns that Saddam was trying to reconstitute his weapons of mass destruction programs, the Security Council created UNMOVIC in December 1999. UNMOVIC was to replace UNSCOM and continue with the latter's mandate to disarm Iraq of its weapons of mass destruction and to operate a system of ongoing monitoring and verification of Iraq's compliance with its obligations not to reacquire the weapons prohibited to it by the Security Council. But only in November 2002 did Saddam allow UN inspectors to return to Iraq (probably in an effort to prevent a Security Council consensus on using military force against his regime). UNMOVIC led inspections of possible chemical and biological facilities in Iraq until shortly before the US invasion of Iraq in March 2003; it did not find any weapons of mass destruction. Likewise, the IAEA found nothing to substantiate the judgment that the nuclear weapon program was being reconstituted in any significant way.

tion"; "he aspired to develop a nuclear capability"; "the events in the 1980s and early 1990s shaped Saddam's belief in the value of WMD"; "In Saddam's view, WMD helped to save the Regime multiple times."[7]

US Intelligence Judgments on Iraq's WMD Programs

Despite Iraq's development efforts, *no one*, including within the US Intelligence Community, believed that Saddam had or was even close to developing nuclear weapons. The Key Judgments in the October 2002 NIE, especially the State Department's Bureau of Intelligence and Research opinion casting doubt on Saddam's progress in reconstituting his nuclear weapon program, demonstrate that (see Appendix L). All, however, believed that he desired them, and many experts believed that Iraq had made some headway in reconstituting its nuclear weapon program after 1998. The real question was how much progress had been made in the absence of UN inspections, and there were clear differences of view within the IC on the answer. The majority view in the 2002 NIE was that "if left unchecked, it [Iraq] probably will have a nuclear weapon during this decade." The CIA and other agencies concluded that because of Iraq's aggressive attempts to obtain what they believed were high-strength aluminum tubes for centrifuge rotors, Saddam's nuclear weapon program was moving forward. The Department of Energy agreed that reconstitution of the nuclear program was underway, but it concluded that the aluminum tubes were not part of the program.

The State Department's Bureau of Intelligence and Research (INR), persuaded by the Energy Department's analysis of the aluminum tubes issue, had the most conservative view and stated that "Saddam continues to want nuclear weapons and available evidence indicates that Baghdad is pursuing at least a limited effort to maintain and acquire nuclear weapon-related capabilities." However, INR concluded that the detected activities did not represent an integrated and comprehensive approach. The aluminum tubes were subsequently proved to be for conventional weapons and were entirely unsuitable for use as centrifuge components. Unfortunately, the aluminum tubes and the imaginary mobile bioweapon labs referred to by the German liaison source "Curveball," who was later discredited, were included in Secretary Powell's speech to the UN Security Council presenting the United States' case for war. US policymakers and the IC were seriously discredited as a result. Summarizing to here, the differences within the IC were over how much progress Saddam had made in reconstituting his nuclear weapon program, not whether he was attempting to do so.

One of the better-researched analyses of the debates within the Intelligence Community is provided by Jeffrey Richelson in *Spying on the Bomb: American Nuclear Intelligence from Nazi Germany to Iran and North Korea*. In his detailed account, Richelson concludes that the IC had made reasonable assumptions about Saddam's desires and intent but that senior IC management allowed the views of the CIA and the Defense Intelligence Agency (DIA) to override those of nuclear experts in the Department of Energy, and there was insufficient effort by the community to get to the bottom of their technical differences.[8] Moreover, imagery, signals intelligence, and human source information seemed to confirm CIA's assumptions. Liaison information also confirmed what CIA analysts believed to be true.

One of the issues that received significant play in the press was the possibility that Iraq had sought highly enriched uranium to bolster its own allegedly inadequate stocks of this critical material. The NIE noted that "a foreign government service reported that as of early 2001, Niger planned to send several tons of 'pure uranium' (yellowcake) to Iraq. . . . As of early 2001, Niger and Iraq were still working out arrangements for this deal. We do not know the status of this arrangement." The NIE went on to state, "We cannot confirm whether Iraq succeeded in acquiring uranium ore and yellowcake (a refined form of natural uranium) from these sources." The INR added its opinion that "the claims of Iraqi pursuit of natural uranium in Africa are . . . highly dubious." Richelson claims that multiple African sources, mainly from British and Italian intelligence, asserted that Iraq had sought uranium. The United States could not confirm that sales had taken place, especially from Niger, but it could not conclude that contracts had not been signed. In October 2002, an Italian journalist passed documents, which purported to support an Iraqi purchase of uranium from Niger, to the US embassy and ultimately to the CIA. The INR's analyst thought them to be forgeries and circulated this view around the IC. The United States supplied copies of the documents to the IAEA, and in March 2003 the IAEA replied, almost immediately, that the documents were without question forgeries. CIA analysts were reportedly also skeptical about the documents.[9]

All agencies agreed with the 2002 NIE forecast that it would likely be years before Saddam might achieve a nuclear weapon capability, and they judged that "although Saddam does not yet have nuclear weapons or sufficient material to make any, he remains intent on acquiring them." However, they differed in their estimates on timing. The majority, apparently led by the CIA, as noted earlier, judged that if unconstrained, Iraq probably would have such a weapon by the end of the decade (by 2010). Consistent with INR's doubt that Iraq had progressed as far in reconstituting its nuclear weapon program as most other agencies judged, INR stated that it was "unable to predict when Iraq could acquire a nuclear device or weapon."

Chemical and Biological Weapons. In 1986, the United Nations accused Iraq of using chemical weapons (CW), including mustard and nerve gases, against Iranian forces during the Iran-Iraq War, which resulted in some fifty thousand Iranian casualties. And in 1988, Saddam used chemical weapons against his own Kurdish population in northern Iraq. Subsequent UN inspections revealed that before the 1991 Gulf War, Iraq had maintained one of the most extensive chemical weapon capabilities in the developing world. At the time of the 1991 Gulf War, Iraq also had a biological weapon (BW) program, which included anthrax and botulinum toxin. Because of the real threat that such weapons posed as Desert Storm approached, President George H.W. Bush warned that

The Niger "Yellowcake" Fiasco

In October 2001, and again in February 2002, the CIA received reports from the Italian military intelligence service that it had evidence that Iraq had contracted to purchase 500 tons of unprocessed "yellowcake" uranium from the African country of Niger. These reports later turned out to be crude forgeries circulated by a former Italian carabinieri with ties to the Italian intelligence service. The CIA and the State Department were skeptical of these reports from the outset because the mines in Niger were controlled by a French consortium; the transportation of 500 tons of uranium could not go undetected; Iraq did not have the ability to process 500 tons of yellowcake at that time; and it already had 550 tons in storage under IAEA seal.[10]

However, the report caught the attention of Vice President Cheney's office, and a call to Valerie Plame Wilson's office at the CIA from the Vice President's office in February 2002 asked for more information. At the time, Ms. Plame was not aware of the "unprecedented number of visits that the Vice President had made to [CIA] Headquarters to meet with analysts and look for any available evidence to support the Iraq WMD claims that the Administration was beginning to make."[11]

While struggling to respond to this unusual request, Plame discussed with others in her office whom the CIA could send to Niger to verify this information. Another mid-level official suggested Plame's husband, former Ambassador Joseph Wilson, who had extensive experience in Africa, had taken a sensitive trip to Africa three years before, and had been the acting ambassador in Iraq at the time of the 1991 Gulf War.[12]

The suggestion was approved at higher levels. Ambassador Wilson agreed to the trip on a pro bono (expenses-only) basis, and in late February 2002, after consultations with the State Department, he undertook an eight-day fact-finding trip to Niger. While there he met with Nigerois officials and other contacts. Wilson found nothing in Niger to support the claim that Iraq had made any purchase—and for the same reasons the CIA had been skeptical to begin with. Further, he noted that the French consortium and Niger's uranium were under a high degree of oversight. Within hours of his return he briefed CIA officers at his home; a few days later the CIA completed a report on Wilson's findings and distributed it around the government. Just weeks earlier, reports by a former US ambassador to Niger and an army four-star general, who also concluded that the yellowcake story was bogus, had been circulated as well.[13] However, the White House and the Vice President would not let the story die. Director George Tenet was able to keep it out of a presidential speech in October, but White House staff maneuvered it into the president's State of the Union speech in January 2003: "We also know that [Saddam Hussein] has recently sought to buy uranium in Africa." A few weeks later, the IAEA obtained the documents and promptly declared them to be forgeries. IAEA Director-General ElBaradei reported the same to the UN

Security Council. Then came the invasion of Iraq and the subsequent failure to find any weapons of mass destruction. Ambassador Wilson, therefore, had reason to believe that the White House should have known its intelligence claims were, to put it mildly, overstated.

In May 2003 Ambassador Wilson participated in a panel discussion with Nicholas Kristof of the *New York Times* at a retreat for Democratic senators. Kristof asked Wilson if he could write an article on the issue, and Wilson agreed on the condition that his name not be used. He was referred to as a "retired former ambassador." In June, Wilson was warned by a journalist friend that his name likely would surface in the ongoing controversy. Then, on June 8, National Security Adviser Rice stated on "Meet the Press" that no one at the top levels of the government was aware of the inaccuracy of the Niger claim. Wilson knew this to be false, given the distribution of his and others' reports, and he decided to do something about it. On July 6, 2003, the *New York Times* published Wilson's op-ed article "What I Did Not Find in Africa," which refuted the administration's claims that Iraq sought uranium in Niger. Shortly thereafter, he repeated his assertions on "Meet the Press."[14]

Two days after the article appeared, a business acquaintance of Wilson's encountered Robert Novak, the columnist, who asserted that Ambassador Wilson was unreliable, that he was sent by the CIA, and that his wife was working for the CIA. Wilson and Novak spoke on the telephone not long after, and while Novak retracted his expletives about Wilson, he pressed for information—unsuccessfully—about where his wife worked. On July 14, Novak's column in the *Washington Post* stated, "Wilson never worked for the CIA, but his wife, Valerie Plame, is an Agency operative on weapons of mass destruction."[15] It now appears that in retaliation for the July 6 op-ed piece and to discredit Wilson's views, the White House destroyed the career of his wife. As Karl Rove told Chris Matthews of *Hardball*, "Wilson's wife is fair game."[16]

Valerie Plame's unit targeted students and foreign businessmen who had possible knowledge of links to Iraqi weapons programs. A separate CIA unit, the National Resources Division, recruited US-resident relatives of Iraqi scientists and officials to travel to Baghdad and seek information—surreptitiously—from their relatives in Iraq. As chronicled by James Risen in *State of War*, some thirty US-based relatives of Iraqi weapon scientists agreed to return to Baghdad to gain information. Their debriefing reports were filed by the CIA on their return. The informants all said the same thing, "that Iraq's program to develop nuclear, chemical, and biological weapons had long been abandoned." Indeed, one Iraqi in Baghdad asked his sister, "Where do they come up with these questions? Don't they know there is no nuclear program?" He asserted that the nuclear program had been dead since 1991. According to Risen, the CIA, which was under heavy pressure from the White House, ignored this evidence, as well as other information.[17]

"the American people would demand the strongest possible response . . . and [Iraq] will pay a terrible price" for the use of such weapons against coalition forces.[18]

Following the Gulf War, UNSCOM and later UNMOVIC, repeatedly claimed that Iraq had failed to fully disclose and account for its WMD programs, especially its chemical and biological agents stockpiles. Although UN specialists destroyed a large amount of chemical agents, UN officials doubted that the entire stockpile had been found and hypothesized that chemical agents and precursors remained in secret depots. (Iraq had never joined the Chemical Weapons Convention.) In 1996, five years after the end of the Gulf War, UNSCOM reported to the Security Council that "the Commission has serious concerns that a full accounting and disposal of Iraq's holdings of prohibited items has not been made."[19] As a result of this history and lingering doubts related to Saddam's efforts to conceal his chemical and biological programs, and the fact that Iraq barred UN inspectors after 1998, the US Intelligence Community, along with most of the international community, believed in late 2002 that Saddam had biological and chemical weapons in his inventory.

In response to the question whether it was clear in early 2003 that there were no weapons of mass destruction in Iraq, Hans Blix, in the aforementioned March 2004 interview with Jim Lehrer, responded, "No, that is going too far . . . there were lots of question marks . . . there were lots of things that were unaccounted for . . . they had had quantities of mustard gas and anthrax and other things, and they could not give us any evidence of where it had gone." Blix continued that in March 2003 "we could not have excluded that there still were weapons of mass destruction; it was only a little later I think that that conclusion, I think, was clear." Blix subsequently informed us that the reason he did "a little later" positively exclude weapons of mass destruction was that after the invasion, the United States had interviewed numerous relevant Iraqis, who now had little fear of telling what they knew but could rather expect rewards for providing information about weapons. He was impressed also by his former opposite Iraqi number, Amir al-Saadi, voluntarily surrendering himself to the United States and saying before television cameras, "There are no weapons of mass destruction and time will bear me out." Blix admits that this is not compelling evidence, but he believes that al-Saadi had no reason at this point to lie.[20] He commented further in the Lehrer interview that "by April-May, I think it was pretty clear to me that there weren't any weapons of mass destruction."

As would be expected, from 1998 to early 2003 there was a steady flow of intelligence analysis and reporting to senior policymakers on activities inside Iraq, including on Saddam's efforts to reconstitute his WMD programs. Most of the reporting is classified and not in the public domain. However, political pressure from Congress to explain what intelligence had been provided to policymakers (and to congressional oversight committees) prior to the use of military force in March 2003 induced the administration to authorize later in 2003 the declassification and release of the Key Judgments from the October 2002 National Intelligence Estimate (NIE) "Iraq's Continuing Program for Weapons of Mass Destruction" (see Appendix L). At the beginning of the NIE, the Intelligence Community categorically stated, "We judge that Iraq has continued its weapons of mass destruction (WMD) programs. . . . Baghdad has chemical and biological weapons." It further stated that "since inspections ended in 1998, Iraq has maintained its chemical weapons effort . . . and invested more heavily in biological weapons." It concluded that "Iraq has largely rebuilt . . . biological weapons facilities . . . and has expanded its chemical and biological infrastructure under the cover of civilian production." The IC added that "an array of clandestine reporting reveals that Baghdad has procured covertly the types and quantities of chemicals and equipment sufficient to allow limited CW agent production hidden within Iraq's legitimate chemical industry. Although we have little specific information on Iraq's CW stockpile, Saddam probably has stocked at least 100 metric tons and possibly as much as 500 metric tons of CW agents—much of it added in the last year."

Thus, there was little doubt in the US Intelligence Community, nor in the international arena, including UN inspectors, that Saddam had such weapons in his inventory. When the UN Security Council voted in November 2002 to allow Iraq one more opportunity to update its declared disposition of WMD facilities and stocks, it was hoped that Saddam would clarify the situation. The fact is that his declaration shed no new light on his unaccounted stocks of chemical and biological agents and provided no further understanding of progress in reconstituting his nuclear weapon program. Given Saddam's consistent efforts to deny access, deceive inspectors, and hide activities, the IC had little to base its judgments on other than the fact that Saddam was continuing to hide his WMD programs.

Iraqi Support for Terrorist WMD Attacks. Along with its assessment of Iraq's WMD programs, the 2002 NIE touched on the likelihood of Saddam conducting terrorist attacks using chemical or biological weapons against the United States or cooperating with and giving aid to terrorist organizations such as al-

Qaeda. The Intelligence Community saw either possibility as only a last resort for Saddam and concluded that "if sufficiently desperate . . . [Saddam] might decide that only an organization such as al-Qa'ida with world-wide reach . . . could perpetrate the type of terrorist attack that he would hope to conduct."

Some policymakers' comments about intelligence on Saddam's WMD programs and his relations with terrorist groups made the threat sound more imminent than the IC had conveyed, at least in the declassified NIE. The disparity was likely due in part to policymakers basing their comments on analysis that had been provided by sources other than the US Intelligence Community. This seems evident from a statement by the Pentagon's inspector general in April 2007 that the Defense Department had inappropriately undercut the IC's analysis by issuing its own reports claiming close Iraqi-terrorist connections. According to an article that appeared in the publication *Truthout* in April 2007, the Pentagon had established its own intelligence cell called the Policy Counterterrorism Evaluation Group, which reported to Undersecretary for Policy Douglas Feith, because senior Pentagon officials believed the IC was improperly assessing information.[21] In a *New York Times* article of April 6, 2007, Senator Carl Levin, chairman of the Armed Services Committee, commenting on the Defense Department's announcement, was quoted as saying that "the analysis of Mr. Feith's office was not supported by available intelligence and was contrary to the consensus view of the intelligence community."[22]

This smells of an attempt by some policymakers to create their own intelligence basis for decisions and actions when the IC's analyses and judgments did not provide sufficient justification for a preferred policy. It also appears that the new Secretary of Defense, Robert Gates, who had been a career intelligence officer and former Director of Central Intelligence, decided to eliminate the competing intelligence cell promptly on assuming office in early 2007. Former DCI George Tenet comments in his book *At the Center of the Storm: My Years at the CIA* that Feith's team showed none of the professional skills or discipline required for good intelligence analysis; they focused on nuggets of information that supported their position, but they never put it in the context of other available information.[23] In his recent book *War and Decision*, Feith responded by denouncing the CIA, accusing it of producing poor intelligence, intruding on the formulation of policy, and then using leaks to the media to defend itself and attack its bureaucratic opponents. Most notably, Feith defends the Pentagon's intelligence activities on grounds that the CIA was "politicizing" intelligence by ignoring evidence in its own reports of ties between Saddam and international terrorists. He charges that intelligence officials ignored and refused to investigate possible links between al-Qaeda and Saddam's govern-ment.[24] This is clearly an example of a policy official dismissing the IC's care-ful evaluation of the available intelligence and choosing to believe reports that supported his policy.

Policymakers have the right to seek information and opinions from any source they choose; however, the creation of an organization for the express purpose of conforming "intelligence" to policymakers' preferences distorts and corrupts the vital relationship between the IC and policymakers (described in Chapter 4)—a relationship that was designed to provide good intelligence in the service of good policy.

It is legitimate to ask what sources the IC had and whether it was sufficiently plugged into the situation on the ground in Iraq. The US Intelligence Com-munity apparently had access to all reporting from UN and IAEA inspections. But in a speech given at Georgetown University on February 5, 2004, Tenet admitted that the IC had precious few human sources of its own and greatly depended on friendly liaison intelligence services that had sources. This was echoed in a subsequent speech by the former Deputy Director for Operations, James Pavitt, who explained the United States' difficulty in recruiting and vet-ting reliable sources on Saddam's regime.[25]

One challenge is using information from defectors and émigrés, who usu-ally have a personal agenda when providing information to the United States. As in the run-up to the Bay of Pigs covert action fiasco in 1961, many volunteer sources were hoping that the United States would accomplish something they were powerless to achieve on their own. Thus, such sources often oversell the prospects for a course of action to persuade the United States to act. As US policymakers were finalizing their policy on the Saddam regime, they were ap-parently receptive to such views.

Obtaining credible human source intelligence was key to understanding Saddam's motivations and plans, but it was difficult. In his book, Tenet dis-cusses the challenge of dealing with human source information, especially that which came from non-CIA sources. He points to the German-run source "Curveball," an Iraqi chemical engineer who volunteered to provide informa-tion and claimed that Iraq had a biological weapon program located in mobile laboratories. However, there were concerns about the source's reliability, and the Germans refused to give US intelligence officials direct access to him. Af-ter a time the Germans began to claim that their source was not sane. Tyler

Drumheller, chief of the CIA's European Division, which handled the liaison relationship with the Germans, claims in his own book *On the Brink: An Insider's Account of How the White House Compromised American Intelligence* that he informed Tenet of the problems with Curveball.[26] However, Tenet claims that none of the doubts were ever communicated to him. Secretary Powell's speech to the UN Security Council contained information from this source on the purported mobile bioweapon laboratories. Using information from human sources is risky, especially when it is a single source reporting on an issue. Tenet notes further that information from another source, who also proved to be a fabricator, got into the NIE without anyone catching it.[27]

Technical collection systems, as impressive and sophisticated as they are, rarely provide unambiguous information on plans and intentions. Granted, the intercept of a critical conversation can be quite helpful, but obtaining that golden nugget is often fortuitous. Images of activity on the ground can give clues as to what is planned or transpiring, but they must be seen within the context of a broader base of information. According to Tenet, US imagery collection in Iraq showed a pattern of activity that was designed to conceal the movement of material from places where chemical weapons had been stored in the past. And US intelligence observed the reconstruction of dual-purpose facilities that had previously been used to make biological agents or chemical precursors.[28]

Intelligence Failure? Why did US intelligence overestimate the status of Iraq's chemical and biological weapons programs? As mentioned, it now appears that UN inspections had successfully stopped the chemical and biological weapons programs by 1998 despite incomplete Iraqi declarations. This discrepancy, of course, leads many to conclude that a major failure in US intelligence occurred. Several explanations for this discrepancy are conceivable.

First, Iraq had WMD material but hid it so well that the United States has yet to locate it. While it is true that the physical space required to hide chemical and biological precursors and agents is about the size of a garage, given the time that has passed the probability of this explanation being true is extremely low, indeed virtually nonexistent. If such stocks existed, it is likely that al-Qaeda or sectarian terrorists would have made use of them by now.

Second, Iraq had WMD material but shipped it either to Syria or Lebanon, or to both. The large number of trucks and other vehicles observed leaving Iraq for these countries prior to US military action in 2003 made such a hypothesis initially credible. It is hard to conceive of Saddam being willing to give such precious material to any neighbor, although transports might have been done without his knowledge. The Iraq Survey Group report concluded that this is probably the only way such transfers might have happened. Now, with the passage of so many years, the hypothesis is no longer credible.[29]

Third, Iraq no longer had WMD material, but simply poor accounting kept the Iraqis from making an accurate declaration. While this explanation is possible, it seems unlikely that the Iraqis could not keep track of their own inventories. More likely is that they were intent on keeping up the deception, possibly to keep their enemies Iran and Israel at bay.

Fourth, and the most likely explanation, is that Iraq no longer had WMD material, but the extent of deception and lying within the regime meant that few really knew the truth. Conceivably, Saddam wanted to assert such capabilities to bluff his neighbors. Interviews of senior Iraqi military officers following the fall of Saddam's regime showed that many believed Iraq had at least chemical capabilities. None admitted that such capability existed in their own divisions, but they believed that other divisions had them. Saddam, in a candid interview with an FBI agent (George Piro) after he was captured, said that he knew he didn't have any weapons of mass destruction, but he was maintaining a pretence of having them to keep Iran at bay. He also said that he wanted to reconstitute his entire WMD program.[30] It was all probably a house of cards, and Saddam seems to have made a gross miscalculation regarding the likelihood of US military action.

Tenet's Critique of the 2002 NIE. In his book, former DCI George Tenet gives his perspective on why the intelligence provided to policymakers in the run-up to US military strikes against Iraq in March 2003 appears to have been incorrect in its judgments about chemical and biological weapons. First, he acknowledged that the Intelligence Community had been slow in providing an up-to-date interagency assessment of Iraq's WMD programs—one had not been done in several years, although a steady flow of current intelligence reporting had been given to policymakers. It took pressure from members of the Senate Select Committee on Intelligence (SSCI), including a letter from Chairman Bob Graham, to get the ball rolling on a new national intelligence estimate (NIE). In retrospect, Tenet believes that the IC should have taken the initiative to launch a series of estimates on Iraq, including on the implications of conflict in Iraq.[31]

According to Tenet, the terms of reference for the 2002 NIE were focused on answering two questions: did Saddam have WMD and, if not, when could he get them? The time given to produce the NIE was three weeks, which meant that the entire process of drafting, coordinating, and reviewing the NIE was quite short. Normally, one to several months is allowed for the process, unless there is a crisis. Clearly, the US government was in a crisis over the threat of going to war. As a result of the time frame, analysts pasted together large chunks of analysis from already published papers and did not take the time to take a fresh look at the basis and assumptions for the judgments in those papers. Tenet believes the community could have done a better job on the NIE if it had begun the process earlier, but he acknowledges that the shortness of time did not relieve the community of the responsibility to get the information right.[32] This seems to prove the commonly used expression that "if you want it bad (that is, you refuse to allow sufficient time for a well thought-out and vetted analysis), you get it bad."

As mentioned earlier, the final NIE gave full exposure to alternative views held within the IC, particularly on details regarding Saddam's nuclear weapon program. Tenet claims that the Niger yellowcake issue was not a major pillar of the judgments, but the aluminum tubes were. He explains that during the final review by the National Foreign Intelligence Board, the Department of Energy's representative was unable to provide a clear explanation for the department's dissenting view on the tubes. This made the majority of agencies stick to their position that the tubes were most likely part of a nuclear weapon program. In contrast, none of the agencies took exception to the judgment that Saddam had chemical and biological weapons programs and stockpiles.[33] We note here, although the NIE did not, that the IAEA also did not believe that the tubes were related to a nuclear program and had said so publicly.

In April 2001, the *Senior Executive Intelligence Brief*, one of the IC's current intelligence publications, informed its readers about the tubes and said that they "have little use other than for a uranium enrichment program." This judgment is believed to have been made by a single CIA intelligence analyst, the only analyst the agency possessed with hands-on experience with centrifuges. The official, who had spent many years at Oak Ridge National Laboratory, drove the issue for the CIA in 2001 and 2002. During this period the CIA produced at least ten additional reports, all of which echoed the first report. The CIA analyst did not convince the Department of Energy, however, which judged that the tube specifications were not consistent for use as centrifuges, and which on further investigation discovered that Iraq had purchased tens of thousands of tubes with identical specifications for use in rocket technology. State Department/INR analysts were not persuaded either, while the Defense Intelligence Agency sided with the CIA. The issue of the tubes, driven by essentially one analyst who was backed by his agency superiors, was so controversial that it should never have found its way into an NIE in the conclusory form that it did. More weight should have been given to the Energy Department's views.[34]

Looking back, Tenet faults the NIE principally on three accounts: (1) the human source information was much weaker than judgments in the estimate indicated; (2) the Key Judgments (the portion read by most senior policymakers) were not as nuanced and cautious as the Main Text on the evidence for continued WMD programs; and (3) the IC's technical analysis of Saddam's WMD programs was too divorced from its understanding of Iraqi culture. On the first point, Tenet particularly regrets that so much emphasis was put on information provided by the German-run human source Curveball. As we said earlier, this appears to be a case where liaison information, while shared in an effort to be helpful, was not vetted sufficiently to recognize its weakness. However, Tenet claims there was a very sensitive source in Iraq who appeared to be providing reliable and credible information, which reinforced the IC's confidence about information on Saddam's WMD programs, presumably including that obtained from Curveball. Nevertheless, he believes that the Key Judgments were too assertive and conveyed a level of certainty not supported by the main discussion in the estimate. On the third point, Tenet concedes that the judgments were consistent with a regime that had tried to deceive inspectors and had refused to account for WMD material missing after the 1991 Gulf War. However, the IC failed to think "outside the box" and consider that Saddam might have been bluffing. Tenet concludes that the IC got it wrong "partly because the truth was so implausible."[35]

Tenet claims finally that the IC's judgments were not politicized (inappropriately influenced) by policymakers and were consistent with the judgments that had been provided to two consecutive presidents. However, he notes that policymakers and members of Congress made political use of the judgments. For example, Democratic senators insisted on having an unclassified text of the NIE to use in speeches and for the press, and members of the administration put spin on the IC's judgments to bolster the case for going to war against Saddam. In the end, Tenet confesses that the IC should have done a more careful job of crafting and providing its judgments, and that the failings of the NIE constituted one of the lowest moments of his tenure as DCI.[36]

Critiques of US Intelligence on Iraq's WMD Programs

After many months of investigation following the March 2003 military defeat of the Saddam regime, the United States was unsuccessful in uncovering
significant evidence of Iraqi WMD programs, especially chemical and biological, as had been believed to exist. To most it seemed that the US Intelligence
Community had overestimated Saddam's success in reconstituting his programs after the departure of UN inspectors in 1998. As a result, several studies (both within and outside the executive branch) were conducted to identify
what had gone wrong leading to the judgments in the October 2002 NIE. The
situation was certainly clouded by what policymakers had said about the intelligence.

   SSCI Report. In its July 2004 report, the Senate Select Committee on Intelligence (SSCI) reached the following overall conclusions: (1) most of the major
Key Judgments of the NIE were either overstated or were not supported by the
underlying intelligence reporting; (2) the IC did not accurately or adequately
explain to policymakers the uncertainties behind the judgments; (3) IC mecha-
nisms established to challenge assumptions and groupthink were not utilized;
(4) assessments were built on previous judgments without carrying forward
the uncertainties associated with those judgments; (5) IC managers failed to
fully consider alternative arguments; and (6) the IC had no sources collecting
against Iraqi WMD programs after 1998.[37] It appears that the SSCI's approach
was to criticize any judgment that was not backed by an explicit piece of intelligence reporting which said the same thing as the judgment. By doing so, the
committee was discounting informed intelligence analysis in favor of pure reporting.

   From Tenet's confession that the Key Judgments did not adequately reflect
the nuances surrounding IC judgments, which were contained in the Main
Text of the NIE, conclusion (1) may be a legitimate criticism. Without knowing what intelligence officials had communicated orally to policy consumers,
however, one cannot confidently judge the veracity of conclusion (2). However,
it is reasonable to suspect that Tenet's confession would apply to this point as
well. Conclusion (3) seems to be correct, as far as the public record shows. The
problem here was probably the lack of time, although that does not excuse the
IC from using whatever time it had to include a critical review of its judgments.
However, as explained earlier, groupthink in this case was not unreasonable
given the historical record of the Saddam regime and its efforts to deny and

conceal its activities. Likewise, conclusion (4) seems to be correct, at least based on how Tenet described the NIE process. Again, due to the shortness of time, previous analyses and judgments were likely included in the NIE without sufficient critical questioning of the underlying assumptions. Conclusion (5) is correct: the NIE should at least have posed alternative explanations for what might have been the truth. Although such alternatives might have seemed unlikely, it was possible that the rampant deception within the Saddam regime masked the truth that Saddam, along with others in his regime, knew Iraq had **no** chemical and biological weapons, but they pretended that they did. Finally, conclusion (6) appears to be correct for US human sources, although the United States did have access, for better or worse, to the sources of liaison intelligence services. There is no question, however, that the lack of US presence and the absence of inspectors in Iraq from 1998 through 2002 put the US Intelligence Community at a definite disadvantage.

Second SSCI Report on Pre-War Intelligence on Iraq. On June 5, 2008, the Senate Select Committee on Intelligence issued a public version of the long-awaited and politically charged report titled "Whether Public Statements Regarding Iraq by U.S. Government Officials Were Substantiated by Intelligence Information." All eight Democrats and two of the seven Republican members voted in support of the report. In releasing the document, Chairman Rockefeller was quoted as saying, "The President and his advisors undertook a relentless public campaign in the aftermath of the [9/11] attacks to use the war against al-Qaeda as a justification for overthrowing Saddam Hussein." He added that the administration's linking of Iraq and al-Qaeda as a single indistinguishable threat was "fundamentally misleading and led the nation to war on false pretenses."[38]

The report generally credits senior officials' statements on Iraqi nuclear, chemical, and biological weapons programs as being substantiated by the intelligence provided. Its main criticism, apart from the Iraq–al-Qaeda connection, is that policymakers overstated the WMD threat by not adequately explaining the differences in judgments and uncertainties reported by the IC.

The report provides the following conclusions:

1. *Nuclear weapons.* Statements by the President, Vice President, Secretary of State, and the National Security Advisor regarding a possible Iraqi nuclear weapon program were generally substantiated by Intelligence Community estimates but did not convey the substantial disagreements that existed in the IC.

2. *Biological weapons.* Statements in the major speeches analyzed, as well as additional statements, regarding Iraq's possession of biological agents, weapon production capability, and use of mobile biological laboratories were substantiated by intelligence information.

3. *Chemical weapons.* Statements in the major speeches analyzed, as well as additional statements, regarding Iraq's possession of chemical weapons were substantiated by intelligence information.

4. *Chemical weapons.* Statements by the President and Vice President prior to the October 2002 National Intelligence Estimate regarding Iraq's chemical weapon production capability and activities did not reflect the IC's uncertainties as to whether such production was ongoing.

5. *Weapons of mass destruction.* Statements by the President, Vice President, Secretary of State, and Secretary of Defense regarding Iraq's possession of weapons of mass destruction were generally substantiated by intelligence information, though many statements regarding ongoing production prior to late 2002 reflected a higher level of certainty than the intelligence judgments did themselves.[39]

WMD Commission Report. The conclusions of the report by the Commission on the Intelligence Capabilities of the United States Regarding Weapons of Mass Destruction, which appeared in March 2005, were not that different from those of the SSCI. The commission concluded that the intelligence failure was in large part due to analytical shortcomings: analysts were wedded to their assumptions; there was little new information to analyze and much of what existed was misleading and of dubious credibility (such as information provided by the human source Curveball); and the IC had failed to adequately explain how little good information it actually had. Because of the lack of new information, analysts fell back on old assumptions. The commission commented, however, that the assumptions were not foolish or unreasonable, and that failures were not repeated everywhere, pointing to good analyses on Libya, the A. Q. Khan network, and on terrorism. Even though it was understandably hard to conclude that Saddam had abandoned his WMD programs, the NIE failed to communicate how weak the intelligence underlying the judgments was. The IC also failed to give policymakers a full understanding of the frailties of the intelligence on which they were relying. In addition, the commission noted that the demand for current intelligence has prevented sufficient focus on penetrating difficult targets (like Saddam's Iraq), and that more structured debate needs to be fostered among agencies and analysts over the interpretation of information. Despite its criticisms, the commission acknowledged that intelligence will always be imperfect and that surprise can never be completely prevented. It exhorted the Intelligence Community to make the changes necessary to minimize future errors.[40]

DCI Internal Panel Report. Director of Central Intelligence Tenet created a panel of retired CIA analysts led by former Deputy Director of Central Intelligence Richard Kerr to look into the apparent failures of the IC to understand the status of Iraq's WMD programs. The group issued its unclassified study in July 2004, which focused on improving the IC's performance by acknowledging and understanding past mistakes. As in the case of the previous two reports, the Kerr Group concluded that the IC's analysis relied heavily on old information and was strongly influenced by untested, long-held assumptions. Moreover, it echoed the WMD Commission's conclusion that human source information was misleading and often unreliable. The IC was forced to rely heavily on liaison reporting for Key Judgments, and some of that information proved to be false. The panel concluded that quality control was lacking for critical management review of the analysis and underlying assumptions.

In contrast to the analysis of Iraq's WMD programs, intelligence assessments on "post-Saddam" issues were particularly insightful, according to the panel, even though the policy community appeared largely to ignore that analysis. The panel concluded that unfortunately these two lines of analysis (WMD programs and post-Saddam issues) were largely analyzed and reported separately, so that a comprehensive understanding of the Iraqi target was generally lacking. Moreover, intelligence collection against Iraq fell far short of the richness and density of coverage the IC had been used to in analyzing the former USSR. And Saddam's effective use of denial, deception, and intimidation made clandestine collection quite difficult. In the end, the panel concluded that failures of collection, uncritical analytical assumptions, and inadequate management reviews were the main culprits behind the IC's inaccurate understanding and the NIE's flawed judgments.[41] The panel apparently did not examine the Intelligence Community's relations with the White House or Department of Defense, so its report does not shed any light on the bureaucratic dynamics between intelligence and policymaking and whether policymakers misused or dismissed the intelligence provided.

Policymaker Use of Intelligence and Other Information. Although the NIE was not the only intelligence provided to policymakers in 2002 and early 2003 on

Policy Pressure on Intelligence Judgments

Whatever pressure was brought to bear on US intelligence by the policy community with regard to Iraq was not a unique occurrence. In reviewing the article "Rumsfeld Reprise" written by Greg Thielmann, who was the State Department Assistant Secretary for Intelligence and Research in the summer of 2003, one is struck by what Thielmann suggests is a strong sense of déjà vu. He notes that the 1998 Report of the Commission to Assess the Ballistic Missile Threat to the United States, which was chaired by Donald Rumsfeld, had hyped selective pieces of intelligence to support policy goals. In contrast to an earlier Intelligence Community report, which had presented a more benign sense of the future threat from long-range ballistic missiles, the Rumsfeld report suggested that within five years North Korea, Iraq, and Iran would be able to develop long-range strategic missiles—presumably mated with nuclear weapons—which would be able to "inflict major destruction" on US territory. It further asserted that North Korea and Iran placed "a high priority on threatening U.S. territory, and each is even now pursuing advanced ballistic missile capabilities to pose a direct threat to U.S. territory." Five years later (in 2003) none of what the report had predicted had come true. Indeed North Korea and Iran have not tested missiles with even half the range of an intercontinental ballistic missile.[42]

The 1998 report pressured the IC to modify its intelligence judgments on the future ballistic missile threat to the United States to be more dire. The 1998 report and subsequent intelligence judgments (1) served to distract policymakers from the real threats to the country, such as terrorist attack and the growing tactical missile threat; (2) led the United States to abrogate a treaty—the ABM Treaty—which was strongly supported by the international community in general and our allies in particular; and (3) undercut the credibility of the US nuclear deterrent by suggesting that without missile defense the United States would be intimidated by North Korean and Iranian strategic missiles. The hyping of intelligence on Iraq was not initiated by the CIA nor was the hyping of intelligence on the ballistic missile threat. The IC to some extent went along with the missile threat inflation, but the impetus came from policymakers. Sound policy based on sound intelligence depends on responsible political leadership as well as the integrity of IC professionals.[43] Everyone suffers, however, when intelligence judgments are allowed to be colored by policy biases and preferences.

the status of Iraq's WMD programs, it provided a comprehensive status report. How that information was used by policymakers is, of course, another story. As we mentioned in Chapter 4, policymakers are often looking for information that supports their preferred course of action. This leads some to spin the intelligence they receive, especially when they believe the IC has not made as strong a case as they wish or believe possible.

The Bush administration came into office in January 2001 apparently determined to remove Saddam Hussein, even if it meant using military force. As referred to earlier, according to the Secretary of the Treasury, Paul O'Neill as reported to Ron Suskind, at the first principals meeting of the National Security Council on January 30, Iraq and how it was destabilizing the Middle East was the principal subject discussed. The dialogue was about how to weaken or destroy the Saddam regime. At the second meeting, the "why" was made clear: the elimination of the regime could be "a demonstration model of America's new unilateral resolve." If Saddam could be shown to possess, or be trying to build, weapons of mass destruction, creating an "asymmetric threat," then his overthrow would "dissuade" other countries from doing the same. "From the start, we were building the case against Hussein and looking at how we could take him out and change Iraq into a new country. And, if we did that, it would solve everything. It was all about finding a way to do it. That was the tone of it; the President saying, 'Fine! Go find me a way to do this.'"[44]

As reported by Richard Clarke, the National Security Council staff's counterterrorism chief, President Bush was anxious to find Iraq responsible for the World Trade Center and Pentagon attacks. The President had the following exchange with Clarke on September 12, 2001:

Later on the evening of the 12th I left the Video Conferencing Center and there, wandering alone around the Situation Room, was the President. He looked like he wanted something to do. He grabbed a few of us and closed the door to the conference room. "Look," he told us, "I know you have a lot to do and all . . . but I want you, as soon as you can, to go back over everything, everything. See if Saddam did this. See if he is linked in any way."

I was once again taken aback, incredulous, and it showed. "But Mr. President, al-Qaeda did this." "I know, I know, but . . . see if Saddam was involved. Just look. I want to know any shred."

"Absolutely we will look . . . again." I was trying to be more respectful, more responsive. "But you know, we have looked several times for state sponsorship for al-Qaeda and not found any real linkages to Iraq. Iran plays a little, so does Pakistan, and Saudi Arabia, Yemen."

"Look into Iraq, Saddam," the President said testily and left us.[45]

Many reasons were behind the desire to remove Saddam, but the one rationale on which everyone could agree and which could engender public support for this enterprise, according to public admissions of senior officials, was the perceived possession by Saddam of an arsenal of weapons of mass destruction and the alleged threat it would pose to the United States. However, the one thing the Bush administration's Iraqi policy has accomplished is to convince a majority of Americans that it is not wise to initiate major warfare unless the facts supporting the threat are virtually beyond dispute.

Dr. Hans Blix, the director of the United Nations Monitoring, Verification and Inspection Commission for Iraq, believes that if the inspections that were underway in Iraq in early 2003 had been allowed to continue, it was probable they would have demonstrated that there were no weapons of mass destruction in Iraq.[46]

Policymakers are not obliged to believe everything the IC reports, and at times they choose to give other sources of information, such as from academic colleagues or personal contacts, more credence. A case in point as mentioned earlier is the fact that the Department of Defense's Policy Counterterrorism Evaluation Group, under the auspices of its undersecretary for policy, issued its own analysis of Iraq's activities, which more closely aligned with the policy preferences of at least some in the administration. These policymakers chose to base their statements on the Defense Department's analysis rather than on the IC's, particularly with regard to Saddam's ties to fundamentalist Islamic terrorist groups. In his *Foreign Affairs* article on this subject, Paul Pillar, who served as the National Intelligence Officer for the Near East and South Asia during this period, stated that this issue represented the greatest discrepancy between what the IC reported and what policymakers said. He concluded that the administration "wanted to hitch the Iraq expedition to the 'war on terror' and the threat the American public feared most, thereby capitalizing on the country's post-9/11 mood." In contrast, Pillar concludes that "for the most part, the Intelligence Community's own substantive judgments on ties to terrorist groups do not appear to have been compromised."[47] Tenet, in his book, states that the IC did a much better job of "pushing back" against pressure from some in the administration to overstate the case for Iraq's connections to al-Qaeda.[48] A discrepancy also appeared between what the IC reported regarding the likely Iraqi

No Iraqi WMD Discovered

After the defeat of the Saddam regime, the United States searched the country for weapons of mass destruction. The Iraq Survey Group, consisting of a staff of up to 1,400 individuals, was established by DCI Tenet. David Kay, a veteran of the IAEA inspections after the 1991 Gulf War and a WMD expert, was appointed "special advisor" to Tenet in the spring of 2003 and attached to the Iraq Survey Group. Kay submitted an interim report to Congress in October 2003, in which he admitted that "we all were wrong" about the existence of WMD stockpiles in Iraq.

Charles Duelfer took over the Iraq Survey Group in January 2004, and eight months later the final report of the group was submitted and briefed to the Congress. Contrary to the assertions of the 2002 National Intelligence Estimate, the Iraq Survey Group reported that no nuclear infrastructure was found, no stockpiles of chemical or biological weapons were found, no significant infrastructure to produce chemical and biological weapons was found, the aluminum tubes were proven to be for rockets, and no mobile bioweapon labs existed. At the same time, the IC's skepticism on the alleged Iraqi purchase of uranium in Niger was vindicated by the revelation that the information was based on forged documents—although the IC had been slow in turning these documents over to experts who could easily have ascertained they were forgeries. The IAEA very quickly reached the same conclusion after receipt of the documents.[49]

It turned out to be true, as reported in the October 2002 NIE, that Saddam's regime had produced ballistic missiles which exceeded the ranges allowed under UN sanctions. Nevertheless, the reality on the ground in Iraq with respect to chemical and biological weapons significantly differed from the IC's judgment, and there was also a discrepancy between the status of Iraq's nuclear weapon program and the portrayal of that status by the majority view in the NIE. These discrepancies had serious repercussions on the US Intelligence Community, leading some to call for an investigation and overhaul of the IC's structure.

reaction to US military action and what some senior policymakers claimed. In the run-up to the invasion, senior administration officials, such as Vice President Cheney and Deputy Defense Secretary Wolfowitz, frequently and publicly stated—without any support whatsoever from the IC—that American forces would be greeted as "liberators" and showered with flowers, this in spite of the CIA having delivered two other reports on Iraq in late 2002 and early 2003, correctly warning that far from being considered liberators, US forces would face chaos and a serious insurgency.

In retrospect, public speeches made by members of the administration seemed to be a mixed bag. Some speeches were quite consistent with IC judgments, while others chose to emphasize points that were not supported by the IC's findings. An example of the former was Secretary Powell's presentation to the UN Security Council on February 5, 2003, which he used to make the case for taking military action against Saddam. During that presentation he outlined an unprecedented amount of detail on available intelligence and what US policymakers derived from it. This was one of the most detailed public uses of intelligence in history to support policy. Powell's speech included examples of human source intelligence (reports from Iraqi informants and agents), signals intelligence (intercepted phone conversations of Iraqi officials), and imagery intelligence (photos of Iraqi equipment and facilities).

Secretary Powell's points on Saddam's clandestine WMD programs were generally consistent with the NIE's judgments, although they were less nuanced than even the Key Judgments. Because the aluminum tubes were included in the NIE, Powell unfortunately chose to emphasize them, as well as what were mistakenly thought to be mobile biological laboratories, based on information from the discredited human source Curveball. He did mention the difference in analytic judgments on the aluminum tubes, but he nevertheless put forth the NIE's majority view and cited the tubes as evidence for a nuclear program. This emphasis may reflect the fact that he reportedly had spent considerable time with CIA analysts in preparing his speech. But it is noteworthy that while Powell cited differences in analytical judgments within the IC, he did not mention that among the dissenters were the two organizations most knowledgeable on centrifuge technology: the US Department of Energy and the IAEA. Powell's effort to show that his presentation was backed by the US Intelligence Community was enhanced by the fact that the DCI George Tenet sat behind Powell in the Security Council chamber during the presentation. Only in the area of Iraqi ties to terrorists did Powell seem to stretch the IC's judgments, perhaps being influenced more by the Defense Department's independent and more alarmist analysis of this issue.

Subsequently, Powell said that he regrets not scrubbing the intelligence more thoroughly before making his UN Security Council presentation and that he considers this presentation to be one of the low points of his otherwise distinguished career in the federal government. It is interesting that Powell reportedly had said in February 2001 that Saddam did not have "any significant capability with respect to weapons of mass destruction."[50] It is unclear what changed his mind during the following two years.

Pronouncements by other policymakers were less carefully pegged to the NIE's judgments. Several speeches mentioned the possibility of a "mushroom cloud" arising from Iraq, hyping the nuclear threat from Saddam. National Security Advisor Rice said on television that "we don't want the smoking gun to be a mushroom cloud." Secretaries Powell and Rumsfeld, along with the President and Vice President, made similar references in public statements on Iraq's nuclear threat. While not directly contrary to the IC's judgments, these comments were perceived as making Iraq's nuclear program appear more advanced and the threat more imminent than was warranted from those judgments. Pillar criticizes the administration for "cherry-picking," that is, selectively using intelligence rather than using the IC's judgments in full. In particular, he criticizes the vice president for stating that "many of us are convinced that Saddam will acquire nuclear weapons fairly soon," which was contrary to the NIE's judgment.[51]

In our society, policymakers, at least at senior levels, are also politicians. When they believe that certain intelligence is appropriate for public discourse, they will say something about it. Usually, intelligence will be discussed in a way that supports administration policies. For example, the Bush administration believed, probably correctly, that the nuclear program in Iran is not just for peaceful power production but also a weapon program. So when policymakers say something in public about intelligence information on the nuclear program in Iran, it is always to lend credence to this belief. In all administrations, policymakers, at least in the national security field, have a built-in bias toward the worst case. They do not want to be seen as minimizing a threat to national security. This bias is difficult to eradicate, and it can lead to misjudgment and overreaction.

The IC tries to restrain policymakers' use of intelligence information, especially if it appears dubious. DCI Tenet's unsuccessful efforts to extract a sentence about the Niger uranium issue from the President's State of the Union speech in January 2003 is a clear example of policymakers using information that the IC did not consider credible. Prior to the 2003 invasion of Iraq, some intelligence on weapons of mass destruction and on Saddam's ties to international terrorists was misused, distorted, or ignored in public pronouncements by administration officials to support a case for war. Policymakers may, at their peril, make statements and use any information they choose to believe, and most will use that which justifies their policy.

The following examples are from public sources of information provided by the IC and statements by policymakers, which are chronicled along with other references in an appendix to Frank Rich's book *The Greatest Story Ever Sold.*[52] The examples are categorized according to the type of WMD being discussed and the purported ties between Saddam's regime and international terrorists. Listed below is what Rich, based on public sources, indicates the IC reported (beyond the October 2002 NIE) and then what policymakers said. In reading Rich's list, one must keep in mind that with regard to weapons of mass destruction the IC did, as noted above, reach and report some erroneous judgments, while with regard to terrorist connections the administration propounded views that were counter to the IC's judgments.

On Iraqi WMD programs generally, the IC reported:

December 17, 2001—A CIA-administered polygraph determined that an Iraqi defector who said that he helped Saddam Hussein's men secretly bury tons of biological, chemical, and nuclear weapons was lying. (Reported by James Bamford in his book *A Pretext for War*, June 2004, and in an article for *Rolling Stone*, December 1, 2005.)[53]

Mid-September 2002—The CIA director informed President Bush, Vice President Cheney, and National Security Adviser Rice that a member of Saddam Hussein's inner circle who was providing information to the CIA reported that there was "no active weapons of mass destruction program." (First reported by "60 Minutes," April 23, 2006.)[54]

On Iraq's nuclear weapon program, the IC reported:

October 15, 2001—A possible uranium yellowcake sales agreement between Niger and Iraq first came to the attention of the US Intelligence Community. (From the Senate Intelligence Committee's "Report on U.S. Intelligence Community's Prewar Intelligence Assessments on Iraq.")[55]

February 2002—Former ambassador to Niger, Joseph Wilson, traveled to the capital, Niamey, and determined the alleged sale to be unfounded. (The documents were later declassified and made public by Senator Carl Levin, D-Mich., in November 2005.)[56]

March 4, 2002—A high-level intelligence assessment concluded that the sale of uranium from Niger to Iraq was "unlikely." (The memo was declassified in early 2006 through a Freedom of Information request filed by Judicial Watch and reported in the *New York Times*, January 18, 2006.)[57]

Mid-September 2002—The CIA director informed the president that with respect to aluminum tubes purchased by Iraq, the State and Energy Departments and some in the CIA are not certain that that tubes are meant for nuclear weapons. (First reported in *National Journal*, March 30, 2006.)[58]

January 2003—In response to a request from the Pentagon, the National Intelligence Council prepared a memorandum stating that the claim that Iraq attempted to procure uranium from Niger was baseless. The memorandum was also delivered to the White House. (First reported in the *Washington Post*, April 9, 2006.)[59]

January 10, 2003—An intelligence assessment circulated among senior officials, including the Vice President and the National Security Advisor, stated that the Departments of Energy and State, along with the IAEA, all believed that Iraq was using aluminum tubes for conventional weapons programs. (First reported in *National Journal*, March 2, 2006.)[60]

On Iraq's nuclear weapon program, policymakers publicly said:

August 7, 2002—Vice President Cheney, in a speech at the Commonwealth Club in San Francisco, said, "What we now know, from various sources, is that he [Saddam Hussein] has continued to improve the, if you can put it in those terms, the capabilities of his nuclear . . . and he continues to pursue a nuclear weapon."[61]

September 8, 2002—A *New York Times* story citing Vice President Cheney, National Security Advisor Rice, Secretary of Defense Rumsfeld, and Secretary of State Powell reported that Saddam Hussein had sought to acquire thousands of aluminum tubes believed to be intended as components for centrifuges to enrich uranium for bomb materials.[62]

September 8, 2002—Vice President Cheney on "Meet the Press" said, "And what we have seen recently has raised our level of concern to the current state of unrest . . . is that he is trying through his [Saddam Hussein's] illicit procurement network, to acquire the equipment he needs to be able to enrich uranium to make the bombs."

Vice President Cheney—". . . specifically aluminum tubes. . . . We know we have a part of the picture and that part of the picture tells us that he is, in fact, actively and aggressively seeking to acquire nuclear weapons."[63]

September 8, 2002—Secretary of State Powell on Fox News Sunday said, "With respect to nuclear weapons, we are quite confident that he continues to try to pursue the technology that would allow him to develop a nuclear weapon. . . . And as we saw in reporting just this morning, he is still trying to acquire, for example, some of the specialized aluminum tubing one needs to develop centrifuges that would give you an enrichment capability."[64]

October 7, 2002—President Bush, in a speech in Cincinnati, said, "Iraq has attempted to purchase high-strength aluminum tubes and other equipment for gas centrifuges, which are used to enrich uranium for nuclear weapons."[65]

January 23, 2003—National Security Advisor Rice, in an op-ed piece in the *New York Times* detailing deficiencies of Iraq's weapons declaration, asserted that the "declaration fails to account for or explain Iraq's effort to get uranium from abroad."[66]

January 28, 2003—In President Bush's State of the Union Speech, he said, "The International Atomic Energy Agency confirmed in the 1990s that Saddam Hussein had an advanced nuclear weapon program, had a design for a nuclear weapon and was working on five different methods of enriching uranium for a bomb. The British government has learned that Saddam Hussein recently sought significant quantities of uranium from Africa. Our intelligence sources tell us that he has attempted to purchase high-strength aluminum tubes suitable for weapons production."[67]

On Iraq's biological weapon program, the IC reported:

May 2002—A warning posted in US intelligence databases stated in reference to the most important of three CIA sources, who supported claims about Iraqi mobile labs, that he was judged by the CIA and DIA to be a liar. (First reported in the *Los Angeles Times*, November 30, 2005.)[68]

On Iraq's biological weapon program, policymakers said:

January 28, 2003—In President Bush's State of the Union Speech, he said, "From three Iraqi defectors we know that Iraq, in the late 1990s, had several mobile biological weapons labs. . . . Saddam Hussein has not disclosed these facilities. He's given no evidence that he has destroyed them."[69]

February 6, 2003—President Bush said, "The Iraqi regime has actively and secretly attempted to obtain equipment needed to produce chemical, biological and nuclear weapons. First-hand witnesses have informed us that Iraq has at least seven mobile factories for the production of biological agents, equipment mounted on trucks and rails to evade discovery. Using these factories, Iraq has produced within just months hundreds of pounds of biological poisons."[70]

On the Saddam-terrorist connection, the IC reported:

September 21, 2001—"The President was told in the President's Daily Brief that there is no evidence of Iraq's participation in the attacks on September 11, 2001 and that there is scant credible evidence" of any "significant collaborative ties" between Iraq and al-Qaeda and "other theocratic Islamist organizations." This assessment was also sent to Vice President Cheney, National Security Advisor Rice, Deputy National Security Advisor Hadley, Secretary of Defense Rumsfeld, Deputy

Secretary of Defense Wolfowitz, Secretary of State Powell, as well as others. (First reported in *National Journal*, November 22, 2005.)[71]

February 2002—The DIA issued a report in which claims by a senior member of al-Qaeda in American custody that Iraq provided biological and chemical weapons training to al-Qaeda members are said to be fabrications. (The documents were later declassified and made public by Senator Carl Levin, D-Mich., in November 2005.)[72]

June 21, 2002—A CIA report notes "many critical gaps" in knowledge of Iraqi links to al-Qaeda due to "limited reporting" and "the questionable reliability of many of our sources." (First reported in *Newsweek*, July 19, 2004.)[73]

On the Saddam-terrorist connection, policymakers said:

December 9, 2001—Vice President Cheney on "Meet the Press" said that "it's been pretty well confirmed that [Mohammed Atta] did go to Prague and he did meet with a senior official of the Iraqi intelligence service in Czechoslovakia last April."[74]

September 8, 2003—Vice President Cheney on "Meet the Press" said, "I'm not here to make a specific allegation that Iraq was somehow responsible for 9/11. On the other hand . . . we spent time looking at the relationship between Iraq, on the one hand, and the Al Qaeda organization on the other. And there has been reporting that suggests that there have been a number of contacts over the years. We've seen in connection with the hijackers, of course, Mohammed Atta, who was the lead hijacker, [who] did apparently travel to Prague on a number of occasions, we have reporting that places him in Prague [on] a number of occasions. And on at least one occasion, we have reporting that places him in Prague with a senior Iraqi intelligence officer a few months before the attack on the World Trade Center."[75]

September 26, 2002—Secretary of Defense Rumsfeld at a department briefing said, "We have what we believe to be credible information that Iraq and Al Qaeda have discussed safe haven opportunities. . . . We do have—I believe it's in one report indicating that Iraq provided unspecified training relating to chemical and/or biological matters for Al Qaeda members."[76]

September 28, 2002—President Bush in his weekly radio address said that the Iraqi regime "has longstanding and continuing ties to terrorist groups, and there are Al Qaeda terrorists inside Iraq."[77]

October 7, 2002—President Bush in a speech in Cincinnati said, "We know that Iraq and Al Qaeda have had high level contacts that go back a decade."[78]

January 26, 2003—Secretary of State Powell in a European press interview said, "We do have evidence of it [Iraq–Al Qaeda link]. We are not suggesting a 9/11 link, but we are suggesting we do have evidence—of connections over the years between Iraq and Al Qaeda and other terrorist organizations."[79]

9, 2003—National Security Advisor Rice on "Face the Nation" said, "We ▯ a detainee that the head of training for Al Qaeda—that they sought ...▯ ▯▯ ▯▯veloping chemical and biological weapons because they weren't doing well on their own. They sought it in Iraq. They received the help."[80]

Members of Congress were not exempt from culpability in the public use or misuse of intelligence on these subjects. In the debate over the legitimacy of the administration's push to use military force, some in Congress seemed to have selective memory about what they had been told by the IC or had read in its publications, including the NIE of October 2002. Although it was Congress, and not the administration, that had requested the NIE, Pillar asserts that few members of Congress actually read it.[81] The debate on the Hill over US policy on Iraq became manifestly political, particularly in the critiques that followed the initiation of hostilities and the failure to uncover strong evidence of WMD programs in Iraq. Not surprisingly, the political battle between the White House and Congress soon proceeded along party lines.

Conclusions and Lessons Learned

So, what do we conclude about the Intelligence Community's performance on Iraq during the Bush administration and what are the lessons that should be learned?

Policymaker Mind-set. We have discussed the difficulty of maintaining a strong policy process when at least some policymakers are looking for justification for their preferred policy and disavowing any information or analysis that does not provide them the support they are seeking. In addition to cherry-picking the available intelligence, these policymakers seek outside justification for their policies. This appears to have been behind the Pentagon's "intelligence" cell (the Policy Counterterrorism Evaluation Group), which, as mentioned earlier, was established to second-guess IC judgments, particularly on Saddam's ties to international terrorists.

In his book, Tenet acknowledges that policymakers may legitimately arrive at independent judgments about what the intelligence may mean and what risks they will tolerate. However, they should not overstate the intelligence itself.[82] It is natural for policymakers to look for information that supports their policy preferences. Some in the Bush administration did this in referring to an "imminent" nuclear threat and by going beyond intelligence judgments regarding Saddam's ties to international terrorists.

But in addition to going beyond intelligence, did senior policymakers *ignore* available intelligence when it contradicted their preferred policy? Ron Suskind, a former White House staffer, reports a number of such incidents in his book *The Way of the World.* (*We are aware that there may be a number of inaccuracies in Suskind's book regarding the Intelligence Community, but we believe the following appears to have credibility.*) Suskind relates that Naji Sabri, Saddam Hussein's last foreign minister, had established by the summer of 2002 a relationship with French intelligence. The French put the CIA on to Sabri. With the support of President Bush, Vice President Cheney, and National Security Advisor Rice, CIA arranged to put questions to Sabri through an intermediary when Sabri visited New York in September. According to Suskind, the essence of Sabri's account was that Saddam "neither possessed WMD nor was trying very hard to procure or develop them. If Saddam was eager for a nuclear weapon, he was as far as ever from having one and was making no progress on that front; any vestige of a bioweapons program was negligible; and if any chemical weapons remained in Iraq, they were no longer in the hands of Saddam or his military." When briefed by Tenet on this information the next day, the White House dismissed the intelligence as disinformation.[83] This matter was disclosed by NBC in March 2006. Shortly thereafter, Tim Russert on "Meet the Press" questioned Secretary of State Rice about the incident. She confirmed it by responding, "Of course, Tim. . . . This was a single source among multiple sources."[84]

Further, as reported by Suskind, the British government had shared information with Washington in February 2003, which cast doubt on the US Intelligence Community judgment that some chemical and biological weapons remained in Iraq. The information, reportedly given to Michael Shipster, the Middle East chief for SIS (British intelligence), by the chief of the Iraqi Intelligence Service, Tahir Jaliol Habbush, was that Iraq had no weapons of mass destruction. Habbush reportedly explained that Saddam was worried that his neighbors, particularly Iran, would discover that he had none of these weapons. Habbush noted that if the United States invaded Iraq, it would find no WMD. He claimed that Saddam had ended his nuclear program in 1991, the same year he destroyed his chemical stockpile, and that Saddam had no intention of restarting either program. Further, since the destruction of the Al Hakam biological weapons facility in 1996, there was no biological weapon program.

Suskind subsequently interviewed Sir Richard Dearlove, retired former head of MI6, about this exchange of intelligence. "Yes, it did happen," Dearlove confirmed. He said the purpose of the Shipster mission was a last-minute effort to "attempt to try, as it were, I'd say to diffuse the whole situation." Suskind reports that Dearlove speculated on why the report made no impact in Washington: "The problem . . . was the Cheney crowd was in too much of a hurry, really, Bush never resisted them quite strongly enough. Yes, it was probably too late I imagine, for Cheney. I'm not sure that it was too late for Bush."[85]

According to Suskind, this information came out in a series of secret weekly meetings between Michael Shipster and Tahir Jalil Habbush in Jordan from early January 2003 to early February 2003. In the Suskind account, Dearlove himself presented the report to Tenet, but the White House apparently decided to dismiss the British report on Habbush as disinformation. As it turned out, Habbush simply could not persuasively prove a negative.[86]

Although the concern attributed to Saddam about Iran is credible and was likely behind his concealing Iraq's real inventory of weapons, it is curious that nothing was said about the administration ignoring such information from the British in either the Senate or WMD Commission reports. Moreover, in his book Tenet made no mention of such information from the Iraqi Intelligence Service. However, in a speech at Georgetown University in February 2004, Tenet acknowledged that he had received reliable, sensitive reports from foreign partners, one from a source with direct access to Saddam and his inner circle, who said that Iraq was not in possession of a nuclear weapon but that it was stockpiling chemical weapons. Tenet added that a second reliable liaison source confirmed that the production of chemical and biological weapons was taking place.[87]

These sources and reports are good examples of the challenges the IC and policymakers face in sorting through conflicting intelligence information. It is clear that by February 2003 senior policymakers had made up their minds regarding the policy they planned to pursue. As a consequence, they appeared to be seeking information that supported rather than questioned the basis for their preferred policy toward Saddam.

While (as we stated in Chapter 4) it is natural for policymakers to look for information that supports their policy preferences, they ignore contrary intelligence at their risk. As indicated, some policymakers did just this in referring to an "imminent threat" from Saddam's WMD programs, particularly his nuclear program, and by going beyond intelligence judgments regarding Saddam's ties to international terrorists.

Vetting the Credibility of Human Sources. There were critical gaps in available information, especially human source intelligence, due to the lack of any presence on the ground in Iraq once international inspectors had been barred from the country after 1998. Some of the human sources were "feeding" information to the IC based not only on what they believed to be true, however incorrect, but also on what they wanted the United States to believe—and do—on their behalf. Finally, heavy reliance on liaison information, particularly from human sources, introduced further complexity and potential disinformation into the mix.

These facts lead to two lessons—the need to properly vet sources and to ensure the reliability of liaison information. One of the risks of using information from human sources is that people typically have something they wish the intelligence service or its country to do as a result of the information they provide. These aims can range from a personal vendetta against an individual or one's own country, to the need for money, or to ideological commitment. Thus, determining the potential source's motivations, credibility, and access to required information is essential to recruitment and to subsequent use of the information provided. The risk increases when the source belongs to a liaison intelligence service, which means that the IC would most likely not have direct access to the source to satisfy itself that the source was telling the truth, at least as that person understood it. Whether sources are direct or not, their information must, if at all possible, be checked against other information. Unfortunately, according to critiques of the Iraqi case, lying and misinformation were rampant among human sources. Of particular note, as mentioned earlier, was the case of the German source, code-named Curveball. From separate accounts by Tenet and Drumheller mentioned above, some debate exists as to what was told to whom about this source.[88]

Getting Too Close to Policy? As mentioned in Chapter 4, intelligence officers must walk a fine line when working closely in support of policymakers, especially in times of crisis, to avoid becoming policy advocates rather than suppliers of objective intelligence whether or not it supports the particular policy. Some argue that DCI Tenet allowed himself to get too close to the White House and, therefore, did not provide available information that was contrary to the administration's preferred policies and that might have kept policymakers from being blinded by their own enthusiastic and optimistic calculations of what their policies might achieve in Iraq. In the aforementioned article, Pillar faults the administration for failing to ask for critical analysis and, rather, seeking judgments that bolstered its preconceived policy preferences.[89] While undoubtedly true, this does not excuse the IC, especially the DCI (now DNI), from giving policymakers the information they need to make good decisions, whether they like it, or ask for it, or not—even when the messenger might be "shot" for providing intelligence that calls into question the wisdom of their policy preferences. Therefore, even when policymakers do not request critical analysis, it is the job of the IC to provide it. When providing warning, the IC is expected to take the initiative and not wait to be asked.

Sounding a warning is different from advising on the implications and potential downsides of a policy decision that appears likely to be made. One particularly difficult problem in the run-up to the war in Iraq may have been the absence of a clear decision point. Without such a defined point it is difficult to know when to give such advice—that is, to warn of potential pitfalls shortly before a decision is made—and when to support whatever that decision is. The IC provided an analysis of the likely implications of removing Saddam, but the IC's judgments may have been received too late to influence the policy decision, or perhaps they were just disregarded. Tenet appeared to be intimately involved in the decision process, so it is hard to believe that he would not have had a good feel for when the final decision to use military force was made. If Tenet had in fact moved so close to the President and his senior policy advisors that he was trapped by their thinking, then he had lost the ability to look beyond their desires to their real need for information and insight, as well as to give them objective intelligence. Such indirect politicization of intelligence can be as damaging as direct efforts by policymakers to influence intelligence judgments.

Was There Politicization? Pillar responds in the affirmative, albeit indirect politicization. In his view the Intelligence Community was being asked by policymakers to produce information and judgments that would help sell the administration's policy rather than produce critical analysis to inform it. However, the report issued jointly by the SSCI and the HPSCI (the two congressional intelligence committees) as well as the WMD Commission's report did not assert any evidence of overt politicization of intelligence judgments by policymakers; but they did not address the more subtle form of politicization mentioned by Pillar. Rather, they criticized the IC for lacking good information and being trapped by assumptions on the nature of Saddam's regime and his likely actions. While the reports conceded that such assumptions were somewhat warranted, the IC should have given policymakers a better feel for the thinness of the information on which its judgments were based. The reports also concluded that some of the information was misleading; in particular, the

CIA failed to point out to policymakers serious doubts about the reliability of the human source Curveball on Iraq's biological weapon program.[90]

Conclusions. Having reviewed the record, which is now available publicly, we offer the following conclusions about the US Intelligence Community's understanding and reporting of Iraq's intentions and capabilities with respect to nuclear weapons and other weapons of mass destruction:

(1) The IC made reasonable assumptions based on the context, history, and intentions of the Iraqi regime; that is, Saddam's history of possessing and using chemical weapons, evidence that he had produced biological weapons, his having made surprising progress in his nuclear weapon program prior to 1991, his failure to account for missing chemical inventories, and his repeated efforts to deceive and lie to the international community and UN inspectors. Nevertheless, the IC appears to have been wrong in believing that Iraq had stockpiles of chemical and biological precursors and agents. In its final report in October 2004, the IC's Iraq Survey Group (ISG) concluded that Saddam was attempting to preserve the capability to reconstitute his WMD when sanctions were lifted; in Saddam's view, as stated earlier, WMD had helped to save the regime many times. Therefore, he wanted to recreate the WMD capabilities that had been destroyed in 1991 and aspired to develop a nuclear weapon capability, but he intended to focus on tactical chemical warfare capabilities. On whether WMD-related material had been moved out of Iraq prior to the 2003 war, the ISG concluded that it was unlikely this had been done officially, but there may have been unofficial transport of such material to Syria.[91]

(2) The IC had it basically right with regard to Saddam's nuclear weapon program; it judged that he did not have and was not close to having such weapons. Regarding the value of alternative views and scenarios, there were different views on how much progress Iraq had made in reconstituting its nuclear weapon program after its dismantlement by IAEA inspectors following the 1991 Gulf War. Such views demonstrated that significant uncertainty existed, which was important for policymakers to know. The State Department's INR was the most conservative, while the CIA judged that Iraq had made more progress. In a similar way, the use of alternative *scenarios* can help to sort out the variables and how they may play out, particularly in the face of significant gaps in information. Even in the context of a strong, unidirectional policy environment, the IC would have been well advised to at least acknowledge other plausible possibilities, such as Iraq's climate of rampant disinformation and lying as well

as Saddam's concern about Iran, for explaining contradictory information and the lack of good information on the status of Iraq's nuclear as well as chemical and biological weapons programs.

Although the probability is extremely low to the point of being virtually nonexistent, it is perhaps still conceivable that very small amounts of chemical and biological precursors and agents could still be hidden inside Iraq. Indeed, until July 1, 2007, the United Nations continued to retain UNMOVIC with a roster of weapons experts from fifty countries, who were on call to serve, including reviewing satellite images of former Iraqi weapon sites. The United States opposed the continuation of UN inspections, while Russia insisted that Iraq's disarmament be formally confirmed by UN inspectors.[92] A small minority of observers continue to suspect that with the help of Russia, Saddam shipped WMD materials to either Syria or Lebanon, or to both, just prior to the outbreak of military hostilities in March 2003, and that these materials remain buried there.[93] However, no evidence has yet been uncovered, and this hypothesis lacks credibility.

(3) The gap between what the Iraq Survey Group eventually reported in 2004 and the judgments provided by the IC prior to the invasion in 2003 reveals an urgent need for the IC to enhance its capabilities to monitor and correctly understand small clandestine WMD programs.[94] Richelson, in *Spying on the Bomb*, concludes that in the case of North Korea the US Intelligence Community "through satellites and other means, has uncovered much that the North Koreans undoubtedly wish had remained hidden. That has allowed the IAEA or the United States to confront North Korea when, predictably, it has failed to live up to its promises to refrain from taking steps toward producing fissile material, whether plutonium or uranium." He acknowledges, however, that "much remains unknown about the North Korean program." But he concludes that "the failure to find a satisfactory solution to the problem of the Iranian or North Korean nuclear programs is not a failure that can be laid at the door of the U.S. Intelligence Community."[95] Richelson is correct: the IC's responsibility is to monitor and establish the facts as best it can; it is the job of policymakers to come up with appropriate solutions that limit and, if possible, halt proliferation activities.

The Iraqi case shows that it is also critical for the IC to have a sophisticated understanding of the countries that are pursuing clandestine WMD programs. Former CIA Director Hayden may have correctly identified the problem when he stated that in their analysis of Saddam's progress, CIA analysts put too little reliance on experts on Iraq and too much reliance on technical experts. Perhaps a more insightful understanding of the internal dynamics of the Saddam regime and how it managed its programs would have shed critical light on the actual progress that had been made.[96]

(4) Policymakers did not directly politicize the IC's judgments, but they put sufficient pressure on the IC so that a thorough scrub of the evidence was not made, especially of evidence provided by human sources or of the underlying assumptions. The Vice President's many visits to the CIA were probably somewhat intimidating, particularly when it was impossible to prove the negative. And DCI Tenet appears to have been dangerously close to wanting to provide the intelligence being sought by the White House rather than ensuring that the IC gave warning that their assumptions might not be accurate. Tenet later confessed in his book that more accurate and nuanced findings in the judgments would have made for a more vigorous debate; the IC had let the policy community down by not being more rigorous and precise in its language.[97] It is dubious, however, that such improvements would have led to a change in policy.

Former CIA Director Hayden also claimed that a critical lesson was learned from this episode. While confirming that as Director of NSA in 2002–3 his SIGINT information seemed to confirm IC judgments and that he had agreed with the conclusions of the October 2002 NIE on Iraq's WMD programs, IC analysts did not "think outside the box" sufficiently and explore alternative assumptions on an ambiguous situation.[98] If policy pressure led some members of the IC to selectively report information in the belief that saying anything contrary to policy preferences would be ignored, this would be a travesty and grave corruption of the intelligence-policymaker relationship. As we have stated before, the IC must at all times be willing to provide objective, unbiased information, even when policy consumers do not wish to hear it. It is likely that intelligence managers were frustrated and eventually were willing to look for information that might substantiate policymakers' intentions, but this does not mean that they would have withheld contrary information. Politicization can be a tricky business, but integrity and honesty must nevertheless prevail.

(5) Finally, the preparers of the October 2002 NIE should have at least acknowledged the possibility that due to denial, deception, and lying, both to the outside world and within Saddam's own regime, Iraq may no longer have had chemical and biological weapons in its inventory. An important lesson learned is that human sources out of such a society and regime may be reporting what

---

Intelligence Reporting on Consequences of Military Action in Iraq

The strengths and weaknesses of US intelligence analysis and reporting on Saddam's weapons of mass destruction programs should be seen in the light of other reporting prepared and presented by the Intelligence Community on Iraq. In the early summer of 2007, the Senate Select Committee on Intelligence (SSCI) released a report on pre-war intelligence on the consequences of removing Saddam titled "The Perfect Storm: Planning for Negative Consequences of Invading Iraq." The committee's report stated that the IC described the worst scenarios that could arise after a US-led removal of Saddam. Written seven months before the US invasion, the report speculated that al-Qaeda operatives would take advantage of a destabilized Iraq to establish secure safe havens from which to continue their operations.[99]

In a separate article, Paul Pillar states that the IC's WMD estimate was only one of three classified, community-coordinated assessments on Iraq produced by the IC during the months prior to the war. Although the other two assessments, dealing with the potential consequences of removing Saddam by military force, were apparently not requested by policymakers, Pillar states that he initiated and supervised the reports because it is the duty of intelligence to anticipate future policymaker needs. He gives the SSCI credit for releasing (although belatedly) the reports, which balance the selective attention given to the IC's performance with regard to Iraqi WMD programs. He further claims that the intelligence reorganization of 2004 was predicated on incomplete and incorrect perceptions that intelligence on Iraq had been all wrong. Pillar believes that the judgments reached in the other two assessments proved to be the most important in the war. He concludes by stating that for the most part intelligence judgments on Iraq were correct.[100]

---

they believe to be true, but they themselves may be subject to disinformation and lying.

It is obvious that various components of the IC made mistakes in process (such as insufficient vetting of human sources), analysis, and judgment with regard to Iraq's WMD programs prior to 2003. As noted earlier, the IC has misjudged a few other WMD programs over the decades. But looking at the picture of performance by the IC in the difficult cases of clandestine programs of weapons of mass destruction in recent years, especially in Iraq, columnist David Ignatius's conclusion in the *Washington Post* seems about right: "Sometimes, as in most of its Iraq reporting, the CIA has gotten it dead right. And when we assess the CIA, we should understand that many of its supposed failures really have another address—the White House."[101] While poor intelligence can easily lead to poor policy decisions, in the case of Iraq in 2002–3 it seems clear that even a more accurate assessment of Iraq's WMD programs by the Intelligence Community would not have deterred policymakers from pursuing the course of action they desired.

Implications of the Iraqi Case for Monitoring Other Clandestine WMD Programs

The implications of the Iraqi experience for US efforts to monitor and limit other clandestine WMD programs are likely to be profound. The country became seriously divided over this issue. Some believe that the Intelligence Community did the White House a major disservice by not getting it right on the aluminum tubes and by not warning the administration strongly enough that the Niger contract for yellowcake was a forgery. Some believe that incompetent CIA monitoring, epitomized by Director George Tenet's "slam dunk" statement in referring to the case against Iraq for having illegal weapons of mass destruction, led the United States into a war it did not need to fight—at least on the grounds of Iraq having weapons of mass destruction that were threatening the United States and the world community. In his book Tenet states that his use of the phrase "slam dunk" was taken out of context and exaggerated. He claims that what he was actually trying to communicate to the president was that it was certainly possible to strengthen the public presentation of the case for Iraqi weapons of mass destruction with better, more convincing information, as demonstrated by Secretary Powell in his speech to the UN Security Council.[102] However, others believe that the IC's performance on Iraq, while not without flaws, was reasonable. The community was pressured by the White House to tell it what it wanted to hear, and the White House then distorted the intelligence information that it received by exaggerating the facts and judgments the IC had provided.

Despite the risks in using information provided by liaison intelligence services, there will continue to be situations where such services are likely to be the best source of information available. The United States has little entrée to most of the countries about which it has proliferation concerns, so its ability to identify, recruit, and unilaterally run agents in those countries is severely limited. The United States must also carefully consider any information provided by international inspection activities. Hans Blix states that in the case of Iraq during the period from 2002 to early 2003, UNMOVIC carried out some seven hundred inspections at some five hundred sites, including about three dozen inspections at sites suspected and suggested by US intelligence. As mentioned earlier, UN inspection teams reported no significant WMD-related finds.[103] An administration guided by the facts rather than its policy preferences would have at least taken this into account before launching a war. However, having inspectors on the ground, as helpful as that can be, and even with national intelligence guidance and participation (see the text box "Intelligence Support to International Inspections" in Chapter 6), does not necessarily expose concealment and deception efforts by the country being inspected. Intelligence analysts must take this into account even as they struggle to properly understand and report information provided by human sources. It is the administration's awareness of the factual situation in March 2003, not the fall of 2002, that must determine its bona fides. Human lives in large numbers were at stake.

In the future, congressional committees are likely to be much more skeptical of intelligence estimates and judgments on clandestine weapons of mass destruction programs, at least those that would affect important policy decisions. There will be concerns about White House pressure or "spin" put on intelligence analysis to serve policy goals. Thus, senior intelligence analysts and officials may become less willing to make firm judgments for fear of being accused of simply responding to political pressures. However, the Intelligence Community's issuance of revised judgments on the status of Iran's nuclear weapon program in late 2007, which went against the Bush administration's policy, should be somewhat reassuring.

In addition, congressional funding of intelligence programs might change to emphasize "hard" intelligence collection (satellite reconnaissance, intercepts) and downplay support for human intelligence (defectors, and especially CIA-recruited clandestine agents) as being too subjective and therefore more vulnerable to political pressure. Such reallocation would be most unfortunate in today's world of so-called rogue states, international terrorist organizations, and their small but potentially deadly nuclear, chemical, and biological weapons programs. As already stated, human sources often provide the best information in these contexts, but careful vetting of their reliability is critical. Clandestine WMD programs, especially those involving chemical or biological agents, are simply too small and too well hidden in authoritarian or failing states to make detection by remote technical sensors easy. The future success of US intelligence efforts against small clandestine WMD programs depends on drawing the appropriate lessons from the Iraqi case and avoiding an overreaction.

And this may be what happened in 2007 with regard to Syria's nuclear program. In a public speech given in the early fall of 2008, then CIA Director Hayden seemed to be trying to reassure the public that the CIA along with the entire US Intelligence Community had indeed learned important lessons from the Iraqi WMD episode. He stated that the quality of tradecraft, in terms of collection and analysis, and the value of collaboration, both within the US government and with liaison intelligence services, had led to the discovery and destruction of Syria's secret effort to build a nuclear reactor with North Korean assistance. Hayden noted that US analysts early on had discovered the suspicious facility at Al Kibar, which a foreign partner subsequently identified as a nuclear reactor. However, US analysts remained open to alternative possibilities, such as a conventional power plant or a water treatment facility. As they laid out the available information, the analysts concluded that the reactor hypothesis was the most difficult to refute. Hayden claimed that successfully identifying the facility as a nuclear reactor and as being built with the assistance of North Korean nuclear experts was the result of close cooperation among US intelligence agencies and foreign liaison services. Hayden concluded that the rigor of sourcing, the emphasis on alternative analysis, and the integration of US and foreign expertise was the key to this successful counterproliferation effort.[104]

Meanwhile, in late November 2008, the IAEA's inspection and analysis confirmed that the bombed facility at Al Kibar resembled a nuclear reactor. Moreover, soil samples collected near the site contained significant amounts of uranium, which should not have been there. The IAEA's report at least partly bolstered the US case and discounted the Syrian claim that detected uranium came from the Israeli bombs used to destroy the facility.[105]

6   National and International Efforts to Thwart Proliferation

As with many countries, the United States has both national and multinational options for ensuring its national security. The tools the United States may use for a given situation depend on many factors, and the tools that are likely to be effective depend on whether the target is a nation-state or a non-state actor, such as an international terrorist group, or both. Independent intelligence capabilities, effective diplomacy, economic sanctions, and, when appropriate, military force are the bedrock of a country's national tools for dealing with proliferation activities by nation-states and for preventing the acquisition and use of weapons of mass destruction by terrorists. However, the United States has learned that some adjustments in the way it employs its national capabilities, including intelligence, have been required to deal with the challenge of terrorism.

Despite its power, the United States is rarely able to do anything effectively beyond its borders without the cooperation of one or more other countries. Multinational approaches are normally most effective in dealing with threats in the international arena. Even during World War II, the United States found it necessary, in spite of its unparalleled industrial and military might, to form military alliances (including with the Soviet Union, its ideological enemy) to fight the Japanese Imperialists and German Nazis. This was followed by the formation of the United Nations and the North Atlantic Treaty Organization, among other international arrangements, to bolster US national security during the Cold War. However, US leaders have always viewed international efforts as supplementary to, not replacing, strong, independent national security capabilities.

As we discussed in our book *Spy Satellites and Other Intelligence Technologies That Changed History*, during the early days of the Cold War US policymakers were in desperate need of more detailed and reliable information on Soviet military capabilities and intentions. This led to the development of a large and capable intelligence establishment, which sought on the collection side of the business to make up for the lack of effective human sources with increasingly sophisticated remote technical collection systems. These technical collection capabilities eventually were referred to publicly as national technical means (NTM) of verification once negotiations had begun with the Soviet Union to halt and roll back the increasingly dangerous nuclear arms race.[1] However, US actions during the Cold War were rarely taken without the cooperation of allies, such as through NATO.

Israel has provided the prime examples of unilateral action to thwart proliferation in its military air strikes against Iraq's Osiraq reactor in 1981 and more recently against the suspected Syrian reactor in 2007. The closest that the United States has come to taking unilateral action in the counterproliferation arena has been (1) its opposition to the entry into force of the Comprehensive Nuclear Test Ban Treaty (CTBT), which many countries view as a valuable international tool to fight proliferation; (2) its opposition to more-stringent verification provisions for the Biological Weapons Convention; and (3) in the use of military force to depose the Saddam regime in Iraq. Most of the international community has viewed all three actions negatively. The Bush administration's decision in 2001 not to support more effective measures against biological weapons nor to seek ratification of the CTBT after the United States had led the negotiation of this treaty, irritated even close US allies and undercut international efforts to forge a permanent ban on nuclear testing. In the case of Iraq, the United States tried to secure international consensus on using military force against the Saddam regime, but key members of the UN Security Council, including China, France, and Russia, refused to go along. As a result, the United States, with several like-minded countries, proceeded to oust Saddam by military force. The international repercussions of what have appeared to many countries to be unwise unilateral actions have been significant.

Enhancing and Adjusting National Capabilities

To improve its ability to monitor and protect itself from the effects of WMD proliferation, especially from a potential attack by international terrorists, the United States since the terrorist attacks in September 2001 has taken several steps at the national and local levels. Most notably, the Bush administration and Congress established the Department of Homeland Security (DHS) to bolster

US National Technical Means of Verification

By the late 1960s, the United States was well along in using sophisticated remote technical collection systems to monitor primarily the military activities of the Soviet Union and the Warsaw Pact, as well as China. In addition, analytic processes were developed to understand and integrate technical data with other data collected from human sources and open-source information. Together these capabilities are commonly referred to in the intelligence world as sensitive sources and methods, which include all efforts to collect and analyze data on foreign adversaries, particularly those that are military threats.

Many people understand remote technical collection to be limited to photographic satellites, given that such satellites are perhaps the best-known collection system and are designed to circle the globe and collect information on otherwise denied areas. To be sure, technical collection includes reconnaissance satellites of various types, but it also includes capabilities such as aerial, sea-based, and ground-based sensors. The products of these collection systems include photographs or digital images, electronic signals, communications intercepts, seismic data, and radionuclide samples from nuclear test explosions. The details of such systems are largely and necessarily classified to ensure their continued effectiveness, that is, for protection against efforts to spoof them.

The challenge for the United States is to use these remote collection systems—which were developed mainly to monitor the large and technically sophisticated Soviet weapon systems and military forces supported by a large industrial infrastructure—to monitor the small, clandestine nuclear, chemical, and biological weapon programs within various countries, as well as terrorists' efforts to gain access to such programs, their lethal materials, or the actual weapons themselves.

Meanwhile, the international community has been less enthusiastic about the use of national intelligence capabilities, especially when only a few countries appear to have such sophisticated monitoring tools and because of fears that the United States in particular might use its tools as a pretext to justify inspections, accusations of misconduct, or even the use of force. Such reservations have been reinforced by unfortunate incidents, such as when US Secretary of State Colin Powell made a comprehensive presentation to the UN Security Council on Iraq's WMD programs based largely on data collected by US technical intelligence collection systems and human sources, the information from which was proven to be somewhat incorrect. Clearly, the United States and other countries must learn how to use most effectively national and multinational collection and analytic capabilities to better understand and counter proliferation efforts by various countries and by terrorists. The activities of terrorist groups are quite distinct from those of nation-states, so additional tools have had to be developed to monitor and prevent proliferation to, and by, terrorists.

and better coordinate efforts at the federal and local levels to defend the United States from another terrorist attack, especially one involving nuclear, chemical, or biological agents or weapons. The DHS's intelligence division became the newest member of the US Intelligence Community in an effort to enhance the systematic sharing and merging of foreign and domestic intelligence, as well as information obtained from local authorities, on potential terrorist threats.

In addition, the Bush administration and Congress, prodded by the 9/11 and Iraqi WMD Commission reports and bowing to political pressure to make significant changes in the management of US intelligence activities, agreed in 2004 to reorganize the top leadership of the Intelligence Community. The position of Director of National Intelligence (DNI) was created to replace the former position of Director of Central Intelligence, who had also been the director of the Central Intelligence Agency. By separating the top IC position from day-to-day management responsibilities for any single intelligence entity, it was hoped that the DNI would be able to ensure better information sharing throughout the community and to focus the community more effectively on critical issues. It remains to be seen whether or not this change—not having to manage a large intelligence agency—will be successful in creating a director who can do a better job. The risk is that the new position will succeed only in adding a new layer of bureaucracy because the DNI does not directly control any collection or analytic part of the IC.

More recently, in the spring of 2008, Congress established the Commission on the Prevention of Weapons of Mass Destruction Proliferation and Terrorism. This was the outgrowth of the legislation Congress passed in 2007 to fully implement the recommendations of the 9/11 Commission, which had criticized Congress for not doing enough to prevent proliferation and terrorist attacks. The commission is responsible for assessing federal programs intended to secure all nuclear weapon material; evaluating the roles and structure of relevant government departments and other actors; promoting coordination between the United States and international regimes and organizations; and analyzing the threat posed by international black market networks and the effectiveness of US responses. Only time will tell how effective the commission will be in bolstering US efforts to monitor and limit the proliferation of weapons of mass destruction, especially to terrorists.[2]

Perhaps one of the best national defenses is to use political action against, and the threat of punishment on, any state failing to take appropriate measures to prevent its territory from being used by terrorists. To effectively carry out a strategy of defense against WMD terrorism, the United States would need to announce that its response to the use of any chemical, biological, or nuclear weapons against the United States would be powerful and sustained. And as the post-Saddam Iraqi situation has shown, an effective strategy requires also the general support of the international community. If necessary, the United States would violate sovereignty and attack preemptively, deep into other nations; would act on "reasonable" evidence; and would make assumptions about who is supporting terrorists in possessing WMD. The United States would make it clear that it would punish vigorously, not only active supporters but even states that merely tolerated terrorists or indirectly facilitated them. The purpose would be to instill fear of an American reprisal and so deter through influence.[3] In the case of a terrorist group acquiring WMD without a state sponsor, and without the state from whose territory it operates even being aware of such activity, the unwitting host state would presumably act just as aggressively as the United States when apprised of the situation.

National Versus International Monitoring

The proliferation of nuclear, chemical, or biological weapons has normally involved clandestine cooperation among those countries that want to obtain such weapons and those countries (or private black market traders, such as the A. Q. Khan network) that are willing to supply the associated technologies, expertise, and materials. The challenge of monitoring terrorist organizations' efforts to obtain such weapons (or at least the relevant expertise, components, or agents) must go beyond national means and include cooperation by local police authorities and international organizations, such as the International Criminal Police Organization (INTERPOL). The United States, along with many other countries, uses both national and international tools to monitor and limit proliferation activities. How to balance the use of national and international capabilities to optimize US national security is the challenge that all administrations face.

In negotiating the first Strategic Arms Limitation Treaty agreements (SALT I), which put at least a cap on further deployments of strategic nuclear weapon systems, the United States and the USSR had to rely on their respective intelligence capabilities to verify compliance with the agreements. Because neither wanted to record in a public document any specifics of its verification methods, they agreed to the euphemism "national technical means of verification" as the codeword in the treaty texts for national intelligence capabilities—principally, but not exclusively, satellite reconnaissance.

During the same period, the international community successfully concluded agreements such as the Nuclear Non-Proliferation Treaty (NPT) designed to halt further proliferation. The multinational agreements necessarily included international monitoring and verification. Consequently, in the case of nuclear proliferation, the International Atomic Energy Agency was charged with monitoring compliance with the NPT through on-site inspections. Nevertheless, the United States continued to rely heavily on its own monitoring capabilities to verify the compliance of other countries.

The use of national technical means of verification took on an international focus following the end of the Cold War. During the negotiation of the Conventional Armed Forces in Europe Treaty, which was concluded in 1991 between the nations of the Warsaw Pact and NATO, all participants (including the United States and Soviet Union) agreed to internationalize the application of technical means of verification by referring in the treaty to "national or multinational" technical means of verification. This codified an arrangement by which many countries could pool their national resources and even establish cooperative efforts to monitor compliance.[4]

Later, in the mid-1990s, the international community reached almost unanimous agreement on a Comprehensive Nuclear Test Ban Treaty (CTBT) designed to ban all further nuclear test explosions in any environment. The total ban was backed up by a verification approach, after much discussion and considerable resistance, which allowed individual countries to use their national technical means to monitor nuclear testing—a provision that was championed by the United States along with several other countries, including Russia. However, there was significant resistance from countries such as China, India, and Pakistan, which argued that the superpowers would use their superior monitoring capabilities to the disadvantage of less capable countries. As a result, agreement was also reached to develop an International Monitoring System (IMS), which consists of 321 monitoring stations in over two hundred countries, on which most of the world would rely for verifying compliance with the CTBT. All countries, including the United States, promoted this international approach to monitoring the CTBT, although there was intense discussion and debate within the US government on the appropriate reliance to be put on national versus international nuclear test monitoring capabilities.

Having led the international effort to negotiate the CTBT, the Clinton ad-

---

CTBT Verification Regime

The Comprehensive Nuclear Test Ban Treaty's verification regime consists of the International Monitoring System (IMS), with global seismological, radionuclide, hydroacoustic, and infrasound networks, as well as possible on-site inspections on a challenge basis. It also includes voluntary data exchanges. The CTBT explicitly provides that parties may use information from national technical means of verification, as well as the IMS, as the basis for on-site inspection requests.

The detection systems in the IMS compose a huge international monitoring system for verifying the treaty. The primary system consists of 50 seismic stations worldwide to monitor underground events (earthquakes and explosions) and 120 auxiliary seismic stations, 80 radionuclide stations along with 16 radionuclide laboratories to monitor radioactive particles associated with a nuclear explosion, 11 hydroacoustic stations to listen for explosions under water, and 60 infrasound stations to monitor sound waves in the atmosphere. The data flows continuously into an international data center, which is part of the technical secretariat of the future CTBT organization. An on-site inspection request, based on data provided by the IMS or by national monitoring or both, would be granted pursuant to an affirmative vote of at least thirty of the fifty-one members of the CTBT Executive Council (composed of states parties with worldwide geographic balance).

Such monitoring capabilities, when combined with national capabilities, gave the international community the ability to detect the Indian and Pakistani tests in May 1998 (although they were publicly announced) and to detect and measure the yield of the North Korean nuclear test in October 2006. However, because of opposition from several key countries, including India, North Korea, and especially the United States, the CTBT has not yet entered into force.

---

ministration nevertheless was divided on how much stock to put in the International Monitoring System. There was some concern in Washington that the IMS would not be as capable as the US Atomic Energy Detection System (USAEDS), the primary US capability to monitor nuclear test explosions around the globe. This issue was one that arose during the brief and unsuccessful effort by the Clinton administration to achieve the Senate's advice and consent to the CTBT during the fall of 1999. In anticipation of the debate, the administration proposed to the Senate six conditions (so-called safeguards) for attachment to US ratification of the treaty. One condition called for the enhancement of national monitoring capabilities, particularly additional funding for the USAEDS.[5]

As one of us, Keith Hansen, describes in *The Comprehensive Nuclear Test Ban Treaty: An Insider's Perspective,* the US ratification effort failed for political and technical reasons. But the debate within the US government over the appropriate approach to monitoring nuclear testing did not stop with the Clinton administration. The George W. Bush administration came into office in 2001 with a definite bias against the CTBT, because of doubts about the wisdom of forever giving up the right to test, concerns that the IMS would not be sufficient to the task of verification, and suspicions that India and North Korea would never sign the Treaty. In the late summer of 2001, the new administration decided against any further efforts to seek US ratification of the CTBT, although it supported the continued development of the International Monitoring System.

US Atomic Energy Detection System (USAEDS)

Beginning in the late 1940s, the United States began to monitor the nuclear tests of other countries. That effort, which includes various types of technical sensors located in the air, on the ground, and under water, evolved into the USAEDS. The US Air Force Technical Applications Center (AFTAC), which is located at Patrick Air Force Base in Florida, operates the system. The center operates 24 hours a day, 365 days a year, and the system has been monitoring nuclear tests around the world since the 1950s.[6]

As agreements to limit nuclear testing have been negotiated over the years, AFTAC has been charged successively with monitoring the Limited Test Ban Treaty, the Threshold Test Ban Treaty, and the Peaceful Nuclear Explosion Treaty. In addition, AFTAC provides assistance to the International Atomic Energy Agency and serves as the US laboratory for supporting the agency's analysis of samples collected during inspections.

In the case of the Comprehensive Nuclear Test Ban Treaty, AFTAC sent experts to advise the US delegation during negotiations in Geneva and provided leadership in developing the treaty's International Monitoring System, the IMS. AFTAC experts remain deeply involved in supporting the treaty's Provisional Technical Secretariat through operating and maintaining USAEDS stations that are also part of the IMS, and as a resource of expertise to ensure a smooth buildup of the IMS.

Even though the United States has continued to fund its portion of development costs for the IMS, the bias in the Bush administration was clearly to rely more on US national than international monitoring capabilities; as of publication of this book, it is too early to know how the Obama administration will decide this issue, although the new administration favors CTBT ratification by the United States. The international community's reaction to the change in US priorities was extremely negative, and most countries believed the United States was being shortsighted, given that it could have both its national monitoring capabilities and the IMS working in its favor. As a result of US resistance to ratifying the CTBT, along with the resistance of several other key countries (primarily India and North Korea), the IMS to this day is unable to function on behalf of the international community in the manner envisioned by the negotiators.[7] While the IMS was successful in detecting the Indian, Pakistani, and North Korean nuclear tests over a ten-year period, at best this international tool thus far provides only a nominal deterrent to future clandestine tests. Most expect the Obama administration to renew efforts to achieve US ratification of the CTBT and to encourage the signature and ratification of India and the other holdout states.

Criticisms that the George W. Bush administration chose to walk away from international efforts to monitor proliferation in favor of "unilateralism" are not limited to the CTBT. The Bush administration also thwarted international efforts in the early 2000s to forge a verification protocol to the Biological Weapons Convention, which hitherto had not contained meaningful verification provisions to back up its ban on such weapons. The administration argued that the new protocol's provisions would not be effective. Some critics of the administration suspected that US pharmaceutical companies had complained that the provisions would be too intrusive and possibly compromise proprietary data. Further, the Bush administration called into question considerations for the verification provisions of a possible Fissile Material Cutoff Treaty (FMCT), which if negotiated as envisioned by most countries would ban future production of nuclear fissile material.[8] Although China and Pakistan have blocked the negotiation of an FMCT for nearly a decade, US-expressed doubts about the verifiability of such an agreement have reduced its negotiability.

Finally, in making the decision to use military force to remove Saddam Hussein, the Bush administration clearly discounted the results in late 2002 and early 2003 of UN and IAEA inspections of Iraq's efforts to reconstitute its nuclear weapon program, despite the administration's willingness to supply intelligence to those inspections. In contrast, the Bush administration was instrumental in launching the multinational Proliferation Security Initiative and the UN Security Council's Resolution 1540, both of which require international cooperation to monitor and prevent further proliferation.

It is safe to say that deliberations over the balance between national and international monitoring efforts will plague future US administrations just as they have the last two. However, the United States cannot go it alone in the face of an international web of activities that make proliferation possible. A combination of robust national and international monitoring capabilities as well as effective cooperation will be required to prevent further WMD proliferation, especially into the hands of international terrorists.

International Efforts to Prevent Proliferation

Monitoring and limiting the proliferation of weapons of mass destruction programs are concerns not only of the United States, of course. As mentioned, the international community has given considerable attention to the issues. The United Nations Security Council (UNSC) has frequently deliberated on and passed resolutions to prevent, stop, or roll back such programs. As we discussed in Chapter 5, the United Nations deployed inspectors to Iraq (from 1991 to 1998, and from late 2002 to early 2003) to investigate and dismantle Saddam's clandestine WMD programs. In addition, the International Atomic Energy Agency (IAEA) has been the watchdog for adherence to the Nuclear Non-Proliferation Treaty by states parties since the early 1970s. Finally, numerous treaties and arrangements, such as the Nuclear Suppliers Group, Nuclear-Weapon-Free Zones, Chemical Weapons Convention, and the Biological Weapons Convention, have been negotiated, and in most cases implemented, to establish international norms against the acquisition and use of nuclear, chemical, or biological weapons. However, the track record of international efforts has been mixed.

On September 29, 2008, an organization known as the World Institute for Nuclear Security was established in Vienna by the Nuclear Threat Initiative, a private organization led by former US senator Sam Nunn. It was launched with a donation of $6 million and a staff of perhaps a dozen specialists. The new organization will seek to bolster security at thousands of nuclear sites around the world to block the theft of nuclear material and thwart its use by terrorists. It will promote best security practices and eliminate weak links in the global nuclear security system. Senator Nunn noted, "The stakes are very high, there's no doubt that terrorists are trying to get this material." The new institute will be located near the IAEA headquarters in Vienna, Austria, and Director-General ElBaradei wrote to Senator Nunn that he believed the new organization will help establish "a global nuclear security regime."[9]

Beyond direct national or regional efforts to preserve security, there are in a sense three ways through international arrangements to monitor and inhibit weapon proliferation. The three methods need not be in conflict with one another; indeed they are complementary. The *first* consists of classic nonproliferation treaty arrangements, represented most notably by the Nuclear Non-Proliferation Treaty, the Chemical Weapons Convention, and the Biological Weapons Convention. Of course, the effectiveness of such treaties depends on convincing skeptical countries that their security requirements are best met by joining such regimes. The first of these treaties, the NPT was intended to limit the spread of nuclear weapons beyond the recognized five nuclear weapon states: the United States, Britain, France, Russia, and China. The other two treaties prohibit the production and possession of chemical and biological weapons on a worldwide basis. Closely related measures include the Comprehensive Test Ban Treaty and possible negotiations directed toward terminating the production of fissile material. The NPT through the auspices of the International Atomic Energy Agency, and the CTBT through its own International Monitoring System, provide sophisticated technical capabilities and methodologies to monitor and verify compliance. Both allow the provision of information from national technical collection and analysis to inform the international community. The United States is involved quite heavily with the IAEA, and as mentioned above, has remained involved in the development of the International Monitoring System. The failure of the CTBT thus far to enter into force demonstrates that efforts to establish international norms for inhibiting proliferation can be undermined by domestic politics, national aspirations, and policy objectives which conflict with, and at times override, commitments to the international community.

Ultimately, countries tend to look to national capabilities or to their allies for security rather than to international organizations or agreements, which are often difficult to influence or control, and which at times are either too slow to act or are incapable of acting in a decisive manner. One exception to this tendency has been the negotiation of regional nuclear-weapon-free zones (NWFZs), which thus far have been adopted by the countries in Latin America, Africa, Southeast Asia, and the South Pacific. These agreements have been a boon to the nuclear nonproliferation regime. However, the regions where such treaties would offer the greatest contribution are precisely those where insecurities have already bred or are breeding efforts toward nuclear proliferation. Calls have been made for years for the establishment of NWFZs in the Middle East and South Asia. After the 1998 nuclear tests conducted by India and Pakistan, it appears to be too late for South Asia. And Iran's striving for nuclear weapon status, when added to Israel's existing nuclear arsenal, makes it highly unlikely that an agreement to ban nuclear weapons in the Middle East is achievable.[10] Nevertheless, in July 2008, forty-three nations (including Israel but not Iran) met in Paris and issued a declaration to pursue a mutually verifiable Middle East Zone free of weapons of mass destruction.[11] Given Jerusalem's policy of ambiguity regarding its own nuclear arsenal, Israel probably saw this declaration as a means of building international pressure against Iran's efforts to develop a nuclear weapon capability. Israel would be highly unlikely to actually comply with such a ban unless there was complete transparency from all others in the region, including Tehran, and a comprehensive peace treaty in place between Israel and all other countries in the region. Also, it is noteworthy that on September 8, 2006, five Central Asian nations (Uzbekistan, Tajikistan, Turkmenistan, Kazakhstan, and Kyrgystan) concluded a Central Asian Nuclear Weapon Free Zone Treaty after years of negotiation. The Treaty entered into force on December 11, 2008.

The *second* approach is commonly referred to as counterproliferation—the prevention of the proliferation of nuclear, chemical, or biological weapons by force of one kind or another, normally through international organizations. Such measures are normally effective only if applied by the United Nations Security Council or some other organization or arrangement, such as the IAEA, representing a united world community. Measures include political or diplomatic pressure, economic sanctions—most commonly applied under Chapter 7 of the UN Charter by the Security Council or by national sanctions legislation—and the use of preventive military force, such as by Israel against Iraq and Syria, as well as the United States and a selected number of other countries against the Saddam regime's occupation of Kuwait during the 1991 Gulf War which led to the dismantling of Iraq's WMD programs. Military actions, as the 2003 invasion of Iraq has demonstrated, carry with them high risk when not backed by a majority of the world community.

The *third* approach is international cooperation outside of treaty arrangements, such as the US-led Proliferation Security Initiative (see Appendix M). Such measures are not based on international legal arrangements but rather are made among like-minded states to prevent the proliferation of WMD. The measures require the capabilities to detect, attribute, monitor, interdict, and render safe suspicious and potentially dangerous materials and information being proliferated. Participating states call on their independent national (and at times cooperative) collection and analytic expertise to understand what is transpiring and then share at least some of their information with one another. An example is the US Department of Energy's material protection, control, and accounting effort designed to monitor the production, use, and storage of fissile material. And through the Proliferation Security Initiative states have agreed to cooperate to share information and intercept suspicious cargos on the high seas. It appears that the identification of such cargos generally comes from sensitive national or joint technical collection systems or human sources. In 2008, the United States was apparently able to thwart a suspected shipment of sophisticated technology from North Korea to Iran by persuading the government of India to deny clearance through Indian airspace for a North Korean aircraft. India is not a member of the Proliferation Security Initiative, but US intelligence convinced New Delhi of the importance of this move.[12] Such multinational cooperation, although not related to the Proliferation Security Initiative itself, also proved effective in terminating Libya's clandestine nuclear weapon program. Another example is cooperation arrangements among the intelligence agencies of various countries to share information on proliferation threats.

International Treaties

Nuclear Non-Proliferation Treaty. To focus efforts on nonproliferation, multinational treaties have established international norms of behavior among nations. The basic document of international nuclear nonproliferation is of course the Nuclear Non-Proliferation Treaty (NPT), which has been relatively successful (see Appendix N). The Nuclear Non-Proliferation Treaty is the centerpiece of world security and for almost four decades has been the bedrock for international norms against nuclear proliferation. The treaty is at the heart of the larger nuclear nonproliferation regime. From one standpoint, the regime seems to have inhibited some countries from acquiring a nuclear weapon capability; in other ways, it has been ineffective. Since the late 1990s, international strains stemming from the Iraqi, Iranian, and North Korean episodes have put considerable pressure on the treaty's viability as a counter to proliferation.

The primary reason that President Kennedy's concern in the early 1960s that some fifteen to twenty countries could have nuclear weapons within a decade[13] was not realized was the negotiation of the NPT and its entry into force in 1970, along with the associated extended deterrence policies—"the nuclear umbrella"—pursued by the United States and the Soviet Union during the Cold War. Indeed, since that year only five nations—beyond the original five—have acquired nuclear weapons: Israel, India, Pakistan, South Africa, and North Korea. Two, Israel and India, already had nuclear weapon programs prior to 1970, and a third, South Africa, subsequently gave up its weapons and joined the NPT as a nonnuclear weapon state. As of this writing, some 183 nations, including a few that have abandoned their nuclear weapon programs, remain committed to the principle of not acquiring nuclear weapons and remaining NPT nonnuclear weapon states—with their status verified by international inspection (although there is a serious question about the commitment of one of them—Iran). This is far from the fears expressed by President Kennedy.

Meanwhile, the refusal of India, Israel, and Pakistan to join the NPT indicated that they intended to keep open the option of becoming nuclear weapon states. This intention was confirmed when first India and then Pakistan exploded nuclear devices in 1998. Subsequently, both have declared themselves to be nuclear weapon states, even though under the NPT only five countries (China, France, Russia, the United Kingdom, and the United States) are formally recognized as such.[14] In contrast, Israel has never acknowledged having nuclear weapons, although no one doubts that Israel possesses a modern nuclear arsenal, either with no tests or possibly one having been conducted. It has intentionally pursued a policy of ambiguity to deter aggression from its neighbors while denying them an excuse to acquire their own nuclear weapons. Although Israel has never acknowledged conducting a nuclear weapon test, there is some evidence, as we mentioned in Chapter 3, that it did so in the South Atlantic with the assistance of South Africa in 1979.[15]

But the success of the NPT is no accident. It is rooted in a carefully crafted bargain whereby NPT nonnuclear weapon states agree to never acquire nuclear weapons—a major limitation on state sovereignty—in exchange for commitments by the five NPT nuclear weapon states to share peaceful nuclear technology and (pursuant to Article 6 of the treaty) to pursue the eventual elimination of their own nuclear weapon stockpiles. Prominent among these disarmament

Nuclear Nonproliferation Regime

The nuclear nonproliferation regime came into being during the Cold War as a global and regional effort to stop the spread of nuclear weapons. The "regime" represents an international norm against the possession, testing, and proliferation of nuclear weapons and their components, such as weapons-grade fissile material.

The heart of the regime has been the Nuclear Non-Proliferation Treaty (NPT), signed in 1968 and now subscribed to by 188 countries. (A total of 189 countries have joined the NPT, but North Korea withdrew from the treaty in January 2003, and Taiwan's position was taken over by the People's Republic of China in 1979; East Timor joined the NPT in 2003.) India, Israel, and Pakistan are the only states that have never signed the treaty. The NPT recognizes two categories of countries: nuclear weapon states (those that had developed and exploded a nuclear weapon as of January 1, 1967), and nonnuclear weapon states (those that had not). The treaty requires the nuclear weapon states to (1) refrain from transferring such weapons "to any recipient whatsoever," (2) share nuclear technology with nonnuclear weapon states for peaceful purposes, and (3) reduce and eventually eliminate their nuclear weapons. In return, the nonnuclear weapon states must refrain from developing or obtaining nuclear weapons, although they may pursue peaceful uses of nuclear energy, such as reactors for research or for generating power.

The NPT followed earlier treaties, which ban nuclear weapons in the Antarctic, outer space, and in Latin America. Subsequently, the NPT has been joined by other treaties codifying nuclear-weapon-free zones in Africa, Southeast Asia, the South Pacific, and most recently in Central Asia. The monitoring of nuclear facilities under the NPT was turned over to the International Atomic Energy Agency, which routinely inspects nuclear facilities declared by member states.

The NPT calls for review conferences every five years to examine the status of implementation; the next review conference is scheduled for 2010. These conferences have been used by the nonnuclear weapon states in large measure to hold the nuclear weapon states accountable for their obligations to share technology and to disarm. The treaty also allowed for a one-time opportunity after twenty-five years to extend its duration without an amendment. The NPT was extended indefinitely in 1995, and as part of the bargain to do so, the nuclear weapon states promised again, among other things, to negotiate a Comprehensive Nuclear Test Ban Treaty by 1996 and a Fissile Material Cutoff Treaty. Most countries believed that the negotiation of a CTBT would be a major contribution to the nuclear nonproliferation regime, but it has not yet entered into force, as mentioned above. Further, the Conference on Disarmament has been unable for over a decade to begin the negotiation of a FMCT.

Because the history of the NPT has been mixed and given the inherent limits of the NPT to prevent all nuclear proliferation, some countries have undertaken nonproliferation efforts outside the treaty. And in response to the UN Security Council's Resolution 1540, calling on all states to take measures to prevent proliferation to terrorists, other unilateral or cooperative measures may be undertaken in the future.

obligations, and recognized as such at the signing of the NPT in 1968, are a nuclear test-ban treaty prohibiting all nuclear weapon tests and an agreement to terminate the production of nuclear weapon explosive material—or fissile material—also on a global basis. As explained above, the first of these, the Comprehensive Nuclear Test Ban Treaty, has been negotiated but as yet has not entered into force. The second, the Fissile Material Cutoff Treaty, has not yet been negotiated. These two measures, if achieved, would contribute greatly to nonproliferation efforts through their provisions and through strengthening the nuclear nonproliferation regime by fulfilling, at least in part, the obligations of Article 6 of the NPT.

Convention on the Prohibition of Chemical Weapons. With the collapse of the Soviet Union and the end of the Cold War, the international community was able to begin considering and eventually to negotiate a convention banning the stockpiling and use of chemical agents and offensive weapons. The Chemical Weapons Convention (CWC) was completed in 1993 and entered into force in 1997. The Organization for the Prevention of Chemical Weapons (OPCW) was established in The Hague to monitor the implementation of the convention, which calls for intrusive, routine, and challenge international inspections.

The CWC prohibits on a worldwide basis the possession, manufacture, and use of chemical weapons (such as poison gas). The CWC consists of twenty-four articles and two annexes, the Annex on Implementation and Verification and the Annex on the Protection of Confidential Information. Article 1 mirrors the first article of the Biological and Toxin Weapons Convention (BWC) in that each party undertakes "never in any circumstances" to develop, acquire, and retain chemical weapons—even if attacked by another state using chemical weapons. Thus, it is a universal prohibition intended to apply to all states everywhere. The CWC defines chemical weapons as toxic chemicals or their precursors. It establishes a broad on-site inspection process, providing for intrusive on-site inspections while protecting sensitive facilities through a system of managed access.

Article 3 of the CWC requires states parties to make declarations of their inventories of chemical weapons and production facilities, and Article 4 provides for the destruction of such weapons and facilities. Article 1 extends the prohibition on weapons to engagement in military preparations for the use of chemical weapons, such as troop training, required if chemical weapons are to be intelligently used in the field of battle. Such preparations are largely verifiable.

Article 4 requires the destruction of chemical weapons and facilities to begin two years after entry into force and be completed no later than ten years after entry into force. Meeting this obligation has been a particular problem for Russia, given the vast stockpile created by the Soviet Union. The declaration and destruction of declared weapons and facilities are to be verified pursuant to the Verification Annex, which details provisions for on-site inspection, including challenge inspections with managed access. "Managed access" means that if sensitive facilities are declared by the party to be inspected, then the parameters of the on-site inspection are to be negotiated so as to protect the party's unrelated sensitive facilities.

Pursuant to Article 8 of the treaty, the states parties established the CWC implementing body, the Organization for the Prohibition of Chemical Weapons. The Executive Council of the OPCW (composed of forty-one members with worldwide geographic balance) addresses compliance issues, regulates the conduct of inspections, and oversees the day-to-day management of the OPCW. The OPCW technical secretariat actually conducts the inspections called for by the CWC. Each state party has the right to submit an on-site challenge inspection request to the council. If a request meets the requirements set forth in the Verification Annex, the party to be inspected must allow the technical secretariat to conduct the inspection pursuant to the rules of the Inspection Annex. The inspection will go forward unless within twelve hours of receiving the inspection request the Executive Council decides by a three-quarters vote to disallow it. If the OPCW decides, however, that an act of noncompliance has taken place, the ultimate appeal for action (as with the IAEA board with respect to nuclear issues) is to the UN Security Council.

Most observers consider the convention to be a deterrent to a country that might want to possess such weapons, but as discussed in Chapter 2, it is unlikely to prevent countries bent on pursuing such weapons from doing so clandestinely. To date, there have been no challenge inspections of suspected countries because of the international political sensitivities of even hinting that a country may be involved in suspect activities that are inconsistent with the convention.[16] Moreover, as of the tenth anniversary of the convention in 2007, six parties (Albania, India, Libya, Russia, South Korea, and the United States) were believed to still possess chemical weapon stockpiles. The deadline for eliminating all inventories was April 2007, but various difficulties, such as finances, are hampering this objective. Russia has the largest stockpile, and some see it as a security concern for the international community.[17]

Biological and Toxin Weapons Convention. The international effort to ban the production and possession of biological and toxin weapons was concluded in a convention, which entered into force in 1975. Unlike the CWC, the BWC does not ban the "use" of biological weapons; such a ban was adopted in the 1925 Geneva Protocol. However, unlike the CWC, the BWC was never given verification teeth to enforce its ban on possession. When the Soviets' clandestine biological weapon program was finally acknowledged in the early 1990s following the collapse of the Soviet Union (see Chapter 3), the international community tried to negotiate a verification protocol that would make the ban more credible and enforceable.

With the precedent of the Chemical Weapons Convention, a multinational effort began in Geneva to develop an on-site inspection protocol for the BWC. Six years of negotiations on a BWC verification and enforcement protocol led to the tabling of a draft by an ad hoc group of states in 1999. After further negotiation, a vote was scheduled for all BWC parties in November 2001 on the proposed protocol, which called for routine plant inspections by four-person teams on two weeks' notice. These efforts in Geneva were spurred by the revelation after the 1991 Gulf War of Iraq's sizable undertaking to develop biological weapons, combined with the confirmation in the early 1990s that the Soviet Union had continued a huge biological weapon program in massive violation of its BWC obligations. Nevertheless, by the summer of 2001, the new Bush administration decided at the last minute that an intrusive system of inspections and verification would be ineffective—and detrimental to the US pharmaceutical industry. When Washington refused to give its consent, the proposals collapsed. As a consequence, the convention continues without significant enforcement, although the United States and other countries have tried to come up with alternatives for holding states accountable to their obligations.[18]

The BWC declares that states parties will "never under any circumstances" develop or acquire "biological agents or toxins . . . of types and in quantities" that cannot be justified for "prophylactic, protective or other peaceful purposes" as well as equipment to use such agents for hostile purposes. Thus, whether a biological agent qualifies as a biological weapon is based on whether it is possessed in types and amounts that have no apparent justification for peaceful purposes.

As mentioned above, the BWC contains no real verification provisions; a state party to the convention has the right only to lodge a complaint of a detected violation with the UN Security Council, and all parties are to cooperate

---

Russia's Clandestine Biological Weapon Program

Five years after the BWC entered into force and just weeks before the first review conference was to take place in 1980, the international community learned that an explosion had occurred in a laboratory in Sverdlovsk (now Ekaterinburg), which apparently released deadly anthrax spores and caused a number of deaths. Anthrax is a primary biological weapon agent, and this information suggested that the Soviets were violating the BWC. The United States learned of this violation essentially through intelligence means—the interview of defectors. The review conference was held just a few weeks later, and the United States raised the issue with vigor. The Soviets denied the event, of course, and claimed that no one had contracted anthrax, but rather the illness that had spread was something they called Siberian ulcer.[19]

Other than the charges and countercharges, not much was accomplished at this first BWC review conference, but the issue of Soviet compliance was joined, and the United States had considerable support from the other BWC parties at the conference. The Sverdlovsk issue was discussed again at the second Review Conference of the BWC in 1986. At that conference the United States alleged Soviet involvement in the production, transfer, and use of myotoxins as weapons of war (the poisonous "yellow rain" in Southeast Asia) and that the Soviet Union maintained an offensive biological warfare program in direct violation of the BWC.

Finally, in the early 1990s following the breakup of the Soviet Union, irrefutable evidence was publicly revealed that the USSR had secretly and massively violated the BWC and had in place a vast offensive biological weapon development and production establishment. Russian President Boris Yeltsin acknowledged that the Soviet Union had been in violation of the BWC from the very beginning and had constructed a huge, illegal infrastructure. Negotiations with the Russian government in the 1990s led to gradual immobilization of the program and to partial conversion of the infrastructure to peaceful purposes. The episode reignited international efforts to create a verification regime for the BWC. However, the international community has yet to devise a verification approach that is both effective and acceptable to all—most significantly to the United States because of the intrusive measures it would entail.[20]

---

with any investigation the Security Council may order. Thus, the BWC adds little to the effort to control the proliferation of weapons of mass destruction, except for the international norm it attempts to establish, which is designed to prohibit biological weapons to all states.

Comprehensive Nuclear Test Ban Treaty. During the mid-1990s, the interna-

tional community also made an effort to reinforce a norm against the proliferation of nuclear weapons by negotiating a total ban on any type of nuclear
explosion, in any environment, in all locations. The CTBT was seen as the logi-
cal successor to previous international agreements that had banned nuclear
explosions in outer space, in the atmosphere, and under water as well as limited
the size of nuclear weapon tests and restricted all subsequent testing to below
ground. The pressure to negotiate such a ban had increased dramatically after the end of the Cold War as the nonnuclear weapon states under the NPT
wanted to hold the five nuclear weapon states, especially the United States and
Russia, accountable to their NPT promise to work toward total denuclearization and, in particular, a comprehensive ban on nuclear tests. The nonnuclear
weapon states saw the effort as a disarmament initiative, while the nuclear
weapon states saw it more as counterproliferation. The United States and Russia were finally willing to engage in such a negotiation in large measure because
the end of the Cold War had made the banning of nuclear testing something
the two superpowers could consider with less risk to their national security.

The pressure to achieve a total ban on testing reached its climax during the
negotiation of the indefinite extension of the Nuclear Non-Proliferation Treaty
in the spring of 1995. As part of the inducement to achieve this extension, the
nuclear weapon states promised to negotiate a comprehensive ban on testing
by 1996. The treaty was concluded by the Conference on Disarmament in Geneva in August 1996, and it was seen by most countries as a major accomplishment after decades of efforts to move beyond partial test bans. However, the
euphoria and optimism of the international community was dashed, first by
India's refusal in 1996 to go along (later joined by Pakistan and North Korea)
and then by the rejection of the treaty in 1999 by the US Senate.

Consistent with its long-standing refusal to join the NPT, India began showing signs of opposing the CTBT during the latter stage of negotiations, despite
its intense involvement in those negotiations. By the early summer of 1996,
India stated that it could not support the treaty being negotiated and called
it non-comprehensive (because it permitted the "subcritical" testing of nonnuclear bomb components) and discriminatory against nonnuclear weapon
states. After failing to prevent the passing of the treaty text to the United Nations in New York for a vote by the General Assembly, India fought a losing
battle to prevent the General Assembly from adopting the treaty in September
1996 and opening it up for signature. In the end, only Iraq and Bhutan voted
with India to oppose opening the CTBT for signature. Pakistan announced that

it could not join the treaty unless India did, and North Korea announced that it refused to join, too, in solidarity with India.[21]

Most observers believed that India's opposition to both the NPT and CTBT was based on holding out the option of testing and becoming a nuclear weapon state. Any doubt was erased when in May 1998 India tested several nuclear devices and announced to the world that it was now a nuclear weapon state. Pakistan, not to be left behind, within days tested several nuclear devices of its own. Both nations have thus become de facto nuclear weapon states, although under the NPT neither is granted that status by the international community. Nevertheless, both have proven that clandestine nuclear weapon programs can proceed, and succeed, even in the face of an international norm against such efforts, in this case established by the NPT. Furthermore, North Korea eventually followed through on its opposition to the CTBT by testing a nuclear device in the fall of 2006. The three countries demonstrate that international efforts to monitor and prevent nuclear proliferation have had only a limited effect. A country's national security concerns and aspirations often appear to prevail over a commitment to collective security and international norms.

India, Pakistan, and North Korea are not alone to blame for the international community's failure to inhibit nuclear proliferation through the CTBT. After the United States led the charge during treaty negotiations and then during the early years of implementing the treaty's provisions, the Senate, as noted earlier, shocked the world in the fall of 1999 by refusing to consent to the treaty's ratification. The failure to follow through was in part due to substantive concerns but most immediately because of domestic political issues between President Clinton and the Republican-controlled Senate.[22] The result was the elimination of pressure on India and others to join the treaty. Prior to this the hope had been that having proven their nuclear capabilities through testing, India (and then Pakistan) would be ready to sign; significant efforts had been made to bring India and Pakistan on board prior to the fall of 1999. The treaty continues to languish in a semicomatose state because by its own terms it cannot enter into force until the United States, along with several other holdouts, sign and ratify it. Meanwhile, because the United States for the past half-dozen years has chosen not to fund its whole portion of the annual costs associated with treaty implementation, it is significantly behind in its financial obligations to the CTBTO Preparatory Commission, and has lost its voting rights.[23]

With the failure of the CTBT to enter into force, the failure to initiate negotiations on a Fissile Material Cutoff Treaty, and the failure to provide an effective verification provision to the BWC, the international community has lost further ground in its effort to strengthen the nuclear nonproliferation regime. This and the failure of international efforts to prevent Iran (and North Korea) from developing nuclear weapon capabilities has taken some of the steam out of the international nuclear nonproliferation effort, and some believe that the NPT has been seriously weakened.

The United States has not conducted a nuclear test since its self-imposed suspension of testing in 1992, but it nevertheless has a large advantage over the rest of the world in the sophistication of its nuclear arsenal and the depth of knowledge of its nuclear scientists. This advantage was developed by conducting 1,054 announced nuclear explosive tests (greater than the combined total of nuclear tests conducted by the rest of the world) and translates into a nuclear force of unmatched effectiveness. The Soviet Union/Russia conducted 715 tests; France, 210; and China, 45. Britain, which has had access to US test data, also has conducted 45 tests. Thus, many argue that the United States can and should support the entry into force of the Comprehensive Nuclear Test Ban Treaty, which establishes a complete and verifiable ban throughout the world on all nuclear test explosions and provides for a vast international monitoring system composed of hundreds of seismic stations and other technical stations spread around the globe. Op-ed articles authored by senior statesmen George Shultz, William Perry, Sam Nunn, and Henry Kissinger and supported by other former senior officials appeared on January 4, 2007, and January 15, 2008, and argued for the CTBT's entry into force along with a number of other steps that support a stronger NPT—and an eventual nuclear-weapon-free world.[24]

Were the CTBT to come into force, it would advance significantly the effort to halt the proliferation of nuclear weapons. Entry into force of the CTBT would largely inhibit the acquisition of reliable nuclear weapons by additional states. Countries could still develop crude, difficult-to-deliver, Hiroshima-type nuclear weapons without testing. But in advanced nuclear weapon states a nuclear explosive testing program involving full-scale testing is normally necessary to prove the reliability of newly designed nuclear weapons, which are extremely complex. No responsible political leadership, no competent modern military authority, and no nation depending on nuclear weapons for its security could be expected to deploy a modern nuclear weapon without a full-scale test program. In terms of US security concerns, the CTBT would significantly inhibit the introduction of new advanced weapons into the stockpiles of Russia and China and other states with nuclear weapon programs. Nevertheless, we expect the effort by the Obama administration to push for ratification will lead to a lively debate between those who favor the CTBT and those who will continue to argue that a total ban on testing is incompatible with US security interests.

Fissile Material Cutoff Treaty. An international treaty prohibiting all states from additional—or new—production of fissile material (highly enriched uranium or plutonium) to fuel nuclear weapons would also inhibit the proliferation of nuclear weapons. As mentioned earlier, a fissile material cutoff treaty was an important measure considered for Article 6 at the signing of the NPT in 1968, and was listed as one of the nonproliferation and disarmament commitments made in exchange for the indefinite extension of the NPT in 1995. Despite the calls for action, the treaty's negotiation has been stalemated at the Geneva disarmament negotiations for over a decade, even though the NPT nuclear weapon states have all terminated production. The current problems essentially are twofold. First, India and Pakistan refuse to agree to negotiate such a ban, and states such as China and Russia are unwilling to enter into binding legal agreements and commitments not to produce fissile material unless India and Pakistan stop production. Second, the United States under the Bush administration called the verification measures being proposed for such a treaty to be ineffective. Although an FMCT is a promising tool for nonproliferation, its short-term prospects are bleak given the lack of will of key countries, particularly China, India, and Pakistan, to move forward. It is unclear how the Obama administration will deal with this issue.

Other Counterproliferation Measures

Political pressure, sanctions, and preventive military force make up the other options for counterproliferation approaches.

Preventive Military Force. The 1981 Israeli attack on the Iraqi Osiraq reactor and the inspections in Iraq following the 1991 Gulf War by a united international community put an end, at least temporarily, to Saddam's ambitions to acquire nuclear weapons and other weapons of mass destruction. After extensive inspections following the US invasion of Iraq in 2003, the world learned that sanctions and enforcement measures adopted by the UN Security Council following the 1991 Gulf War had successfully eliminated the Iraqi nuclear infrastructure. More recently, Israel's destruction of the suspected nuclear reactor in northern Syria in September 2007 demonstrated the use of preventive military force to stop proliferation. However, if Damascus is committed to developing a nuclear weapon program, it likely will try another route to achieve its objective.

As the case of Iraq has shown, military intervention in a world that supports the concept of international law can be truly effective only if supported by the international community. And military force should only be used in extremity, as routine gunboat diplomacy—even if backed by the UN Security Council—would eventually lose its effectiveness since resistance would grow in response to frequent use. The entire world condemned the Israeli strike on Iraq's reactor in 1981. Although the strike was effective in setting back the Iraqi program for a few years, it ultimately drove the Iraqi nuclear weapon program underground, and by 1990, the program was not broadly understood as being a threat. Responding to Iraq's invasion of Kuwait gave the international community another chance to eliminate the Iraqi nuclear weapon program by force. Unfortunately as mentioned in Chapter 5, the community allowed Saddam to refuse the resumption of UN inspections in 1998, which in principle freed him to reconstitute his nuclear program as well as his chemical and biological weapons programs. Nevertheless, as mentioned in Chapters 3 and 5, the United States was unable to gain wide support for its military intervention in Iraq in 2003. The US case was not seen as persuasive, and few countries viewed Saddam's Iraq as a severe threat requiring military action.

Political Pressure and Sanctions. These two methods are closely allied and have had mixed results. They were successful in deterring Taiwan and South Korea from pursuing nuclear weapons in the 1970s. Gradually, political pressure, accompanied by national sanctions in the context of sound diplomacy, appears to be reducing and hopefully permanently eliminating the proliferation threat presented by Libya and, to some extent, North Korea. However, China's and South Korea's lack of full support in applying sanctions to North Korea has diluted the effectiveness of those sanctions.

Meanwhile, international sanctions on Iran, voted for three times by the UN Security Council—and accompanied by national sanctions from the United States and a few other countries—have been thus far ineffective in significantly inhibiting Iran's nuclear program. If Russia and China had been willing to support serious sanctions, the impact of sanctions would likely have been different. With South Africa and Libya it appears that sanctions in place for many years contributed to each country's decision to end its nuclear weapon programs.

International Cooperation

Beyond multilateral treaty arrangements, other forms of international cooperation can contribute to effective policies. For example, cooperation among intelligence agencies from various countries in sharing and seeking information has been an important ingredient in US national security for many years. Intelligence sharing between Britain and the United States proved to be invaluable in the denuclearization of Libya. In another arena, the United States' effort to persuade countries that possess research reactors fueled by highly enriched uranium to convert to low enriched uranium, which cannot be used for weapons, is having marked success. Although the initiative remains a significant challenge, within a few years the conversion of reactors could be complete and a positive step in promoting nonproliferation will have been taken.

The world has now realized, after the exposure of the illegal black market nuclear proliferation ring headed by the senior Pakistani scientist Abdul Qadeer Khan, that innocent-appearing commercial activities can be used to disguise proliferation activities. Partly in response to this, as stated earlier, the United States has organized through the Proliferation Security Initiative (PSI) a good number of important seafaring countries to interdict suspicious shipments on the high seas. Although not an accomplishment of the PSI, a shipment of nuclear technology from Malaysia to Libya on the vessel *BBC China* was interdicted as a result of alert cooperative action by the CIA and MI6. This action led to the exposure and eventual abandonment of the Libyan nuclear program.

The PSI is not an organization; rather it is a multilateral arrangement among sovereign seafaring countries to carry out interdictions under the general policy guidance of UN Security Council Resolution 1540, which also was initiated and promoted by the United States to counter proliferation to terrorists. The resolution makes it illegal on an international basis to provide any support to non-state actors in acquiring weapons of mass destruction and calls on all states to adopt national measures to prevent the proliferation of WMD. It includes export controls to impede the acquisition of nuclear weapons and make it illegal for private subjects (such as terrorists) to develop WMD. It is too early to judge the effectiveness of the Proliferation Security Initiative itself, but unquestionably such arrangements have a place in the list of international tools to inhibit proliferation. Some countries, however, fear that the PSI may be used as a mechanism to bless the unilateral use of military force. (For more information on the PSI and Resolution 1540, see Appendixes M and O.)

Bilateral Negotiations. Finally, bilateral negotiations with proliferating countries are at times possible but have had limited success. During the Cold War, the United States provided security guarantees to its allies under its nuclear umbrella. This influenced a number of countries to forego nuclear weapons. However, the United States has seen how bilateral negotiations with North Korea, particularly the Framework Agreement of 1994, have fallen short of expectations. It became apparent that negotiation needed to include the other key players in the region—China, Japan, Russia, and South Korea. Thus, the Bush administration insisted on the Six-Party Talks as the primary method to achieve the denuclearization of North Korea, although the administration also ultimately agreed to limited bilateral discussions with North Korea as part of the Six-Party negotiations. With regard to Iran, the Bush administration avoided participation in or support for negotiations for a number of years; however, it finally supported multilateral negotiations led by members of the European Union to deal with Iran's nuclear weapon program. However, neither these negotiations nor UN Security Council sanctions have halted Iran's drive toward a nuclear weapon capability. Needless to say, conducting negotiations— bilateral or multilateral—with international terrorists is not a viable option for most countries, certainly not for the United States.

International Organizations

United Nations Security Council. In discussing the contribution of international organizations and treaty regimes to constraining the proliferation of weapons of mass destruction, we must first consider the role of the United Nations Security Council. The Council is the primary source of world community influence in the field of nonproliferation of weapons of mass destruction. It is also the principal means of enforcement of international treaty obligations designed to prevent proliferation.

After the Cold War the president of the Security Council issued a statement—not the same as a resolution of the Council but a formal statement nonetheless—that the proliferation of WMD is a threat to world peace. This position established, among other things, the basis for applying sanctions on countries in accordance with Chapter 7 of the UN Charter to enforce obligations of international nonproliferation treaty arrangements and to support the underlying policies of those treaties. As mentioned, in 2004 the Council adopted Resolution 1540, which calls on all members of the United Nations to adopt appropriate national laws to prevent the proliferation of weapons of mass destruction to terrorists. The resolution supports the Proliferation Security Initiative and other comparable regimes to come in the future. However, to date UN members have been slow to respond, and it is not possible to determine what impact the resolution has had on inhibiting the proliferation of WMD to terrorists. Nevertheless, the UN Security Council agreed in 2008 to extend the 1540 Committee, which was established to collect and report on country submissions, for an additional three years.[25]

The Security Council's track record in dealing with proliferation by nation-states is mixed. In the aftermath of the 1991 Gulf War and pursuant to Resolution 687 (adopted in April 1991), the council required the elimination of all weapons and infrastructure in Iraq associated with WMD, and established the UN Special Commission (UNSCOM) to implement this task with respect to chemical and biological weapons while calling on the IAEA to carry out the assignment with respect to Iraq's nuclear program. The IAEA and UNSCOM operated in Iraq from 1992 until 1998, when Iraq prevented them from continuing (see Chapter 5), but they were confident that virtually all of the Iraqi chemical and biological weapons and associated infrastructure, as well as all of its nuclear weapon infrastructure, had been eliminated. Nevertheless, according to then IAEA Director-General Hans Blix, many things remained unaccounted for.[26] When in 2002 Saddam again faced the threat of international military action against his country, he allowed UN inspectors to resume inspections. As in the past, he tried to use concealment and denial techniques to mask his secret facilities and activities, although according to Blix on no occasion were inspectors denied access to sites they asked to visit.[27] The United States and a few other countries believed that Saddam was in fact hiding from UN inspectors and the international community WMD efforts he had resumed since 1998.

The case of North Korea was brought to the UNSC by a vote of the board of the International Atomic Energy Agency. The IAEA had on several occasions requested an inspection (in part based on US intelligence) of two suspicious waste storage areas (once in late 1992 and twice in early 1993), which had not been cited in the safeguards declaration by North Korea as required. North Korea had signed the Safeguards Agreement with the IAEA only in early 1992. All three requests were refused by North Korea. Director-General Blix then requested a board resolution insisting on such an inspection. Prior to its vote on February 25, 1993, the IAEA board accepted intelligence provided by the United States as a legitimate basis for international verification. The board resolution called on North Korea to permit "full and prompt" implementation of the Safeguards Agreement including the requested inspection. This was rejected by North Korea the next day. On March 12, North Korea announced that it was withdrawing from the NPT, giving the required ninety days' notice. On April 1, 1993, after North Korea rejected another request to inspect the two waste storage sites, the IAEA board declared that it could not verify that there had been no diversion of safeguarded nuclear material and instructed Blix to report this finding to the UNSC. Reflecting the view that North Korea should not be pushed into a corner, China voted against the board resolution thereby implying it would veto a sanctions decision in the council.

The consideration by the UN Security Council of the North Korean case raised the possibility of a major public debate in the council on the subject of Chapter 7 sanctions, even though China made clear that it was not inclined to support sanctions. However, not long after the board decision, the United States and North Korea signaled to each other that they were prepared to negotiate. North Korea's NPT withdrawal statement had left the door open to this and had hinted at compromise. The United States offered to hold high-level talks with North Korea, and the offer was accepted. The talks began at the US mission to the United Nations in Geneva on June 2, and an agreement in principle was reached on June 11, 1993, a day before the North Korean withdrawal from the NPT would have become effective. It was clear that North Korea did not want to leave the NPT nor be the subject of a sanctions debate in the United Nations. The IAEA verification and enforcement process was thus partially effective, but many years of uncertainty and crisis lay ahead.[28] The negotiations that began in June 1993 led to the Framework Agreement in 1994, which kept the peace for a time. But there would not have been a successful outcome to the negotiation—indeed, there might have been war with North Korea—but for the intervention of former President Jimmy Carter. Carter traveled to Pyongyang and told the North Korean dictator, alone among his American interlocutors, what would happen if he did cooperate with the United States, as opposed to what would happen if he didn't.[29] It is important to note that the progress made on the North Korean nuclear issues in recent years has been in the context of the Six-Party Talks, not the UN Security Council.

With regard to Iran, the council has three times voted for Chapter 7 sanctions: first in December 2006, then in March 2007, and most recently in early 2008. The sanctions are largely financial and travel restrictions, which are focused on particular individuals and organizations, and an arms embargo added by the second sanctions resolution. The rationale for these sanctions is Iran's failure to properly report the acquisition of uranium enrichment capability, which is required by its NPT Safeguards Agreement with the IAEA, and its subsequent refusal to suspend its current enrichment activities, pending negotiations. The Iranian case was placed on the agenda of the council by the IAEA board in a divided vote with several abstentions in February 2006. Thus far the UN Security Council's sanctions have had no effect on Iran, and in fact have led to a hardening of Iran's position.

At times, however, the United Nations is unable to take decisive action. In the 1990s the United States deemed military intervention into violently disintegrating Yugoslavia (on the borders of NATO) to be essential to national security, even though the United Kingdom, along with other European countries, opposed such intervention for a long time. It was not possible to undertake such action pursuant to a UN Security Council mandate given the threat of a Russian veto. Finally, NATO, as a regional security organization, took action.

Action by the United Nations is possible only when key countries are in agreement. Within the UN Security Council, the Permanent Five members have the right of veto; as sovereign states, they normally put their own national interests ahead of what many might consider the world's bests interests. At the same time, the United Nations can act as a constraint on the unilateral action of member countries. In the case of Iraq, the United States was unsuccessful in late 2002 and early 2003 in getting UN agreement to dislodge Saddam by force, so it sought support by selected countries outside the United Nations.

In dealing with proliferation to terrorists, the adoption of Resolution 1540 by the United Nations in 2004 was an unprecedented step to register an international norm against the spread of WMD among non-state actors, especially international terrorists. Of course, such a resolution can only be as effective as individual states are willing to adhere to the letter and spirit of the text. As of mid-2007, 137 of the UN members had complied with the resolution and submitted the required national reports on implementation. However, Iran and North Korea were among the remaining states that had not submitted such reports.[30] (For the text of UNSC Resolution 1540, see Appendix O.)

International Atomic Energy Agency. After the NPT's entry into force in 1970, the IAEA was given an important monitoring role in the treaty's effort to prevent the proliferation of nuclear weapons. As the implementing body for the treaty's verification system, the IAEA was charged to detect any diversion of nuclear materials from peaceful to weapon use by states parties. Article 3 of the NPT requires each nonnuclear weapon state party to the treaty to accept safeguards set forth in an agreement negotiated and concluded in accordance with the agency's safeguards system. Further, to allay the concerns of nonnuclear weapon states parties that having IAEA safeguards on their nuclear facilities might place them at a commercial disadvantage, the nuclear weapon states parties over time have negotiated voluntary safeguards for their civil nuclear facilities, even though there was no issue of diversion because these states already possessed nuclear weapons. Even the nonsignatories to the NPT (India, Pakistan, and Israel) submitted to at least some of the old declared facility-related inspections by the IAEA.

Over time the IAEA built up a highly effective inspectorate, which has been supported by intelligence provided by various member states. Since 1970, only one country that became an NPT nonnuclear weapon state party—North Korea—has developed weapons, and that country's program had been suspicious from the start. North Korea joined the NPT in 1985 under pressure from the Soviet Union, but its IAEA Safeguards Agreement was only completed and signed in January 1992. Just a few months later, in late 1992, the IAEA first requested inspection of the two waste storage sites in North Korea—which were not declared as required by the Safeguards Agreement—and as explained earlier, this action led some months later to North Korea's move to withdraw from the NPT. North Korea rescinded this withdrawal, but a decade later (in early 2003) it finally carried out its withdrawal from the NPT.

One problem always has been that the original IAEA safeguards only verified the correctness of a country's declaration; getting information on activities beyond declared facilities, therefore, largely depended on monitoring efforts by member states. Under the original authorities the IAEA could inspect essentially only declared facilities, such as power and research reactors, and nowhere else. To address this limitation after the discovery of Iraq's advanced nuclear weapon program following the 1991 Gulf War and the decision to indefinitely extend the NPT in 1995, which included a commitment to improved verification, a Model Additional Protocol on NPT verification was negotiated and adopted by the IAEA in 1997 for NPT states parties to follow. The protocol is negotiated by the IAEA bilaterally with each country. Intended to verify the "completeness" of a country's declaration, it will significantly improve NPT verification as it becomes more widely accepted by expanding the authority to conduct off-site inspections; for example, sampling river water to disclose upstream nuclear activity. On the whole, the IAEA-managed NPT verification system has worked well supplemented by the efforts of national intelligence

Intelligence Support to International Inspections

Intelligence support to the IAEA by various member states has been critical to the success of many of its inspections but at times has created political tensions. During the Iraqi WMD episode a seeming conflict arose between what UN, and to some extent IAEA, inspection teams were reporting about the status of Iraq's programs prior to March 2003 and what the US Intelligence Community was telling US policymakers. Members of the UN Security Council were trying to decide what to conclude about Saddam's WMD efforts given the differences between UNMOVIC's reports and US statements exemplified by Secretary of State Colin Powell's presentation to the council on February 5, 2003. This begs for some explanation of how the United States (and presumably other countries) supported, and benefited from, the inspections particularly with regard to intelligence.

It appears to be standard practice for member states of the IAEA to provide national intelligence to support international inspections. Indeed, diplomats having good contacts with the IAEA reported in early April 2008 that even China had provided intelligence linked to Iran's alleged attempts to make nuclear weapons. They commented that China was the most surprising entry among a fairly substantial list of nations recently forwarding information to the IAEA that adds to previously provided intelligence on Iran's nuclear weapon research.[31] The IAEA apparently expects member countries to provide national information to help its international inspections be more effective. In April 2008, some seven months after Israel had destroyed an alleged nuclear facility in northern Syria (see Chapter 3), IAEA Director-General Mohamed ElBaradei complained that the United States and Israel had failed to notify his agency in a timely manner of their concerns about the facility and North Korea's alleged assistance. The evidence apparently consisted of photographs from ground level and from satellites after the Israeli strike. ElBaradei stated that Israel's unilateral use of force had undermined the due process of verification that is at the heart of the nonproliferation regime. In response to ElBaradei's complaint, a US intelligence team was reportedly sent to Vienna to brief the IAEA.[32]

As reported by Hans Blix, US intelligence had not only provided intelligence information to UNSCOM inspections in Iraq during the 1991–98 period to help guide the inspectors, but US intelligence officers had actually participated in some of the inspections. Blix indicated that the head of UNSCOM, Rolf Ekeus, tried to prevent his inspections from being covers for intelligence collection. Blix believes that the direct participation of US intelligence officers was unwise given that it risked the integrity and credibility of UN inspections.[33] He suspects that some of the Iraqis' resistance to inspections can be explained by their awareness that intelligence-linked inspectors might help identify targets for bombing. Richard Clarke, former US National Security Council official, has asserted that he and Robert Gallucci actually prepared one of the UNSCOM inspections to ensure that it focused on the correct sites and facilities.[34]

Considerable discussion subsequently arose in the press about US intelligence's use of the inspections. Scott Ritter, who had led many of the inspections, publicly testified to the presence of US intelligence officers at inspections. It appears that the UN Security Council finally reacted to these reports when it authorized the establishment of the United Nations Monitoring, Verification and Inspection Commission (UNMOVIC), which Blix headed, to resume inspections in Iraq in 2002–3. In drafting Resolution 1284, which set up UNMOVIC, the council stipulated that inspections staff should be international civil servants, who should not take instructions from any government.[35]

Blix's sentiments are correct and commendable: all countries benefit (except perhaps those that are objects of inspections) when the integrity of UN operations is maintained. Unfortunately, almost all countries also try to benefit from inspections to gain intelligence for their national decision making, and this can lead to attempts to influence the staffing and operation of inspections. When a country has no "on the ground" presence, as with the United States in Iraq during most of the 1990s, international inspections offer a unique opportunity to collect information firsthand. Furthermore, when there is good reason to suspect that the inspected country is using every means to conceal and to deceive inspectors, motivation is strong to ensure that suspicious sites and facilities are in fact inspected and that all means are used to defeat the inspected country's countermeasures. Finally, it is only realistic that the international staff of operations such as UNSCOM and UNMOVIC, which were essentially information-gathering "intelligence" activities (albeit sanctioned by the United Nations), includes officers with intelligence experience from a number of the countries represented. But there is a difference between intelligence experience and an inspector who continues to follow guidance from his home country.

agencies, which share nuclear proliferation information with the IAEA and elsewhere. Concern over the nuclear program in Iran, as noted earlier, surfaced in 2002 with a report by the National Council of Resistance of Iran—itself a former terrorist organization in Iran and by the time of the disclosure virtually a wholly owned subsidiary of Iraq. Iranian activity turned out to be in violation of the reporting provision in Iran's original IAEA Safeguards Agreement.

International Atomic Energy Agency's Nuclear Monitoring

The IAEA was created in 1957, following President Eisenhower's "Atoms for Peace" address to the UN General Assembly in 1953, to address three issues: nuclear verification, security and safety, and technology transfer. With the negotiation of the NPT in 1968, the international community turned to the IAEA to be the primary monitor of peaceful nuclear activities around the world.

The safeguards included in the IAEA's statute were designed chiefly to cover individual nuclear facilities and stockpiles of fissile material declared by member states. However, the discovery in 1991 of Iraq's clandestine nuclear weapon program demonstrated the inadequacy of the safeguards, and IAEA members agreed to take steps to enhance NPT safeguards to deal with possible undeclared nuclear activities. The additional measures have been accepted by many NPT parties, but not all; as of January 21, 2009, the number of NPT states parties that had ratified additional protocols based on the 1997 IAEA Model Additional Protocol was 90 out of 188.[36] Another 29 countries have signed but not ratified. India, Israel, and Pakistan, not being signatories to the NPT, have not accepted full-scope safeguards under the IAEA; and as stated earlier, in 2003 North Korea withdrew from both the NPT and the IAEA.

The United States has favored the additional measures and put pressure on other countries, such as Iran, to comply. In a speech at the National Defense University in February 2004, President George W. Bush urged all NPT parties to ratify the additional protocol to their NPT safeguards agreements and announced that the United States would actively seek its own ratification. But in spite of all the rhetoric over the years, the United States only finally ratified its additional protocol on January 6, 2009. There was no evidence of opposition within the United States; the slowness by the Bush administration was probably due to the bureaucratic process and competing priorities in the White House and Senate. Now all NPT nuclear weapon states have ratified the protocol.

Despite UN Security Council calls for the denuclearization of North Korea, Pyongyang has only intermittently allowed IAEA inspectors to monitor its nuclear facilities. Following the Framework Agreement with the United States and South Korea in 1994, North Korea allowed the IAEA to conduct a baseline inspection of the Yongbyon nuclear reactor and to place seals on its reprocessing equipment. However, when that agreement fell apart after the meeting with Assistant Secretary of State James Kelly in October 2002, North Korea halted the inspections, removed the seals, and resumed the reprocessing of plutonium.

It also withdrew from participation with the IAEA and from the NPT in early 2003.

In more recent years, the UNSC and the IAEA have been increasingly concerned about Iran's circumventing its NPT obligations by developing the capability to enrich uranium to a weapons-grade level. Iran has refused to adhere to international calls for compliance, arguing that under the NPT it has the right to enrich uranium. This is true, at least to the low level required for power reactors, but it exposes a problem in the NPT and the nuclear nonproliferation regime. IAEA Director-General ElBaradei has acknowledged this so-called loophole and called for multinational enrichment activities that will prevent individual countries from taking advantage of the situation.[37] Subsequently, in a joint article, ElBaradei and Norwegian Minister of Foreign Affairs Jonas Gahr Støre claimed that "if all enrichment operations were brought under multinational control, it would become far more difficult for any country to divert enriched uranium for use in weapons." In addition, they called for highly enriched uranium in research reactors to be returned to the countries of origin for downblending and reuse and for an international agreement to halt the production of further fissile material for nuclear weapons. Such steps, they claimed, would reduce substantially the risk of nuclear terrorism.[38] Other fuel-leasing schemes have been proposed to address the fact that the pursuit of nuclear energy, which is legitimate under the NPT, can bring countries close to weapon capabilities.

Despite efforts by the United States and other countries to press Iran to sign and implement the additional protocol to strengthen the IAEA's ability to monitor Tehran's nuclear program activities, thus far the UNSC has refused to take stronger measures to force Iran to abide by its safeguards commitments. Because of differences among members of the council, likely due in part to commercial agreements with Iran, differing security concerns, or different perceptions of which measures are most likely to succeed, UNSC members have been unable to come to a consensus on anything more than moderate sanctions on Iran. The lack of consensus on Iran shows that UN efforts, while potentially useful in halting proliferation, are often made ineffective by differences among key countries, especially when some—such as Russia, in building nuclear reactors for Iran—are benefiting commercially by the status quo.

Conclusion: Is It Possible
to Prevent Future Proliferation?

This book has attempted to show that efforts to monitor and limit the proliferation of nuclear, chemical, and biological weapon programs pose unique challenges not only to the United States but also to the international community. While proliferation (and an intelligence focus on it) is not a new, twenty-first century phenomenon, the urgency of detecting and correctly understanding clandestine weapon programs, especially nuclear, has increased with the possibility of international terrorists obtaining and using nuclear, chemical, or biological agents or weapons. Consequently, the Intelligence Community and policymakers have had to adjust their thinking about the nature of the threat, the approach that needs to be taken to deal with it, and the likelihood of achieving positive results.

As we have explained in this book, over the past fifty years the United States and international community have had considerable success in slowing down the proliferation of nuclear weapons by nation-states through measures such as the Nuclear Non-Proliferation Treaty, although the cases of India, Iran, Iraq, Israel, Libya, North Korea, Pakistan, and possibly Syria demonstrate that clandestine programs are often not easy to detect and stop. And the challenge posed in understanding the extent of the A. Q. Khan black market nuclear proliferation network demonstrated that the supply of technology and equipment is difficult to track, especially when in the hands of non-state actors. The chemical and biological weapons conventions have undoubtedly contributed to the international effort to harness the proliferation of those weapons, but as we have discussed, the clandestine production of such agents is much less problematic for nation-states than is the clandestine production of nuclear weapons.

However, past accomplishments in identifying and preventing proliferation are no guarantee of future success. Good intelligence, wise policymaking, good cooperation among federal and local law enforcement and intelligence organizations, and effective international cooperation will clearly be required to prevent weapons from reaching the hands of international terrorists. As the Iraqi, Iranian, Libyan, and North Korean cases have demonstrated, intelligence analysis and judgments are often less than perfect, even on the activities of nation-states. International agreements and inspections may inhibit proliferation but certainly do not ensure that proliferation efforts are not under way, especially with non-state actors. Additional creative, cooperative approaches are required.

Given the inaccurate intelligence estimate prepared and disseminated by the IC on Iraq's WMD programs in October 2002, some have asked whether the US Intelligence Community is up to the task of monitoring and correctly reporting on the status of small, clandestine nuclear, chemical, and biological weapons programs. The IC has tried to learn from its past mistakes and to correct its shortcomings. As the preface to the unclassified judgments from the national intelligence estimate on Iran's nuclear weapon program, released in December 2007, indicated, the IC has adopted changes, such as a more thorough vetting of sources, in preparing and presenting its findings—along with explaining more carefully the basis for findings—to avoid repeating past mistakes and misunderstandings regarding its judgments. However, since no two situations are exactly alike, success in discovering a clandestine program in one country does not guarantee success in another. Moreover, some of the "fixes" to the Intelligence Community, especially those that are purely bureaucratic at upper levels, can create as many difficulties as they are designed to solve. And as discussed, the effort to monitor and prevent the proliferation of WMD technology, expertise, and equipment to international terrorists is even more challenging than monitoring the activities of nation-states. It requires effective cooperation at multiple levels within and across national boundaries.

The United States adopted structural and bureaucratic changes following the 9/11 attacks that have most likely improved information sharing and policy coordination against potential terrorist attacks, especially those that might involve nuclear, chemical, or biological weapons. Less clear is whether these changes have improved the IC's ability to monitor and understand clandestine proliferation efforts by nation-states. Establishing the Department of Homeland Security has certainly improved information sharing between federal and local intelligence and law enforcement organizations as well as the coordination of defensive measures against future terrorist attacks. And establishing the position of Director of National Intelligence based on recommendations from the 9/11 Commission Report promises to improve the IC's information sharing and performance at least in certain areas.

However, measures such as restructuring at the top (sometimes referred to as rearranging the chairs on the A deck of a cruise ship), throwing in more money, and creating a new organization chart do not necessarily affect activities or improve performance lower down in the bureaucracy, where actual collection and analytic activities are performed. Some of the IC's responsibilities may have been made even more difficult, including the monitoring and analysis of clandestine WMD programs. For example, because foreign intelligence services are probably somewhat unsure as to who is actually running US intelligence, they may be more hesitant to share key pieces of information. Should they establish liaison with members of the DNI's growing staff or retain their traditional liaison relationship with the CIA? Most are probably doing a little of both until they are sure which address really counts![1]

Moreover, making structural changes in response to one crisis (such as the lack of tactical warning about the attacks of September 11, 2001) does not necessarily make the Intelligence Community immune to future failures in other areas, such as detecting and accurately understanding proliferation activities. The reorganization did not alter any of the essential levers of power, such as Department of Defense control over most intelligence resources. From what has been described in this book, there seems little relationship between the problems the IC faced in assessing Iraq's WMD programs and the restructuring of the Intelligence Community in 2004. Nevertheless, the Senate Report, WMD Commission, and Kerr internal study (see Chapter 5) did offer helpful observations on pitfalls to avoid and approaches to improve intelligence collection and analysis with regard to proliferation issues.

As we have noted, the task of understanding whether a WMD program exists, as well as determining its status, depends on the type of weapon in question. It also depends on understanding and factoring in what we know about context, motives, intentions, ongoing efforts, and capabilities achieved by potential state or non-state proliferators. This knowledge in turn requires effective and thoughtful management and use of all collection disciplines and appropriate analytical methodologies. It also requires that collectors and analysts work together as a team, especially to ensure that reliability and motives of human sources are vetted properly and that information is understood in the appropriate context.

Future success in collecting information for the effective monitoring of clandestine proliferation activities in the twenty-first century is not assured, just as it was not during Cold War efforts to monitor Soviet military forces. Effective human source and technical collection require careful analysis of the problems the United States faces, careful planning and execution of agent recruitment and development programs, diligent vetting of human sources, and patience. Hiring officers with appropriate cultural and linguistic skills must go hand in hand with training in human collection tradecraft, if the US Intelligence Community ever hopes to recruit foreign agents with the access and reliability required to penetrate proliferation programs. For technical collection, creativity and ingenuity are required for breaking into the covert activities of those who will use every means available to deny, conceal, and mislead. For analysts, success in understanding the collected bits of information requires, as learned from the Iraqi case, the ability to think "outside the box" and to apply the relevant cultural and historical lenses. Challenging assumptions and considering alternative explanations are critical to effective analysis and to reaching accurate judgments. The IC must train its intelligence analysts to be bold in making informed judgments and to be diligent in explaining what they know, what they do not know, and expressing the level of confidence in their judgments. This tradecraft of intelligence analysis is not new, but the stakes are quite high when the IC fails to learn from the past or fails to apply due diligence in analyzing available data, both with respect to credibility and importance. And policymakers must work cooperatively with intelligence officers, challenging them to be thorough but avoiding efforts to politicize judgments.

Thus, one should not assume that the post–9/11 legislation establishing the Department of Homeland Security and the Director of National Intelligence will have fixed all problems or will prevent intelligence failures in the future. To think so would show a lack of understanding of the intelligence business, which deals with uncertainty, ambiguity, incomplete data, and a dynamically evolving world.

Apart from the alleged shortcomings of the Intelligence Community's reorganization in Washington and potential misuse of intelligence judgments by policymakers in the future, the IC must keep in mind that one of its chief responsibilities is to warn policymakers and help them avoid potentially tragic blind spots on what is surfacing in the world around them. Intelligence officers must have the courage to report to policymakers what they need to hear, whether or not they wish to hear it.

On the intelligence task of detecting and monitoring clandestine nuclear, chemical, and biological weapons programs it appears appropriate to para-phrase former DCI Tenet's concluding remarks from his speech at Georgetown University in February 2004. The remarks are not a rationalization for the IC's failure to assess correctly the status of Saddam's WMD programs but rather a realistic recognition of the challenges intelligence faces. In sum, he said that intelligence deals with the unclear, the unknown, and the deliberately hidden. Uncertainties in intelligence information are significant, and analysts must fill in the gaps with informed judgments. Tenet ended by saying that in the intel-ligence business one is almost never completely wrong nor completely right. Mistakes are disappointing and dangerous, and when the IC makes them it must figure out why and fix the problem.[2] That certainly is the community's duty to the nation; in turn the American people must give the IC their full support to maximize its effectiveness as the first line of defense against threats in the twenty-first century, which most likely will include WMD proliferation, especially to terrorists.

The United States must recognize that terrorist use of one or more WMD is the principal external threat that it faces as a nation and as a member of the world community. While it is possible to make it more difficult for na-tion-states to acquire or proliferate these types of weapons, it may be overly optimistic to think that such activities can be prevented. Even benign assistance in the field of nuclear technology for purposes sanctioned by the Nuclear Non-Proliferation Treaty, such as the enrichment of uranium for research or power reactors, can lead to the clandestine misuse of nuclear expertise, facilities, and material by nation-states that can then be passed on to or stolen by terrorists. As we stated earlier, the war on terror will be easier to win if terrorists have only conventional means with which to strike; however, if more rogue states acquire WMD, especially nuclear, the chances will increase that international terror-ists will acquire and use them. The consequences could be catastrophic for the world community.

It is of the greatest importance, therefore, to inhibit and, if possible, prevent the further spread of nuclear weapons, along with other WMD, to states not committed to the world community such as Iran and North Korea. The more widely weapons proliferate, the more likely they will be used in warfare and the greater the risk they will be acquired, and used, by international terrorists. The administration and Congress must give the Intelligence Community the resources, authorities, and support it needs to effectively monitor proliferation activities. For its part, the IC must remain diligent, apolitical, and objective in its judgments. It must also adapt and think outside the box to detect and understand novel efforts to proliferate, especially to non-state actors. And for its part, the policy community must responsibly use the intelligence it is given without trying to politicize intelligence judgments or misuse them to fit policy biases and preferences. It must also weigh carefully intelligence provided by other countries and information from international inspections.

The world has seen what happens when intelligence is off the mark, when the international community is unable to cooperate, and when policymakers choose to misconstrue intelligence judgments to justify their preferred policy. We, the authors, judge that the George W. Bush administration has left a legacy on US intelligence which is—as often the case with administrations led by either party—a mixed bag (see Appendix K). While the administration gave the US Intelligence Community strong support in many areas, the intelligence-policymaker relationship was put under considerable strain. Its handling of intense political criticism for its decision to use military force to remove Saddam Hussein led it to blame the Intelligence Community for a poorly conceived policy; some in the administration sought analysis outside of the IC to support its policy decisions. We underscore the words of columnist David Ignatius quoted in Chapter 5: "When we assess the CIA, we should understand that many of its supposed failures really have another address—the White House." Exaggerating and misconstruing available intelligence can lead to bad policy decisions. This does not excuse the shortcomings of the IC, however, which as we stated in Chapter 5 should have offered a more thorough and accurate assessment of Iraq's WMD capabilities and perhaps provided an even more forceful warning about the risks of using military force in Iraq.

To be successful in future nonproliferation efforts, the United States will need to heal its internal bureaucratic wounds and establish a collegiality that will fuse good intelligence collection and analysis with good policy making. Such fusion is essential to national security, and fortunately it normally prevails. There are ups and downs within every administration (see Appendix K), and wounds from the Iraqi WMD crisis will also heal. But the nation has come through a particularly difficult time. There is a real danger that the general mistrust of US intelligence which has resulted from the criticisms and various investigations following the 9/11 and Iraqi WMD episodes may be spilling over into criticisms of, and constraints on, US corporations, which have patriotically supported intelligence activities against proliferation and international terrorists. This is particularly true of telecommunications companies that assisted the Bush administration's terrorist surveillance programs which have come under attack. Companies that have in the past supported intelligence efforts can rightfully fear that they will be exposed and subject to legal consequences for aiding such efforts in the future. If this proves to be the case, the country (and the international community) will have suffered a significant loss of security.[3]

In addition, the United States must find a way to weave together national and local intelligence more effectively as well as cooperate more harmoniously with the international community, despite differences of perception and national interest. In conjunction with the international community, the United States must pressure countries to control the supply side of proliferation (transferring critical technology, material, or actual weapons) as well as promote arms control, nonproliferation and counterproliferation measures to deter nations and terrorists from clandestinely acquiring WMD. US intelligence and policymakers must take advantage of international inspections and liaison information from like-minded countries to ensure that all channels of information are available and shared, especially in areas of the world where the United States does not have a presence. The increasing availability of commercial overhead photography from satellites with ever-increasing resolution should be helpful. The public must be included, where possible, to help Washington pursue this difficult task. Even Internet users, using Google Earth, should be persuaded to be part of the battle against international terrorism.

We conclude that the path ahead will be difficult. We live in a far more dangerous world than was ever imagined at the end of the Cold War. The continued efforts of an extremist Islamic regime in Iran to achieve nuclear weapons capability and the possibility of a future Pakistani government taking a Taliban-like course would certainly increase the risks of nuclear proliferation among Arab states in the Middle East as well as the provision of nuclear expertise and material to terrorist organizations such as Hamas, Hezbollah, or al-Qaeda. Moreover, a failure to denuclearize North Korea, especially if that state became more aggressive and bellicose as a result, would increase the chances that Japan and South Korea would choose to go nuclear.

The first line of defense is good intelligence, and the US Intelligence Community is the finest the world has ever seen. Mistakes have been made and will be made in the future, for that is the nature of the uncertain and ambiguous world of intelligence. But for the most part the dedicated professionals in the CIA and its sister organizations in the Intelligence Community have served the United States and its citizens well. Through the ups and downs of attempting to understand dynamic world events and trying to give insightful support to administrations, Intelligence Community professionals must maintain their integrity, honesty, perseverance, courage, and commitment to serve the national security needs of the United States. And the citizens of the United States must ensure that the Intelligence Community has the best and brightest individuals the country can offer, as well as the resources they need to give us the security we need.

Postscript: What If the International Community Fails to Prevent Further Proliferation?

Because past achievements in preventing and reversing proliferation do not guarantee future success, especially with regard to nuclear, chemical, and biological weapons and terrorists, this discussion would not be complete if the serious implications of failing to monitor and limit proliferation in the future were not addressed.

The United States and the international community have not been entirely successful in preventing the proliferation of nuclear weapons. India, Israel, North Korea, and Pakistan are the most obvious examples. Unfortunately, more countries likely will attempt to enter the nuclear club.

Arguably because of its history as the target of nuclear weapons, Japan has resisted the urge to become a nuclear weapon power to counter North Korea. However, an overt, unconstrained North Korean nuclear arsenal likely would cause Japan to put these inhibitions aside and proceed to develop nuclear weapons, which it is capable of doing quickly. That development would lead promptly to a nuclear-armed South Korea and conceivably to nuclear weapons in Taiwan. And Iran appears determined to join the rank of countries that possess nuclear weapons. An overt Iranian nuclear weapon capability likely would lead to similar programs in Egypt, Saudi Arabia, and perhaps Syria. Such developments would deal a body blow to the international effort to restrain nuclear weapon proliferation among nation-states and would increase the risk of nuclear weapons, or at least fissile material, getting into the hands of terrorists.

In May 2008, the IAEA reported that at least forty countries, including several in the Middle East such as Egypt, Kuwait, Yemen, and Algeria, had approached the agency to signal their interest in nuclear power. Moreover, a half-dozen or so countries indicated their intention to enrich or reprocess nuclear fuel, which, as we explained, provides a latent ability to covertly develop nuclear weapons.

Many—such as Joseph Cirincione, one of the most prestigious US non-governmental experts on WMD programs—suspect that the interest of these countries in nuclear power is in reaction to the threat of a nuclear-weapon-capable Iran as much as to rising fuel prices or finite oil supplies. However, many countries around the world truly want nuclear technology in order to meet their carbon-free energy targets. They have demonstrated that they not only are not pursuing enrichment and reprocessing technology but also are willing to formally foreswear that technology—as the United Arab Emirates, to its credit, did in its white paper on nuclear energy in 2007. Nevertheless, Mohamed ElBaradei, IAEA Director-General, likened the pursuit of "latent" nuclear capability to buying an insurance policy. Once a country has the basic nuclear capability, it can just sit on it as a deterrent. And Egypt's ambassador to the United States warned that a nuclear arms race in the Middle East may be inevitable unless leaders in that region agree to ban such weapons. At a minimum, an increase in the number of countries that possess and ship nuclear material around the world would give terrorists more opportunities to purchase, if not steal, the fissile material for at least crude nuclear or radiological devices.[1]

The case of Iran demonstrates that ambiguities surrounding legitimate nuclear research and power activities—such as access to peaceful nuclear technology, including uranium enrichment, which are permitted and in fact guaranteed by the NPT—and limits on the effectiveness of on-site inspections due to concealment and denial measures, make it difficult for anyone to determine what is actually going on. The clandestine acquisition of chemical or biological weapons is particularly difficult to monitor and stop due to legitimate commercial activities, which can mask the production of key agents. Moreover, both the supply and demand sides of proliferation tend to be international in scope, and a complex web of financial and technical activities must be monitored to understand what is transpiring. The case of Saddam's Iraq demonstrated that significant uncertainties can accompany efforts to understand clandestine proliferation activities.

What is likely to happen if there is further WMD proliferation by nation-states? Would proliferation increase the risk that nuclear, biological, or chemical weapons will get into the hands of terrorists and be used? If so, how effective are possible defenses against such attacks?

Other authors have explored these questions in more depth, but we wish to briefly share our perspective. As mentioned, the advent of a radical regime in Pakistan would increase the chances of Pakistan's nuclear expertise—if not actual fissile material or weapons—being provided to an international terror-ist organization such as al-Qaeda. And if the government of Iran succeeds in its apparent quest for a nuclear weapon capability, the likelihood that Arab countries would also go down that path would increase, as would the chances that the two Iranian-sponsored terrorist organizations, Hamas and Hezbollah, would gain access to nuclear expertise or fissile material. One worrisome fact is that Iran is not a unitary state; the central government entities might be deter-mined not to share nuclear technology, but a substate organization such as the Revolutionary Guards might do so on its own. These situations would increase the likelihood of a catastrophe.

Since the attacks of September 11, 2001, the United States and international community have taken steps to hinder the acquisition of nuclear, biological, and chemical weapons by terrorists and have implemented measures to de-fend against attacks resulting from such proliferation. However, little has been done to strengthen the nuclear nonproliferation regime, and many argue that the regime has been weakened during the past decade; the entry into force of the Comprehensive Nuclear Test Ban Treaty and the negotiation of a Fissile Material Cutoff Treaty would improve the situation. On the national level, the United States and other countries have taken unilateral and cooperative mea-sures to protect against terrorist attacks. Thus far, the measures appear to have helped; however, much remains to be done.

Because of ongoing concerns that terrorists might get access to fissile ma-terial located in hundreds of storage sites in dozens of countries around the world, Harvard University's Belfer Center for Science and International Affairs issued its seventh annual study "Securing the Bomb 2008" at the end of 2008. The study reported that the attempt in November 2007 of four armed men to break into South Africa's most closely guarded nuclear facility at Pelindaba, which holds hundreds of pounds of weapons-grade nuclear material (highly enriched uranium probably from South Africa's dismantled nuclear weapons), demonstrated the global challenge of keeping such material out of the hands of terrorists. The report urged the incoming US administration to launch a global campaign to lock down every nuclear weapon and every significant stock of weapons-grade material worldwide because a sophisticated terrorist group could make a crude nuclear weapon. While the study acknowledges that using a nuclear bomb would be among the most difficult types of attack for terrorists to accomplish and thus far none has, the potential results make nuclear weap-ons a priority for terrorists.[2]

Notwithstanding such measures, some continue to question whether the United States or other countries can successfully defend themselves from terrorist attacks using WMD. Terrorists must be successful only once to create havoc and terror, whereas defenders must be successful one hundred percent of the time. Given the number of tanker cars and trucks hauling hazardous materials around the United States, it is not hard to envision a terrorist attack on commercial transports (principally trains) and spreading toxic material in populated areas. Moreover, with the number of shipping containers entering the United States every day, the chances are uncomfortably high that nuclear, biological, or chemical material could slip through the screening process. The Aum Shinrikyo chemical attacks in the Tokyo subway in the early 1990s and the anthrax-tainted letters anonymously mailed in the United States in 2001, demonstrate that even a small amount of lethal agents can cause major disruption and panic. The real surprise and good news is that, at the writing of this book, no significant attacks with weapons of mass destruction have been successfully undertaken thus far in this century.

Once again, past success in disrupting clandestine proliferation activities and thwarting terrorist attacks is no guarantee of future success. The time it took the United States and international community to understand the broad extent of the A. Q. Khan black market nuclear proliferation network is troublesome. And it remains unclear whether the international community has fully understood the full scope of this network. David Albright said that "the busting up was handled far better than the rounding up." He went on to say that it is likely other smugglers will seek to take Khan's place and that some may have already done so. He even thought it might be unwise to count Khan himself out.[3]

Indeed, in early February 2009, a Pakistani court declared A. Q. Khan a "free man." It is now clear that virtually none of the members of the network have or will face significant prison time. Blueprints of nuclear weapons have been discovered on computers in Switzerland and Dubai, and serious questions are being raised as to whether the network has been contained or even understood. US officials concede that it is possible that Khan and his allies may have shared nuclear secrets with still unknown countries and, perhaps, terrorist groups.[4]

This reality brings us back to the main thrust of this book: the United States and international community must make every effort to prevent further proliferation by nation-states, especially that which might lead to international terrorists gaining access to weapons of mass destruction—most importantly to nuclear explosive devices but also to lethal chemical or biological agents. Unfortunately, the United States and world community must always be willing to think the unthinkable and prepare for the worst-case scenario if collective efforts to monitor and prevent the proliferation and use of weapons by terror- ists should fail. Perpetual vigilance must remain the guiding principle.

Epilogue

In early April 2009, President Obama announced significant new initiatives in dealing with WMD proliferation by nation states and terrorist groups. Moreover, the Obama administration essentially had its senior national security leadership in place, including Intelligence Community leaders: Admiral Dennis Blair as the Director of National Intelligence and Leon Panetta as Director of CIA. Meanwhile, the countries of primary proliferation concern continued on their former paths.

Iran. As reported in the *New York Times* (David E. Sanger and William J. Broad, *New York Times*, March 14, 2009, p. WK 1), in early March 2009 Israel reacted harshly to the February 2009 announcement by the International Atomic Energy Agency that Iran had enriched uranium to reactor grade so as to possess enough fissile material, should a decision be made to enrich such uranium upwards to weapons-grade, for one nuclear weapon. The chief of Israeli military intelligence, Amos Yadlin, said in Jerusalem that Iran had "crossed the technological threshold" and that Iran's reaching "military nuclear capabilities" was "a matter of adapting its strategy to the target of manufacturing a nuclear bomb." This alarmist reaction by Israel came about a year after Israel allegedly made a private, unsuccessful request to the Bush administration for bunker-busting bombs, the right to overfly Iraq, and refueling capabilities so that Israeli warplanes would be able to attack the principal Iranian uranium enrichment facility at Natanz.

However, there seemed to be serious differences between the United States and Israel as to how urgently to treat this threat. Israel declared that it wanted to see diplomacy with Iran begin promptly and to end "by late spring or early summer." Otherwise, it was argued, the Iranians would simply drag on negotiations endlessly while continuing their nuclear weapon program. By contrast, the Obama administration was only planning to begin serious discussions after the Iranian presidential election in June. According to the *New York Times* report, the Intelligence Community estimated that Iran might have enough HEU for a nuclear weapon by the end of 2009, but more likely somewhere between 2010 and 2015. Moreover, in response to reports of Iranian uranium enrichment progress, the new Director of National Intelligence, Admiral Blair, said in Washington in congressional testimony a few days after the date of the *New York Times* report from Israel that there was "potential for an Iran-Israeli confrontation or crisis," adding that the Israelis took "more of a worst case approach to these things." Secretary of Defense Gates had stated a few days earlier that it would be several years before Iran could build a nuclear weapon arsenal.

The question of how the Obama administration should deal with growing Iranian nuclear capabilities may have been a factor in the controversy in March 2009 over the prospect that Charles W. Freeman, Jr., a former US Ambassador to Saudi Arabia and sometime critic of Israeli policy, would become chairman of the National Intelligence Council—the Intelligence Community body that produces National Intelligence Estimates. As a result of the controversy, Freeman withdrew his name.

North Korea. About the same time, North Korea was busily creating a new issue with the international community. In early March 2009, the DPRK issued a notice to international aviation and maritime agencies that it planned to launch a communication satellite between April 4 and 8. Washington believed that this was merely a pretext to test the Taepodong-2, the first North Korean ballistic missile technically capable of reaching North America. US Air Force General Kevin P. Chilton, Commander of the US Strategic Command, noted that such a launch would "help advance [North Korea's] technology of long-range missiles" (see Walter Pincus, "U.S. Could Hit N. Korean Missile," *Washington Post*, March 20, 2009, A-9). North Korea is prohibited by United Nations sanctions from testing long-range ballistic missiles, so that calling the launch a satellite launch seemed to be a subterfuge to get around the prohibition. Japan declared that if the launch occurred, it would place more sanctions on North Korea and would raise the issue at the United Nations Security Council. Meanwhile, North Korea had removed 75 percent of its spent fuel rods from the Yongbyon reactor.

There was speculation regarding when North Korea would be capable of building a nuclear warhead to fit on its mid- or long-range missiles. According to David Albright, North Korea was likely able to build a crude nuclear warhead for its mid-range missiles that target Japan, and its strategy was to keep everyone confused and wondering. Lieutenant General Michael Maples, Director of the Defense Intelligence Agency, stated in March testimony to the Senate that North Korea might have the capability to mate a nuclear warhead to ballistic missiles. (See Blaine Harden, "North Korean Nuclear Test a Growing Possibility," washingtonpost.com, March 27, 2009.) And "North Korea defied the United States, China and a series of United Nations resolutions by launching a rocket on Sunday [April 5] . . . that much of the world viewed as an effort to . . . shoot a nuclear warhead on a longer-range missile." (See Choe Sang-Hun and David E. Sanger, "North Koreans Launch Rocket Over the Pacific," *New York Times*, April 5, 2009, A-1.) Experts judged the North Korean launch to have been a failure.

Syria. Also in March 2009, there surfaced a report by Hans Ruehle, former chief of the planning staff of the German Defense Ministry, claiming that an Iranian defector, a retired General from the Revolutionary Guards in Iran, had provided considerable information concerning the Iranian nuclear program in February 2007. (See Alexander Higgins, "Report: Iranian Defector Tipped Syria Nuke Plans," Associated Press, March 19, 2009.) Included in the report was the general's assertion that "Iran was financing a secret nuclear project of Syria and North Korea." Ruehle said no one in US or Israeli intelligence at the time knew of this. Further investigation led to the conclusion that what was being constructed at Al Kibar was a North Korean type gas graphite nuclear reactor. The Israeli air raid of September 6, 2007 followed, and Israel estimated that Iran had given North Korea one to two billion dollars for the project. However, according to a US official speaking without attribution, "only two countries were involved in building the Syrian covert nuclear reactor at Al Kibar—Syria and North Korea."

As can be seen from these reports, the threat of nuclear or nuclear-related programs in dangerous states continues. It was reported that the Obama administration planned to appoint a new White House official to coordinate efforts to prevent terrorists from obtaining nuclear or biological weapons (see Bryan Bender, "New Leadership Planned to Fight WMD Terrorism," *Boston Globe*, December 3, 2008, p. 1). This White House appointment was apparently in response to the Report of the Commission on the Prevention of WMD Proliferation and Terrorism, "WORLD AT RISK," released in early December 2008, which had been ordered by Congress in accordance with implementing recommendations of the 9/11 Commission Act of 2007 (P.L. 110-53). This sobering report concluded that "unless the world community acts decisively and with great urgency, it is more likely than not that a weapon of mass destruction will be used in a terrorist attack somewhere in the world by the end of 2013." The Commission believed that terrorists are more likely to obtain and use a biological weapon than a nuclear weapon and criticized the US government's approach to bioterrorism for having placed too little emphasis on prevention. In addition to urging the appointment of a White House principal advisor for WMD proliferation and terrorism, the Commission issued a call for increased cooperation and international support, a halt to the Iranian and North Korean nuclear weapon programs, implementation of a comprehensive policy toward Pakistan including measures to secure nuclear and biological materials, more effective congressional oversight of intelligence and other efforts to prevent WMD proliferation and terrorism, and the adoption of a counterterrorism strategy that effectively counters the ideology behind WMD terrorism.

On April 5, 2009, President Obama presented in a speech in Prague some details regarding his administration's arms control/nonproliferation policy for the future. Among other things, the President said: "I state clearly and with conviction America's commitment to seek the peace and security of a world without nuclear weapons. . . . To reduce our warheads and stockpiles, we will negotiate a new Strategic Arms Reduction Treaty with the Russians this year. . . . And this will set the stage for further cuts, and we will seek to include all nuclear weapons states in this endeavor. . . . my administration will immediately and aggressively pursue U.S. ratification of the Comprehensive Test Ban Treaty. . . . the United States will seek a new treaty that verifiably ends the production of fissile materials intended for use in state nuclear weapons. . . . we will strengthen the Nuclear Non-Proliferation Treaty as a basis for cooperation. . . . we should build a new framework for civil nuclear cooperation. . . . Just this morning, we were reminded again of why we need a new and more rigorous approach to address this [nuclear weapon proliferation] threat. North Korea broke the rules once again by testing a rocket that could be used for long range missiles. . . . Iran has yet to build a nuclear weapon. . . . We believe in dialogue. But in that dialogue we will present a clear choice. . . . Iran's nuclear and ballistic missile activity poses a real threat, not just to the United States, but to Iran's neighbors and our allies. . . . Finally, we must ensure that terrorists never acquire a nuclear weapon. . . . I am announcing a new international effort to secure all vulnerable nuclear material around the world within four years."

We support these initiatives and are eager to see how the Obama administration moves forward to implement them. We very much agree that a multifront, multitiered approach is required, but the first line of defense of the United States will remain an effective and capable Intelligence Community supported by the Obama administration, Congress, and the American people.

Appendix A
Glossary of Acronyms and Terms

The following acronyms and terms are commonly used when discussing intelligence and WMD proliferation issues, and are used in the text:

AFTAC   Air Force Technical Applications Center; conducts US monitoring of foreign nuclear programs and testing

BW   biological weapons

BWC   Biological and Toxin Weapons Convention; signed in 1972, entered into force in 1975

CD   Conference on Disarmament; the international community's sole body for negotiating multilateral arms control agreements

C,D&D   concealment, denial, and deception; practices used by countries and non-state actors to avoid detection by foreign intelligence services or to mislead them

CIA   Central Intelligence Agency

CTBT   Comprehensive Nuclear Test Ban Treaty; signed in 1996 but has yet to enter into force

CW   chemical weapons

CWC   Convention on the Prohibition of Chemical Weapons; signed in 1993, entered into force in 1997

DCI   Director of Central Intelligence

DHS   Department of Homeland Security

DIA   Defense Intelligence Agency

DNI   Director of National Intelligence

DoD   Department of Defense

DPRK   Democratic Peoples' Republic of Korea (North Korea)

FISA   Foreign Intelligence Surveillance Act

FMCT   Fissile Material Cutoff Treaty; an agreement that has never been negotiated but is intended to ban the production of weapons-grade fissile material

HEU   highly enriched uranium (weapon-grade nuclear material)

HPSCI	House Permanent Select Committee on Intelligence
HUMINT	clandestine human source intelligence; derived through volunteering by or recruitment of foreign nationals who agree to provide nonpublic information
IAEA	International Atomic Energy Agency; responsible for monitoring peaceful nuclear activities under the Nuclear Non-Proliferation Treaty
IC	Intelligence Community; a collection of sixteen US organizations that collect and analyze information on foreign or domestic activities of national security concern
IMINT	imagery intelligence; derived primarily from air- and space-based reconnaissance systems
INTERPOL	International Criminal Police Organization
INR	Bureau of Intelligence and Research, Department of State
MASINT	measurement intelligence; information on the efforts to produce or test weapons of mass destruction
Monitoring	The process of tracking foreign activities, including those relevant to an arms control agreement to verify parties' compliance
MTR	nuclear materials testing reactor
NATO	North Atlantic Treaty Organization
NGA	National Geospatial-Intelligence Agency
NIB	National Intelligence Board; the group of senior Intelligence Community officials, chaired by the Director of National Intelligence, which considers and passes judgment on national intelligence estimates and other interagency analyses before sending them to policymakers. Before the 2004 Intelligence Community reorganization which strengthened the integration of foreign and domestic intelligence, it was called the National Foreign Intelligence Board (NFIB).
NIC	National Intelligence Council; the group of senior analysts (NIOs) who manage the production of interagency intelligence reports on various subjects
NIE	National Intelligence Estimate; an interagency effort by the Intelligence Community to report on the status of an issue or forecast a future direction or capability
NIO	National Intelligence Officer; a senior analyst serving in the NIC who is responsible for a substantive area and the production of interagency reports in that area
NPT	Nuclear Non-Proliferation Treaty; signed in 1968, entered into force in 1970
NSA	National Security Agency

NTM	national technical means of verification
NWFZ	nuclear weapon free zone
OPCW	Organization for the Prohibition of Chemical Weapons; established by the CWC to oversee inspections and verification proceedings
PDB	President's Daily Brief
PSI	Proliferation Security Initiative
SIGINT	signals intelligence; intercepted communications and electronic emissions
SSCI	Senate Select Committee on Intelligence
UAV	unmanned aerial vehicle
UNGA	United Nations General Assembly
UNMOVIC	United Nations Monitoring, Verification and Inspection Commission
UNSC	United Nations Security Council
UNSCOM	United Nations Special Commission
UNSYG	United Nations Secretary General
USAEDS	United States Atomic Energy Detection System
WMD	weapons of mass destruction; normally nuclear, chemical, or biological weapons

Appendix B

Technical Descriptions of Nuclear, Chemical, and Biological Weapons

Nuclear Weapons. Two basic types of nuclear weapons exist: atomic (fission) and thermonuclear (fission and fusion). Atomic weapons are devices that yield explosive energy derived from fission (uranium or plutonium design, or a combination of both). Thermonuclear weapons, which are many times more destructive than atomic weapons, use both fission and the fusion of isotopes of the hydrogen atom. This combination allows designers to get a higher yield than with a pure nuclear fission weapon (with uranium or plutonium) and at a much lower weight.

Atomic and thermonuclear weapons cause catastrophic damage with blast, high temperatures, and radiation. Thermonuclear weapons are the most destructive weapons ever created by humankind, but they are also the most sophisticated and difficult to manufacture or acquire.

The production of nuclear weapons requires an expensive infrastructure, sophisticated manufacturing capabilities, and a special isotope of uranium (U-235) or plutonium (PU-239) to achieve the chain reaction that results in its destructive power. U-235 can be obtained only through the enrichment of natural uranium; plutonium is produced in reactors and must be extracted from spent fuel by chemical processes. Both processes require specialized facilities.

Only nine nations (China, France, India, Israel, North Korea, Pakistan, Russia, United Kingdom, and United States) have built the required infrastructures (some with outside help) and currently acknowledge having nuclear weapons of one or both types (except for Israel, which does not confirm or demonstrate that it possesses nuclear weapons). In addition, South Africa until the early 1990s had a secret arsenal of six nuclear weapons. A number of other countries (Canada, Sweden, Switzerland, Taiwan, Australia, Brazil, Argentina, Libya, Iraq, Iran, and possibly Syria) have pursued nuclear weapon capabilities. Most have either turned back or have been forced to dismantle their efforts. Iran, North Korea, and potentially Syria remain of concern to the United States and the international community. Following the collapse of the Soviet Union in 1991, Ukraine, Belarus, and Kazakhstan inherited the Soviet nuclear weapons located on their now independent territories.

For several years, Ukraine tried to retain the weapons and considered becoming a nuclear weapon state.

Being the most sophisticated of the three types of WMD, nuclear weapons require the largest infrastructure and highest level of expertise for their development, production, and deployment. Only advanced countries typically have the wealth, industrial capacity, and scientific depth to conduct research, produce specialized materials, and manufacture weapons and delivery systems that are normally associated with modern nuclear arsenals. The United States, USSR/Russia, United Kingdom, France, and China were for years the only states to have developed and deployed nuclear weapon systems. These states are referred to as first-tier countries and are best able to proliferate weapon designs, knowledge, and technology, if not weapons themselves, to other countries. However, all of these countries, including China more recently, have joined the major nonproliferation agreements, and their governments appear to be fully supportive of the international nonproliferation regime.

A second tier of countries includes India, Pakistan, Israel, South Africa (until the early 1990s), and most recently North Korea, all of which joined the ranks of countries possessing nuclear weapons. They most likely benefited from technology transfers (dual-use if not clandestine transfers) from some of the first-tier countries, such as China (to Pakistan, and perhaps Iran) and France (to Israel). Moreover, civilian nuclear programs, such as for research and power reactors, have provided, along with the ability to enrich natural uranium, some of the essential building blocks for their governments' nuclear weapon programs. And perhaps with the assistance of other, more advanced nuclear countries, a nation can develop most of the capabilities supporting nuclear weapons under the cover of a civilian nuclear program. Such clandestine development can take place even under the umbrella of the Nuclear Non-Proliferation Treaty when International Atomic Energy Agency inspectors are denied access to the facilities where clandestine work is taking place.

Second-tier countries have taken longer than first-tier countries to achieve success, but through clandestine methods and some indigenous work they eventually have acquired the capability to produce and, in most cases, deliver a nuclear explosive device to a target. While these countries may be less able to transfer knowledge and technology to other countries or to terrorists, some of them may have greater motivation to do so than the first-tier countries. The world learned in recent years that the private underground network of Pakistani nuclear expert A. Q. Khan contributed significantly to the proliferation of nuclear design, technology, and expertise for use by second-tier countries. The challenge of the Intelligence Community and policymakers, therefore, is to distinguish between activities which are legal and those which are not. With Iran, this has become a particularly contentious issue.

The infrastructure, expertise, complexities, and costs associated with the development of nuclear weapons makes the production of such weapons difficult for terrorist organizations. Enrichment of uranium and the chemical processing required to produce plutonium is beyond the capabilities of non-state actors. However, millions of kilograms of fissile material exist throughout the world, and terrorists may be able to steal sufficient quantities of it for use in the manufacture of crude nuclear devices—either a relatively simple Hiroshima gun-type bomb or radiological.

Radiological Weapons. A derivative of nuclear weapons, but much less powerful, is a crude device, sometimes referred to as a dirty bomb, which uses explosives such as dynamite or C-4 to disperse radioactive materials. The radioactive material might be highly enriched uranium or plutonium but more likely a potent radioactive decay product (Cs-137, Co-60, or Ir-192), which can be found in hospitals and nuclear research laboratories. If terrorists were able to steal the required fissile material, they might choose to build and use such weapons.

The explosion of such a crude nuclear device in a densely populated area would cause much damage in the immediate vicinity, would lead to radiological poisoning of those directly affected, and would contaminate the damaged area for an unspecified duration. Even though such a bomb would not cause mass destruction, as would a more powerful sophisticated nuclear device, the resulting civil disruption and casualties might be all that terrorists would need to create havoc and panic.

Chemical and Biological Weapons. In contrast to nuclear weapons, developing or acquiring chemical or biological weapons is relatively easy for most countries, though there are important qualitative distinctions between these two types of weapons and how they are produced. Many countries have developed or acquired one or both types, or at least have prepared for eventual production of appropriate lethal agents if needed. This results largely from the dual-use of the critical ingredients and production processes required for these weapons (most fertilizer plants can also produce chemical agents, and most pharmaceutical laboratories can produce dangerous biological agents). Further, the deployment of such agents, while tricky, generally requires less sophistication than the delivery of nuclear weapons. Indeed, various countries have used chemical weapons on the battlefield: chemical weapons were used during World War I, and Saddam Hussein used such weapons against the Iranians in the 1980s (and against his own Kurdish population). In contrast, the use of biological weapons in warfare has been rare. The Japanese reportedly dropped infected fleas and contaminated rice over China during World War II. The letter-borne anthrax attacks in the United States in October 2001 and the use of sarin gas by Japanese terrorists in the mid-1990s demonstrate that terrorists possibly would choose either type of weapon to create panic and mass casualties—although the ability of these weapons to cause mass destruction is nothing compared to nuclear weapons. While the first-world medical establishment likely would contain a major attack from biological weapons, the same might not be true if multiple attacks were employed. The effect on a developing country would be devastating. In recent years we have witnessed the use of chlorine gas by terrorists in Iraq.

Chemical substances, such as chlorine or nerve gas, when spread by conventional explosives can produce physical or physiological effects on target populations. These weapons, being basically suitable for battlefield use, can be delivered through bombs, rockets, artillery shells, or missile warheads and are dispersed through explosions. Chemical agents can be dispersed also through spraying.

Biological weapons intentionally disperse biological agents (pathogens), such as bacteria (anthrax), viruses (smallpox), or toxins (ricin), which spread infectious diseases. Because some of these agents, such as smallpox, are live organisms, they may replicate and spread, increasing their lethality. Any country possessing a pharmaceutical or food storage infrastructure has the inherent capability to produce offensive biological agents. Such agents can be dispersed through an explosive device or through aerosol delivery.[1]

Note: An excellent resource, which clearly explains the important differences among these types of weapons, along with the efforts of countries to acquire them, is Joseph Cirincione's *Deadly Arsenals: Tracking Weapons of Mass Destruction*, Second Edition (Carnegie Endowment for International Peace, 2005).

Appendix C
How Easy Is It to Produce Nuclear Weapons?

The major challenge in all nuclear weapon designs is to ensure that a significant fraction of the nuclear fuel is consumed before the weapon destroys itself. Of course, no nuclear weapon can be built without the requisite nuclear material. *Highly enriched uranium* is uranium whose isotope U-235 has been artificially concentrated to a high degree (more than 90 percent is considered best, but lower concentrations can also be used in weapons). By contrast, naturally occurring uranium has a concentration of only 0.7 percent U-235, and nuclear power plants require uranium with only a low level of enrichment (generally 3 to 5 percent). The process of increasing the concentration of U-235 takes place in a uranium enrichment plant, which typically uses either the gaseous diffusion method or the high-speed gas centrifuge method. The latter method is more efficient and uses less energy than the former method. Gas centrifuges are linked together in what is referred to as a cascade to achieve the enrichment desired. Pakistan (and possibly North Korea) has used this method, and this is also what Iran appears to be intent on developing.

Producing plutonium requires additional, expensive facilities, such as a plutonium reactor or a reprocessing plant. Such facilities are difficult to hide. This has been the primary means of producing weapons by India, North Korea, presumably Israel, and to some extent Pakistan.

Nonmilitary nuclear power reactors may also be used to produce plutonium. Most power reactors use uranium fuel enriched to 3 to 5 percent, and various countries have commercial uranium enrichment plants to fuel these power reactors. Gas centrifuge enrichment facilities that produce low-enriched uranium for fuel can be reconfigured to produce highly enriched uranium for weapons. This points to an inherent weakness in traditional nonproliferation measures designed to stop the production of highly enriched uranium, and is part of the concern about Iran obtaining a uranium enrichment capability. Also, conventional commercial nuclear fuel produces "reactor grade" plutonium in its spent fuel as a result of operations. It has been demonstrated that reactor-grade plutonium can be used in a workable nuclear weapon.[1] Experts believe that 25 kilograms (55 pounds) of highly enriched uranium or 8 kilograms (18 pounds) of plutonium is all it takes to manufacture a nuclear weapon.

Beyond the need to obtain appropriate weapon-grade nuclear material, a proliferator must also have a weapon design, the ability to produce a weapon, and the capability to test the nonnuclear components of the weapon. Given the relative availability of design information through open-source literature and black-market sales, such as the A. Q. Khan network, it is possible to design a fission weapon (a gun-type design is the simplest) without the need for a full-scale nuclear explosive test. Plutonium weapons require a more complicated "implosion" design. All proliferators, such as India, Pakistan, and North Korea, have succeeded in building nuclear weapons by concentrating their resources and by obtaining assistance from other countries or private individuals. For example, India's program took advantage of Canadian and US assistance to its peaceful nuclear research, and Pakistan relied on assistance from China along with technology and equipment secretly obtained from Western European suppliers. Iran was aided by Russia in the construction of a reactor and along with North Korea, through other means, as by the A. Q. Khan network.

As discussed in Appendix B, the complexity and expense of nuclear weapon production makes it less likely that international terrorists would be able to independently produce weapons that have any degree of sophistication. Terrorists are more likely to try stealing a small nuclear weapon, acquiring fissile material to construct a crude gun-type bomb similar to the Hiroshima weapon, or resorting to the production of a crude radiological device, which uses relatively low-grade nuclear material stolen from hospitals or research reactors and surrounded by high explosives that disperse nuclear contamination, so as to create mass panic and terror.

Appendix D
US Intelligence Community

Note: This entire text was copied from the DNI website (dni.gov).

The United States Intelligence Community (IC) is a collection of sixteen agencies and organizations within the Executive Branch that conduct diverse intelligence activities in support of US policymaker requirements. These agencies and organizations are responsible for the development and operation of collection systems and activities as well as for the analysis of all-source data to understand the threats to US national security.

Most of the IC organizations belong to the various policy departments of the Executive Branch and support their specific missions (see IC organizational chart below). The Department of Defense contains the majority of these components to support military planning and operations. Only the Central Intelligence Agency was created to be independent of any policy department in order to serve the intelligence needs of the President and National Security Council as a whole. Except for the domestic counterintelligence and counterterrorism functions of the Federal Bureau of Investigation and the Department of Homeland Security, all IC components are focused only on foreign intelligence as specified in the National Security Act of 1947 and by Executive Order 12333 of 1981.

The position of *Director of National Intelligence* (DNI) was created by the Intelligence Reform Act of 2004 to strengthen the management of the Community and to improve the sharing of critical intelligence information among IC components. Supporting the DNI are various interagency groups, including the National Counterterrorism Center and the National Intelligence Council, which is the senior substantive analytic body of the Community responsible for producing national intelligence estimates and other interagency analysis for national decision makers.

Those IC components that contribute most directly to the effort to understand foreign military forces and to monitor arms control agreements are the following:

—The *Central Intelligence Agency* (CIA) provides comprehensive, all-source, intelligence on national security topics; conducts counterintelligence activities overseas; and conducts special activities and other functions related to foreign intelligence as directed by the President. CIA's three principle components are the National Clandestine Service, which collects information from human sources not obtainable through other means; the Directorate of Intelligence, which analyzes and interprets information collected from all sources; and the Directorate of Science and Technology, which applies innovative scientific, engineering, and technical solutions to intelligence collection and analytic problems.

—The *Defense Intelligence Agency* (DIA) provides and coordinates all-source military analysis to the Secretary of Defense; the Chairman, Joint Chiefs of Staff; and to force planners and war fighters world-wide. DIA manages and integrates defense intelligence resources, both for analysis and collection.

—The *National Security Agency* (NSA) is the nation's cryptologic organization that coordinates, directs, and performs the exploitation of foreign signals intelligence (SIGINT) and protects US and allied information. NSA serves the needs of both the Department of Defense and national policymakers.

—The *National Geospatial-Intelligence Agency* (NGA) supports national policymakers and military forces by providing intelligence derived from the exploitation and analysis of overhead imagery and geospatial information.

—The *National Reconnaissance Office* (NRO) develops and operates space reconnaissance systems. It ensures the availability of the technology and spaceborne systems needed to meet the requirements of national policymakers and military forces.

—The *Army, Navy, Marine Corps, and Air Force* intelligence services support military acquisition and development programs as well as ensure that critical technical intelligence is provided to the rest of the IC and to the warfighters, along with targeting information in the support of military operations.

—The *Department of Energy* (DOE) provides the Intelligence Community key technical expertise and information on foreign nuclear weapon programs and proliferation efforts, energy issues, as well as on science and technology developments.

—The *Department of State's Bureau of Intelligence and Research* (INR) provides the Secretary of State and the IC with analysis of global developments, drawing on all-source intelligence, diplomatic reporting, and interaction with scholars.

The remaining members of the Intelligence Community have specific departmental as well as national functions:

—The *Federal Bureau of Investigation* (FBI) is the principal investigative arm of the Department of Justice. With respect to counterintelligence, it is responsible for detecting and countering foreign intelligence activity targeted against US national security interests. It also helps to counter terrorist threats to the United States.

—The *Department of Homeland Security* (DHS), a new member of the US Intelli-

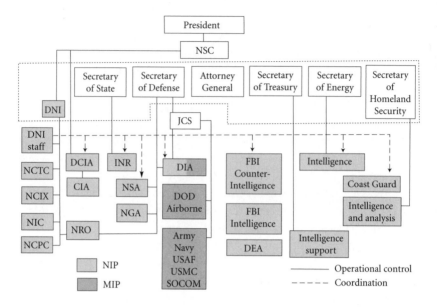

Acronyms: CIA = Central Intelligence Agency; DCIA = Director of CIA; DEA = Drug Enforcement Agency; DIA = Defense Intelligence Agency; DNI = Director of National Intelligence; FBI = Federal Bureau of Investigation; INR = Bureau of Intelligence and Research; JCS = Joint Chiefs of Staff; MIP = Joint Military Intelligence Program; NCIX = National Counterintelligence Executive; NCPC = National Counterproliferation Center; NCTC = National Counterterrorism Center; NGA = National Geospatial-Intelligence Agency; NIC = National Intelligence Council; NIP = National Intelligence Program; NRO = National Reconnaissance Office; NSA = National Security Agency; NSC = National Security Council.

This figure offers an organizational view of the Intelligence Community emphasizing vertical lines of authority, operational control, and coordination. The National Security Council (NSC) has authority over the Director of National Intelligence (DNI), but the Secretary of Defense controls 75–80 percent of the IC's personnel and budget on a daily basis. The CIA, unlike the INR or the DIA, has no cabinet-level policy patron but rather reports to the DNI. The CIA's main clients are the President and the NSC.

The figure also shows the IC's two main budget sectors: the National Intelligence Program which covers all civilian programs, including domestic intelligence (FBI) and homeland security, as well as most of the national-level military programs (NSA, NGA, and half of DIA); the Military Intelligence Program includes those Defense Department components that are responsible for tactical support to military operations and report directly to the Joint Chiefs of Staff.

Source: Mark M. Lowenthal, *Intelligence: From Secrets to Policy*, 4th ed. (Washington, DC: CQ Press, 2009), fig. 3-1, page 32. Copyright © 2009 CQ Press, a division of SAGE Publications.

gence Community, contributes to the IC's efforts to understand and thwart terrorist threats to the homeland by fusing law enforcement and intelligence information.

—The *Coast Guard*, which is now part of DHS, deals with maritime security and homeland defense.

—The *Department of the Treasury* collects and processes information that may affect US fiscal and monetary policies, and it covers the terrorist financing issue.

—The *Drug Enforcement Administration* (DEA) is responsible for enforcing US controlled substances laws and regulations.

Appendix E
The Intelligence Cycle

To make the policymaker-intelligence relationship work smoothly, a cycle of activity exists. The provision of intelligence begins with policy requirements—the need for information articulated by the policy community. Some of these requirements are obvious and are of continuing duration. For example, during the Cold War the best intelligence possible on Soviet intentions and military capabilities was a standing requirement. And today, detecting and understanding the status of clandestine WMD programs and learning where terrorists are likely to strike next are standing requirements. However, many requirements, such as reporting on a political crisis in a country of concern, can be ad hoc. Thus, policymakers' requirements for intelligence are dynamic and ever changing in response to the evolving international situation and threat to US national security. It is the responsibility of the policy community, beginning with the president, to articulate its intelligence needs and prioritize them. Only in the case of warning does the Intelligence Community have the responsibility to take the initiative to inform policymakers of a trend or potential crisis on the horizon, about which they might otherwise be ignorant. Policymakers do not like to be surprised by what they read in the morning newspaper or hear on CNN!

Once the requirements are identified, senior managers in the Intelligence Community decide how best to respond. If the desired information is essentially available, then analysts gather, organize, and put it into perspective to address the situation at hand. The information requested may require a blend of both open-source information (press reports, speeches, journals, magazines) and intelligence information, which is acquired through sensitive clandestine human or technical sources and methods. After appropriate analysis, the resulting "finished" intelligence is disseminated to the requestor (and normally to other policymakers and members of Congress who have a legitimate need to know). If, however, additional information is required to answer the question, then collection efforts of one sort or another are launched to fill the gaps before further analysis and dissemination can take place. At times, the collection of information requires new assets or techniques; if so, then those need to be developed so that the lacking information can be collected and integrated into the available information.

However the process proceeds, it ends with analysis and judgments that are communicated back to the policy requestor. Communication is most frequently in the form of a written report, but it may also be an oral briefing. Depending on the nature and urgency of the request, the policymaker may also be shown the "raw" (unanalyzed) intelligence collected from human or technical sources; however, this is usually done only in the presence of an intelligence professional who can ensure that the information is understood in the proper context. In the case of some raw, vice-finished (that is, analyzed) intelligence, such as intercepts of communications or images of targets, some processing and possible explanation is required so that the non-expert will properly understand the information.

Appendix F

Supply vs. Demand: Two Sides of the Proliferation Coin

Any effort to monitor or limit proliferation must deal with both the supply and demand sides of the issue. Supply-side action requires focusing on countries that either because of capabilities or instabilities are most likely to be a source of WMD expertise and materials. However, even benign assistance in the field of nuclear technology for legitimate purposes, such as for research or power reactors, can lead to clandestine misuse of nuclear expertise and material. Most first-tier nuclear countries, including the United States and France, bear some responsibility for supplying technology that has led to the development of nuclear weapons. And the recent US-Indian nuclear technology agreement, while it helps to bring India into the nonproliferation mainstream, has raised concerns in some quarters that it rewards an overt proliferator and might undermine efforts to halt nuclear proliferation in other countries.

Fears regarding the relative lack of security and accounting for nuclear material during the breakup of the Soviet Union led to calls for increased collection and analysis of information on the activities surrounding the former Soviet nuclear arsenal and infrastructure, which became resident in four newly independent states. The Cooperative Threat Reduction Program was a key policy response to the threat of former Soviet nuclear material, if not nuclear devices themselves, being sold or stolen. In addition, the world has witnessed an increasingly active Russian Federation selling nuclear expertise and technology to countries such as Iran. As the market (demand side) for nuclear power grows, Russia appears ready to meet that demand. Unfortunately, this readiness raises the odds that technology and material will be misused by recipient states. Moreover, efforts to halt state-to-state proliferation transactions can and have been undermined by activities of black markets, such as the A. Q. Khan network.

China's traditionally loose controls were also of concern to those trying to strengthen the nonproliferation regime, especially after it became known that China had assisted Pakistan with its nuclear program in the 1970s and 1980s. Although China later joined the Nuclear Suppliers Group in 1998 and has recently updated its export controls on nuclear technology, some remain concerned about Chinese nuclear assistance to Iran as well as Pakistan. An August 2005 Department of State report indicated that Beijing may be aiding two unnamed countries' nuclear weapon programs (that is, Iran and Pakistan).[1] Moreover, former Assistant Secretary of State for Nonproliferation John S. Wolf admitted that China's record in controlling chemical weapons and missile exports has been less than desirable.[2]

Finally, exposure of the A. Q. Khan black market supply network for nuclear design and technology showed how the supply-demand equation could work outside normal nation-state control. Besides North Korea and Libya, it appears that the Khan network approached Iran, Iraq, and perhaps other countries (possibly Syria) with offers of nuclear weapon-related deals.[3] Israel's strike in September 2007 against the facility in northern Syria was perhaps linked to information regarding Khan's network.

International Arrangements. Multilateral export control regimes, such as the Nuclear Suppliers Group, and safeguards of the International Atomic Energy Agency (IAEA), which were established under the Nuclear Non-Proliferation Treaty (NPT), are among the international efforts designed to inhibit the transfer of nuclear technology and material that is contrary to the treaty. But these supply-side measures are most effective against first-tier nuclear states, and they require the adherence of those states. It was Germany, not Russia, that initially provided centrifuge technology to Iraq.

By the early 1990s, the cases of North Korea and Iraq had demonstrated that safeguards arrangements under the NPT could be sidestepped through the use of covert (undeclared) facilities. However, North Korea's cheating was discovered when the samples provided by Pyongyang to the IAEA, along with a sample collected by inspectors, showed that there had been at least two reprocessing campaigns. When this information was combined with intelligence information from the United States, the board was convinced.[4] As a result of the Iraq and North Korea cases, the IAEA secretariat proposed to the board that they strengthen safeguards as far as possible without new agreements with governments. Work commenced at the IAEA in 1995 on a model additional NPT Safeguards Protocol, initially called 93+2 (agreed to in 1993 and originally intended to be completed in 1995—hence "93+2"), which was adopted by the General Conference finally in 1997. The strengthened safeguards require greater intrusion and go to the heart of the uneasy bargain between the treaty's nuclear weapon states and nonnuclear weapon states.[5] Naturally, the effectiveness of these enhanced safeguards depends on the cooperation of nation-states. Implementation has been slow.

Appendix G
Concealment, Denial, and Deception

Countries that want to hide their military or proliferation activities from the outside world often implement efforts to prevent access or observation through denial, concealment, or deceptive practices. In general, their intent is to reduce collection effectiveness by controlling what intelligence collectors (human or technical) can observe, manipulating information, or otherwise managing perceptions of foreign intelligence analysts and shape the decisions and actions of their policymakers.

—*Denial* refers specifically to activities and programs designed to eliminate, impair, degrade, or neutralize the effectiveness of human source, signals intercepts, imagery, and other types of collection efforts.

—*Concealment* refers to camouflage or to the management of activities in order to hide clandestine programs from detection and observation.

—*Deception* refers to the manipulation of intelligence collection, analysis, or public opinion by introducing false, misleading, or even true but tailored information into foreign intelligence channels. Again, the intent is to influence the judgments made by intelligence analysts as well as the perceptions and actions of their policymakers.

Appendix H

National Intelligence Estimate, Iran: Nuclear Intentions and Capabilities, November 2007

Note: An unclassified version of the Key Judgments from an NIE produced in the early fall of 2007 was released to the public in December 2007 (http://www.dni. gov/press_releases/20071203_release.pdf). The text of the release is presented here along with several explanatory notes from the Office of the Director of National Intelligence.

OFFICE OF THE DIRECTOR OF NATIONAL INTELLIGENCE

The Director of National Intelligence serves as the head of the Intelligence Community (IC), overseeing and directing the implementation of the National Intelligence Program and acting as the principal advisor to the President, the National Security Council, and the Homeland Security Council for intelligence matters.

The Office of the Director of National Intelligence is charged with:

- Integrating the domestic and foreign dimensions of US intelligence so that there are no gaps in our understanding of threats to our national security;
- Bringing more depth and accuracy to intelligence analysis; and
- Ensuring that US intelligence resources generate future capabilities as well as present results.

NATIONAL INTELLIGENCE COUNCIL

Since its formation in 1973, the National Intelligence Council (NIC) has served as a bridge between the intelligence and policy communities, a source of deep substantive expertise on critical national security issues, and as a focal point for Intelligence Community collaboration. The NIC's key goal is to provide policymakers with the best, unvarnished, and unbiased information—regardless of whether analytic judgments conform to US policy. Its primary functions are to:

- Support the DNI in his role as Principal Intelligence Advisor to the President and other senior policymakers.

- Lead the Intelligence Community's effort to produce National Intelligence Estimates (NIEs) and other NIC products that address key national security concerns.
- Provide a focal point for policymakers, warfighters, and Congressional leaders to task the Intelligence Community for answers to important questions.
- Reach out to nongovernment experts in academia and the private sector—and use alternative analyses and new analytic tools—to broaden and deepen the Intelligence Community's perspective.

NATIONAL INTELLIGENCE ESTIMATES AND THE NIE PROCESS

National Intelligence Estimates (NIEs) are the Intelligence Community's (IC) most authoritative written judgments on national security issues and designed to help US civilian and military leaders develop policies to protect US national security interests. NIEs usually provide information on the current state of play but are primarily "estimative"—that is, they make judgments about the likely course of future events and identify the implications for US policy.

The NIEs are typically requested by senior civilian and military policymakers, Congressional leaders and at times are initiated by the National Intelligence Council (NIC). Before a NIE is drafted, the relevant NIO is responsible for producing a concept paper or terms of reference (TOR) and circulates it throughout the Intelligence Community for comment. The TOR defines the key estimative questions, determines drafting responsibilities, and sets the drafting and publication schedule. One or more IC analysts are usually assigned to produce the initial text. The NIC then meets to critique the draft before it is circulated to the broader IC. Representatives from the relevant IC agencies meet to hone and coordinate line-by-line the full text of the NIE. Working with their Agencies, reps also assign the level of confidence they have in each key judgment. IC reps discuss the quality of sources with collectors, and the National Clandestine Service vets the sources used to ensure the draft does not include any that have been recalled or otherwise seriously questioned.

All NIEs are reviewed by the National Intelligence Board, which is chaired by the DNI and is composed of the heads of relevant IC agencies. Once approved by the NIB, NIEs are briefed to the President and senior policymakers. The whole process of producing NIEs normally takes at least several months.

The NIC has undertaken a number of steps to improve the NIE process under the DNI. These steps are in accordance with the goals and recommendations set out in the SSCI and WMD Commission reports and the 2004 Intelligence Reform and Prevention of Terrorism Act. Most notably, over the last year and a half, the IC has:

- *Created new procedures to integrate formal reviews of source reporting and technical judgments.* The Directors of the National Clandestine Service, NSA, NGA, and DIA and the Assistant Secretary/INR are now required to submit formal assessments that highlight the strengths, weaknesses, and overall credibility of their sources used in developing the critical judgments of the NIE.
- *Applied more rigorous standards.* A textbox is incorporated into all NIEs that explains what we mean by such terms as "we judge" and that clarifies the difference between judgments of likelihood and confidence levels. We have made a concerted effort to not only highlight differences among agencies but to explain the reasons for such differences and to prominently display them in the Key Judgments.

Scope Note

This National Intelligence Estimate (NIE) assesses the status of Iran's nuclear program, and the program's outlook over the next 10 years. This time frame is more appropriate for estimating capabilities than intentions and foreign reactions, which are more difficult to estimate over a decade. In presenting the Intelligence Community's assessment of Iranian nuclear intentions and capabilities, the NIE thoroughly reviews all available information on these questions, examines the range of reasonable scenarios consistent with this information, and describes the key factors we judge would drive or impede nuclear progress in Iran. This NIE is an extensive reexamination of the issues in the May 2005 assessment.

This Estimate focuses on the following key questions:

- What are Iran's intentions toward developing nuclear weapons?
- What domestic factors affect Iran's decisionmaking on whether to develop nuclear weapons?
- What external factors affect Iran's decisionmaking on whether to develop nuclear weapons?
- What is the range of potential Iranian actions concerning the development of nuclear weapons, and the decisive factors that would lead Iran to choose one course of action over another?
- What is Iran's current and projected capability to develop nuclear weapons? What are our key assumptions, and Iran's key chokepoints/vulnerabilities?

This NIE does *not* assume that Iran intends to acquire nuclear weapons. Rather, it examines the intelligence to assess Iran's capability and intent (or lack thereof) to acquire nuclear weapons, taking full account of Iran's dual-use uranium fuel cycle and those nuclear activities that are at least partly civil in nature.

This Estimate does assume that the strategic goals and basic structure of Iran's senior leadership and government will remain similar to those that have endured since the death of Ayatollah Khomeini in 1989. We acknowledge the potential for these to change during the time frame of the Estimate, but are unable to confidently predict such changes or their implications. This Estimate does not assess how Iran may conduct future negotiations with the West on the nuclear issue.

This Estimate incorporates intelligence reporting available as of 31 October 2007.

Key Judgments

A. We judge with high confidence that in fall 2003, Tehran halted its nuclear weapons program*; we also assess with moderate-to-high confidence that Tehran at a minimum is keeping open the option to develop nuclear weapons. We judge with high confidence that the halt, and Tehran's announcement of its decision to suspend its declared uranium enrichment program and sign an Additional Protocol to its Nuclear Non-Proliferation Treaty Safeguards Agreement, was directed primarily in response to increasing international scrutiny and pressure resulting from exposure of Iran's previously undeclared nuclear work.

- We assess with high confidence that until fall 2003, Iranian military entities were working under government direction to develop nuclear weapons.
- We judge with high confidence that the halt lasted at least several years. (Because of intelligence gaps discussed elsewhere in this Estimate, however, DOE and the NIC assess with only moderate confidence that the halt to those activities represents a halt to Iran's entire nuclear weapons program.)
- We assess with moderate confidence Tehran had not restarted its nuclear weapons program as of mid-2007, but we do not know whether it currently intends to develop nuclear weapons.
- We continue to assess with moderate-to-high confidence that Iran does not currently have a nuclear weapon.
- Tehran's decision to halt its nuclear weapons program suggests it is less determined to develop nuclear weapons than we have been judging since 2005. Our assessment that the program probably was halted primarily in response to international pressure suggests Iran may be more vulnerable to influence on the issue than we judged previously.

B. We continue to assess with low confidence that Iran probably has imported at least some weapons-usable fissile material, but still judge with moderate-to-high

*For the purposes of this Estimate, by "nuclear weapons program" we mean Iran's nuclear weapon design and weaponization work and covert uranium conversion-related and uranium enrichment-related work; we do not mean Iran's declared civil work related to uranium conversion and enrichment.

What We Mean When We Say: An Explanation of Estimative Language

We use phrases such as *we judge, we assess,* and *we estimate*—and probabilistic terms such as *probably* and *likely*—to convey analytical assessments and judgments. Such statements are not facts, proof, or knowledge. These assessments and judgments generally are based on collected information, which often is incomplete or fragmentary. Some assessments are built on previous judgments. In all cases, assessments and judgments are not intended to imply that we have "proof" that shows something to be a fact or that definitively links two items or issues.

In addition to conveying judgments rather than certainty, our estimative language also often conveys 1) our assessed likelihood or probability of an event; and 2) the level of confidence we ascribe to the judgment.

Estimates of Likelihood. Because analytical judgments are not certain, we use probabilistic language to reflect the Community's estimates of the likelihood of developments or events. Terms such as *probably, likely, very likely,* or *almost certainly* indicate a greater than even chance. The terms *unlikely* and *remote* indicate a less then even chance that an event will occur; they do not imply that an event will not occur. Terms such as *might* or *may* reflect situations in which we are unable to assess the likelihood, generally because relevant information is unavailable, sketchy, or fragmented. Terms such as *we cannot dismiss, we cannot rule out,* or *we cannot discount* reflect an unlikely, improbable, or remote event whose consequences are such that it warrants mentioning. The chart provides a rough idea of the relationship of some of these terms to each other.

Remote	Very unlikely	Unlikely	Even chance	Probably/ Likely	Very likely	Almost certainly

Confidence in Assessments. Our assessments and estimates are supported by information that varies in scope, quality and sourcing. Consequently, we ascribe *high, moderate,* or *low* confidence to our assessments, as follows:

- *High confidence* generally indicates that our judgments are based on high-quality information, and/or that the nature of the issue makes it possible to render a solid judgment. A "high confidence" judgment is not a fact or a certainty, however, and such judgments still carry a risk of being wrong.

- *Moderate confidence* generally means that the information is credibly sourced and plausible but not of sufficient quality or corroborated sufficiently to warrant a higher level of confidence.

- *Low confidence* generally means that the information's credibility and/or plausibility is questionable, or that the information is too fragmented or poorly corroborated to make solid analytic inferences, or that we have significant concerns or problems with the sources.

confidence it has not obtained enough for a nuclear weapon. We cannot rule out that Iran has acquired from abroad—or will acquire in the future—a nuclear weapon or enough fissile material for a weapon. Barring such acquisitions, if Iran wants to have nuclear weapons it would need to produce sufficient amounts of fissile material indigenously—which we judge with high confidence it has not yet done.

C. We assess centrifuge enrichment is how Iran probably could first produce enough fissile material for a weapon, if it decides to do so. Iran resumed its declared

Key Differences Between the Key Judgments of This Estimate on Iran's Nuclear Program and the May 2005 Assessment

2005 IC Estimate	2007 National Intelligence Estimate
Assess with high confidence that Iran currently is determined to develop nuclear weapons despite its international obligations and international pressure, but we do not assess that Iran is immovable.	Judge with high confidence that in fall 2003, Tehran halted its nuclear weapons program. Judge with high confidence that the halt lasted at least several years. (DOE and the NIC have moderate confidence that the halt to those activities represents a halt to Iran's entire nuclear weapons program.) Assess with moderate confidence Tehran had not restarted its nuclear weapons program as of mid-2007, but we do not know whether it currently intends to develop nuclear weapons. Judge with high confidence that the halt was directed primarily in response to increasing international scrutiny and pressure resulting from exposure of Iran's previously undeclared nuclear work. Assess with moderate-to-high confidence that Tehran at a minimum is keeping open the option to develop nuclear weapons.
We have moderate confidence in projecting when Iran is likely to make a nuclear weapon; we assess that it is unlikely before early-to-mid next decade.	We judge with moderate confidence that the earliest possible date Iran would be technically capable of producing enough highly enriched uranium (HEU) for a weapon is late 2009, but that this is very unlikely. We judge with moderate confidence Iran probably would be technically capable of producing enough HEU for a weapon sometime during the 2010–2015 time frame. (INR judges that Iran is unlikely to achieve this capability before 2013 because of foreseeable technical and programmatic problems.)
Iran could produce enough fissile material for a weapon by the end of this decade if it were to make more rapid and successful progress than we have seen to date.	We judge with moderate confidence that the earliest possible date Iran would be technically capable of producing enough highly enriched uranium (HEU) for a weapon is late 2009, but that this is very unlikely.

centrifuge enrichment activities in January 2006, despite the continued halt in the nuclear weapons program. Iran made significant progress in 2007 installing centrifuges at Natanz, but we judge with moderate confidence it still faces significant technical problems operating them.

- We judge with moderate confidence that the earliest possible date Iran would be technically capable of producing enough HEU for a weapon is late 2009, but that this is very unlikely.

- We judge with moderate confidence Iran probably would be technically capable of producing enough HEU for a weapon sometime during the 2010–15 time frame. (INR judges Iran is unlikely to achieve this capability before 2013 because of foreseeable technical and programmatic problems.) All agencies recognize the possibility that this capability may not be attained until *after* 2015.

D. Iranian entities are continuing to develop a range of technical capabilities that could be applied to producing nuclear weapons, if a decision is made to do so. For example, Iran's civilian uranium enrichment program is continuing. We also assess with high confidence that since fall 2003, Iran has been conducting research and development projects with commercial and conventional military applications—some of which would also be of limited use for nuclear weapons.

E. We do not have sufficient intelligence to judge confidently whether Tehran is willing to maintain the halt of its nuclear weapons program indefinitely while it weighs its options, or whether it will or already has set specific deadlines or criteria that will prompt it to restart the program.

- Our assessment that Iran halted the program in 2003 primarily in response to international pressure indicates Tehran's decisions are guided by a cost-benefit approach rather than a rush to a weapon irrespective of the political, economic, and military costs. This, in turn, suggests that some combination of threats of intensified international scrutiny and pressures, along with opportunities for Iran to achieve its security, prestige, and goals for regional influence in other ways, might—if perceived by Iran's leaders as credible—prompt Tehran to extend the current halt to its nuclear weapons program. It is difficult to specify what such a combination might be.

- We assess with moderate confidence that convincing the Iranian leadership to forgo the eventual development of nuclear weapons will be difficult given the linkage many within the leadership probably see between nuclear weapons development and Iran's key national security and foreign policy objectives, and given Iran's considerable effort from at least the late 1980s to 2003 to develop such weapons. In our judgment, only an Iranian political decision to abandon a nuclear weapons objective would plausibly keep Iran from eventually producing nuclear weapons—and such a decision is inherently reversible.

F. We assess with moderate confidence that Iran probably would use covert facilities—rather than its declared nuclear sites—for the production of highly enriched uranium for a weapon. A growing amount of intelligence indicates Iran was engaged in covert uranium conversion and uranium enrichment activity, but we judge that these efforts probably were halted in response to the fall 2003 halt, and that these efforts probably had not been restarted through at least mid-2007.

G. We judge with high confidence that Iran will not be technically capable of producing and reprocessing enough plutonium for a weapon before about 2015.

H. We assess with high confidence that Iran has the scientific, technical, and industrial capacity eventually to produce nuclear weapons if it decides to do so.

Appendix I
Oversight of US Intelligence Activities

Given the number of critiques of intelligence performance that have been produced since the 9/11 attacks and the US invasion of Iraq, understanding how oversight of the US Intelligence Community is conducted can be confusing.

The White House has the primary responsibility within the executive branch for monitoring intelligence activities. This is done mainly through the National Security Council staff, although each president normally appoints members to the President's Foreign Intelligence Advisory Board (PFIAB) and directs them to selectively investigate substantive and bureaucratic intelligence issues. And within each of the intelligence organizations are inspectors-general, who monitor activities, and general counsels, who ensure that activities are consistent with US laws.

Prior to the mid-1970s, congressional oversight of intelligence activities was quite informal and relaxed. Bipartisan support for the fight against communism during the early Cold War years meant that Congress did not pay much attention to the details of intelligence activities and pretty much provided requested funds in the battle against the Soviet Union and international communism. Successive DCIs informed Senate and House leadership of key activities, and defense subcommittees were briefed on budgets and programs, but not much other interaction took place.

This rather passive approach to oversight came to an abrupt halt in the 1970s with congressional concerns about the Vietnam War, the Watergate cover-up, and the exposure of a few illegal intelligence activities. On learning that assassination attempts against foreign leaders had been made during the late 1950s and early 1960s, Congress launched investigations into past intelligence activities. The good news is that despite some minor infractions of legal restrictions, the CIA and other parts of the IC were found to have been operating as directed by the White House—they were not "rogue elephants" conducting their own operations overseas and domestically.

With new congressional assertiveness that followed and a recognition by members of Congress that they had not been playing a responsible oversight role, both houses established permanent select committees on intelligence—the Senate Select Committee on Intelligence (SSCI) and the House Permanent Select Committee on Intelligence (HPSCI)—to monitor all future intelligence activities. Some responsibilities for defense intelligence activities were retained by the defense committees, but the two new select committees took the lead. Subsequently, both committees began to review and critique all annual budgets and programs, and from time to time launched special investigations into particular issues, such as the IC's performance relative to the terrorist attacks on September 11, 2001, and more recently on the quality of intelligence on Iraqi WMD programs leading to the decision to use military force against the Saddam regime. Both committees have also become avid recipients of IC reports and frequently request their own tailor-made intelligence reporting. Thus, Congress is now better informed and better able to carry out its constitutional mandate to monitor the executive branch including the Intelligence Community.

Appendix J
The Production of a National Intelligence Estimate

The production of a national intelligence estimate (NIE) is a multifaceted and intense enterprise, as is the case with most intelligence products. Because NIEs are interagency products, the process is more involved and complex than the production of single-agency analyses. What follows is a generic description of the NIE production process which can be adjusted somewhat depending on the subject matter and its complexity.

Requirement: The request for a national intelligence estimate normally comes from the policy community, but an NIE may be initiated by the Intelligence Community (IC) in anticipation of a policy need. The National Intelligence Council (NIC), now part of the Office of the Director of National Intelligence (ODNI) determines the feasibility of producing the desired NIE and decides which of the national intelligence officers (NIOs) should take primary responsibility for its production.

Drafting: The relevant NIO proposes the scope, content, and timing for the NIE, which is then circulated and considered at an interagency meeting of IC experts. The NIO identifies a primary drafter, sets the schedule for the NIE's production, and solicits substantive inputs from IC agencies, depending on their particular expertise.

Coordination: Once the NIO is satisfied that a reasonable draft has been prepared, it is circulated to all IC agencies for review, and a meeting is scheduled to coordinate the draft and to prepare the Key Judgments. It is important that any alternative views are vetted and included, especially where gaps in information prevent a confident judgment.

Substantive review: Once the draft has been coordinated, it is submitted to a panel of outside experts to review for content, accuracy, completeness, and responsiveness to the policy need. The NIO considers the results of this review and determines if any adjustments should be made to the draft NIE.

Final IC review: When the NIO and NIC chairman conclude that the draft NIE is ready for final IC review, it is discussed at a meeting of the National Intelligence

Board (heads of all IC agencies chaired by the DNI) to determine whether the NIE is ready for dissemination to policymakers.

Dissemination: The published NIE is disseminated to relevant policymakers (including members of Congress) who have a legitimate need to know normally under a cover letter signed by the DNI. If it is of sufficient importance, a short summary of the NIE's judgments will be included in the president's daily intelligence briefing, and oral briefings of senior policymakers may also be scheduled.

Follow-up: The IC solicits feedback from policymakers to ensure their need has been met and to provide further explanations as well as to respond to questions. If the production of the NIE uncovers significant collection or analytic gaps, the NIC will instruct IC agencies to take steps to fill in the gaps.

Appendix K
History of Presidential Influence on US Intelligence

Note: The best comprehensive history of how the US Intelligence Community became what it is today is Christopher Andrew's *For the President's Eyes Only: Secret
Intelligence and the American Presidency from Washington to Bush*. All historical
facts in this appendix, except for the Clinton and George W. Bush administrations,
are drawn from this source, unless otherwise noted.

All presidents and their administrations, particularly since World War II, have
made decisions that have shaped the scope and capabilities of US intelligence. Most
presidential administrations have had a mixed record (both positive and negative
impact on the capabilities and effectiveness of the Intelligence Community), due in
part to their strong biases or reactions to events that occurred during their time in
office. And all have been guilty to one degree or another of attempting to politicize
intelligence to support their policy objectives. Moreover, all have had to deal with
imperfect intelligence and even intelligence failures, and some have ignored the intelligence provided even when it was accurate. A few administrations have blamed
the Intelligence Community, especially the CIA, for national security failures that
were in fact failures of policy, not intelligence. Thus, the dynamic and difficult relationship between policy and intelligence is a consistent part of the political and bureaucratic landscape in Washington, no matter which party is in the White House.
And since the mid-1970s, Congress has compounded the complexity of that relationship through its increased influence on Intelligence Community activities.

The United States was late in recognizing the need for any type of peacetime intelligence efforts against other countries. Only during times of military conflict did
the United States resort to intelligence activities, in order to win the war. The sense
of being an "island state" separated from the "old world" by the Atlantic Ocean
certainly contributed to the belief that the United States could exist apart from the
rest of the world. However, the nation ultimately discovered not once but twice that
conflicts in Europe, and subsequently in Asia, would affect its own security interests. It was only following World War II when its commercial and political interests
had become global and were threatened by communist expansion that the United
States reluctantly understood that it had to be better informed about what the rest

of the world was doing in peacetime. Even with this recognition tension continues between the conduct of secret activities on behalf of national security and concerns that such activities threaten civil liberties.

It was only in the 1960s that the United States, and therefore the Intelligence Community, began to focus on the proliferation of weapons of mass destruction, especially nuclear. Various administrations, along with an assertive Congress, have strengthened or weakened intelligence capabilities, particularly those targeted on WMD. While the earliest concerns were over nuclear proliferation, by the late 1970s biological and chemical weapons were also part of the mix.

Early US Military Intelligence Activities

During the Revolutionary War, *General Washington* faced a superior military force and resorted to all sorts of intelligence activities to learn about British troop movements and to deceive the British as to US capabilities and intentions. He ran his own group of spies, used coded messages, and employed deception to mislead British commanders. At the same time, the Continental Congress conducted its own intelligence activities through its Committee of Secret Correspondence, and it dispatched Benjamin Franklin to Paris as an agent of influence to ensure French support against the British.[1]

Following the war of independence, the United States saw no requirement for foreign intelligence and did not recreate some of General Washington's earlier capabilities until the Civil War. During that conflict, both Union and Confederate political and military leaders used intelligence to understand the intentions and capabilities of the other side in order to fight with superior knowledge. Moreover, advances in technology made it possible for both sides to improve on techniques used during the Revolutionary War. However, once the Civil War was over, the United States again relaxed and failed to pursue any peacetime intelligence activities. Only in the 1880s did the navy, and then the army, set up small intelligence units to be ready for any future military conflict.

Once *President Wilson* joined the struggle against the German Empire during World War I, he appreciated the benefit of good intelligence. For the first time, the United States developed, with the help of the British, a signals intelligence capability to read German and other codes. Even after the war, this capability (now incorporated into what was called the Black Chamber) provided useful information and tactical advantage during peace negotiations with Germany and later during the Washington Naval Conference. However, true to the past pattern, postconflict euphoria and the desire for "normalcy" resulted in the gutting of US intelligence capabilities by presidents Harding, Coolidge, and Hoover; the latter finally dismantled the Black Chamber. It was in this context that Secretary of State Stimson stated that "gentlemen do not read other gentlemen's mail," and he added his voice to those advocating an end to peacetime signals intelligence collection, calling it "highly unethical."

The rise of Nazi Germany and expansion of the Japanese Empire in the 1930s awoke Washington once again to the need for foreign intelligence (not yet, unfortunately, domestic intelligence or counterintelligence), especially code breaking. After the attack on Pearl Harbor, *President Roosevelt* established the first national intelligence effort, the Office of Strategic Services (OSS), which was devoted to supporting the war effort. The OSS made its biggest contribution in the European theater of operations. In the Pacific, General MacArthur refused to allow the OSS to participate, preferring rather to depend on the army's and navy's intelligence capabilities. Once again, the British joined forces with the United States and taught the Americans essentially everything they needed to know about espionage and covert actions, as together they sought to support the French resistance and infiltrate Nazi Germany. The United States also used deception effectively, which made the landings at Normandy on D-Day successful by misleading the Germans about where the main landing was to take place. Nevertheless, before his death, Roosevelt resisted suggestions that he establish a peacetime intelligence capability.

Establishing the US Intelligence Community

At the end of World War II, a yearning for "normalcy" and perhaps a false hope that establishing the United Nations would end international conflict led to the dismantling of the OSS (along with general military demobilization), despite warnings about a growing Soviet threat. Ultimately, *President Truman* and others recognized the need to prevent another nasty surprise, as had been the case with the Japanese attack on Pearl Harbor, and signed into law the National Security Act of 1947, which established the National Security Council and the Department of Defense along with the Central Intelligence Agency (CIA), the first peacetime intelligence organization in US history. The act made clear, however, that the CIA was to deal only with foreign intelligence, not domestic. There was considerable concern that the government not create a Gestapo or KGB type organization with both foreign intelligence and domestic intelligence/policy responsibilities, and moreover the FBI under J. Edgar Hoover resisted any encroachment on its turf. Thus, from the beginning of the modern-day US Intelligence Community a legal and bureaucratic wall was built between foreign and domestic intelligence activities. One of the United States' difficulties in sharing information within the Intelligence Community and understanding the terrorist threat in 2001 was the rigid separation between foreign and domestic intelligence.

When President Truman found himself facing a growing Soviet and international communist threat, he resorted to covert actions (such as efforts to clandestinely support pro-Western political parties in Turkey, Greece, and Italy) in an effort to blunt Soviet attempts to turn countries in Eastern Europe and outside the Soviet sphere to communism. Through additional, classified executive orders, the CIA was given the responsibilities to conduct clandestine human source collection activities overseas (espionage or spying) and to organize and execute covert actions.

Covert actions, in contrast to typical intelligence activities, are policy efforts to influence the political, economic, military, and leadership situations in other countries. They are ordered by the president with the advice of the National Security Council when neither diplomacy nor the use of US military power is deemed appropriate, effective, or desirable. In the case of paramilitary operations, the intent is to train and support foreign fighters to accomplish a military objective, such as overthrowing Fidel Castro, as in the failed Bay of Pigs invasion in 1961, and driving Soviet military forces out of Afghanistan in the 1980s. Covert actions are to be carried out without exposing the US government's hand, thereby providing plausible deniability to the administration. Since the mid-1970s, the president has been required to notify both intelligence committees in the Congress when he has decided to pursue such a policy in a particular case. Because the same skill set required to conduct clandestine human source collection (spying) is generally needed to organize and implement covert actions, the Truman administration decided that the CIA would be responsible for their execution. However, covert actions are not intelligence activities in the traditional sense; they are policy actions, not efforts to collect, analyze, or inform policymakers about the hostile world they face.[2]

Having benefited from OSS successes during the war in Europe, *President Eisenhower* continued the active use of covert actions (as in Iran and Guatemala). Moreover, his administration became increasingly concerned with understanding the nature and capabilities of the Soviet nuclear threat. Because of the closed nature of the USSR and the difficulty of recruiting and running human agents, he launched projects to create remote technical collection capabilities (U-2 reconnaissance aircraft and photographic satellites) that would hopefully provide information to make reasonable decisions about defense issues and to avoid making worst-case assessments of Soviet intentions and capabilities. Indeed, the Eisenhower administration launched the US Intelligence Community in earnest by establishing the National Security Agency in 1952 to manage the collection of signals intelligence and by setting an aggressive pattern of collecting intelligence on the Soviet Union and its overseas activities (along with other closed countries, such as China and Castro's Cuba). His administration's support for peacetime intelligence enabled the development of US intelligence capabilities during the early Cold War. However, his plans for a covert action to invade Cuba and overthrow Castro inadvertently set the stage for a major setback in the reputation of the United States and the CIA.

President Kennedy's agreement in the spring of 1961 to launch covert action against Cuba marred his administration and gave the CIA and the United States a black eye. Most likely he was overly optimistic due to the success of previous covert actions under the Truman and Eisenhower administrations. Moreover, his administration pushed the CIA to launch plans to assassinate Castro, which later came to light, causing considerable bad press for the CIA and leading in the 1970s to congressional investigations of its misdeeds. However, during the 1962 Cuban Missile Crisis, when U-2 photographs showed that the Soviets were indeed placing offensive, medium-range nuclear missiles in Cuba, Kennedy learned that good intelligence was essential for the success of US policy. In another arena, he began a White House-intelligence relationship that continues today, namely, the daily provision of current intelligence known as the President's Daily Brief. Kennedy was also concerned about nuclear proliferation and directed an intelligence focus on that issue.

The Johnson administration continued to expand intelligence capabilities, as evidenced by the public disclosure of the SR-71 reconnaissance aircraft, a replacement for the U-2. When China joined the nuclear club in 1964, concern about the further spread of nuclear capabilities increased, which had a direct impact on the IC. But most of that progress was overshadowed by the Vietnam war effort, which had an impact on intelligence priorities and activities. Johnson and his closest advisors tried to ignore the CIA's analysis during the Vietnam war when a debate was raging between the Department of Defense and the CIA over the progress of the war effort and the likelihood of the South winning against the North.

According to one CIA expert, any criticism of the South Vietnamese army's shortcomings was off-limits. This came to a head in the preparation of a national intelligence estimate (NIE) in 1963, in which analysts concluded that the South's key weaknesses included a lack of aggressive and firm leadership, poor morale among the troops, a lack of trust between peasants and soldiers, and obvious Communist penetration of the South's military organization. The criticisms raised a firestorm among policymakers, and DCI McCone agreed to have a more rosy NIE written. This was not one of the CIA's proudest moments. Clearly, decisions on what to do in Vietnam and how to do it were taking place in a highly charged political arena. For some years the Democratic Party had been vulnerable for having "lost" China and having been "soft" in Korea. Presidents Kennedy and Johnson repeatedly stated that they were not going to be the presidents who lost Vietnam and Southeast Asia.[3] Only at the end of his presidency did Johnson finally agree to hear the intelligence analysis, which led to his acknowledgment that he had been blind to the situation on the ground.

President Nixon came to office with disdain for the CIA, because he believed that the IC had cost him the 1960 election by its unwillingness to disclose publicly that the Democratic Party's accusations of a missile gap with the USSR had been false.

Consequently, he kept the CIA in particular at arm's length by using his national security advisor, Henry Kissinger, as the gatekeeper for all incoming intelligence. Only in the case of strategic nuclear arms control negotiations did the Nixon administration appreciate the contribution that intelligence could make to informing policy. But even in this arena, the Nixon administration took issue with the IC's analysis of the capabilities of the Soviet intercontinental ballistic missile (ICBM) force, and it put pressure on the IC to change its judgments, believing that the analysis would undercut the administration's efforts to get the Safeguard antiballistic missile (ABM) system approved and funded by Congress.

In contrast to the IC's judgment in a 1968 NIE that the large Soviet SS-9 ICBM, even in its three-warhead version, was capable of hitting only one target, not three independent targets, Secretary of Defense Laird publicly claimed that the SS-9 could carry three multiple, independently targetable reentry vehicles (MIRVs), which would allow it to strike three different targets, thereby giving the Soviets a disarming first-strike capability.[4] The IC's analysis eventually proved to be correct when the Soviets tested a real MIRV capability in 1973 and then deployed MIRVs on their new SS-19 missiles in 1974. The replacement for the SS-9, the large SS-18 ICBM, also appeared later with a MIRV capability.

Even after the Senate approved the ABM program, the Pentagon continued to lean on the IC to not undercut the administration's characterization of Soviet strategic capability. When the next NIE on Soviet strategic offensive forces was about to come out in 1969, pressure was put on DCI Richard Helms to delete a paragraph that said, "We consider it unlikely that they (the Soviets) will attempt within the period of this estimate . . . to achieve a first-strike capability." Helms was subsequently criticized within the IC for having caved to political pressure, and the 1975 congressional investigations concluded that the DCI had been put under unusual pressure by the Nixon administration.[5]

However, the Nixon administration's biggest abuse of intelligence came in its use of the CIA to collect against domestic antiwar demonstrators and, as the Watergate fiasco unfolded, in its efforts to use the CIA in its cover-up scheme. Nixon's establishing the "Plumbers" as a private intelligence cell inside the White House compromised domestic intelligence efforts. When Helms refused Nixon's order to implicate the CIA in the cover-up scheme, Nixon fired him. And it was during the Nixon presidency that India conducted what it referred to as a peaceful nuclear explosion. Thus, proliferation within the developing world was becoming a serious concern for the United States during this time.

President Ford's short time in office was overshadowed by the aftermath of Watergate, the "loss" of Vietnam, and the subsequent congressional investigations into the "misdeeds" of the IC under previous presidents. However, the silver lining is that the US Congress finally began taking its oversight responsibilities for intelligence activities seriously through the establishment of two permanent intelligence oversight committees. Moreover, this led to Congress being not only a watchdog of intelligence activities but also an insatiable consumer of intelligence information.[6] This dark period in the history of US intelligence ultimately led to a healthier functioning of the government through dedicated congressional oversight and to a sense of relief that US intelligence activities were now being conducted in accordance with the law. In the so-called Team B affair, Ford did allow the US Intelligence Community's reputation to be challenged by conservative ideologues who believed that the United States was underestimating the intentions and capabilities of the Soviet Union to wage and win a nuclear war. While the judgments of the IC should always be put to the test, this was a highly political episode that led to few new insights into the USSR. However, the episode once again reminded the IC that its credibility is well served by allowing outside experts (and even critics) to review its work and ensure that it is not suffering from a closed mind-set.

President Carter began his administration with considerable anxiety about intelligence activities and a definite bias against clandestine human collection (espionage) and the use of covert actions. In addition, Carter began what some believe is the politicization of the Intelligence Community's leadership by insisting on replacing George H.W. Bush, a staunch Republican, with Admiral Stansfield Turner as Director of Central Intelligence. Because of its bias, this administration gutted the CIA's clandestine human collection capabilities in favor of technical collection capabilities, which were in fact becoming quite impressive. Nevertheless, by the end of his presidency international events forced Carter to rethink the role of espionage as a national security tool.

With regard to Iran, the Carter administration followed several predecessor administrations in prohibiting the CIA from developing clandestine links to opposition figures in order not to offend the Shah. As a result, CIA had to base its assessments of Iran's internal situation largely on liaison information provided by SAVAK, the Shah's secret police. Despite increasing unrest in 1978, CIA was not able to provide warning that a revolution was about to happen. When the coup by the Ayatollah Khomeini took place the following year, the White House called it an intelligence failure. US intelligence certainly failed to provide warning of the revolution, but there was also a policy failure for restricting CIA's ability to collect relevant information and for downplaying the importance of clandestine human collection. DCI Turner was convinced that he had been set up as the scapegoat. In addition, Carter launched what became the largest US paramilitary covert action in history: the effort to drive the Soviets out of Afghanistan. Finally in 1979 on Carter's watch, a US VELA satellite detected a bright flash from the South Atlantic, which some suspected was a nuclear explosion. The IC was never able to confirm that judgment through the collection of radionuclide material or other intelligence analyses, but in the 1990s there were assertions that the "flash" had in fact been a joint South African-Israeli nuclear test.[7]

When *President Reagan* took office with a clearly stated agenda to rebuild US defense and intelligence capabilities, concerns about the politicization of intelligence arose with the appointment of William Casey as DCI. Casey was a committed Republican and anticommunist who had OSS experience, and he set about to use the IC to do battle with the Soviet Union. This led to accusations that the CIA's analysis was being biased by a mind-set that was looking only for proof of Soviet misdeeds rather than understanding the realities of the USSR. Reagan and Casey began to rebuild intelligence capabilities, especially in the realm of clandestine human source collection—the very area that Carter and Turner had gutted. In addition, Reagan, with considerable push from members of Congress, expanded US support to the Mujahedin against Soviet forces in Afghanistan, which ultimately led to the withdrawal of Soviet troops. But it also resulted in the exposure of the government's hand in the covert action (thereby compromising plausible deniability) and led to the longer-term, unintended consequence of trained and armed Islamic fundamentalists now opposed to Western, particularly US, interests. On the positive side, the Reagan administration fully supported a robust and effective IC, and it put intelligence capabilities to good use in the negotiation and monitoring of treaties that dramatically reduced, and in some cases eliminated, key elements of the Soviet nuclear threat.

President George H.W. Bush, having served as DCI under President Ford, was a strong supporter of intelligence. His administration faced the collapse of the USSR and did not accept accusations that it had been let down by the Intelligence Community for not predicting the event with any precision. The CIA and the community as a whole had provided strategic warning that collapse was under way, but it was not possible to forecast how quickly or in what form that collapse would take. The passing of the USSR into history led to concerns about "loose nukes"—that positive control of the former Soviet nuclear arsenal would be compromised or that now under- or unemployed Soviet nuclear experts might sell their expertise (and possibly nuclear secrets or material) to other countries or to non-state entities. Equally significant for the IC was the Gulf War of 1991, during which it was discovered that national intelligence capabilities developed during the Cold War were not well suited to support tactical military operations in remote places of the globe. This led to a refocus of intelligence capabilities. The administration was also under considerable pressure from Congress to contribute to what became known as the "peace dividend"—savings from reduced post–Cold War spending on defense and intelligence. Congress began pushing for adjustments in intelligence priorities and reductions in resources, which threatened some core capabilities.

The Clinton administration took the new post–Cold War reality to heart and began to reduce intelligence capabilities, once again generally in the area of clandestine human source collection. Thus, for the second time in two decades, the CIA was being told to "stand down" on agent recruitment and to focus on other issues. No one denied that reorientation was required, but it was a struggle to prevent post–Cold War euphoria from leading to unwise decisions. Intelligence budgets were slashed. The highest concern was the possibility of nuclear weapons, technology, expertise, or material from the former USSR getting into the wrong hands. Moreover, with the Saddam Hussein regime, the festering problems of regional instability and possibly proliferating weapons of mass destruction were taking shape. Despite efforts by the previous Bush and now Clinton administrations to launch covert actions to topple the Saddam regime, no success was achieved. Fortunately, the CIA was increasing the allocation of its declining resources to counterterrorism, and Osama Bin Laden and his growing organization, al-Qaeda, were clearly on the radar scope. Meanwhile, North Korea's nuclear weapon program was of increasing concern, which led the IC to increase its focus on proliferation issues.

By the time the *George W. Bush* administration appeared in 2001, proliferation and terrorist issues were at the top of the list of priorities for the US Intelligence Community. However, because it was still in transition from its Cold War posture, the IC was not yet optimally positioned to deal with these threats to national security.

The new administration began its first term with a positive boost for the IC in terms of management continuity: it agreed to retain DCI George Tenet, who had been appointed by President Clinton in 1997. Keeping Tenet provided critical continuity in senior management after several decades of successive administrations bringing in a new DCI (three during the Clinton administration). Moreover, the new administration, perhaps due to the influence of the new president's father, had a positive attitude toward intelligence and sought appropriate funding and support after the post–Cold War downturn in intelligence resources of the Clinton administration.

The terrorist attacks on New York and Washington on September 11, 2001, which took place barely eight months after the new administration had taken office, led to changes in Washington, and especially the Intelligence Community, which are still being sorted out. The record shows that the IC provided loud and clear "strategic" warning that al-Qaeda was intent on doing something dramatic against US interests either overseas or possibly within the United States itself. There is a question as to how seriously the Bush administration took the warnings. It was no doubt frustrating to policymakers that the available intelligence was not actionable: the IC was unable to provide "tactical" warnings on the exact time or place that an attack would occur, or on the manner of an attack.[8]

All serious studies after the tragic incident show that there was precious little information on the plans of the terrorists. Nevertheless, the inability of the IC to provide tactical warning evoked memories of the surprise attack on Pearl Harbor, which had been a key reason for establishing the Intelligence Community, particularly the CIA, after World War II. The failure to give precise warning on the September 11 attacks led to severe criticism of US intelligence and led to calls for the revamping of the IC. An immediate and dramatic shift in priorities occurred, and resources were realigned to support what became known as the war on terror.

Other than the tactical mistakes in both the foreign (CIA) and domestic (FBI) arenas, the most important intelligence shortcoming identified in the terrorist attacks of September 11 was the inability of domestic and foreign intelligence to come together consistently and comprehensively. This was due in large measure to the legal and bureaucratic wall that successive administrations and congresses since 1947 had built and reinforced between foreign and domestic intelligence activities to protect civil liberties and privacy. To correct this situation, the administration established the Department of Homeland Security (DHS), which added a new component to the Intelligence Community—one the administration hoped would enhance the sharing and blending of foreign and domestic intelligence as well as local law enforcement information. The FBI put more resources on domestic counterintelligence and counterproliferation. In addition, the 9/11 Commission recommended, and the Congress pressed for, establishing the position of Director of National Intelligence (DNI) to draw together foreign and domestic intelligence at the top, particularly in the area of counterterrorism to support the DHS. This was followed by the realization that intelligence provided to policymakers on Iraq's WMD programs appeared to have been incorrect, which added fuel to the calls for changes to the Intelligence Community.

Unfortunately, the legislation that came out in the fall of 2004 did so in the midst of a presidential election, when eyes were on winning elections rather than on doing the best thing for the country. When the Democratic nominee for president, Senator John Kerry, endorsed the 9/11 Commission recommendations as a whole, President Bush apparently felt obliged to avoid being seen as dragging his feet on fixing the intelligence problem. Having made some administrative adjustments through executive orders, he finally added his support to the new legislation. As it turned out, some of the changes, such as splitting the DCI's three roles into two portfolios (the DNI became the president's senior intelligence advisor and chief of the IC, while the directorship of the CIA was split away), have probably improved information sharing within the Intelligence Community, especially between domestic and foreign intelligence agencies. However, because of bureaucratic realities, such as the relative power of the Secretary of Defense, a gap remains between the responsibilities and the authorities of the DNI—a situation that had plagued every DCI since 1947. Moreover, the responsibilities are so diffuse that an "intelligence failure," which is likely at some point, might lead to finger pointing in several directions rather than one. Thus, it is not surprising that already Congress and the first two DNIs have complained that the DNI is not able to do all that had been envisioned by the 9/11 Commission and the drafters of the 2004 legislation. Such complaints reinforce a conclusion that the George W. Bush administration allowed itself to be swept along in the political arena into agreeing to a new Intelligence Community management structure that had not been fully vetted and thought through.

For the relations among various intelligence agencies, the 2004 legislation in one respect served as "payback time" for the CIA. Because the DCI had also been the director of the CIA, criticism of the IC's judgments regarding Iraqi WMD programs fell largely on the CIA. Moreover, since its inception in 1947, the CIA has been seen at least by the White House as the first among equals in providing all-source analysis, especially to the President. This status has grated on other intelligence agencies, which have perceived that CIA judgments were always given more weight than their own and that they were second-class citizens in the community. Once criticisms of the incorrect NIE judgments on Iraq's WMD were pegged largely (though incorrectly) on the CIA, the agency was put on the defensive. The legislation and reorganization seem to have taken pride of place away from the CIA, and more influence has been given to other agencies, especially the Department of State's Bureau of Intelligence and Research. We hope that the rough ride of this bureaucratic change and acrimony will be smoothed out over time with the help of cooler heads. It is critical that the US Intelligence Community function in a collegial and positive manner; all components of the community are essential to its success.

Finally, the George W. Bush administration's handling of intense political criticism over its using military force to oust Saddam's regime and then occupying the country has led it to put the blame for poor policy implementation on the Intelligence Community. After prominent members of the administration had hyped the imminence of the regime's WMD threat by declaring that the administration didn't want "the smoking gun" to be "a mushroom cloud" and by alleging entirely unfounded links between the regime and al-Qaeda (and by implication to 9/11), the administration then tried to blame the IC and its management for getting it wrong. As explained in Chapter 5, the IC was guilty of definite shortcomings in not offering a more thorough assessment of Iraq's WMD capabilities. In contrast, the two NIEs produced in late 2002 and early 2003 as companions to the 2002 NIE on Iraqi WMD were prescient in offering a clear and forceful warning about the risks in using military force to replace Saddam. However, some in the administration chose to listen to voices outside the IC and shape the intelligence to fit the policy rather than vice versa; ultimately, they took the easier path of letting blame for a mistaken policy fall on the shoulders of the IC.

As fallout from the increased political fighting over US military involvement in Iraq, DCI Tenet lost the confidence of the administration and felt compelled to resign. His replacement, former congressman Porter Goss, faced a tough job in rebuilding the confidence and reputation of the IC, particularly of the CIA, but unfortunately he did not go about it in a positive manner. By bringing in with him a cadre of inexperienced, arrogant staffers from the Hill, his tenure caused additional strains and resulted in the resignation of a large number of senior and midlevel competent CIA officials. After a disastrous eighteen months, President Bush finally replaced Goss with General Michael Hayden as director of the CIA. Hayden was a professional military intelligence officer and former director of the National Security Agency and deputy DNI, who appears to have brought good management and helped restore the morale and competence of the agency. (We believe it unfortunate that the Obama administration, due largely to political considerations, was unwilling to allow Hayden (a professional intelligence officer) to remain in his post at least for a period of time.)

We conclude that the George W. Bush administration's intelligence legacy will be viewed negatively. Although the administration supported the Intelligence Community in many areas, the intelligence-policymaker relationship was put under strain that is comparable to what occurred under presidents Nixon and Johnson. Under this administration there were unprecedented efforts to shape and deliberately distort intelligence to serve political objectives. To prevail in the battle against international terrorism and to prevent further WMD proliferation, it is essential that the United States protect the intelligence process and its product from such misuse. It will take time for the restructuring and reorienting of US intelligence capabilities to sort out and for the bureaucratic wounds to heal. Meanwhile, we hope that the American public will not complacently believe that changes made as a result of the 2004 legislation have solved all problems and will prevent future intelligence failures or terrorist attacks, especially an attack involving weapons of mass destruction.

Appendix L

National Intelligence Estimate, Key Judgments: Iraq's Continuing Programs for Weapons of Mass Destruction, October 2002

Federation of American Scientists (FAS) Note: The following excerpts from an October 2002 National Intelligence Estimate were declassified on July 18, 2003, and presented at a *White House background briefing* on weapons of mass destruction in Iraq.

Key Judgments [from October 2002 NIE][1]

Iraq's Continuing Programs for Weapons of Mass Destruction

We judge that Iraq has continued its weapons of mass destruction (WMD) programs in defiance of UN resolutions and restrictions. Baghdad has chemical and biological weapons as well as missiles with ranges in excess of UN restrictions; if left unchecked, it probably will have a nuclear weapon during this decade. (See INR alternative view at the end of these Key Judgments.)

We judge that we are seeing only a portion of Iraq's WMD efforts, owing to Baghdad's vigorous denial and deception efforts. Revelations after the Gulf war starkly demonstrate the extensive efforts undertaken by Iraq to deny information. We lack specific information on many key aspects of Iraq's WMD programs.

Since inspections ended in 1998, Iraq has maintained its chemical weapons effort, energized its missile program, and invested more heavily in biological weapons; in the view of most agencies, Baghdad is reconstituting its nuclear weapons program.

- Iraq's growing ability to sell oil illicitly increases Baghdad's capabilities to finance WMD programs; annual earnings in cash and goods have more than quadrupled, from $580 million in 1998 to about $3 billion this year.
- Iraq has largely rebuilt missile and biological weapons facilities damaged during Operation Desert Fox and has expanded its chemical and biological infrastructure under the cover of civilian production.
- Baghdad has exceeded UN range limits of 150 km with its ballistic missiles and is working with unmanned aerial vehicles (UAVs), which allow for a more lethal means to deliver biological and, less likely, chemical warfare agents.

- Although we assess that Saddam does not yet have nuclear weapons or sufficient material to make any, he remains intent on acquiring them. Most agencies assess that Baghdad started reconstituting its nuclear program about the time that UNSCOM inspectors departed—December 1998.

How quickly Iraq will obtain its first nuclear weapon depends on when it acquires sufficient weapons-grade fissile material.

- If Baghdad acquires sufficient fissile material from abroad it could make a nuclear weapon within several months to a year.
- Without such material from abroad, Iraq probably would not be able to make a weapon until 2007 to 2009, owing to inexperience in building and operating centrifuge facilities to produce highly enriched uranium and challenges in procuring the necessary equipment and expertise.
  - o Most agencies believe that Saddam's personal interest in and Iraq's aggressive attempts to obtain high-strength aluminum tubes for centrifuge rotors—as well as Iraq's attempts to acquire magnets, high-speed balancing machines, and machine tools—provide compelling evidence that Saddam is reconstituting a uranium enrichment effort for Baghdad's nuclear weapons program. (DOE agrees that reconstitution of the nuclear program is underway but assesses that the tubes probably are not part of the program.)
  - o Iraq's efforts to re-establish and enhance its cadre of weapons personnel as well as activities at several suspect nuclear sites further indicate that reconstitution is underway.
  - o All agencies agree that about 25,000 centrifuges based on tubes of the size Iraq is trying to acquire would be capable of producing approximately two weapons' worth of highly enriched uranium per year.
- In a much less likely scenario, Baghdad could make enough fissile material for a nuclear weapon by 2005 to 2007 if it obtains suitable centrifuge tubes this year and has all the other materials and technological expertise necessary to build production-scale uranium enrichment facilities.

We assess that Baghdad has begun renewed production of mustard, sarin, GF (cyclosarin), and VX; its capability probably is more limited now than it was at the time of the Gulf war, although VX production and agent storage life probably have been improved.

- An array of clandestine reporting reveals that Baghdad has procured covertly the types and quantities of chemicals and equipment sufficient to allow limited CW agent production hidden within Iraq's legitimate chemical industry.
- Although we have little specific information on Iraq's CW stockpile, Saddam

probably has stocked at least 100 metric tons (MT) and possibly as much as 500 MT of CW agents—much of it added in the last year.

- The Iraqis have experience in manufacturing CW bombs, artillery rockets, and projectiles. We assess that they possess CW bulk fills for SRBM warheads, including for a limited number of covertly stored Scuds, possibly a few with extended ranges.

We judge that all key aspects—R&D, production, and weaponization—of Iraq's offensive BW program are active and that most elements are larger and more advanced than they were before the Gulf war.

- We judge Iraq has some lethal and incapacitating BW agents and is capable of quickly producing and weaponizing a variety of such agents, including anthrax, for delivery by bombs, missiles, aerial sprayers, and covert operatives.
  - o Chances are even that smallpox is part of Iraq's offensive BW program.
  - o Baghdad probably has developed genetically engineered BW agents.
- Baghdad has established a large-scale, redundant, and concealed BW agent production capability.
  - o Baghdad has mobile facilities for producing bacterial and toxin BW agents; these facilities can evade detection and are highly survivable. Within three to six months [Corrected per Errata sheet issued in October 2002] these units probably could produce an amount of agent equal to the total that Iraq produced in the years prior to the Gulf war.

Iraq maintains a small missile force and several development programs, including for a UAV probably intended to deliver biological warfare agent.

- Gaps in Iraqi accounting to UNSCOM suggest that Saddam retains a covert force of up to a few dozen Scud-variant SRBMs with ranges of 650 to 900 km.
- Iraq is deploying its new al-Samoud and Ababil-100 SRBMs, which are capable of flying beyond the UN-authorized 150-km range limit; Iraq has tested an al-Samoud variant beyond 150 km—perhaps as far as 300 km.
- Baghdad's UAVs could threaten Iraq's neighbors, U.S. forces in the Persian Gulf, *and if brought close to, or into, the United States, the U.S. Homeland.*
  - o An Iraqi UAV procurement network attempted to procure commercially available route planning software and an associated topographic database that would be able to support targeting of the United States, according to analysis of special intelligence.
  - o The Director, Intelligence, Surveillance, and Reconnaissance, U.S. Air Force, does not agree that Iraq is developing UAVs *primarily* intended to be delivery platforms for chemical and biological warfare (CBW) agents. The small

size of Iraq's new UAV strongly suggests a primary role of reconnaissance, although CBW delivery is an inherent capability.

- Iraq is developing medium-range ballistic missile capabilities, largely through foreign assistance in building specialized facilities, including a test stand for engines more powerful than those in its current missile force.

We have low confidence in our ability to assess when Saddam would use WMD.

- Saddam could decide to use chemical and biological warfare (CBW) preemptively against U.S. forces, friends, and allies in the region in an attempt to disrupt U.S. war preparations and undermine the political will of the Coalition.
- Saddam might use CBW after an initial advance into Iraqi territory, but early use of WMD could foreclose diplomatic options for stalling the US advance.
- He probably would use CBW when he perceived he irretrievably had lost control of the military and security situation, but we are unlikely to know when Saddam reaches that point.
- We judge that Saddam would be more likely to use chemical weapons than biological weapons on the battlefield.
- Saddam historically has maintained tight control over the use of WMD; however, he probably has provided contingency instructions to his commanders to use CBW in specific circumstances.

Baghdad for now appears to be drawing a line short of conducting terrorist attacks with conventional or CBW against the United States, fearing that exposure of Iraqi involvement would provide Washington a stronger cause for making war.

Iraq probably would attempt clandestine attacks against the U.S. Homeland if Baghdad feared an attack that threatened the survival of the regime were imminent or unavoidable, or possibly for revenge. Such attacks—more likely with biological than chemical agents—probably would be carried out by special forces or intelligence operatives.

- The Iraqi Intelligence Service (IIS) probably has been directed to conduct clandestine attacks against US and Allied interests in the Middle East in the event the United States takes action against Iraq. The US probably would be the primary means by which Iraq would attempt to conduct any CBW attacks on the US Homeland, although we have no specific intelligence information that Saddam's regime has directed attacks against US territory.

Saddam, if sufficiently desperate, might decide that only an organization such as al-Qa'ida—with worldwide reach and extensive terrorist infrastructure, and already engaged in a life-or-death struggle against the United States—could perpetrate the type of terrorist attack that he would hope to conduct.

- In such circumstances, he might decide that the extreme step of assisting the Islamist terrorists in conducting a CBW attack against the United States would be his last chance to exact vengeance by taking a large number of victims with him.

Confidence Levels for Selected Key Judgments in This Estimate

High Confidence:

- Iraq is continuing, and in some areas expanding, its chemical, biological, nuclear and missile programs contrary to UN resolutions.
- We are not detecting portions of these weapons programs.
- Iraq possesses proscribed chemical and biological weapons and missiles.
- Iraq could make a nuclear weapon in months to a year once it acquires sufficient weapons-grade fissile material

Moderate Confidence:

- Iraq does not yet have a nuclear weapon or sufficient material to make one but is likely to have a weapon by 2007 to 2009. (See INR alternative view, page 84).

Low Confidence:

- When Saddam would use weapons of mass destruction.
- Whether Saddam would engage in clandestine attacks against the US Homeland.
- Whether in desperation Saddam would share chemical or biological weapons with al-Qa'ida.

[NIE page 24]

Uranium Acquisition. Iraq retains approximately two-and-a-half tons of 2.5 percent enriched uranium oxide, which the IAEA permits. This low-enriched material could be used as feed material to produce enough HEU for about two nuclear weapons. The use of enriched feed material also would reduce the initial number of centrifuges that Baghdad would need by about half. Iraq could divert this material—the IAEA inspects it only once a year—and enrich it to weapons grade before a subsequent inspection discovered it was missing. The IAEA last inspected this material in late January 2002.

Iraq has about 500 metric tons of yellowcake[2] and low enriched uranium at Tuwaitha, which is inspected annually by the IAEA. Iraq also began vigorously trying to procure uranium ore and yellowcake; acquiring either would shorten the time Baghdad needs to produce nuclear weapons.

- A foreign government service reported that as of early 2001, Niger planned to send several tons of "pure uranium" (probably yellowcake) to Iraq. As of early 2001, Niger and Iraq reportedly were still working out arrangements for this deal, which could be for up to 500 tons of yellowcake. We do not know the status of this arrangement.

- Reports indicate Iraq also has sought uranium ore from Somalia and possibly the Democratic Republic of the Congo.

We cannot confirm whether Iraq succeeded in acquiring uranium ore and/or yellowcake from these sources. Reports suggest Iraq is shifting from domestic mining and milling of uranium to foreign acquisition. Iraq possesses significant phosphate deposits, from which uranium had been chemically extracted before Operation Desert Storm. Intelligence information on whether nuclear-related phosphate mining and/or processing has been reestablished is inconclusive, however.

Annex A

Iraq's Attempts to Acquire Aluminum Tubes

(This excerpt from a longer view includes INR's position on the African uranium issue)

INR's Alternative View: Iraq's Attempts to Acquire Aluminum Tubes

Some of the specialized but dual-use items being sought are, by all indications, bound for Iraq's missile program. Other cases are ambiguous such as that of a planned magnet-production line whose suitability for centrifuge operations remains unknown. Some efforts involve non-controlled industrial material and equipment—including a variety of machine tools—and are troubling because they would help establish the infrastructure for a renewed nuclear program. But such efforts (which began well before the inspectors departed) are not clearly linked to a nuclear end-use. Finally, the claims of Iraqi pursuit of natural uranium in African are, in INR's assessment, highly dubious.

State/INR's Alternative view of Iraq's Nuclear Program

The Assistant Secretary of State for Intelligence and Research (INR) believes that Saddam continues to want nuclear weapons and that available evidence indicates that Baghdad is pursuing at least a limited effort to maintain and acquire nuclear weapon-related capabilities. The activities we have detected do not, however, add up to a compelling case that Iraq is currently pursuing what INR would consider to be an integrated and comprehensive approach to acquire nuclear weapons. Iraq may be doing so, but INR considers the available evidence inadequate to support such a judgment. Lacking persuasive evidence that Baghdad has launched a coherent effort to reconstitute its nuclear weapon program, INR is unwilling to speculate that such an effort began soon after the departure of UN inspectors or to project a timeline for the completion of activities it does not now see happening. As a result, INR is unable to predict when Iraq could acquire a nuclear device or weapon.

In INR's view, Iraq's efforts to acquire aluminum tubes is central to the argument that Baghdad is reconstituting its nuclear weapon program, but INR is not persuaded that the tubes in question are intended for use as centrifuge rotors. INR accepts the judgment of technical experts at the U.S. Department of Energy (DOE) who have concluded that the tubes Iraq seeks to acquire are poorly suited for use in gas centrifuges to be used for uranium enrichment and finds unpersuasive the arguments advanced by others to make the case that they are intended for that purpose. INR considers it far more likely that the tubes are intended for another purpose, most likely the production of artillery rockets. The very large quantities being sought, the way the tubes were tested by the Iraqis and the atypical lack of attention to operational security in the procurement efforts are among the factors, in addition to the DOE assessment, that lead INR to conclude that the tubes are not intended for use in Iraq's nuclear weapon program.

Appendix M
Proliferation Security Initiative

(*Source*: Proliferation Security Initiative: Statement of Interdiction Principles, http://www.whitehouse.gov/news/releases/2003/09/20030904-11.html)

Fact Sheet

The White House, Office of the Press Secretary
Washington, DC
September 4, 2003

Proliferation Security Initiative: Statement of Interdiction Principles

The Proliferation Security Initiative (PSI) is a response to the growing challenge posed by the proliferation of weapons of mass destruction (WMD), their delivery systems, and related materials worldwide. The PSI builds on efforts by the international community to prevent proliferation of such items, including existing treaties and regimes. It is consistent with and a step in the implementation of the UN Security Council Presidential Statement of January 1992, which states that the proliferation of all WMD constitutes a threat to international peace and security, and underlines the need for member states of the UN to prevent proliferation. The PSI is also consistent with recent statements of the G8 and the European Union, establishing that more coherent and concerted efforts are needed to prevent the proliferation of WMD, their delivery systems, and related materials. PSI participants are deeply concerned about this threat and of the danger that these items could fall into the hands of terrorists, and are committed to working together to stop the flow of these items to and from states and non-state actors of proliferation concern.

The PSI seeks to involve in some capacity all states that have a stake in nonproliferation and the ability and willingness to take steps to stop the flow of such items at sea, in the air, or on land. The PSI also seeks cooperation from any state whose vessels, flags, ports, territorial waters, airspace, or land might be used for proliferation purposes by states and non-state actors of proliferation concern. The increasingly aggressive efforts by proliferators to stand outside or to circumvent existing nonproliferation norms, and to profit from such trade, requires new and stronger actions by the international community. We look forward to working with all concerned states on measures they are able and willing to take in support of the PSI, as outlined in the following set of "Interdiction Principles."

Interdiction Principles for the Proliferation Security Initiative

PSI participants are committed to the following interdiction principles to establish a more coordinated and effective basis through which to impede and stop shipments of WMD, delivery systems, and related materials flowing to and from states and non-state actors of proliferation concern, consistent with national legal authorities and relevant international law and frameworks, including the UN Security Council. They call on all states concerned with this threat to international peace and security to join in similarly committing to:

1. Undertake effective measures, either alone or in concert with other states, for interdicting the transfer or transport of WMD, their delivery systems, and related materials to and from states and non-state actors of proliferation concern. "States or non-state actors of proliferation concern" generally refers to those countries or entities that the PSI participants involved establish should be subject to interdiction activities because they are engaged in proliferation through: (1) efforts to develop or acquire chemical, biological, or nuclear weapons and associated delivery systems; or (2) transfers (either selling, receiving, or facilitating) of WMD, their delivery systems, or related materials.

2. Adopt streamlined procedures for rapid exchange of relevant information concerning suspected proliferation activity, protecting the confidential character of classified information provided by other states as part of this initiative, dedicate appropriate resources and efforts to interdiction operations and capabilities, and maximize coordination among participants in interdiction efforts.

3. Review and work to strengthen their relevant national legal authorities where necessary to accomplish these objectives, and work to strengthen when necessary relevant international law and frameworks in appropriate ways to support these commitments.

4. Take specific actions in support of interdiction efforts regarding cargoes of WMD, their delivery systems, or related materials, to the extent their national legal authorities permit and consistent with their obligations under international law and frameworks, to include:

a. Not to transport or assist in the transport of any such cargoes to or from states or non-state actors of proliferation concern, and not to allow any persons subject to their jurisdiction to do so.

b. At their own initiative, or at the request and good cause shown by another state, to take action to board and search any vessel flying their flag in their internal waters or territorial seas, or areas beyond the territorial seas of any other state, that is reasonably suspected of transporting such cargoes to or from states or non-state actors of proliferation concern, and to seize such cargoes that are identified.

c. To seriously consider providing consent under the appropriate circumstances to the boarding and searching of its own flag vessels by other states, and to the seizure of such WMD-related cargoes in such vessels that may be identified by such states.

d. To take appropriate actions to (1) stop and/or search in their internal waters, territorial seas, or contiguous zones (when declared) vessels that are reasonably suspected of carrying such cargoes to or from states or non-state actors of proliferation concern and to seize such cargoes that are identified; and (2) to enforce conditions on vessels entering or leaving their ports, internal waters or territorial seas that are reasonably suspected of carrying such cargoes, such as requiring that such vessels be subject to boarding, search, and seizure of such cargoes prior to entry.

e. At their own initiative or upon the request and good cause shown by another state, to (a) require aircraft that are reasonably suspected of carrying such cargoes to or from states or non-state actors of proliferation concern and that are transiting their airspace to land for inspection and seize any such cargoes that are identified; and/or (b) deny aircraft reasonably suspected of carrying such cargoes transit rights through their airspace in advance of such flights.

f. If their ports, airfields, or other facilities are used as transshipment points for shipment of such cargoes to or from states or non-state actors of proliferation concern, to inspect vessels, aircraft, or other modes of transport reasonably suspected of carrying such cargoes, and to seize such cargoes that are identified.

Appendix N

Nuclear Non-Proliferation Treaty

Signed at Washington, London, and Moscow July 1, 1968
Ratification advised by U.S. Senate March 13, 1969
Ratified by U.S. President November 24, 1969
U.S. ratification deposited at Washington, London, and Moscow March 5, 1970
Proclaimed by U.S. President March 5, 1970
Entered into force March 5, 1970
(*Source*: Treaty on the Non-proliferation of Nuclear Weapons, *http://www.iaea.org/
Publications/Documents/Treaties/npt.html*)

TREATY ON THE NON-PROLIFERATION OF NUCLEAR WEAPONS

The States concluding this Treaty, hereinafter referred to as the "Parties to the
Treaty,"

Considering the devastation that would be visited upon all mankind by a nuclear war and the consequent need to make every effort to avert the danger of such
a war and to take measures to safeguard the security of peoples,

Believing that the proliferation of nuclear weapons would seriously enhance the
danger of nuclear war,

In conformity with resolutions of the United Nations General Assembly calling
for the conclusion of an agreement on the prevention of wider dissemination of
nuclear weapons,

Undertaking to cooperate in facilitating the application of International Atomic
Energy Agency safeguards on peaceful nuclear activities,

Expressing their support for research, development and other efforts to further
the application, within the framework of the International Atomic Energy Agency
safeguards system, of the principle of safeguarding effectively the flow of source
and special fissionable materials by use of instruments and other techniques at certain strategic points,

Affirming the principle that the benefits of peaceful applications of nuclear
technology, including any technological by-products which may be derived by nu-

clear-weapon States from the development of nuclear explosive devices, should be available for peaceful purposes to all Parties of the Treaty, whether nuclear-weapon or non-nuclear weapon States,

Convinced that, in furtherance of this principle, all Parties to the Treaty are entitled to participate in the fullest possible exchange of scientific information for, and to contribute alone or in cooperation with other States to, the further development of the applications of atomic energy for peaceful purposes,

Declaring their intention to achieve at the earliest possible date the cessation of the nuclear arms race and to undertake effective measures in the direction of nuclear disarmament,

Urging the cooperation of all States in the attainment of this objective,

Recalling the determination expressed by the Parties to the 1963 Treaty banning nuclear weapon tests in the atmosphere, in outer space and under water in its Preamble to seek to achieve the discontinuance of all test explosions of nuclear weapons for all time and to continue negotiations to this end,

Desiring to further the easing of international tension and the strengthening of trust between States in order to facilitate the cessation of the manufacture of nuclear weapons, the liquidation of all their existing stockpiles, and the elimination from national arsenals of nuclear weapons and the means of their delivery pursuant to a Treaty on general and complete disarmament under strict and effective international control,

Recalling that, in accordance with the Charter of the United Nations, States must refrain in their international relations from the threat or use of force against the territorial integrity or political independence of any State, or in any other manner inconsistent with the Purposes of the United Nations, and that the establishment and maintenance of international peace and security are to be promoted with the least diversion for armaments of the world's human and economic resources,

Have agreed as follows:

Article I

Each nuclear-weapon State Party to the Treaty undertakes not to transfer to any recipient whatsoever nuclear weapons or other nuclear explosive devices or control over such weapons or explosive devices directly, or indirectly; and not in any way to assist, encourage, or induce any non-nuclear weapon State to manufacture or otherwise acquire nuclear weapons or other nuclear explosive devices, or control over such weapons or explosive devices.

Article II

Each non-nuclear-weapon State Party to the Treaty undertakes not to receive the transfer from any transferor whatsoever of nuclear weapons or other nuclear explosive devices or of control over such weapons or explosive devices directly, or indirectly; not to manufacture or otherwise acquire nuclear weapons or other nuclear explosive devices; and not to seek or receive any assistance in the manufacture of nuclear weapons or other nuclear explosive devices.

Article III

1. Each non-nuclear-weapon State Party to the Treaty undertakes to accept safeguards, as set forth in an agreement to be negotiated and concluded with the International Atomic Energy Agency in accordance with the Statute of the International Atomic Energy Agency and the Agency's safeguards system, for the exclusive purpose of verification of the fulfillment of its obligations assumed under this Treaty with a view to preventing diversion of nuclear energy from peaceful uses to nuclear weapons or other nuclear explosive devices. Procedures for the safeguards required by this article shall be followed with respect to source or special fissionable material whether it is being produced, processed or used in any principal nuclear facility or is outside any such facility. The safeguards required by this article shall be applied to all source or special fissionable material in all peaceful nuclear activities within the territory of such State, under its jurisdiction, or carried out under its control anywhere.

2. Each State Party to the Treaty undertakes not to provide: (a) source or special fissionable material, or (b) equipment or material especially designed or prepared for the processing, use or production of special fissionable material, to any non-nuclear-weapon State for peaceful purposes, unless the source or special fissionable material shall be subject to the safeguards required by this article.

3. The safeguards required by this article shall be implemented in a manner designed to comply with article IV of this Treaty, and to avoid hampering the economic or technological development of the Parties or international cooperation in the field of peaceful nuclear activities, including the international exchange of nuclear material and equipment for the processing, use or production of nuclear material for peaceful purposes in accordance with the provisions of this article and the principle of safeguarding set forth in the Preamble of the Treaty.

4. Non-nuclear-weapon States Party to the Treaty shall conclude agreements with the International Atomic Energy Agency to meet the requirements of this article either individually or together with other States in accordance with the Statute of the International Atomic Energy Agency. Negotiation of such agreements shall commence within 180 days from the original entry into force of this Treaty. For States depositing their instruments of ratification or accession after the 180-day period, negotiation of such agreements shall commence not later than the date of such deposit. Such agreements shall enter into force not later than eighteen months after the date of initiation of negotiations.

Article IV

1. Nothing in this Treaty shall be interpreted as affecting the inalienable right of all the Parties to the Treaty to develop research, production and use of nuclear energy for peaceful purposes without discrimination and in conformity with articles I and II of this Treaty.

2. All the Parties to the Treaty undertake to facilitate, and have the right to participate in, the fullest possible exchange of equipment, materials and scientific and technological information for the peaceful uses of nuclear energy. Parties to the Treaty in a position to do so shall also cooperate in contributing alone or together with other States or international organizations to the further development of the applications of nuclear energy for peaceful purposes, especially in the territories of non-nuclear-weapon States Party to the Treaty, with due consideration for the needs of the developing areas of the world.

Article V

Each Party to the Treaty undertakes to take appropriate measures to ensure that, in accordance with this Treaty, under appropriate international observation and through appropriate international procedures, potential benefits from any peaceful applications of nuclear explosions will be made available to non-nuclear-weapon States Party to the Treaty on a nondiscriminatory basis and that the charge to such Parties for the explosive devices used will be as low as possible and exclude any charge for research and development. Non-nuclear-weapon States Party to the Treaty shall be able to obtain such benefits, pursuant to a special international agreement or agreements, through an appropriate international body with adequate representation of non-nuclear-weapon States. Negotiations on this subject shall commence as soon as possible after the Treaty enters into force. Non-nuclear-weapon States Party to the Treaty so desiring may also obtain such benefits pursuant to bilateral agreements.

Article VI

Each of the Parties to the Treaty undertakes to pursue negotiations in good faith on effective measures relating to cessation of the nuclear arms race at an early date and to nuclear disarmament, and on a Treaty on general and complete disarmament under strict and effective international control.

Article VII

Nothing in this Treaty affects the right of any group of States to conclude regional treaties in order to assure the total absence of nuclear weapons in their respective territories.

Article VIII

1. Any Party to the Treaty may propose amendments to this Treaty. The text of any proposed amendment shall be submitted to the Depositary Governments which shall circulate it to all Parties to the Treaty. Thereupon, if requested to do so by one-third or more of the Parties to the Treaty, the Depositary Governments shall convene a conference, to which they shall invite all the Parties to the Treaty, to consider such an amendment.

2. Any amendment to this Treaty must be approved by a majority of the votes of all the Parties to the Treaty, including the votes of all nuclear-weapon States Party to the Treaty and all other Parties which, on the date the amendment is circulated, are members of the Board of Governors of the International Atomic Energy Agency. The amendment shall enter into force for each Party that deposits its instrument of ratification of the amendment upon the deposit of such instruments of ratification by a majority of all the Parties, including the instruments of ratification of all nuclear-weapon States Party to the Treaty and all other Parties which, on the date the amendment is circulated, are members of the Board of Governors of the International Atomic Energy Agency. Thereafter, it shall enter into force for any other Party upon the deposit of its instrument of ratification of the amendment.

3. Five years after the entry into force of this Treaty, a conference of Parties to the Treaty shall be held in Geneva, Switzerland, in order to review the operation of this Treaty with a view to assuring that the purposes of the Preamble and the provisions of the Treaty are being realized. At intervals of five years thereafter, a majority of the Parties to the Treaty may obtain, by submitting a proposal to this effect to the Depositary Governments, the convening of further conferences with the same objective of reviewing the operation of the Treaty.

Article IX

1. This Treaty shall be open to all States for signature. Any State which does not sign the Treaty before its entry into force in accordance with paragraph 3 of this article may accede to it at any time.

2. This Treaty shall be subject to ratification by signatory States. Instruments of ratification and instruments of accession shall be deposited with the Governments of the United States of America, the United Kingdom of Great Britain and Northern Ireland and the Union of Soviet Socialist Republics, which are hereby designated the Depositary Governments.

3. This Treaty shall enter into force after its ratification by the States, the Governments of which are designated Depositaries of the Treaty, and forty other States signatory to this Treaty and the deposit of their instruments of ratification. For the purposes of this Treaty, a nuclear-weapon State is one which has manufactured and

exploded a nuclear weapon or other nuclear explosive device prior to January 1, 1967.

4. For States whose instruments of ratification or accession are deposited subsequent to the entry into force of this Treaty, it shall enter into force on the date of the deposit of their instruments of ratification or accession.

5. The Depositary Governments shall promptly inform all signatory and acceding States of the date of each signature, the date of deposit of each instrument of ratification or of accession, the date of the entry into force of this Treaty, and the date of receipt of any requests for convening a conference or other notices.

6. This Treaty shall be registered by the Depositary Governments pursuant to article 102 of the Charter of the United Nations.

Article X

1. Each Party shall in exercising its national sovereignty have the right to withdraw from the Treaty if it decides that extraordinary events, related to the subject matter of this Treaty, have jeopardized the supreme interests of its country. It shall give notice of such withdrawal to all other Parties to the Treaty and to the United Nations Security Council three months in advance. Such notice shall include a statement of the extraordinary events it regards as having jeopardized its supreme interests.

2. Twenty-five years after the entry into force of the Treaty, a conference shall be convened to decide whether the Treaty shall continue in force indefinitely, or shall be extended for an additional fixed period or periods. This decision shall be taken by a majority of the Parties to the Treaty.

Article XI

This Treaty, the English, Russian, French, Spanish and Chinese texts of which are equally authentic, shall be deposited in the archives of the Depositary Governments. Duly certified copies of this Treaty shall be transmitted by the Depositary Governments to the Governments of the signatory and acceding States.

IN WITNESS WHEREOF the undersigned, duly authorized, have signed this Treaty.

DONE in triplicate, at the cities of Washington, London and Moscow, this first day of July one thousand nine hundred sixty-eight.

Appendix O

UN Security Council Resolution 1540

(*Source*: U.N. Security Council Resolution 1540, http://www.un.org/Docs/sc/unsc_resolutionso4.html)

Resolution 1540 (2004)

Adopted by the Security Council at its 4956th meeting, on 28 April 2004

The Security Council,

Affirming that proliferation of nuclear, chemical and biological weapons, as well as their means of delivery,* constitutes a threat to international peace and security,

Reaffirming, in this context, the Statement of its President adopted at the Council's meeting at the level of Heads of State and Government on 31 January 1992 (S/23500), including the need for all Member States to fulfil their obligations in relation to arms control and disarmament and to prevent proliferation in all its aspects of all weapons of mass destruction,

Recalling also that the Statement underlined the need for all Member States to resolve peacefully in accordance with the Charter any problems in that context threatening or disrupting the maintenance of regional and global stability,

Affirming its resolve to take appropriate and effective actions against any threat to international peace and security caused by the proliferation of nuclear, chemical and biological weapons and their means of delivery, in conformity with its primary responsibilities, as provided for in the United Nations Charter,

Affirming its support for the multilateral treaties whose aim is to eliminate or

---

*Definitions for the purpose of this resolution only:

Means of delivery: missiles, rockets and other unmanned systems capable of delivering nuclear, chemical, or biological weapons, that are specially designed for such use.

Non-State actor: individual or entity, not acting under the lawful authority of any State in conducting activities which come within the scope of this resolution.

Related materials: materials, equipment and technology covered by relevant multilateral treaties and arrangements, or included on national control lists, which could be used for the design, development, production or use of nuclear, chemical and biological weapons and their means of delivery.

prevent the proliferation of nuclear, chemical or biological weapons and the importance for all States parties to these treaties to implement them fully in order to promote international stability,

Welcoming efforts in this context by multilateral arrangements which contribute to non-proliferation,

Affirming that prevention of proliferation of nuclear, chemical and biological weapons should not hamper international cooperation in materials, equipment and technology for peaceful purposes while goals of peaceful utilization should not be used as a cover for proliferation,

Gravely concerned by the threat of terrorism and the risk that non-State actors* such as those identified in the United Nations list established and maintained by the Committee established under Security Council resolution 1267 and those to whom resolution 1373 applies, may acquire, develop, traffic in or use nuclear, chemical and biological weapons and their means of delivery,

Gravely concerned by the threat of illicit trafficking in nuclear, chemical, or biological weapons and their means of delivery, and related materials,* which adds a new dimension to the issue of proliferation of such weapons and also poses a threat to international peace and security,

Recognizing the need to enhance coordination of efforts on national, subregional, regional and international levels in order to strengthen a global response to this serious challenge and threat to international security,

Recognizing that most States have undertaken binding legal obligations under treaties to which they are parties, or have made other commitments aimed at preventing the proliferation of nuclear, chemical or biological weapons, and have taken effective measures to account for, secure and physically protect sensitive materials, such as those required by the Convention on the Physical Protection of Nuclear Materials and those recommended by the IAEA Code of Conduct on the Safety and Security of Radioactive Sources,

Recognizing further the urgent need for all States to take additional effective measures to prevent the proliferation of nuclear, chemical or biological weapons and their means of delivery,

Encouraging all Member States to implement fully the disarmament treaties and agreements to which they are party,

Reaffirming the need to combat by all means, in accordance with the Charter of the United Nations, threats to international peace and security caused by terrorist acts,

Determined to facilitate henceforth an effective response to global threats in the area of non-proliferation,

Acting under Chapter VII of the Charter of the United Nations,

1. *Decides that* all States shall refrain from providing any form of support to

non-State actors that attempt to develop, acquire, manufacture, possess, transport, transfer or use nuclear, chemical or biological weapons and their means of delivery;

2.   *Decides also* that all States, in accordance with their national procedures, shall adopt and enforce appropriate effective laws which prohibit any non-State actor to manufacture, acquire, possess, develop, transport, transfer or use nuclear, chemical or biological weapons and their means of delivery, in particular for terrorist purposes, as well as attempts to engage in any of the foregoing activities, participate in them as an accomplice, assist or finance them;

3.   *Decides also* that all States shall take and enforce effective measures to establish domestic controls to prevent the proliferation of nuclear, chemical, or biological weapons and their means of delivery, including by establishing appropriate controls over related materials and to this end shall:

(a)   Develop and maintain appropriate effective measures to account for and secure such items in production, use, storage or transport;

(b)   Develop and maintain appropriate effective physical protection measures;

(c)   Develop and maintain appropriate effective border controls and law enforcement efforts to detect, deter, prevent and combat, including through international cooperation when necessary, the illicit trafficking and brokering in such items in accordance with their national legal authorities and legislation and consistent with international law;

(d)   Establish, develop, review and maintain appropriate effective national export and trans-shipment controls over such items, including appropriate laws and regulations to control export, transit, trans-shipment and re-export and controls on providing funds and services related to such export and trans-shipment such as financing, and transporting that would contribute to proliferation, as well as establishing end-user controls; and establishing and enforcing appropriate criminal or civil penalties for violations of such export control laws and regulations;

4.   *Decides* to establish, in accordance with rule 28 of its provisional rules of procedure, for a period of no longer than two years, a Committee of the Security Council, consisting of all members of the Council, which will, calling as appropriate on other expertise, report to the Security Council for its examination, on the implementation of this resolution, and to this end calls upon States to present a first report no later than six months from the adoption of this resolution to the Committee on steps they have taken or intend to take to implement this resolution;

5.   *Decides* that none of the obligations set forth in this resolution shall be interpreted so as to conflict with or alter the rights and obligations of State Parties to the Nuclear Non-Proliferation Treaty, the Chemical Weapons Convention and the Biological and Toxin Weapons Convention or alter the responsibilities of the

International Atomic Energy Agency or the Organization for the Prohibition of Chemical Weapons;

6. *Recognizes* the utility in implementing this resolution of effective national control lists and calls upon all Member States, when necessary, to pursue at the earliest opportunity the development of such lists;

7. *Recognizes* that some States may require assistance in implementing the provisions of this resolution within their territories and invites States in a position to do so to offer assistance as appropriate in response to specific requests to the States lacking the legal and regulatory infrastructure, implementation experience and/or resources for fulfilling the above provisions;

8. *Calls upon* all States:

(a) To promote the universal adoption and full implementation, and, where necessary, strengthening of multilateral treaties to which they are parties, whose aim is to prevent the proliferation of nuclear, biological or chemical weapons;

(b) To adopt national rules and regulations, where it has not yet been done, to ensure compliance with their commitments under the key multilateral non-proliferation treaties;

(c) To renew and fulfil their commitment to multilateral cooperation, in particular within the framework of the International Atomic Energy Agency, the Organization for the Prohibition of Chemical Weapons and the Biological and Toxin Weapons Convention, as important means of pursuing and achieving their common objectives in the area of non-proliferation and of promoting international cooperation for peaceful purposes;

(d) To develop appropriate ways to work with and inform industry and the public regarding their obligations under such laws;

9. *Calls upon* all States to promote dialogue and cooperation on non-proliferation so as to address the threat posed by proliferation of nuclear, chemical, or biological weapons, and their means of delivery;

10. Further to counter that threat, *calls upon* all States, in accordance with their national legal authorities and legislation and consistent with international law, to take cooperative action to prevent illicit trafficking in nuclear, chemical or biological weapons, their means of delivery, and related materials;

11. *Expresses* its intention to monitor closely the implementation of this resolution and, at the appropriate level, to take further decisions which may be required to this end;

12. *Decides* to remain seized of the matter.

Notes

Chapter 1

1. Kurt M. Campbell, Robert J. Einhorn, and Mitchell B. Reiss, eds., *The Nuclear Tipping Point: Why States Reconsider Their Nuclear Choices* (Washington, DC: Brooking Institution Press, 2004), 237.

2. Sidney David Drell and James E. Goodby, *The Gravest Danger: Nuclear Weapons* (Stanford, CA: Hoover Press, 2003), 32–33.

3. Barry Kellman, *Bioviolence* (Cambridge, UK: Cambridge University Press, 2007), 13.

4. Jeffrey T. Richelson, *Spying on the Bomb: American Nuclear Intelligence from Nazi Germany to Iran and North Korea* (New York: W. W. Norton, 2006), 133.

5. Lawrence Freedman, *The Evolution of Nuclear Strategy*, 3rd ed. (New York: Palgrave Macmillan, 2003), 295.

6. Thomas Graham Jr., *Common Sense on Weapons of Mass Destruction* (Seattle and London: University of Washington Press, 2004), 66.

7. Ibid.

8. Anthony Faiola, "As His Country Stumbles, the Practical 'Lula' Soars; Candidate Taps Into Brazilians' Desire for Respect," *Washington Post*, September 22, 2002, A16.

9. Graham, *Common Sense*, 162–64.

10. Thomas Graham Jr. and Damien J. La Vera, *Cornerstones of Security* (Seattle and London: University of Washington Press, 2003), 29.

11. Jacques E. C. Hymans, *The Psychology of Nuclear Proliferation* (Cambridge, UK: Cambridge University Press, 2006), 85, 89.

12. Ibid., 93.

13. Richelson, *Spying on the Bomb*, 328.

14. Joseph Cirincione, Jon Wolfsthal, and Miriam Rajkumar, *Deadly Arsenals: Nuclear, Biological, and Chemical Threats*, 2nd ed. (Washington, DC: Carnegie Endowment for International Peace, 2005), 265–66.

15. Cirincione, *Deadly Arsenals*, 8, 55.

16. Robert Dallek, *An Unfinished Life: John F. Kennedy, 1917–1963* (Boston: Little, Brown, 2003), 615.

17. Keith A. Hansen, *The Comprehensive Nuclear Test Ban Treaty: An Insider's Perspective* (Stanford, CA: Stanford University Press, 2006), 123, 126–27.

18. Ibid., 11, 82.

19. Ibid., 13, 81.

20. Lawrence Wein, "Biological and Chemical Safety Nets," *Wall Street Journal*, February 28, 2007.

21. D. W. Brackett, *Holy Terror: Armageddon in Tokyo* (New York: Weatherhill, 1996), 6.

22. Cirincione, *Deadly Arsenals*, 64.

23. Ibid., 12, 59–60.

24. Lara Jakes Jordan and David Dishneau, "Anthrax Scientist Commits Suicide as FBI Closes In," Associated Press, August 1, 2008, http://www.firstcoastnews.com/news/waronterror/news-article.aspx?storyid=115292&catid=33; Amy Goldstein, Anne Hull, and Julie Tate, "Acquaintances and Counselor Recall the Scientist's Dark Side," *Washington Post*, August 7, 2008, A1.

25. Kellman, *Bioviolence*, 13, 22.

26. Michael Levi, *On Nuclear Terrorism* (Cambridge, MA: Harvard University Press, November 2007), http://www.armscontrol.org/act/2008_04/BookReview.

Chapter 2

1. "Members of the Intelligence Community," http://www.dni.gov.

2. Peter Eisler, "Commercial satellites alter global security," *USA Today*, November 7, 2008, 13.

3. Mark M. Lowenthal, *Intelligence: From Secrets to Policy*, 3rd ed. (Washington, DC: CQ Press, 2006), 237.

4. John Deutch, "DCI Statement to the Public on the Ames Damage Assessment," CIA Press Release, October 31, 1995.

5. Lowenthal, *Intelligence*, 100.

6. Ibid.

7. Robert Lindsey, *The Falcon and the Snowman* (New York: Simon & Schuster, 1979), 75.

8. Lowenthal, *Intelligence*, 153.

9. Pete Earley, *Comrade J: The Untold Secrets of Russia's Master Spy in America After the End of the Cold War* (New York: Penguin Group, 2007), 8.

10. "American charged with giving secrets to Israel," MSNBC News, Apr. 22, 2008.

11. Lowenthal, *Intelligence*, 153–55.

12. Joby Warrick and Carrie Johnson, "Chinese Spying on the Rise, U.S. Says," *Washington Post*, April 3, 2008.

13. "U.S. probing two espionage cases," *USA Today* (Associated Press), February 11, 2008, http://www.usatoday.com/news/washington/2008-02-11-spying_n.htm.

14. Gudrun Harrer, "Dismantling the Iraqi Program," Private Monograph (International Atomic Energy Agency, December 2007 version), 521.

15. Christopher Andrew, *For the President's Eyes Only: Secret Intelligence and the American Presidency from Washington to Bush* (New York: HarperCollins, 1995), 39.

16. Ibid., 94.

17. George Tenet, *At the Center of the Storm: My Years at the CIA* (New York: HarperCollins, 2007), 174.

18. Lowenthal, *Intelligence*, 303.

19. Ibid., 146.

20. Harrer, "Dismantling the Iraqi Program," 165.

21. Lowenthal, *Intelligence*, 96–97.

Chapter 3

1. Richelson, *Spying on the Bomb*, 342–45.

2. George Perkovich, *India's Nuclear Bomb* (Berkeley and Los Angeles: University of California Press, 1999), 90–91.

3. Richelson, *Spying on the Bomb*, 231.

4. Ibid., 233.

5. Ibid., 234.

6. Ibid., 428.

7. Cirincione, *Deadly Arsenals*, 221.

8. Richelson, *Spying on the Bomb*, 429–31.

9. Ibid., 442.

10. Ibid., 443.

11. Ibid., 433–42.

12. Ibid., 446.

13. Ibid., 435–36.

14. Gordon Corera, *Shopping for Bombs: Nuclear Proliferation, Global Insecurity, and the Rise and Fall of the A. Q. Khan Network* (Oxford, New York: Oxford University Press, 2006), 48–49.

15. Richelson, *Spying on the Bomb*, 329–31.

16. Ibid., 345.

17. Ibid., 342–43.

18. Reiss, *Bridled Ambition*, 192.

19. Avner Cohen, *Israel and the Bomb* (New York: Columbia UP, 1998), 12, 31.

20. Cirincione, *Deadly Arsenals*, 264.

21. Richelson, *Spying on the Bomb*, 238–40.

22. Ibid., 241–42.

23. Ibid., 247–53.

24. Ibid., 253–54.

25. Ibid., 272.

26. Ibid., 361.

27. Ibid., 361–67.

28. Ibid., 270–71.
29. Ibid., 278–82.

30. Ibid., 277–82.

31. Reiss, *Bridled Ambition,* 10.

32. Hansen, *Comprehensive Nuclear Test Ban Treaty,* 56.

33. Richelson, *Spying on the Bomb,* 375.

34. Ibid., 324–27.

35. Ibid., 336–37.

36. Corera, *Shopping for Bombs,* 108–9.

37. Ibid., 176–94.

38. http://en.wikipedia.org/wiki/osirak, 2.

39. Richelson, *Spying on the Bomb,* 318–19.

40. http://en.wikipedia.org/wiki/osirak, 2.

41. Ibid., 2–3.

42. Richelson, *Spying on the Bomb,* 322.

43. Ibid., 334.

44. Ibid., 332.

45. Ibid., 332–33.

46. Reiss, *Bridled Ambition,* 289 (n. 3).

47. Siegfried Hecker, private written comments supplied to the authors.

48. Richelson, *Spying on the Bomb,* 351, 357.

49. Ibid., 521; Reiss, *Bridled Ambition,* 249.

50. Reiss, *Bridled Ambition,* 240–52.

51. Richelson, *Spying on the Bomb,* 522.

52. Reiss, *Bridled Ambition,* 251–80.

53. Richelson, *Spying on the Bomb,* 529.

54. Charles L. Pritchard, *Failed Diplomacy: The Tragic Story of How North Korea Got the Bomb* (Washington, DC: Brookings Institution Press, 2007), 27–29.

55. Ibid., 35.

56. Ibid., 35–43.

57. Ibid., 44.

58. Richelson, *Spying on the Bomb,* 529–34.

59. Associated Press, July 12, 2008, www.msnbc.com/id/26651882.

60. Pritchard, *Failed Diplomacy,* 133.

61. Ibid., 15–16.

62. Nicholas Kralev, "Lack of Written Agreement Snags North Korea Talks," *Washington Times,* September 9, 2008.

63. Choe Sang-Hun, *International Herald Tribune,* September 4, 2008, 1.

64. Glenn Kessler, "Far-Reaching U.S. Plan Impaired N. Korea Deal," *Washington Post,* September 26, 2008, A-20.

65. Glenn Kessler, "US Seems Set to Take N. Korea Off Terror List," *Washington Post*, October 10, 2008, A-16.

66. Sean McCormack, Press Statement, October 11, 2008; Glenn Kessler, "North Korea Doesn't Agree to Written Nuclear Agreement; Earlier Verbal Assurances Contradicted," *Washington Post*, December 12, 2008, A-22.

67. Richelson, *Spying on the Bomb*, 504.

68. Ibid., 506.

69. Corera, *Shopping for Bombs*, 68.

70. Richelson, *Spying on the Bomb*, 509.

71. Ibid., 512.

72. Corera, *Shopping for Bombs*, 71.

73. Shahram Chubin, "Iran's Nuclear Ambitions" (Washington, DC: Carnegie Endowment for International Peace, 2006), 36–41, 105–8, 140.

74. George Perkovich, Testimony, U.S. Senate Foreign Relations Committee, May 19, 2005.

75. David Albright, Testimony, U.S. Senate Foreign Relations Committee, May 17, 2006.

76. Edward Turzanski, "Policy Disruption by NIE" (Foreign Policy Research Institute; January 22, 2008), e-notes.

77. Peter Baker and Dafna Linzer, "Diving Deep, Unearthing a Surprise," *Washington Post*, December 8, 2007, A09.

78. "National Intelligence Estimate: Iran: Nuclear Intentions and Capabilities" (National Intelligence Council, November 2007), Unclassified Key Judgments. November 2007, http://www.dni.gov/press_releases/20071203_release.pdf.

79. Mohamed ElBaradei, "Implementation of the NPT Safeguards Agreement and Relevant Provisions of Security Council Resolutions 1737 (2006) and 1747 (2007) in the Islamic Republic of Iran," Report by Director General, IAEA, GOV/2007/58, November 15, 2007.

80. IAEA Staff Report, "Latest Iran Safeguards Report Delivered to IAEA Board," February 22, 2008, http://www.iaea.org/NewsCenter/News/2008/iranreport0208.html.

81. William Broad and David Sanger, "Iran Said to Have Nuclear Fuel for One Weapon," *New York Times*, November 20, 2008, 12.

82. Henry Kissinger, "Misreading the Iran Report: Why Spying and Policymaking Don't Mix," *Washington Post*, December 13, 2007, A35.

83. Michael McConnell, Statement Before the Senate Select Committee on Intelligence, February 5, 2008, http://www.dni.gov/testimonies/20080205_transcript.pdf.

84. Julian Borger, "UK fears Iran still working on nuclear weapon," *The Guard-*

ian, March 6, 2008, http://www.guardian.co.uk/world/2008/mar/06/iran.foreign-policy/print.

85. http://newsvote.bbc.co.uk/mpapps/pagetools/print/news.bbc.co.uk/2/hi/middle_east/727985.

86. "Iran Tests Advanced 'Efficient' Centrifuges," MSNBC News Services, April 8, 2008.

87. "Iran Has More Enriched Uranium Than Thought," *New York Times*, February 20, 2009, http://www.nytimes.com.2009_02_09.world.middleeast.20nuc.html.

88. "Sudan Wants UN to Probe US Bombing of Drug Factory," CNN, August 18, 1999.

89. "World Africa—Clinton defends military strikes," BBC News, August 20, 1998, http://news.bbc.co.uk/2/hi/africa/155252.stm.

90. Daryl Kimball, "The Curious Incident in Northern Syria and Its Potential Proliferation Implications," Prepared Remarks (Arms Control Association, November 1, 2007).

91. Ibid.

92. Ibid.

93. Robin Wright, "North Koreans Taped at Syrian Reactor," *Washington Post*, April 24, 2008, A01.

94. "CIA: Syria reactor could make 1–2 bombs a year," *Reuters*, April 28, 2008, http://www.msnbc.com/id/24359894/.

95. "IAEA Chastises U.S., Israel over Syrian Reactor," MSNBC (Associated Press), April 25, 2008, http://www.msnbc.msn.com/id/24306434/.

96. Peter Crail, "US Shares Information on NK-Syrian Nuclear Ties," *Arms Control Today*, May 2008, http://www.armscontrol.org/act/2007_12/IAEAIran.asp?print.

97. Leonard Spector and Avner Cohen, "Israel's Airstrike on Syrian Reactor: Implications for the Nonproliferation Regime," *Arms Control Today*, July–August 2008, http://www.armscontrol.org/act/2008_07-08/SpectorCohen.

98. Ibid.

99. "IAEA Questions Syria Evidence," *Washington Post*, November 18, 2008, 24.

100. Neil MacFarquhar, "Rates of Nuclear Thefts Disturbingly High, Monitoring Chief Says," *New York Times*, October 28, 2008, 7.

101. Corera, *Shopping for Bombs*, xiii.

102. Douglas Frantz and Catherine Collins, *The Nuclear Jihadist: The True Story of the Man Who Sold the World's Most Dangerous Secrets . . . And How We Could Have Stopped Him* (New York: Hachette Book Group, 2007), 68–71.

103. Ibid., 76–77. 104. Ibid., 78–79.

105. Ibid., 82. 106. Ibid., 84.

107. Ibid., 106–8. 108. Ibid., 126.

109. Ibid., 208–10.

110. Ibid., 222–26.

111. Ibid., 169–71.

112. Ibid., 210.

113. Ibid., 249–51.

114. Ibid.

115. Ibid., 252–60.

116. William Broad, "Swiss Suspect Released in Nuclear Case," *New York Times*, January 24, 2009, A-7.

117. William Broad and David Sanger, "In Nuclear Net's Undoing, a Web of Shadowy Deals," *New York Times*, August 24, 2008, A-1, A-8.

118. Corera, *Shopping for Bombs*, 176–216.

119. Brackett, *Holy Terror*, 6.

120. Cirincione, *Deadly Arsenals*, 12.

Chapter 4

1. Brett Snider, "Sharing Secrets with Lawmakers: Congress as a User of Intelligence," *Studies in Intelligence*, http://www.cia.gov/library/center-for-the-study-of-intelligence/csi-publications/csi-studies/spring98/Congress.html.

2. Robert Blackwill, "A Policymaker's Perspective on Intelligence Analysis," Interviews, 1991–1993, https://www.cia.gov/library/center-for-the-study-of-intelligence/csi-publications/csi-studies/studies/95unclass/Davis.html.

3. Lowenthal, *Intelligence*, 140–41.

4. Richard Helms, "Strategic Arms Limitation and Intelligence," *Studies in Intelligence*, no. 17 (Spring 1973): 38.

5. James Steiner, "Challenging the Red Line Between Intelligence and Policy," Institute for the Study of Diplomacy, Georgetown University, November 2003, 5.

6. Tenet, *At the Center*, 323.

7. Lowenthal, *Intelligence*, 63.

8. "National Intelligence Estimate: Iran: Nuclear Intentions and Capabilities" (National Intelligence Council, November 2007), Unclassified Key Judgments. November 2007, http://www.dni.gov/press_releases/20071203_release.pdf.

9. John Helgerson, *Getting to Know the President: CIA Briefings of Presidential Candidates, 1952–1992* (Washington, DC: CIA/Center for the Study of Intelligence, 1996), 156.

10. Kirsten Lundberg, "The SS-9 Controversy: Intelligence as Political Football," Case Program, Kennedy School of Government, C16-89-884.0, 1989.

11. Lowenthal, *Intelligence*, 178.

12. Ibid.

13. Robert Gates, "A Message to Analysts: Guarding Against Politicization," *Studies in Intelligence*, 36 (1992): 7.

14. One of us, Thomas Graham, was a senior official at the Arms Control and Disarmament Agency in 1979 during the Carter administration. He recalls that

along with several other senior officials, he was given a briefing on Soviet strategic forces by a CIA officer. In 1981, after President Reagan had taken office, Graham and several other senior ACDA officials were given a similar briefing. The facts had not changed much, but the threat level had changed dramatically. Graham attributes this change more to the perspectives of the new administration rather than a significant change in the actual strategic threat posed by the Soviet Union.

15. "The National Intelligence Estimates A-B Team Episode Concerning Soviet Strategic Capability and Objectives," Report of the SSCI, 95th Congress, 2nd Session, February 16, 1978, 1–2.

16. Lowenthal, *Intelligence*, 93, 153.

17. "Prewar Intelligence Assessments About Postwar Iraq," Report of the Senate Select Committee on Intelligence, US Senate, 110th Congress, 1st Session, May 2007, 1–2.

18. "Whether Statements Regarding Iraq by US Government Officials Were Substantiated by Intelligence Information," Report of the Senate Select Committee on Intelligence, US Senate, 110th Congress, 2nd Session, June 2008.

19. James Bruce, "The Consequences of Permissive Neglect: Laws and Leaks of Classified Intelligence," *Studies in Intelligence* 47, no. 1 (2003).

20. Ron Suskind, *The Price of Loyalty: George W. Bush, the White House, and the Education of Paul O'Neill* (New York: Simon & Shuster, 2004), 85–86.

21. Jim Lehrer, Online NewsHour: Commentary by Shields and Lowry, November 11, 2005; Tenet, *At the Center*, 321.

Chapter 5

1. Hans Blix, private letter to authors.

2. "Iraq Survey Group Report, Regime Strategic Intent," October 6, 2004, 1.

3. Michael Gunter, "The Iraqi Opposition and Failure of US Intelligence," *International Journal of Intelligence and Counterintelligence* 12, no. 2 (Summer 1999): 161.

4. Cirincione, *Deadly Arsenals*, 331.

5. Hans Blix, interview with Jim Lehrer, Online News Hour, March 17, 2004, http://pbs.org/newshour/bb/international/jan-june04/blix_3-17.html.

6. Cirincione, *Deadly Arsenals*, 329.

7. "Iraq Survey Group Report, Regime Strategic Intent," October 6, 2004.

8. Richelson, *Spying on the Bomb*, 476–87, 501–2.

9. Ibid., 472–73, 490–91.

10. Valerie Plame Wilson, *Fair Game: My Life as a Spy, My Betrayal by the White House* (New York: Simon & Shuster, 2007), 366–67.

11. Ibid., 109.   12. Ibid., 109–10.

13. Ibid., 111–13.

14. Ibid., 138–40.

15. Ibid., 139–42.

16. Ibid., 147.

17. Ibid., 372–74 (afterword by Laura Rozen); also from James Risen, *State of War: The Secret History of the CIA and the Bush Administration* (New York: Free Press, 2006).

18. Cirincione, *Deadly Arsenals*, 343.

19. UN Special Commission, First Consolidated Report of the Secretary-General Pursuant to Paragraph 9, April 11, 1996.

20. Blix, private letter to authors.

21. Matt Renner, "Pentagon Officer Created Phony Intel on Iraq/al-Qaeda Link," *Truthout* report, April 6, 2007, http://www.truthout.org/article/pentagon-office-created-phony-intel-iraqal-qaeda-link.

22. Carl Levin, "Hussein-Qaeda Link 'Inappropriate,' Report Says," *New York Times*, April 6, 2007, 6.

23. Tenet, *At the Center*, 347.

24. Thomas E. Ricks and Karen DeYoung, "Architect of Iraq War Strategy Blames Powell in New Memoir," *Washington Post*, March 9, 2008, http://www.huffingtonpost.com/2008/03/09/architect-of-iraq-war-str_n_90593.html?page=6.

25. James Pavitt, Remarks at the Foreign Policy Association, June 21, 2004, http://www.cia.gov/news-information/speeches-testimony/2004/ddo_speech_06242004.html.

26. Tyler Drumheller, *On the Brink: An Insider's Account of How the White House Compromised American Intelligence* (Emeryville, CA: Carroll and Graf Publishers, Avalon Publishing Group, 2007), 10–11.

27. Tenet, *At the Center*, 328–29.

28. George Tenet, "Iraq and Weapons of Mass Destruction," Remarks at Georgetown University, February 5, 2004, http://www.fas.org/irp/cia/product/dci020504.html.

29. "Iraq Survey Group Report, Regime Strategic Intent," October 6, 2004.

30. *Wall Street Journal*, February 1, 2008, editorial page, A-14.

31. Tenet, *At the Center*, 321–22.

32. Ibid., 323.

33. Ibid., 325–26.

34. Richelson, *Spying on the Bomb*, 476–80.

35. Tenet, *At the Center,* 327–32.

36. Ibid., 336–39.

37. "Senate Select Committee on Intelligence Report on the US Intelligence Community's Prewar Intelligence Assessments on Iraq," US Senate, 108th Congress, 2nd Session, July 2004.

38. "Senate Select Committee on Intelligence Report on Whether Public Statements Regarding Iraq by US Government Officials Were Substantiated by Intelligence Information," 110th Congress, 2nd Session, June 2008.

39. Ibid.

40. The Commission on Intelligence Capabilities of the United States Regarding Weapons of Mass Destruction, Report to the President of the United States, March 31, 2005, 3–7.

41. "Collection and Analysis on Iraq: Issues for the US Intelligence Community," www.cia.gov/csi/studies, vol.49, no. 3 (2005).

42. Greg Thielmann, "Rumsfeld Reprise? The Missile Report That Foretold the Iraq Intelligence Controversy," *Arms Control Today*, July/August 2003.

43. Ibid.

44. Suskind, *The Price of Loyalty*, 72–76, 82–86.

45. Richard Clarke, *Against All Enemies: Inside America's War on Terror* (New York, London: Free Press, 2004), 32–33.

46. Hans Blix, *Disarming Iraq* (New York: Pantheon Books, 2004), 271–74.

47. Paul Pillar, "Intelligence, Policy, and the War in Iraq," *Foreign Affairs*, March/April 2006, 5.

48. Tenet, *At the Center*, 317.

49. Blix, *Disarming Iraq*, 233–34.

50. Ibid., 229.

51. Pillar, "Intelligence, Policy, and the War in Iraq," 3.

52. Frank Rich, *The Greatest Story Ever Sold* (New York: The Penguin Press, 2006), 277–307.

53. Ibid., 233.
54. Ibid., 247.
55. Ibid., 231.
56. Ibid., 235.
57. Ibid.
58. Ibid., 256.
59. Ibid.
60. Ibid., 257.
61. Ibid., 240.
62. Ibid., 241.
63. Ibid., 241–42.
64. Ibid., 244.
65. Ibid., 252.
66. Ibid., 258.
67. Ibid., 259.
68. Ibid., 236.
69. Ibid., 259.
70. Ibid., 263.
71. Ibid., 230–31.
72. Ibid., 235.
73. Ibid., 237–38.
74. Ibid., 232–33.
75. Ibid., 244.
76. Ibid., 248.
77. Ibid., 249.
78. Ibid., 253.
79. Ibid., 258–59.
80. Ibid., 266.
81. Pillar, "Intelligence, Policy, and the War in Iraq," 2.

82. Tenet, *At the Center*, 316.

83. Ron Suskind, *The Way of the World* (New York: HarperCollins, 2008), 179–82.

84. Ibid., 383–84.

85. Ibid., 192–93.

86. Ibid., 190–94, 362–67.

87. Tenet, "Iraq and Weapons of Mass Destruction," Remarks at Georgetown University, February 5, 2004.

88. Bob Drogin and Greg Miller, "Curveball Debacle Reignites CIA Feud," *Los Angeles Times*, April 2, 2005, A1.

89. Pillar, "Intelligence, Policy, and the War in Iraq," 2.

90. The Commission on Intelligence Capabilities of the United States Regarding Weapons of Mass Destruction, Report to the President of the United States, March 31, 2005, 11.

91. "Iraq Survey Group Report, Regime Strategic Intent," October 6, 2004.

92. Colum Lynch, "U.N. Team Still Looking for Iraq's Arsenal," *Washington Post*, June 2, 2007, 1.

93. Melanie Phillips, "I Found Saddam's WMD Bunkers," April 21, 2007, www.spectator.co.uk/theomagazine/features/29092.

94. Richelson, *Spying on the Bomb*, 502.

95. Ibid., 542–43.

96. Michael Hayden, C-SPAN Interview, April 17, 2007, https://www.cia.gov/news-information/press-releases-statements/press-release-archive-2007/transcript-of-c-span-interview-with-cia-director.html.

97. Tenet, *At the Center*, 338–39.

98. Hayden, C-SPAN Interview, April 17, 2007.

99. Walter Pincus, "Before War, CIA Warned of Negative Outcomes," *Washington Post*, June 3, 2007, 8.

100. Paul Pillar, "The Other Intelligence Assessments on Iraq," *National Interest*, June 6, 2007.

101. David Ignatius, "When the CIA Got it Right," *Washington Post*, September 23, 2007, B7.

102. Tenet, *At the Center*, 362.

103. Blix, private letter to authors.

104. Remarks by Central Intelligence Agency Director Michael Hayden at the Los Angeles World Affairs Council, September 16, 2008.

105. Joby Warrick, "Syrian Facility Looked Like Reactor, UN Says," *Washington Post*, November 20, 2008, 16.

Chapter 6

1. Thomas Graham Jr. and Keith Hansen, *Spy Satellites and Other Intelligence Technologies That Changed History* (Seattle and London: University of Washington Press, 2007), 28.

2. Brittany Griffith, "Panel Formed on WMD, Terrorism," *Arms Control Today*, June 2008.

3. Paul K. Davis and Brian Michael Jenkins, "Deterrence and Influence in Counterterrorism," RAND Monograph, 2002, 1, 40.

4. Graham and Hansen, *Spy Satellites*, 93.

5. White House Fact Sheet, "Comprehensive Test Ban Treaty Safeguards," September 22, 1997.

6. Frank Oliveri, "Secret Air Force Center Monitors Worldwide Treaty Compliance," *Florida Today*, October 20, 1997, 1A–2A.

7. Hansen, *Comprehensive Nuclear Test Ban Treaty*, 72.

8. Graham and Hansen, *Spy Satellites*, 98.

9. William Broad, "New Security Organization Will Try to Prevent Nuclear Theft," *New York Times*, September 29, 2008, A-8.

10. Hansen, *Comprehensive Nuclear Test Ban Treaty*, 83.

11. "43 nations to seek Middle East free of WMDs," MSNBC (Associated Press), July 13, 2008, http://www.msnbc.msn.com/id/25664483/.

12. Glen Kessler, "US Efforts Divert Iran-Bound Cargo," *Washington Post*, November 4, 2008, A-9.

13. Dallek, *An Unfinished Life*, 615.

14. Under the NPT only five countries (China, France, Russia, the United Kingdom, and the United States) are considered nuclear weapon states because they had tested nuclear weapons prior to a specified date set forth in the NPT. All other countries, by definition, are considered to be nonnuclear. Even though India, Pakistan, Israel, and North Korea are now de facto nuclear weapon states, it would take an amendment to the NPT for them to be officially recognized as such under the treaty. Such an amendment would be virtually impossible to achieve in that, pursuant to the treaty, to be effective it would require ratification by all NPT parties on the board of the IAEA and all five NPT nuclear weapon states, along with an overall majority (over ninety) of the NPT states parties.

15. Hansen, *Comprehensive Nuclear Test Ban Treaty*, 56.

16. Ibid., 65.

17. Daryl Kimball, "Grounds for Optimism and Action on Chemical Weapons Convention's 10th Anniversary," Arms Control Association, May 4, 2007, http://www.armscontrol.org/pressroom/2007/20070504_CWC.asp.

18. Graham and Hansen, *Spy Satellites*, 94–95.

19. Ibid., 11–12.

20. Ibid., 12.

21. Hansen, *Comprehensive Nuclear Test Ban Treaty*, 44.

22. Ibid., 50.

23. Daryl Kimball, "Congress Must Remedy Past U.S. Funding Shortfalls for Global Nuclear Test Monitoring System," Arms Control Association, May 21, 2007, http://www.armscontrol.org/pressroom/2007/2007/0521_CTBT.asp.

24. George P. Shultz, William J. Perry, Henry A. Kissinger, and Sam Nunn, "Toward a Nuclear-free World," *Wall Street Journal*, op-ed article, January 15, 2008, http://online.wsj.com/article/SB120036422673589947.html?mod=opinion_main_ commentaries; George P. Shultz, William J. Perry, Henry A. Kissinger, and Sam Nunn, "A World Free of Nuclear Weapons," *Wall Street Journal*, op-ed article, January 4, 2007, A15, http://www.hoover.org/publications/digest/6731276.html.

25. Crail, Peter. "UN Renews Committee on WMD," *Arms Control Today*, June 2008;http://www.armscontrol.org/act/2008_06/UNWMD.

26. Blix, private letter to authors.

27. Ibid.

28. Reiss, *Bridled Ambition*, 252.

29. Marion Creekmore, *A Moment of Crisis: Jimmy Carter, the Power of a Peacemaker, and North Korea's Nuclear Ambitions* (New York: Public Affairs, 2006), 154–64.

30. http://www.un.org/sc/1540/nationalreports.shtml.

31. "China Assists Nuclear Arms Probe of Iran," Associated Press, April 2, 2008.

32. "IAEA Chastises U.S., Israel over Syrian Reactor," Associated Press, April 25, 2008.

33. Blix, private letter to authors.

34. Clarke, *Against All Enemies,* 67–68.

35. Blix, private letter to authors.

36. Mohamed ElBaradei, "Towards a Safer World," *Economist*, October 16, 2003, 48–50.

37. Mohamed ElBaradei and Jonas Gahr Støre, "How the world can combat nuclear terrorism," *Financial Times*, June 15, 2006, http://www.regjeringen.no/nb/dep/ud/dep/utenriksminister_jonas_gahr_store/taler_artikler/2006/How-the-world-can-combat-nuclear-terrorism.html?id=420856.

38. Strengthened Safeguards Systems: States with Additional Protocols, as of January 31, 2009, http://www.iaea.org/OurWork/SV/Safeguards/sg_protocol.html.

Conclusion

1. David Ignatius, "Repairing America's Spy Shop," *Washington Post*, April 6, 2008, B07.

2. Tenet, "Iraq and Weapons of Mass Destruction," Remarks at Georgetown University, February 5, 2004.

3. Ignatius, "Repairing America's Spy Shop."

Postscript

1. Joby Warrick, "Spread of Nuclear Capability Feared," washingtonpost.com, May 11, 2008, http://www.msnbc.msn.com/id/24572974/.

2. David Hoffman, "Report on Nuclear Security Urges Prompt Global Action," *Washington Post*, November 18, 2008, 25.

3. Joby Warrick, "Nuclear Scientist A.Q. Khan Is Freed from House Arrest," *Washington Post*, February 7, 2009, A1 & A9.

4. Ibid.

Appendix B

1. Cirincione, *Deadly Arsenals*, 58–59.

Appendix C

1. US Department of Energy, DOE FACTS, Additional Information Concerning Underground Nuclear Weapon Tests of Reactor-Grade Plutonium, http://www.ccnr.org/plut_bomb.html.

Appendix F

1. Paul Kerr Group Report, "China Updates Nuclear Export Regulations," *Arms Control Today*, January/February 2007, 1–8.

2. Wade Boese, "Congress Questions U.S. Support for China Joining Nuclear Group," *Arms Control Today*, June 2004.

3. Peter Slevin, John Lancaster, and Kamran Khan, "At Least 7 Nations Tied to Pakistani Nuclear Ring," *Washington Post*, February 8, 2004.

4. Blix, letter of January 2008.

5. Chaim Braun and Christopher Chyba, "Proliferation Rings: New Challenges to the Nuclear Nonproliferation Regime," *International Security* 29, no. 2 (Fall 2004): 31.

Appendix K

1. "Intelligence in the War of Independence," CIA/Office of Public Affairs, 14.

2. Lowenthal, *Intelligence*, 157–72.

3. Harold P. Ford, "Why CIA Analysts Were So Doubtful About Vietnam," *Studies in Intelligence* 1, no. 1 (1997).

4. Lundberg, "The SS-9 Controversy," 5.

5. Ibid., 21.

6. Snider, "Sharing Secrets with Lawmakers."

7. Yossi Melman, "The Israel-South Africa Nuclear Tie," *Ha'aretz* (April 21, 1997): FBIS-NES-97-082.

8. DCI George Tenet and D/NSA Michael Hayden, Testimonies to the Senate Select Committee on Intelligence, October 2002.

Appendix L

1. The text of the Key Judgments was downloaded off the Internet.

2. A refined form of natural uranium.

Bibliography

"Agreement reached on North Korea nukes." MSNBC (Associated Press), July 12, 2008, http://www.msnbc.msn.com/id/25651882/.

Albright, David. Testimony. U.S. Senate Foreign Relations Committee, May 17, 2006.

"American charged with giving secrets to Israel." MSNBC News, April 22, 2008, http://www.msnbc.msn.com/id/24256527/.

Andrew, Christopher. *For the President's Eyes Only: Secret Intelligence and the American Presidency from Washington to Bush*. New York: HarperCollins, 1995.

Baker, Peter, and Dafna Linzer. "Diving Deep, Unearthing a Surprise." *Washington Post*, December 8, 2007, A09.

Berkowitz, Bruce, and Jeffrey Richelson. "The CIA vindicated: the Soviet collapse was predicted." *National Interest*, Fall 1995, 36–47.

Blackwill, Robert D. "A Policymaker's Perspective on Intelligence Analysis." Interviews, 1991–1993, https://www.cia.gov/library/center-for-the-study-of-intelligence/csi-publications/csi-studies/studies/95unclass/Davis.html.

Blix, Hans. *Disarming Iraq*. New York: Pantheon Books, 2004.

Blix, Hans. Interview by Jim Lehrer. Online NewsHour, March 17, 2004, http://pbs.org/newshour/bb/international/jan-june04/blix_3-17.html.

Blix, Hans. Private letter to authors.

Boese, Wade. "Congress Questions U.S. Support for China Joining Nuclear Group." *Arms Control Today*, June 2004.

Boese, Wade. "U.S. Disappointed with Worldwide Response to WMD Resolution." *Arms Control Today*, December 2004, http://armscontrol.org/act/2004_12/WMDResolution.asp.

Borger, Julian. "UK fears Iran still working on nuclear weapon." *Guardian*, March 6, 2008, http://www.guardian.co.uk/world/2008/mar/06/iran.foreignpolicy.

Brackett, D. W. *Holy Terror: Armageddon in Tokyo*. New York: Weatherhill, 1996.

Braun, Chaim, and Christopher Chyba. "Proliferation Rings: New Challenges to the Nuclear Nonproliferation Regime." *International Security*, vol. 29, no. 2 (Fall 2004).

Broad, William J., and David E. Sanger. "In Nuclear Net's Undoing, a Web of Shadowy Deals." *New York Times*, August 25, 2008, A-1.

Broad, William J., and David E. Sanger. "Iran Said to Have Fuel for One Nuclear Weapon." *New York Times*, November 20, 2008.

Broad, William J. "New Security Organization Will Try to Prevent Nuclear Theft." *New York Times*, September 29, 2008.

Broad, William J. "Swiss Release Suspect in Nuclear Case." *New York Times*, January 24, 2009.

Bunn, George. "The Nuclear Nonproliferation Treaty: History and Current Problems." *Arms Control Today*, December 2003.

Campbell, Kurt M., Robert J. Einhorn, and Mitchell B. Reiss (eds.). *The Nuclear Tipping Point: Why States Reconsider Their Nuclear Choices.* Washington, DC: Brookings Institution Press, 2004.

"China Assists Nuclear Arms Probe of Iran." Associated Press, April 2, 2008.

Chubin, Shahram. "Iran's Nuclear Ambitions." Washington, DC: Carnegie Endowment for International Peace, 2006.

"CIA: Syria reactor could make 1–2 bombs a year." *MSNBC News* (Reuters), April 28, 2008, http://www.msnbc.msn.com/id/24359894/.

Cirincione, Joseph, Jon Wolfsthal, and Miriam Rajkumar. *Deadly Arsenals: Nuclear, Biological, and Chemical Threats*, 2nd ed. Washington, DC: Carnegie Endowment for International Peace, 2005.

Cirincione, Joseph. *Bomb Scare: The History and Future of Nuclear Weapons.* New York: Columbia University Press, 2007.

Clarke, Richard. *Against All Enemies: Inside America's War on Terror.* New York, London: Free Press, 2004.

"Clinton defends military strikes." BBC News, August 20, 1998, http://news.bbc.co.uk/2/hi/africa/155252.stm.

Cohen, Avner. *Israel and the Bomb.* New York: Columbia University Press, 1998.

Corera, Gordon. *Shopping for Bombs: Nuclear Proliferation, Global Security and the Rise and Fall of the A. Q. Khan Network.* Oxford, New York: Oxford University Press, 2006.

Crail, Peter. "IAEA Issues Mixed Findings on Iran." *Arms Control Today*, December 2007, http://www.armscontrol.org/act/2007_12/IAEAIran.asp?print.

Crail, Peter. "U.S. Shares Information on NK-Syrian Nuclear Ties." *Arms Control Today*, May 2008, http://www.armscontrol.org/act/2008_05/NKSyria.

Crail, Peter. "UN Renews Committee on WMD." *Arms Control Today*, June 2008; http://www.armscontrol.org/act/2008_06/UNWMD.

Creekmore, Marion V. *A Moment of Crisis: Jimmy Carter, the Power of a Peacemaker, and North Korea's Nuclear Ambitions.* New York: Public Affairs, 2006.

Croddy, Eric. *Chemical and Biological Warfare: A Comprehensive Survey for the Concerned Citizen.* New York: Copernicus Books, Springer-Verlag, 2002.

Dallek, Robert. *An Unfinished Life: John F. Kennedy, 1917–1963.* Boston: Little, Brown, 2003.

Davis, Paul K., and Brian Michael Jenkins. *Deterrence and Influence in Counterterrorism.* RAND Monograph, 2002, 1, 40.

Deutch, John. "DCI Statement to the Public on the Ames Damage Assessment." CIA Press Release, October 31, 1995, https://www.cia.gov/news-information/press-releases-statements/press-release-archive-1995/ps103195.html.

Drell, Sidney D. *Nuclear Weapons, Scientists, and the Post–Cold War Challenge: Selected Papers on Arms Control.* Singapore: World Scientific, 2007.

Drell, Sidney D., and James E. Goodby. *The Gravest Danger: Nuclear Weapons.* Stanford, CA: Hoover Press, 2003.

Drogin, Bob, and Greg Miller. "'Curveball' Debacle Reignites CIA Feud." *Los Angeles Times,* April 2, 2005.

Drumheller, Tyler. *On the Brink: An Insider's Account of How the White House Compromised American Intelligence.* Emeryville, CA: Carroll and Graf Publishers, Avalon Publishing Group, 2007.

Earley, Pete. *Comrade J: The Untold Secrets of Russia's Master Spy in America After the End of the Cold War.* New York: Penguin Group, 2007.

Editorial. *Wall Street Journal,* February 1, 2008, A-14.

Eisler, Peter. "Commercial satellites alter global security." *USA Today,* November 7, 2008.

ElBaradei, Mohamed. "Implementation of the NPT Safeguards Agreement and relevant provisions of Security Council resolutions 1737 (2006) and 1747 (2007) in the Islamic Republic of Iran." Report by Director General, IAEA, GOV/2007/58, November 15, 2007.

ElBaradei, Mohamed. "In Search of Security: Finding an Alternative to Nuclear Deterrence." Drell Lecture, Stanford University, November 4, 2004.

ElBaradei, Mohamed. "Towards a Safer World." *Economist,* October 16, 2003, 48–50.

ElBaradei, Mohamed, and Jonas Gahr Støre. "How the world can combat nuclear terrorism." *Financial Times,* June 15, 2006, http://www.regjeringen.no/nb/dep/ud/dep/utenriksminister_jonas_gahr_store/taler_artikler/2006/How-the-world-can-combat-nuclear-terrorism.html?id=420856.

Ellis, Jason D., and Geoffrey D. Kiefer. *Combating Proliferation: Strategic Intelligence and Security Policy.* Baltimore: Johns Hopkins University Press, 2004.

"Ex-Defense Official Assails Colleagues Over Run-Up to War." *Washington Post,* March 8, 2008, A-1, http://www.washingtonpost.com/wp-dyn/context/article/2008/03/08/AR 200803082724.html.

Faiola, Anthony. "As His Country Stumbles, the Practical 'Lula' Soars; Candidate Taps Into Brazilians' Desire for Respect." *Washington Post*, September 22, 2002, A16.

"43 nations to seek Middle East free of WMDs." MSNBC News (Associated Press), July 13, 2008, http://www.msnbc.msn.com/id/25664483/.

Frantz, Douglas, and Catherine Collins. *The Nuclear Jihadist: The True Story of the Man Who Sold the World's Most Dangerous Secrets . . . And How We Could Have Stopped Him.* New York: Twelve Hachette Book Group USA, 2007.

Freedman, Lawrence. *Evolution of Nuclear Strategy*, 3rd ed. New York: Palgrave Macmillan, 2003.

George, Roger, and Robert Kline (eds.). *Intelligence and the National Security Strategist: Enduring Issues and Challenges.* Washington, DC: National Defense University Press, 2004.

Goldstein, Amy, Anne Hull, and Julie Tate. "Acquaintances and Counselor Recall the Scientist's Dark Side." *Washington Post*, August 7, 2008, A-1.

Graham Jr., Thomas. *Disarmament Sketches.* Seattle and London: University of Washington Press, 2002.

Graham Jr., Thomas. *Common Sense on Weapons of Mass Destruction.* Seattle and London: University of Washington Press, 2004.

Graham Jr., Thomas, and Keith Hansen. *Spy Satellites and Other Intelligence Technologies That Changed History.* Seattle and London: University of Washington Press, 2007.

Graham Jr., Thomas, and Damien J. La Vera. *Cornerstones of Security.* Seattle and London: University of Washington Press, 2003.

Griffith, Brittany. "Panel Formed on WMD, Terrorism." *Arms Control Today*, June 2008, http://www.armscontrol.org/act/2008_06/Panel.

Gunter, Michael. "The Iraqi Opposition and the Failure of U.S. Intelligence." *International Journal of Intelligence and Counterintelligence*, vol. 12, no. 2 (Summer 1999).

Hansen, Keith A. *The Comprehensive Nuclear Test Ban Treaty: An Insider's Perspective.* Stanford, CA: Stanford University Press, 2006.

Harrer, Gudrun. "Dismantling the Iraqi Program." Private Monograph. International Atomic Energy Agency, December 2007 version.

Hayden, Michael. Interview. C-SPAN, April 17, 2007, https://www.cia.gov/news-information/press-releases-statements/press-release-archive-2007/transcript-of-c-span-interview-with-cia-director.html.

Hecker, Siegfried. Private written comments supplied to the authors.

Hoffman, David. "Report on Nuclear Security Urges Prompt Global Action." *Washington Post*, November 18, 2008.

Howard, Russell D., and James J. F. Forest. (eds.) *Weapons of Mass Destruction and Terrorism.* New York: McGraw-Hill, 2007.

"Hussein-Qaeda Link 'Inappropriate,' Report Says." *New York Times*, April 6, 2007, A-8.

Hymans, Jacques E. C. *The Psychology of Nuclear Proliferation: Identity, Emotions, and Foreign Policy*. Cambridge, UK: Cambridge University Press, 2006.

"IAEA chastises U.S., Israel over Syrian reactor." MSNBC News (Associated Press), April 25, 2008, http://www.msnbc.msn.com/id/24306434/.

"IAEA Questions Syria Evidence." *Washington Post*, November 18, 2008.

IAEA Staff Report. "Latest Iran Safeguards Report Circulated to IAEA Board," February 23, 2008, http://www.iaea.org/NewsCenter/News/2008/iranreport0208.html.

IAEA Report: "Implementation of the NPT Safeguards Agreement and Relevant Provisions of Security Council Resolutions 1737 (2006), 1747 (2007), 1803 (2008), and 1835 (2008) in the Islamic Republic of Iran," February 20, 2009.

Ignatius, David. "When the CIA Got it Right." *Washington Post*, September 23, 2007, B-7.

Ignatius, David. "Repairing America's Spy Shop." *Washington Post*, April 6, 2008, B07.

"Iran Has More Enriched Uranium Than Thought." *New York Times*, February 20, 2009; http://www.nytimes.com/2009_02_09/world.middleeast.20nuc.html.

"Iran Tests Advanced 'Efficient' Centrifuges." *MSNBC News*, April 8, 2008.

Jordan, Lara Jakes, and David Dishneau. "Anthrax Scientist Commits Suicide as FBI Closes In." Associated Press, August 1, 2008, http://www.firstcoastnews.com/news/waronterror/news-article.aspx?storyid=115292&catid=33.

Kellman, Barry. *Bioviolence: Preventing Biological Terror and Crime*. Cambridge, UK: Cambridge University Press, 2007.

Kerr, Paul. "China Updates Nuclear Export Regulations." *Arms Control Today*, January/February 2007.

Kessler, Glenn. "Far-Reaching U.S. Plan Impaired N. Korea Deal." *Washington Post*, September 26, 2008, A-20.

Kessler, Glenn. "North Korea Doesn't Agree to Written Nuclear Agreement; Earlier Verbal Assurances Contradicted." *Washington Post*, December 12, 2008, A-22.

Kessler, Glenn. "US Efforts Divert Iran-Bound Cargo." *Washington Post*, November 4, 2008, A-9.

Kessler, Glenn. "U.S. Seems Set to Take North Korea off Terror List." *Washington Post*, October 10, 2008, A-16.

Kimball, Daryl. "Grounds for Optimism and Action on Chemical Weapons Convention's 10th Anniversary." Arms Control Association Press Room, May 4, 2007, http://www.armscontrol.org/pressroom/2007/20070504_CWC.asp.

Kimball, Daryl. "Congress Must Remedy Past U.S. Funding Shortfalls for Global Nuclear Test Monitoring System." Arms Control Association Press Room, May 21, 2007, http://www.armscontrol.org/pressroom/2007/2007/0521_CTBT.asp.

Kimball, Daryl. "The Curious Incident in Northern Syria and Its Potential Proliferation Implications." Prepared Remarks. Arms Control Association, November 1, 2007, http://www.armscontrol.org/events/20071101_NK_Syria.

Kissinger, Henry. "Misreading the Iran Report: Why Spying and Policymaking Don't Mix." *Washington Post*, December 13, 2007.

Kralev, Nicholas. "Lack of Written Agreement Snags North Korea Talks." *Washington Times*, September 9, 2008.

Levi, Michael. *On Nuclear Terrorism*. Cambridge, MA: Harvard University Press, November 2007, http://www.armscontrol.org/act/2008_04/BookReview.

Levin, Carl. "Hussein-Qaeda Link 'Inappropriate,' Report Says." *New York Times*, April 6, 2007, 6.

Lindsey, Robert. *The Falcon and the Snowman*. New York: Simon & Schuster, 1979.

Lowenthal, Mark. *Intelligence: From Secrets to Policy*, 3rd ed. Washington, DC: CQ Press, 2006.

Lowenthal, Mark. *Intelligence: From Secrets to Policy*, 4th ed. Washington, DC: CQ Press, 2009.

Lundberg, Kristen. "The SS-9 Controversy: Intelligence as Political Football," Case Program, Kennedy School of Government, C16-89-884.0, 1989.

Lynch, Colum. "U.N. Team Still Looking for Iraq's Arsenal." *Washington Post*, June 2, 2007, A-1.

MacFarquhar, Neil. "Rates of Nuclear Thefts Disturbingly High, Monitoring Chief Says." *New York Times*, October 28, 2008, A-7.

Melman, Yossi. "The Israel-South Africa Nuclear Tie." *Ha'aretz*, Tel Aviv, April 21, 1997: FBIS-NES-97-082.

"Members of the Intelligence Community," http://www.dni.gov/.

Norris, Robert. "The Soviet Nuclear Archipelago." *Arms Control Today*, January/February 1992.

Oliveri, Frank. "Secret Air Force Center Monitors Worldwide Treaty Compliance." *Florida Today*, October 20, 1997, 1A-2A.

Perkovich, George. *India's Nuclear Bomb*. Berkeley and Los Angeles: University of California Press, 1999.

Perkovich, George. Testimony. U.S. Senate Foreign Relations Committee, May 19, 2005.

Phillips, Melanie. "I Found Saddam's WMD Bunkers." *Spectator*, April 21, 2007, www.spectator.co.uk/theomagazine/features/29092.

Pillar, Paul. "Intelligence, Policy, and the War in Iraq." *Foreign Affairs*, March/April 2006.

Pillar, Paul. "The Other Intelligence Assessments on Iraq." *National Interest*, June 6, 2007, http://www.nationalinterest.org/.

Pincus, Walter. "Before War, CIA Warned of Negative Outcomes." *Washington Post*, June 3, 2007, A-8.

Pollack, Ken. *The Persian Puzzle: The Conflict Between Iran and America*. Washington, DC: Saban Center, Brookings Institution, 2004.

Powers, Thomas. *The Man Who Kept the Secrets: Richard Helms and the CIA*. New York, Knopf, 1979.

Pritchard, Charles L. *Failed Diplomacy: The Tragic Story of How North Korea Got the Bomb*. Washington, DC: Brookings Institution Press, 2007.

Reiss, Mitchell. *Bridled Ambition: Why Countries Constrain Their Nuclear Capabilities*. Washington, DC: Woodrow Wilson Center Press, 1995.

Renner, Matt. "Pentagon Officer Created Phony Intel on Iraq/al-Qaeda Link." *Truthout report*, April 6, 2007, http://www.truthout.org/article/pentagon-office-created-phony-intel-iraqal-qaeda-link.

Rhodes, Richard. *The Arsenals of Folly*. New York: Knopf, 2007.

Rich, Frank. *The Greatest Story Ever Sold*. New York: Penguin Press, 2006.

Richelson, Jeffrey T. *Spying on the Bomb: American Nuclear Intelligence from Nazi Germany to Iran and North Korea*. New York: W. W. Norton, 2006.

Richelson, Jeffrey T. "The Whole World Is Watching." *Bulletin of the Atomic Scientists*, January/February 2006, 27–35.

Ricks, Thomas E., and Karen DeYoung. "Architect of Iraq War Strategy Blames Powell In New Memoir." *Washington Post*, March 9, 2008, http://www.huffingtonpost.com/2008/03/09/architect-of-iraq-war-str_n_90593.html?page=6.

Risen, James. *State of War: The Secret History of the CIA and the Bush Administration*. New York: Free Press, 2006.

Sang-Hun, Choe. *International Herald Tribune*, September 4, 2008, 1.

Shultz, George P., William J. Perry, Henry A. Kissinger, and Sam Nunn. "Toward a Nuclear-free World" (op-ed). *Wall Street Journal*, January 15, 2008, http://online.wsj.com/article/SB120036422673589947.html?mod=opinion_main_commentaries; Shultz, George P., William J. Perry, Henry A. Kissinger, and Sam Nunn. "A World Free of Nuclear Weapons" (op-ed). *Wall Street Journal*, January 4, 2007, A15, http://www.hoover.org/publications/digest/6731276.html.

Shultz, George P., Steven P. Andreason, Sydney D. Drell, and James E. Goodby (eds.). *Reykjavik Revisited: Steps Toward a World Free of Nuclear Weapons*, Stanford, CA, Hoover Institution Press, 2008.

Slevin, Peter, John Lancaster, and Kamran Khan. "At Least 7 Nations Tied to Pakistani Nuclear Ring." *Washington Post*, February 8, 2004, A-1.

Sokolski, Henry, and Patrick Clawson (eds.). *Checking Iran's Nuclear Ambitions*. Carlisle, PA: Strategic Studies Institute, US Army War College, January 2004, http://www.strategicstudiesinstitute.army.mil/pubs/display.cfm?[ibID=368.

Spector, Leonard S., and Avner Cohen. "Israel's Airstrike on Syria's Reactor: Implications for the Nonproliferation Regime." *Arms Control Today*, July/August 2008, http://www.armscontrol.org/act/2008_07-08/SpectorCohen.

Steiner, James E.. "Challenging the Red Line Between Intelligence and Policy." Institute for the Study of Diplomacy, Georgetown University, November 2003.

Stinson, Jeffrey. "Russia increasingly filling demand for nuclear technology." *USA Today*, June 4, 2007, 6.

Strengthened Safeguards Systems: States with Additional Protocols, as of January 31, 2009, http://www.iaea.org/OurWork/SV/Safeguards/sg_protocol.html.

"Sudan Wants UN to Probe US Bombing of Drug Factory." CNN, August 18, 1999, www.cnn.com/world/africa.

Suskind, Ron. *The Price of Loyalty: George W. Bush, the White House, and the Education of Paul O'Neill.* New York: Simon & Schuster, 2004.

Suskind, Ron. *The Way of the World*, New York, HarperCollins, 2008.

Taubman, Philip. *Secret Empire: Eisenhower, the CIA, and the Hidden Story of America's Space Espionage.* New York: Simon & Schuster, 2003.

Tenet, George. "Iraq and Weapons of Mass Destruction." Remarks at Georgetown University, February 5, 2004, http://www.fas.org/irp/cia/product/dci020504.html.

Tenet, George. *At the Center of the Storm: My Years at the CIA.* New York: HarperCollins, 2007.

Thielmann, Greg. "Rumsfeld Reprise? The Missile Report That Foretold the Iraq Controversy." *Arms Control Today*, July/August 2003.

Treaty on the Non-Proliferation of Nuclear Weapons, http://www.iaea.org/Publications/Documents/Treaties/npt.html.

Turzanski, Edward A. "Policy Disruption by NIE." Foreign Policy Research Institute, January 22, 2008.

U.N. Security Council Resolution 1540, http://www.un.org/Docs/sc/unsc_resolutions04.html.

UN Special Commission (UNSCOM). First Consolidated Report of the Secretary-General Pursuant to Paragraph 9, April 11, 1996.

"U.S. probing two espionage cases." *USA Today* (Associated Press), February 11, 2008, http://www.usatoday.com/news/washington/2008-02-11-spying_n.htm.

Warrick, Joby. "Spread of Nuclear Capability Feared." *Washington Post*, May 12, 2008, A-1.

Warrick, Joby. "Syrian Facility Looked Like Reactor, UN Says." *Washington Post*, November 20, 2008, A-16.

Warrick, Joby. "Nuclear Scientist A.Q. Khan Is Freed from House Arrest." *Washington Post*, February 7, 2009, A1 & A9.

Warrick, Joby, and Carrie Johnson. "Chinese Spying on the Rise, U.S. Says." *Washington Post*, April 3, 2008, http://www.amren.com/mtnews/archives/2008/04/chinese_spying.php.

Wein, Lawrence M. "Biological and Chemical Safety Nets." *Wall Street Journal*, February 28, 2007.

Wilson, Valerie Plame. *Fair Game: My Life as a Spy, My Betrayal by the White House.* New York: Simon & Schuster, 2007.

Wright, Robin. "North Koreans Taped at Syrian Reactor." *Washington Post*, April 24, 2008.

Zegart, Amy B. *Spying Blind: The CIA, the FBI, and the Origins of 9/11.* Princeton, New Jersey: Princeton University Press, 2007.

US Government Documents

"Alleged Assassination Plots Involving Foreign Leaders." Senate Select Committee on Intelligence, 94th Congress, 1st Session, November 20, 1975.

Annual Threat Assessment of the Director of National Intelligence for the Senate Armed Services Committee, February 27, 2007.

Bruce, James B. "The Consequences of Permissive Neglect: Laws and Leaks of Classified Intelligence." *Studies in Intelligence*, vol. 47, no. 1 (2003).

"Collection and Analysis on Iraq: Issues for the US Intelligence Community." www.cia.gov/csi/studies, vol. 49, no. 3 (2005).

"The Commission on Intelligence Capabilities of the United States Regarding Weapons of Mass Destruction." Report to the President of the United States, March 31, 2005.

"Comprehensive Report on the Special Advisor to the DCI on Iraq's WMD & Addendum." March 2005.

DCI John Deutch Statement to the Public on the Ames Damage Assessment, October 31, 1995, http://www.cia.gov/news-information/press-release-statements/press-release-archive-1995/pslo3195.html.

Ford, Harold P. "Why CIA Analysts Were So Doubtful About Vietnam." *Studies in Intelligence*, no. 1 (1997).

Gates, Robert (DCI). "A Message to Analysts: Guarding Against Politicization." March 16, 1992. *Studies in Intelligence*, vol. 36 (1992).

Helgerson, John. *Getting to Know the President: CIA Briefings of Presidential Candidates, 1952–1992.* CIA/Center for the Study of Intelligence, Washington, DC, 1996.

Helms, Richard. "Strategic Arms Limitations and Intelligence." *Studies in Intelligence*, vol. 17 (Spring 1973).

"Intelligence in the Civil War." CIA/Office of Public Affairs, Washington, DC.

"Intelligence in the War of Independence." CIA/Office of Public Affairs, Washington, DC.

"Iraq Survey Group Report, Regime Strategic Intent." October 6, 2004.

"Joint Inquiry into Intelligence Community Activities Before and After the Terrorist Attacks of September 11, 2001." SSCI & HPSCI, 107th Congress, 2nd Session, December 2002.

McConnell, Michael (Director of National Intelligence). Statement Before the Senate Select Committee on Intelligence, February 5, 2008, http://www.dni.gov/testimonies/20080205_transcript.pdf.

National Intelligence Estimate. "Iran: Nuclear Intentions and Capabilities." National Intelligence Council, Unclassified Key Judgments, November 2007, http://www.dni.gov/press_releases/20071203_release.pdf.

"The National Intelligence Estimates A-B Team Episode Concerning Soviet Strategic Capability and Objectives." Report of the SSCI, 95th Congress, 2nd Session, February 16, 1978.

National Intelligence Reform Act of 2004 (S.2845), 108th Congress, 2nd Session, October 6, 2004.

NIE Key Judgments. "Iraq's Continuing Programs for Weapons of Mass Destruction." October 2002; declassified on July 18, 2003, and presented at a White House background briefing, http://www.fas.org/irp/cia/product/iraq-wmd.html.

"The 9/11 Report: The National Commission on Terrorist Attacks Upon the United States." New York: St. Martin's Paperbacks, 2004.

"The Office of Strategic Services: America's First Intelligence Agency." CIA/Office of Public Affairs, Washington, DC.

Pavitt, James. Remarks at the Foreign Policy Association, June 21, 2004, http://www.cia.gov/news-information/speeches-testimony/2004/ddo_speech_06242004.html.

Powell, Colin (Secretary of State). Remarks to the United Nations Security Council, February 5, 2003, http//www.globalsecurity.org/wmd/library/news/iraq/2003/iraq-030205-powell-un-1730opf.html.

Proliferation Security Initiative: Statement of Interdiction Principles, http://www.whitehouse.gov/news/releases/2003/09/20030904-11.html.

Snider, Britt L. "Sharing Secrets with Lawmakers: Congress as a User of Intelligence." *Studies in Intelligence*, Spring 1998, https://www.cia.gov/library/center-for-the-study-of-intelligence/csi-publications/books-and-monographs/sharing-secrets-with-lawmakers-congress-as-a-user-of-intelligence/toc.htm.

Remarks by Central Intelligence Agency Director Michael Hayden at the Los Angeles World Affairs Council, September 16, 2008, http://www.cia.gov/news-information/speeches-testimony/speeches-testimony-archive-2008/directors-remarks-at-lawac.html.

"Senate Select Committee on Intelligence Report on Prewar Intelligence Assessments About Postwar Iraq." US Senate, 110th Congress, 1st Session, May 2007, http://intelligence.senate.gov/11076.pdf.

"Senate Select Committee on Intelligence Report on the US Intelligence Community's Prewar Intelligence Assessments on Iraq." US Senate, 108th Congress, 2nd Session, July 2004, http://intelligence.senate.gov/[?]html.

"Senate Select Committee on Intelligence Report on Whether Public Statements

Regarding Iraq by U.S. Government Officials Were Substantiated by Intelligence Information." US Senate, 110th Congress, 2nd Session, June 2008, http://intelligence.senate.gov/080605/phase2a.pdf.

Tenet, George, and Michael Hayden. Testimonies to Senate Select Committee on Intelligence, October 2002, http://www.fas.org/irp/congress/2002_hr/index.html.

Testimony of the Director of the National Security Agency at the Joint House and Senate Select Intelligence Committees, 107th Congress, 2nd Session, October 17, 2002, Federal News Service.

White House Fact Sheet. "Comprehensive Test Ban Treaty Safeguards." September 22, 1997.

WORLD AT RISK: The Report of the Commission on the Prevention of WMD Proliferation and Terrrorism, December 2, 2008.

Index